Also in the Variorum Collected Studies Series:

LUCIE BOLENS
L'Andalousie du quotidien au sacré (XIe–XIIIe siècles)

ETAN KOHLBERG
Belief and Law in Imāmī Shī'ism

R.B. SERJEANT
Customary and Shari'ah Law in Arabian Society

GEORGE MAKDISI
History and Politics in Eleventh-Century Baghdad

GEORGE MAKDISI
Religion, Law and Learning in Classical Islam

FRANZ ROSENTHAL
Science and Medicine in Islam

NICHOLAS LOWICK
Coinage and History of the Islamic World

NICHOLAS LOWICK
Islamic Coins and Trade in the Medieval World

S.M. STERN
Coins and Documents from the Medieval Middle East

HALIL INALCIK
Studies in Ottoman Social and Economic History

MICHAEL F. HENDY
The Economy, Fiscal Administration and Coinage of Byzantium

ROBERT S. LOPEZ
The Shape of Medieval Monetary History

HARRY A. MISKIMIN
Cash, Credit and Crisis in Europe, 1300–1600

ROBERT-HENRI BAUTIER
Sur l'histoire économique de la France médiévale

Monetary Change and Economic History in the Medieval Muslim World

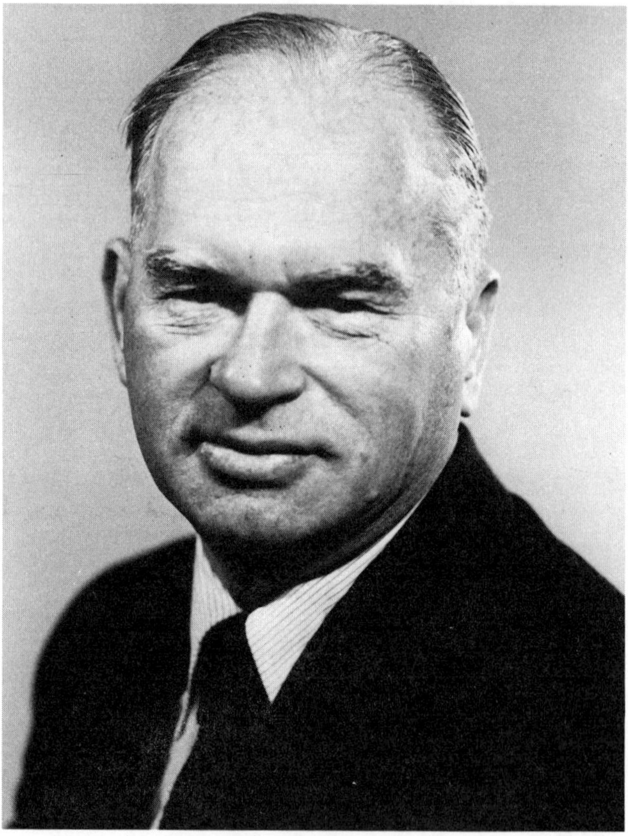

Professor Andrew S. Ehrenkreutz

Andrew S. Ehrenkreutz

Monetary Change and Economic History in the Medieval Muslim World

Edited by Jere L. Bacharach

VARIORUM

Published by VARIORUM

Ashgate Publishing Limited
Gower House, Croft Road,
Hampshire GU11 3HR
Great Britain

Ashgate Publishing Company
Old Post Road
Brookfield, Vermont 05036
U S A

ISBN 0–86078–324–3

A CIP catalogue record for this book is available
from the British Library and the
US Library of Congress.

Printed by Galliard (Printers) Ltd
Great Yarmouth, Norfolk
Great Britain

COLLECTED STUDIES SERIES CS371

CONTENTS

ECONOMIC ISSUES

SALADIN AND THE WORLD OF THE CRUSADERS

This volume contains xii + 290 pages

PREFACE

Born in Poland on December 19, 1921, Andrew S. Ehrenkreutz was the son of two distinguished scholars, Professor Cezaria Baudouin de Courtenay Jedrzejewicz and Professor Stefan L. Ehrenkreutz. Whatever plans he envisioned for himself, World War II brought them to a crashing end. Fighting for a free, democratic Poland has been a constant in Ehrenkreutz's life. After the collapse of Poland he escaped from Poland and joined the Free Polish forces in France. He was decorated with the Croix de Guerre during the 1940 campaign but, ultimately, was taken prisoner, enjoyed a brief spell of freedom after his escape in 1941, and was finally liberated by American troops in April, 1945. Throughout his academic career he has never forgotten his commitment to Poland and during the last decades, in particular, he has been an active participant in Polish-American organizations, both academic and those with a more visible political agenda. One can guarantee that in Australia, he will be just as active.

After World War II, Andrew and Blanche, his wife who had nursed him back to health in a Polish camp hospital, moved to London where he entered the University of London receiving his B.A. in 1950. Trained at the School of Oriental and African Studies under Bernard Lewis for whom he has great admiration and affection, Ehrenkreutz completed his Ph.D. dissertation two years later. His early publications highlighted the career of Saladin and monetary history, two themes which would dominate much of his later research and writings. The interaction of the two topics are encapsulated in the opening to an article published in 1956. "If one judged Saladin's achievements solely by his monetary policy, that great Islamic hero would have been accused by history of dangerously jeopardizing the stability of the official Egyptian currency."[1]

More than any other scholar, I credit Ehrenkreutz with moving the study of Islamic monetary history from the world of curators and collectors into the main stream of medieval Muslim studies. Although he has great respect for Islamic numismatic studies, particularly the contributions of the late George C. Miles, Ehrenkreutz himself was never a numismatist. For him coins and catalogues were ancillary tools

[1] "The Crisis of *Dinar* in the Egypt of Saladin", *JAOS* 76 (1956): 178.

for the exploration of larger issues. In fact, he went beyond what was available in the traditional numismatic sources as illustrated in his study of Ibn Ba'ra's medieval treatise dealing with problems of the Egyptian mint.[2] In order to understand the text, Ehrenkreutz realized that a knowledge of the purity of the coinage, particularly that of the gold dinars, was essential. Using the non-destructive technique of weighing gold coins in air and then in water and then calculating their specific gravity, a method associated with Archimedes, Ehrenkreutz was able to identify specific times and places when coins were debased.

The result was a series of extremely important articles which covered monetary developments in the central Middle East from the Umayyad period into the Mamluk era. In all cases data derived from specific gravity tests was combined with textual information from Arabic sources. Virtually no era of the pre-Ottoman monetary history of Egypt can be written without references to publications by Ehrenkreutz.

By the mid-1960's, Ehrenkreutz turned to another method for studying monetary history. Working with a group of students at the University of Michigan whose faculty he had joined in 1954, he attempted to identify the number of dies produced for specific issues which he then related to changes in coin production, monetary history, and even larger politico-economic issues. Typical of his attitude toward training future scholars, he submitted the article in the name of the four students as well as himself and would only permit it to be published that way.[3]

He used various means of persuasion to have his students present papers at academic meetings always encouraging them with positive reenforcement. At professional meetings his encouragement of younger scholars included calling upon them to comment on presentations when he knew that they had done advanced work on the topics being discussed. In his graduate seminars at Michigan, he exposed his students to a broad range of research tools for the study of medieval Islamic history including practising how to use them. Within the lecture hall, Ehrenkreutz was constantly encouraging students to ask questions, inviting the more advanced ones to give guest lectures, and always making available his extensive bibliography.

The following articles reflect the range of his academic interests behind which was his very strong commitment to teaching. It has been my good fortune to consider him my mentor, my model, and my friend. Having the opportunity to work with Dr John Smedley of Variorum and

2 "Extracts from the Technical Manual of the Ayyubid Mint in Cairo", *BSOAS* 15 (1953): 423–47.

3 "Early Islamic Mint Output", *JESHO* 9 (1966): 212–41.

with the full support of the author of the articles, has been a most pleasant way to say thank you to Andrew S. Ehrenkreutz.

JERE L. BACHARACH

Seattle, WA.,
1991

PUBLISHER'S NOTE

The articles in this volume, as in all others in the Collected Studies Series, have not been given a new, continuous pagination. In order to avoid confusion, and to facilitate their use where these same studies have been referred to elsewhere, the original pagination has been maintained wherever possible.

Each article has been given a Roman number in order of appearance, as listed in the Contents. This number is repeated on each page and quoted in the index entries.

I

Monetary Aspects of Medieval Near Eastern Economic History

To achieve meaningful progress in the field of medieval Near Eastern economic history one must take into account its monetary aspects. This postulate is based on the following premises:

(*a*) Money, or rather a highly elaborate monetary system constituted one of the fundamental institutions in the economic life of medieval Near Eastern society.

(*b*) If properly explored and correlated, historical monetary data may be turned into a heuristic tool permitting an attempt to measure medieval Near Eastern economic accomplishments by means of statistical evaluation.

The Islamic Caliphate was born in a milieu exposed to the circulation of metallic money of Byzantine and Sāsānid origin.[1] Following their victorious expansion in the Near East, Muslim authorities found themselves in control of peoples and territories whose economy had for many centuries been characterized by a sophisticated monetary system. The monetary system inherited by the Muslim conquerors consisted of gold coinage which constituted an imperial monopoly of the Byzantine state, and of silver coinage of the defunct Sāsānid Empire.[2] Military, political, social and economic circumstances produced by the triumph of the Arabs generated major changes with regard to the circulation of money. To begin with, military operations, captures or submissions of towns, palaces, churches and monasteries brought about a process of dethesaurization releasing tremendous quantities of precious metals, coins, jewels, etc., for circulation. Secondly, the territorial extension of the Caliphate resulted in the acquisition of, or at least, accessibility to the rich oriferous and argentiferous areas of the Near East. Finally, by inaugurating the system of *ʿaṭāʾ*, i.e., the institution of regular cash stipends to which all fully-fledged members of the Muslim community were entitled, the Caliphate stimulated production and wide distribution of coinage. One must remember that the beneficiaries of this welfare system were local Near Easterners. In Byzantine times, imperial

[1] Although Ḥimyarite coins were also in circulation (al-Balādhurī, *Futūḥ al-buldān*, ed. de Goeje, 1866, p. 467) they did not seem to play any direct part in the foundation of the Islamic monetary system.

[2] Copper coinage (*fulūs*) because of its inferior, limited and localized function, will not come under consideration in the present paper.

authorities exploited Near Eastern taxpayers and resources to promote the well-being of the court in Constantinople or to finance military campaigns in Europe. Byzantine aristocracy or imperial officials, after serving and earning money in Near Eastern provinces, would retire in the metropolitan district of Constantinople. Indeed, the whole economy of the Byzantine empire was geared to meet the needs of the great consumer and production centre such as Constantinople happened to be. Since the mint of Constantinople was the most important institution producing imperial gold coinage, a lot of Near Eastern gold must have been flowing into the Byzantine capital. Manufacturing activities of gold- and silversmiths of Constantinople must have absorbed substantial quantities of gold and silver bullion imported from Near Eastern provinces. The drainage of Near Eastern gold and silver stopped with the victory of the Muslims. Arab military and administrative aristocracy, or even the rank and file supporting the new regime resided in the Near East. From an economic point of view they represented a class of the nouveau riche consumers, spending money, squandering it or investing it locally, to the benefit of Near Eastern caterers, labourers, producers, merchants, etc. The availability of cash in the hands of the Arab invaders or immigrants stimulated agricultural production, manufacturing and commercial activities and urban developments. All these factors contributed to an intensive circulation of coinage.

Such a situation forced the Caliphate to proceed with appropriate measures to secure an adequate supply of coinage. At first the mints of the new regime continued to strike coins in imitation of traditional Byzantine and Sāsānid types of coins. Before long, however, more precisely towards the end of the seventh century of the Christian era, Muslim administration felt strong enough, politically and economically, to do away with the monetary vestiges of Byzantine and Persian domination of the Near East. In the 690's the mints of the Caliphate began to produce new 'Islamic' coinage consisting of two basic metallic types: silver (*dirham*) and gold (*dīnār*). This event, usually referred to as the monetary reform of ʿAbd al-Malik, received considerable attention in modern scholarly literature but so far its treatment has been mainly limited to numismatic and culturological aspects. Numismatists have registered that event as the inception of a new type of Near Eastern coinage characterized by specific Arab-Islamic stylistic, epigraphical, metrological and other external features. Historians interested in the cultural and ideological evolution of the Caliphate rightly defined the reform of ʿAbd al-Malik as a manifestation of his policy to accomplish arabization of his administration. Still others interpreted the appearance of the purely Islamic, 'impersonal' type of coinage as an expression of a propaganda warfare against the internal and external enemies of the Umayyad regime.

On the other hand little attention has been given to the basic historical function of that reform, namely its economic significance. The reform of ʿAbd al-Malik meant that after a period of transition the new regime established by Arab conquerors decided to assume responsibility with regard to the monetary system of the Caliphate. The very adoption of a uniform bi-metallic coinage was of major economic consequence. It is true that the measure involving silver coins was not too revolutionary in view of the total extinction of the Sāsānid Empire whose function in respect of silver coinage supply was taken over by the Caliphate. In contrast the minting of gold by the Caliphate constituted an outstanding event in medieval economic history. After humiliating the Byzantines on Near Eastern battlefields, the Arab leadership contested the traditional imperial monopoly in respect of gold coinage. This challenge to Byzantine monetary supremacy could not have been undertaken without strong economic foundations and confidence in commercial competitive potentials of Near Eastern society under the new political and religious regime. Thus before the rising silhouettes of Muslim minarets began to dominate Mediterranean horizons, Islamic *dīnārs* had proclaimed the end of economic submissiveness of the Near East and the beginning of its drive in quest of 'international' monetary surpremacy.

The monetary system instituted by the Umayyads entailed more than the adoption of bi-metallic coinage as official currency. Judging by the activities of al-Ḥajjāj and of Hishām[3] the administration of the Caliphate assumed responsibility for the organization of the supply of the official currency. The problems of the procurement of raw materials, in this case of precious metals; of the supervision over the operations of the mints; and of the means of distribution of coinage constituted important areas of governmental involvement in the functioning of Islamic monetary systems.

Subsequent history of that important institution abounded in organizational diversifications and economic modulations. A decentralized network of regional mints replaced the highly centralized Umayyad system of coinage production. The responsibility of the sovereign to safeguard the integrity of coinage was delegated to specially appointed officials. The coinage itself underwent manifold mutations. Money changers and bankers became instrumental agents in the promotion of money circulation. All these historical processes notwithstanding one can hardly question the fact that the monetary system founded by the Umayyads remained one of the fundamental features of the dynamic medieval Near Eastern economy.

How dynamic? To expect a meaningful answer to this question is to presuppose that economic developments in the medieval Near East lend themselves to an analysis by means of some comparative approximation. It

[3] Cf. 'Dār al-ḍarb', *EI*², vol. ii, p. 117.

is precisely in this area of historical comparative interpretation that a proper utilization of our knowledge of the medieval Near Eastern monetary system may produce relevant analytical data.

To begin with one should stress the role of monetary evaluation in the pattern of social stratification. Whether one refers to the early Arab hierarchy or to the Mamlūk regime in Egypt the ascriptive and accomplished status enjoyed by the beneficiaries of the two respective systems was evaluated in strict monetary figures.[4] Fiscal activities of the Caliphate operated according to annual budgetary evaluation.[5] Taxes or salaries were not necessarily paid in cash but their level was always stated in terms of official monetary units. This practice of monetary evaluation was even more striking in other sectors of economic life. Medieval literary sources do not lack quotations of the value of real estate, of land and of housing, produce and rent, of the costs of free, conscript and slave labour, as well as of prices prevalent on internal and external markets.

To utilize such value data for the purpose of a reconstructive analysis of economic history one basic prerequisite must be achieved: the understanding of the value of Islamic money itself. This is necessitated by the fact that besides its basic metallic and denominational categories Islamic coinage was characterized by a lack of uniformity as far as its standards of weight and fineness were concerned. As a result of the decentralization and proliferation of coinage production in the ʿAbbāsid period different mints at different times produced coinage according to their local standards. Consequently the markets of the medieval Near East witnessed the circulation of different types of Muslim currency, of the same basic denominational and metallic categories but of unequal purchasing value. To expedite bookkeeping operations medieval fiscal administrations adopted the system of fictitious account money such for instance as the *dīnār jayshī* in Mamlūk Egypt. Unfortunately medieval sources as a rule quote monetary data not in terms of a standardized money of account but in those of the contemporary market currency. To fail to differentiate between various types of currency is to run the risk of complete misinterpretation of relevant sources of historical information. As an illustration of the danger of such interpretative fallacy one may furnish the following example:

In the seventh century of the Christian era the highest stipend in the ʿ*aṭā*ʾ system as set up by ʿUmar ibn al-Khaṭṭāb was that of ʿĀʾisha, amounting to 12,000 *dirhams* a year.[6] In the fifteenth century the monthly pay (*jāmakiyya*) of a Mamlūk soldier amounted to 2,000 *dirhams*, or 24,000

[4] One may add here that the members of the fiscally underprivileged community, i.e., the *ahl al-dhimmah*, were also stratified according to their economic status.

[5] Cf. the recent article by Makoto Shimizu, 'Les finances publiques de l'Etat ʿabbāsside', *Der Islam*, 42, 1965, pp. 1–24.

[6] Cf. Matti I. Moosa, 'The dīwān of ʿUmar ibn al-Khaṭṭāb', *Studies in Islam*, 2, 1965, p. 68.

dirhams on an annual basis.[7] If uncritically accepted these two statements would suggest that the services of an ordinary warrior in the Mamlūk system were considered twice as valuable as those of the Prophet's widow. However, after investigating the exchange value of the seventh and the fifteenth century *dirhams*, one would find that the rate of exchange of the former was about 14 *dirhams* to a *dīnār*, while that of the latter was 370 to 1 in A.D. 1455 (A.H. 859).[8] In the light of this observation one could deduce that in terms of the seventh century exchange rates the *jāmakiyya* in question amounted to about 900 *dirhams* annually. This amount in turn would appear fairly close to the 500 to 600 *dirhams* payable annually to an ordinary warrior on the *'aṭā'* list of 'Umar ibn al-Khaṭṭāb.[9]

This example has been presented here to stress the importance of the need for exercise of extreme caution in studying monetary data for the purpose of an analysis of economic phenomena in medieval Near Eastern history. As a relevant remark one should observe that medieval Near Eastern units of measure of weight, capacity, volume, etc., were not uniform either. Thus even if the economic status of a particular currency unit happens to be established, there still remains the question of the actual size, weight or volume referred to in a price quotation.

PROBLEMS OF SOURCES

Until recently source materials pertaining to the economic past of the Caliphate have either been mistreated or completely ignored. This regrettable situation has given rise to the opinion that evidence relating to the medieval period is unsystematic and episodic. It is hoped that the following survey of the nature of sources available for the study of monetary developments alone will inspire more confidence in the viability of heuristic undertakings in the field of medieval economic history of the Near East. Truly, historians specializing in that particular field are not as privileged as their colleagues dealing with later periods, and whose research is facilitated by the existence of archival or modern statistical documentation. It is my contention, however, that evidence for the medieval period if properly, systematically and exhaustively handled permits attempts at statistical sampling and even mass interpretation. For the purpose of the present discussion the evidence in question has been arranged into two basic categories: textual and numismatic.

A. Textual evidence

(*i*) *Medieval historical and geographical literature*

This type of evidence is listed first because it constitutes an indispensable base for any endeavours in the field of medieval Near Eastern history.

[7] Cf. D. Ayalon, 'The system of payment in Mamlūk military society', *JESHO*, 1, 1957, p. 54. [8] *Supra*. [9] Matti I. Moosa, *art. cit.*, p. 68.

Historians like al-Balādhurī (d. 892), al-Ṭabarī (d. 923), Ibn al-Jawzī (d. 1201), Ibn al-Athīr (d. 1233), al-Maqrīzī (d. 1442) or Ibn Khaldūn (d. 1406), and geographers like al-Yaʿqūbī (d. 897?), al-Maqdisī (b. 946) or Yāqūt (d. 1229), do not need any introduction to those involved in the study of general or particular aspects of Near Eastern society in the Middle Ages. In the specific field of monetary history, sources included in that broad category are important because of their occasional references to: (*a*) location of gold and silver mines,[10] (*b*) location of mints,[11] (*c*) decisions concerning the operations of the mints,[12] (*d*) decisions concerning the types and quality of coinage,[13] (*e*) monetary exchange rates,[14] (*f*) prices and wages,[15] (*h*) state budgets.[16]

(ii) *Specialized literature dealing with diverse subjects*

This category involves medieval texts containing entire sections devoted to monetary or related problems. Juridical texts such as the *Kitāb al-kharāj* of Abū Yūsuf (d. 798), administrative handbooks such as the *Kitāb al-manāzil* of al-Būzajānī (d. 998) or the *Kitāb qawānīn al-dawāwīn* of Ibn Mammātī (d. 1209), diplomatic compendia such as the *Ṣubḥ al-Aʿshā* of al-Qalqashandī or even mathematical monographs such as the *Kāfī fī'l-ḥisāb* by al-Karajī (d. 1016) may be listed as typical examples of this type of source which should be considered in the pursuit of monetary data.

(iii) *Specialized literature devoted exclusively to monetary or directly pertinent problems*

As perfect examples of this kind of source one has to list the *Shudhūr al-ʿuqūd* of al-Maqrīzī, the *Kashf al-asrār al-ʿilmiyya bidār al-ḍarb al-miṣriyya* by Ibn Baʿra (13th cent.),[17] the *Kitāb al-taysīr* of al-Asadī (15th cent.),[18]

[10] Cf. D. M. Dunlop, 'Sources of gold and silver in Islam according to al-Hamdānī', *Studia Islamica*, 8, 1957, pp. 29–49.

[11] Cf. A. S. Ehrenkreutz, 'Contributions to the knowledge of the fiscal administration of Egypt in the Middle Ages', *Bulletin of the School of Oriental and African Studies*, 16, 1954, pp. 508–9.

[12] Cf. al-Balādhurī, *op. cit.*, pp. 468–9.

[13] Cf. A. S. Ehrenkreutz, 'Studies in the monetary history of the Near East in the Middle Ages', *JESHO*, 2, 1959, p. 138.

[14] Cf. tabulations compiled by W. Popper, *Egypt and Syria under the Circassian sultans, 1382–1468 A.D., Systematic notes* . . . (University of California publications in Semitic philology, vol. 16), 1957, pp. 74–5.

[15] Cf. the latest of the numerous publications of E. Ashtor, 'I salari nel Medio Oriente durante l'epoca medievale', *Rivista Storica Italiana*, 78, 1966, p. 322 f. Also *idem*, 'La recherche des prix dans l'Orient Médiéval. Sources, méthodes et problèmes', *Studia Islamica*, 21, 1964, pp. 101–44.

[16] Cf. A. von Kremer, 'Über das Einnahmebudget des Abbassiden-Reiches vom Jahre 306 H. (918–19)', *Denkschriften der Akademie der Wissenschaften in Wienna, Phil. Hist. Klasse*, 36, 1888, p. 307.

[17] Cf. A. S. Ehrenkreutz, 'Extracts from the technical manual on the Ayyūbid mint in Cairo', *Bulletin of the School of Oriental and African Studies*, 15, 1953, pp. 423–47.

[18] Cf. Subhi Labib, 'Al-Asadī und sein Bericht über Verwaltungs- und Geldreform im 15. Jahrhundert', *JESHO*, 8, 1965, pp. 312–16.

or *al-Dawḥa al-mushtabika fī ḍawābiṭ dār al-sikka* by Abū'l-Ḥasan ʿAlī ibn Yūsuf al-Ḥakīm.[19]

(iv) *Quasi-archival documents*

Albeit disadvantaged by the lack of regular archival materials historians engaged in the study of medieval Near Eastern monetary developments have at their disposal great quantities of documents of quasi-archival nature. I refer here to the Egyptian papyri as well as to the famous Geniza collection. The joint chronological coverage of these materials extends over the entire period of the Islamic Middle Ages, furnishing copious information pertaining to monetary transactions, exchange rates, prices of various commodities, real estate and similar business details. How much one can learn from these otherwise prosaic and very complex materials has been demonstrated by the brilliant editorial accomplishments of A. Grohmann[20] and S. D. Goitein.[21]

To a certain extent the critical remarks expressed in the introduction to the present survey of sources apply to the manner in which textual materials have been treated by modern monetary historians. Any discussion of the modern studies of Islamic monetary developments should begin with a tribute to the monumental accomplishment of Henri Sauvaire (1831–96) who was so successful in carrying out a project of the publication of an impressive body of published and unpublished data pertaining to Near Eastern monetary institutions. The contribution of Sauvaire, which first appeared in a series of articles in *Journal Asiatique* between 1879 and 1887, under the title *Matériaux pour servir à l'histoire de la numismatique et de la métrologie musulmanes*, was of major consequence in the development of this branch of Islamic history. From a methodological point of view the significance of Sauvaire's pioneering achievement results from the fact that he successfully demonstrated the feasibility of a project consisting of establishing and organizing a scattered, dispersed and fragmented mass of historical evidence into a coherent body of information which constitutes a fundamental prerequisite for the study of monetary developments. The merit of Sauvaire's achievement may be fully appreciated when one realizes that ever since their appearance the *Matériaux* have served as a basic reference tool for any historian confronted with Islamic monetary or metrological phenomena. Paradoxically enough, the very accomplishment of Henri Sauvaire dealt a setback to subsequent heuristic activities in the field under present discussion. I mean here that scholars engaged in the

[19] Cf. ed. by Ḥussain Monés, *Regimen de la casa de la moneda*, Madrid 1960.

[20] Cf. A. Grohmann, 'Einführung und Chrestomathie zur arabischen Papyrusurkunde' (*Monografie Archivu Orientálního*, vol. 13, i), 1955.

[21] Cf. his recent contribution 'The exchange rate of gold and silver money in Fatimid and Ayyubid times. A preliminary study of the relevant Geniza material', *JESHO*, 8, 1965, pp. 1–46. Also, S. Shaked, *A tentative bibliography of Geniza documents*, 1964.

study of medieval Near Eastern economic and monetary history were so generously accommodated with the wealth of the published *economica* that they failed to follow up the inspiring example of the French savant. Several decades had elapsed before new published economic data appeared in academic circulation. The contributions of Grohmann who has been engaged in the arduous task of interpreting the contents of the papyri; of Goitein who has been unveiling the dormant resources from the Geniza collection; of Ashtor who has been tabulating economic evidence from all kinds of medieval texts—may serve as instances of heuristic undertakings marking the beginning of a new phase in the field of Near Eastern monetary history. A phase which is characterized by a systematic effort to expand and deepen our research control over textual source materials.

B. Numismatic evidence

If students of medieval Near Eastern monetary history are handicapped by the unsystematic and episodic character of textual evidence, they are overcompensated by the nature of numismatic source materials. The great significance of medieval Islamic numismatic evidence arises from the fact that, as a rule, gold and silver coinage dating from the classical period of the Caliphate displays multiple material features reflecting the religious, political, aesthetic and above all economic background of the institutions or authorities responsible for its production.

The phenomenon of the existence of tremendous quantities of surviving Islamic coin specimens, available in public and private collections, in the hands of coin or antique dealers, or surfacing in treasure troves which keep being discovered in Africa, Asia and Europe has led to the rise of many outstanding specialists excelling in the field of Muslim numismatics. Valuable information derived from Muslim coins and registered by several generations of professional numismatists[22] has eventually attracted the attention of scholars interested in Medieval Near Eastern history. They did not fail to appreciate the services rendered by the ancillary discipline in supplementing textual or other archaeological evidence. Political historians could verify or even reconstruct chronology of political events, the nature of relation between different political regimes, territorial extension of authority of particular rulers, their religious or, if one prefers ideological affiliations, etc. Historians interested in the study of diplomatics could examine the nature

[22] Cf. L. A. Mayer, *Bibliography of Moslem numismatics* (Oriental Translation Fund, 35) 1954; also, A. Kmietowicz, 'Supplements to L. Mayer's "Bibliography of Moslem numismatics" ', *Folia Orientalia*, 2, 1960, pp. 259–75; also George C. Miles, 'Islamic and Sasanian numismatics: retrospect and prospect', *Rapports, Congrès International de Numismatique*, 1953, vol. i, pp. 129–44; also *idem*, 'Islamic numismatics: a progress report', *Relazioni, Congresso Internazionale di Numismatica*, 1961, vol. i, pp. 181–92; also T. Lewicki, 'Nouveaux travaux russes concernant les trésors de monnaies musulmanes trouvés en Europe Orientale et en Asie Centrale (1959–1963)', *JESHO*, 8, 1965, pp. 81–90.

of political and religious titles of the people whose names were mentioned in the inscriptions on the coins. Those concerned with the problem of palaeography, heraldry or of art in general, would eagerly observe stylistic aspects of the coins. Students of the history of science could utilize coinage to study technological, chemical and metallurgical problems involved in the refining and coining of metals. In short, historians have realized the importance of Islamic numismatic materials. They have been aware of the manifold character of historical information to be extracted from this type of evidence. They saw and handled many problems related to or raised by Muslim coinage, but—perhaps because of this topical multiplicity and complexity—they have failed to exploit the availability of these paramount source materials for a serious consideration of the most appropriate subject connected with Islamic coinage. For one can hardly dispute the fact that the most important attribute of Islamic coinage from the point of view of historical discipline, is that it constitutes a direct, physical trace or—to use Bernheim's definition—unintentional material relic of a monetary system. After all, these coins, these *dīnārs*, *dirhams* or *fulūs* were not struck to satisfy the curiosity of historians or vanity of coin collectors of the modern age, but to serve as money, as currency in the monetary system of the medieval Near Eastern world. Consequently, the most logical direct and obvious question which should be asked of surviving medieval Muslim coins is what they can reveal in respect to medieval Near Eastern monetary history.

The situation arising from the underdeveloped state of numismatic evidence in the reconstruction of the monetary history of the Near East is quite absurd. There are millions of Muslim coins available for statistical tabulation and interpretation and yet few steps have been undertaken in this direction. This statement must not be understood as an accusation of carelessness or ineptitude levelled against the established authorities in the field of Islamic numismatics. Our indebtedness to professional numismatists has been registered above. The blame rests with historians studying monetary and economic phenomena of the Islamic Near East, who have failed to utilize or to insist upon the supply of more detailed and analytical information pertaining to numismatic source materials. For a historian differs from a numismatist in his approach to numismatic sources. A numismatist looks for historical information to produce an exhaustive description of a coin specimen. A monetary historian looks for numismatic evidence to help him achieve an exhaustive reconstruction of a historical phenomenon. The difference of approach is also evident in the evaluation of the importance of a numismatic specimen. Some rare specimens, e.g., the 'standing caliph' type of *dīnārs* of the transitional period prior to the great reform of ʿAbd al-Malik, rate as extremely valuable coins on numismatic markets. The monetary historian, on the other hand, may interpret the rarity of these specimens as an indication of their low value or unpopularity as currency units, leading to their withdrawal from circulation and a further drop in their market price. Neither is the numismatist interested in statistical tabulations. And yet the question of the total numbers of preserved Muslim coins is of historical significance. It has been stated above that millions of Muslim coins are available for a study of monetary history. How many millions? What is the total of Muslim coins which have been saved from obliteration? Does not that total represent a certain minimum of precious metal which has been withdrawn from circulation, hurting the economy of the institutions responsible for their production? Should not the number of all specimens of Muslim coins scattered in various collections be tabulated? Should not such tabulations indicate specific totals of specimens according to the year and place of their production?

Any such tabulations must take typological variants into account. Numismatic catalogues normally refer to the precise weight of described specimens but they do not specify the exact nature of their alloy. Traditional segregation into gold and silver category is of a limited pragmatic consequence to the monetary historian for he is interested in knowing how much gold or silver the alloy of a coin contains. After all, if coins struck by the same mint display a deterioration or improvement in their alloy such phenomena must have been produced by some factors or decisions based most frequently—though not always—on economic considerations.

That an inquiry into the nature of the alloy of numismatic specimens lies within the realm of research viability has been demonstrated by a series of recent or even current investigations. The application of the specific gravity measurements for the study of *dīnārs*[23] and *dirhams*,[24] the use of X-ray spectrographic analysis for the study of *dirhams*,[25] and finally the application of the method of radioactivation which reveals the total composition and the percentage of all elements in the alloy structure of examined specimens,[26] these are some of the examples of sustained research efforts aiming at a more exhaustive and analytical exploitation of numismatic evidence.

While the primary function of Islamic numismatic materials is to furnish

[23] Cf. P. Naster, 'Numismatique et méthodes de laboratoire', *Rapports, Congrès International de Numismatique*, 1953, vol. i, pp. 171–92; also E. R. Caley, 'Validity of the specific gravity method for the determination of the fineness of gold objects', *Ohio Journal of Science*, 49, 1949, pp. 73–82; also A. S. Ehrenkreutz, 'Studies in the monetary history of the Near East in the Middle Ages, II.', *JESHO*, 6, 1963, pp. 248–50.

[24] Cf. E. R. Caley, 'Estimation of composition of ancient metal objects', *Analytical Chemistry*, 24, 1952, pp. 676–81.

[25] Cf. J. L. Bacharach, 'History, science and coins', *Michigan Technic*, Jan. 1964, pp. 24–6; also O. I. Smirnova, *Katalog monet gorodishcha Pendzhikent*, 1963; also E. A. Davidovich, 'Iz oblasti denezhnogo obrashcheniya v Sredney Azii', *Numizmatika i Epigrafika*, 2, 1960, p. 102 f.

[26] Cf. J. L. Bacharach and A. A. Gordus, 'Studies on the fineness of silver coins', *JESHO*, 11, 1968, pp. 298–317. Cf. also Alan K. Craig, 'Neutrons and numismatics', *The Numismatist*, 76, 1963, pp. 1085–6.

information concerning the different types of medieval Near Eastern currency, one may also exploit them for the study of the production of coinage. A copious amount of information concerning the identification of geographic, chronological and personal references displayed by Islamic coin specimens, which has been furnished by several generations of outstanding numismatists, has made it possible to trace the evolution of medieval Near Eastern mint production from the vantage point of economic (relation of the mints to the sources of precious metals; to trade routes and markets) and political considerations (relation of the mints to political organization or institutions). The correlating of the external and intrinsic characteristics of the surviving specimens may yield interesting information concerning the quality of production of particular mints.

Another extremely important aspect of the production of coinage is the annual output of individual mints. Without resorting to sophisticated equations defining the relationship between prices and the volume of coins in circulation, one may state that one of the major factors conditioning the price and wage situation in the medieval Near East was the volume of coins available for the needs of its society. One of the salient features of the monetary system of the medieval caliphate was that it depended on its mints for coinage supply. For this reason the problem of Islamic coinage production acquires a significant status in the field of economic history.

In spite of the deplorable lack of textual information,[27] an inquiry into the productivity of Islamic mints can be undertaken by resorting to numismatic evidence, applying the method of the 'coin-die count'. This method involves two basic phases: (i) the estimation of the number of dies employed in the production of a coinage series, and (ii) the estimation of the quantity of coins which the dies were capable of producing. Phase (i) calls for the discernment of traces of coin die variants in a random sample of specimens belonging to a series. The ratio of coin die variants to the number of random samples has been accepted as a basis for calculations aiming at a statistical estimate of the actual number of dies involved in the production of the series.[28] Phase (ii) culminates in the multiplication of the total of estimated dies by the average number of coins which these dies were capable of producing.

Unfortunately, the problem of estimating the capacity or longevity of coin dies can hardly, if at all, be resolved. In spite of this methodological 'cul-de-sac' the application of the coin-die count procedure constitutes a step forward in the attempt at a quantitative assessment of the annual output of

[27] Interpretative limitations arising from the shortage of textual evidence are discussed in a report in *JESHO*, 9, 1966.

[28] For the most recent discussion of the problem of various formulae for establishing die totals see P. Grierson, 'Byzantine coinage as source materials', *Thirteenth International Congress of Byzantine Studies*, Oxford 1966, *Main Papers*, x, pp. 1–17.

individual mints. This point may be illustrated by means of the following hypothetical example. Let us assume that a tabulation of all surviving *dīnār* specimens struck in A.H. 300 would reveal that there are 1,000 specimens from Baghdad and five specimens from Egypt. In the light of such a quantitative contrast one might be inclined to conclude that the output of the Baghdad mint in A.H. 300 was much higher than that of Egypt. And yet upon a closer scrutiny of the Baghdādī specimens one may establish that they were struck by one, only one, set of dies. On the other hand it may be established that each of the five Egyptian specimens was struck by a different set of dies. This revelation would have to force one to postulate that the output of the Egyptian mint in A.H. 300 exceeded five times the total of *dīnārs* struck in Baghdad.

The viability of the coin-die count method and the value of the results yielded by such an inquiry has been successfully tested by a seminar team at the University of Michigan. During the summer of 1966 the members of the seminar undertook a preliminary investigation involving the Umayyad *dīnārs* and *dirhams* and presently they are engaged in a project concerning the annual output of gold coinage by the medieval Egyptian mints.[29]

A final important problem which should be elucidated by means of a proper exploitation of numismatic materials pertains to the geographic extension of the circulation of the medieval Near Eastern currency. This problem is of 'international' interest since it raises the question of monetary relations between Europe and the Near East during the Middle Ages. As far as the West European aspect of this problem is concerned a scholarly debate has for the past few decades revolved around the preliminary but fundamental question as to whether Muslim gold coins were at all in circulation in Christian markets.[30] Following the enunciation of several, sometimes diametrically opposed theories on the subject,[31] a sobering tone was introduced to the debate in question, consisting of an important contribution by J. Duplessy, 'La circulation des monnaies arabes en Europe occidentale du VIIIe au XIIIe siècle'.[32] The main significance of Duplessy's achievement lies in the fact that after having taken stock of earlier contributions on the subject, he boldly challenged the validity of

[29] A full report on the procedures and results of the seminar, entitled 'Early Islamic mint output. A preliminary inquiry into the methodology and application of the "Coin-die count" method' has appeared in *JESHO*, 9, 1966, pp. 212–41.

[30] For a recent succinct summary of the polemics, and pertinent bibliographical references, see Cl. Cahen, 'Quelques problèmes concernant l'expansion économique musulmane au Haut Moyen Age', *L'Occidente e l'Islam nell'alto Medioevo, Settimane di studio del Centro italiano di studi sull' alto medioevo*, 12, 1965, pp. 392–3.

[31] E.g., those postulated by M. Lombard, 'Les bases monétaires d'une suprematie économique. L'or musulman du VII au XI siècle', *Annales (Economies, Sociétés, Civilisations)*, 2, 1947, pp. 143–60, and by Fr. Himly, 'Y a-t-il emprise musulmane sur l'économie des Etats européens du VIII aux X siècle', *Revue Suisse d'Histoire*, 5, 1955, pp. 31–81.

[32] *Revue Numismatique*, V serie, 18, 1956, pp. 101–63.

numismatic foundations on which the arguments supporting some sweeping theories were made to rest. The modest number of Muslim coins (241 whole and fractionary *dīnārs*, 153 whole and fractionary *dirhams*, 1 copper coin) originating from 36 West European treasure troves, can hardly be regarded as adequate numismatic evidence warranting any generalizations. Furthermore, this meagre numismatic evidence was neither properly analysed nor correlated with pertinent textual evidence. To restore the air of methodological integrity to the important debate Duplessy made an essential preliminary step by presenting a survey of relevant numismatic and textual materials.[33] He emphasized, however, that before any definitive and categorical conclusions are formulated many more studies must be undertaken, such as 'étude critique des textes arabes, dépouillement complet et classement par régions des chartes et documents divers de l'Europe occidentale; recherches sur les raisons de chacun des enfouissements connus, sur le pouvoir d'achat des monnaies d'or, sur les relations commerciales et les produits échangés'.[34]

Unlike the situation in Western Europe, numismatic evidence yielded by Central, North and East European hoards is so voluminous that the fact of the presence of Muslim coinage on early medieval Slavic and Scandinavian markets does not constitute a debatable issue. Indeed, according to an authoritative study published in 1960 by R. Kiersnowski, the totals of Islamic numismatic materials registered in those regions consisted of about 1,400 troves and about 200,000 specimens of Arabic coins.[35] It is obvious that, the lack of textual evidence notwithstanding, the tremendous volume of numismatic sources accumulated in Central, Northern and Eastern Europe, warrants serious investigations and reconstructive hypotheses concerning the circulation of Near Eastern currency, based on a quantitative method of statistical analysis.[36]

'*Ars longa – vita brevis*'

Methodological goals outlined in the quoted statement of Duplessy apply to the entire field of medieval Near Eastern monetary history. Naturally, the idea of amassing and interpreting monetary data for the purpose of economic evaluations presents an enormous task, hardly feasible if undertaken by ordinary means of analytical treatment. In this respect the application of modern electronic computing devices is of utmost importance. The

[33] *Ibid.*, pp. 121–52. [34] *Ibid.*, p. 119.

[35] R. Kiersnowski, *Pieniądz kruszcowy w Polsce Średniowiecznej*, 1960, p. 103.

[36] The contribution of Kiersnowski offers an excellent example of such an undertaking. The main topic of his investigation is the question of the role which 'foreign' coins and weights played in the inception of the 'national' monetary and weight system of the Polish state around the turn of the first Christian millenium. His accomplishment is significant not only because of many interesting conclusions but because of its methodological aspects.

above mentioned seminar group of the University of Michigan resorted to electronic computers in its tedious task of tabulating the copious data pertaining to Umayyad coin dies. The results obtained from such a procedure proved to be extremely rewarding. The total number of index cards containing a great diversity of coin and coin-die specifications amounted to 1,440. It is true that preparatory activities such as the typing of special key punch cards or the formulating and executing of the computer programming, were time-consuming. However, once the computer was fed with 1,440 punch cards it took only 1 minute 20·7 seconds to process and type the data consisting of 2,756 lines presented on 53 pages. These results speak for themselves. The value of computers in historical research, whenever large volumes of data are involved—which happens to be the case of monetary history—can hardly be disputed.

From now on those scholars who commit their lives to the task of collecting prosaic monetary data need not fear that they might leave the amassed materials uninterpreted. Indeed, future progress in the field of medieval Near Eastern monetary history will depend on the degree to which historians utilize modern laboratory techniques to control the source materials salvaged from the past.

II

MONEY

By the time of the Arab invasion the Near East had had more than a thousand years of experience with the institution of money. As in other civilizations pre-Islamic money, consisting of coinage made of precious metals, performed a number of functions in the economic life of Near Eastern society. It served as a measure of value of goods and services; it served as standard currency facilitating transactions involving exchanges of commodities; it was used in payment for services; it offered a convenient means of treasuring accumulated wealth; it functioned as international currency, of special importance in the context of pre-Islamic conditions. Finally, Near Eastern coinage was used to disseminate religious and political propaganda.

Both from that thousand-year era and from the subsequent Islamic period there have survived tremendous quantities of numismatic specimens. When treated as historical sources—as unintentional tangible relics of historical phenomena—these numismatic materials yield abundant information about the history of Islamic money, making up for the scantiness of historical data available in textual sources. Moreover, since the scope of circulation of money generally corresponded with prevailing market trends—expanding in times of boom, and contracting during periods of recession—a study of monetary developments constitutes an important element in modern efforts to reconstruct medieval Near Eastern economic history.[1]

On the eve of Islam the major political division which prevailed in the Near East had a parallel in the general monetary situation. The *solidi*, the official currency of the Byzantine Empire,[2] enjoyed monetary supremacy in provinces dominated by Constantinople. On the other

---

[1] A. S. Ehrenkreutz, 'Monetary aspects of medieval Near Eastern economic history', *Studies in the economic history of the Middle East*, ed. by M. A. Cook, London, 1970, p. 37-50; Philip Grierson, *Numismatics and history*, London, 1951; *idem*. 'Byzantine coinage as source material', *Thirteenth International Congress of Byzantine Studies, Main Papers X*, Oxford, 1966.

[2] Ph. Grierson, 'From solidus to hyperperon: the names of Byzantine gold coins', *Numismatic Circular*, 74, 1966, p. 123-124.

hand, the *drachmas*, or silver coins, being the official currency of the Sāsānid dynasty, prevailed in the Persian Empire.[3] In spite of the basic difference of their respective official currencies both empires experimented with other metallic types—the Byzantines with silver issues [4] and the Sāsānids with gold.[5] Moreover, for petty cash transactions, both of them supplied local markets with copper coinage.[6] Nor did the two metallic zones operate in monetary isolation. Under normal political and economic conditions all of the pre-Islamic Near East had no restrictions as far as circulation of divers types of specie were concerned. Byzantine coins were accepted on Sāsānid markets while Sāsānid silver circulated in Christian territories. A typical example of the operation of the monetary open market is provided by the case of pre-Islamic Mekka whose traders were used to handling Byzantine, Sāsānid, and even the less prestigious Yāmānite (Ḥimyarite) coins.[7]

During the decades immediately preceding the Arab invasion, circulation of specie in the Near East appears to have declined, particularly in Byzantine provinces. Oppressive, monopolistic and centripetal fiscal policy of the government in Constantinople worked against the interests of the indigenous Syrian and Egyptian population. Their level of economic activities did not warrant local production of gold coinage then supplied by the mints of Constantinople, Carthage, and Ravenna.[8] Silver coins, introduced in A.D. 619,[9] were struck to meet the military needs of Heraclius rather than in response to market demands. Persian occupation of Syria and Egypt (A.D. 611-628) resulted in a decline of Byzantine specie. Trade routes connecting Near Eastern markets with imperial mints were controlled by Sāsānid troops and those of their allies. Salaried Greek administrators, officials, and military personnel, important in introducing money to local market operations, were eliminated. Local mints, responsible for coining copper, including the major mint of Antioch, were closed down.[10] Precious metals were hoarded

---

[3] R. Göbl, *Sasanidische Numismatik*, Braunschweig, 1968, p. 25.

[4] E.g. the *hexagram* of Heraclius, cf. G. C. Miles, 'Byzantine miliaresion and Arab dirhem: some notes on their relationship', *The American Numismatic Society Museum Notes*, 9, 1963, p. 191.

[5] R. Göbl, *op. cit.*, p. 28.

[6] Ph. Grierson, 'Trace elements in Byzantine copper coins of the 6th and 7th centuries', *Dona Numismatica. Walter Hävernick zum 23. Januar 1965 dargebracht*, Hamburg, p. 29-35; R. Göbl, *op cit.*, p. 29.

[7] Al-Maqrīzī, *Al-nuqūd al-islāmīyah*, al-Najaf, 1967, p. 3-4; E. A. Beliaev, *Arabs, Islam and the Arab caliphate*, New York, 1969, p. 89-90.

[8] W. Wroth, *Catalogue of the Imperial Byzantine coins in the British Museum*, London, 1908, i/civ.

[9] See above, note 4.

[10] George E. Bates, 'Five Byzantine notes — 3. The Antioch mint under Heraclius', *The American Numismatic Society Museum Notes*, 16, 1970, p. 80-82.

privately or thesaurized in churches and monasteries.[11] Several ships were needed to carry some of those treasures in an unsuccessful attempt to save them from falling into Persian hands.[12]

The serious monetary crisis might have been alleviated by the Persian *drachmas* brought by the invasing troops of Khusrau II. The early rule of that dynamic monarch was characterized by the largest number of active mints in Sāsānid history.[13] However, the military exigencies of Khusrau's imperialistic policies seemed to exceed his economic resources; consequently the *drachmas* struck during his expansionist war suffered from a debasement.[14] In spite of territorial gains and of tremendous war booty achieved by the invasion of Syria and Egypt, Sāsānid monetary activities were hampered by oppressive fiscal policies which drained coinage off the markets to the imperial treasury in Ctesiphon.[15] The total collapse of Khusrau's expansionist policy in A.D. 628 brought a further deterioration in the monetary situation. His defeat at the hands of the Heraclius meant not only withdrawal from Byzantine provinces, but a loss of tremendous monetary resources invested in the war effort at the expense of constructive, peaceful economic activities.

The termination of hostilities was not destined to bring any improvement in the monetary situation. Although the return of Byzantine officials and troops, and especially Heraclius' triumphant visit to Jerusalem in A.D. 630, might have increased somewhat the volume of Byzantine coinage on Syrian and Egyptian markets, no major mints reopened their production. In Sāsānid territories the standard of *drachmas* temporarily improved, but the central government was losing control over the mints, exposing its markets to new issues of debased currency.

Consequently, when the first Arab contingents made their appearance in Byzantine and Sāsānid provinces, the monetary sector of the Near Eastern economy faced a serious crisis. While the theoretically standardized money continued to serve as the means of estimating and evaluation in fiscal and commercial operations, the actual transactions and transfers of funds, either local or international, were complicated by the heterogeneous character of available specie. Coins belonging to the same metallic, national or geographic category were of divers intrinsic quality. Chaotic political and economic conditions did not enhance circulation

---

[11] M. Lombard, *Monnaie et histoire d'Alexandre à Mahomet*, Paris, 1971, p. 140.

[12] N. Pigulevskaia, *Vizantiia i Iran na rubezhe VI i VII vekov*, Moskva, 1946, p. 219.

[13] Jere L. Bacharach and Adon A. Gordus, 'The purity of Sasanian silver coins: an introduction', *Journal of the American Oriental Society*, 92, 1972, p. 282.

[14] *Supra.*

[15] N. Pigulevskaia, *op. cit.*, p. 219.

of money. Such production of coinage that still went on was mainly motivated by political and militaristic considerations of the ruling regimes rather than by organic market stimuli. Evidently only an economic regeneration and drastic overhaul of currency could arrest the perilous course of the Near Eastern monetary system.

When the Arabs were invading various Byzantine and Sasanid regions they showed no interest in upsetting the prevailing monetary patterns. The institution of money had been sanctioned by Muhammad and integrated with other economic elements of the Islamic legal system.[16] As stated above the basic monetary types circulating in the conquered territories were not unknown to Arab invaders.[17] Predictably enough, various treaties imposed by Muslim conquerors on subject populations consisted mainly of obligations formulated and expressed in monetary terms—silver coins in former Sāsānid, and gold coins in former Byzantine provinces.[18] The same was true of the tax variants which evolved from the initial tribute agreements.[19] And yet, its original conservative attitude notwithstanding, the victorious Arab regime generated forces which opened a new phase in Near Eastern monetary history. To understand the nature of that significant phenomenon one has to consider the basic aspects of the economic situation arising from the Arab conquest of the Near East.[20]

One of the outstanding aspects of the Arab invasion was the mass migration of the surplus population from the Arabian peninsula to the sedentarized zone of the Near East.[21] Certainly, the members of the Byzantine and Sāsānid ruling establishment were displaced, expelled, or even exterminated by the Arabs, but the number of newcomers exceeded by far the eliminated pre-Islamic elite. To accommodate the mass of the Arab immigrants it was not enough to take over premises vacated by the ousted population. Entire new quarters had to be added to old towns, or completely new urban settlements had to be founded.[22]

---

[16] Al-Maqrīzī, *op. cit.*, p. 6-8; al-Hamdānī, *Kitāb al-ġauharatain*, herausgegeben und übersetzt von Christopher Toll, Uppsala, 1968, p. 50 f.

[17] See above, p. 85.

[19] D. C. Dennett, Jr., *Conversion and the poll tax in Early Islam*, Cambridge, 1950, p. 41-42 and *passim*.

[19] *Ibid.*, p. 22 f. and *passim*.

[20] The following summary is based on this author's article 'Another Orientalist's remarks concerning the Pirenne thesis', *Journal of the Economic and Social History of the Orient*, 15, 1972, p. 94-104.

[21] M. A. Shaban, *The ʿAbbāsid revolution*, Cambridge, 1970, p. 141.

[22] E. Reitemeyer, *Die Städtegründungen der Araber im Islam*, Leipzig, 1912; E. Pauty, 'Villes

With the exception of a small minority, the mass of the Arab immigrants represented unskilled labor which under normal political and social conditions could hardly have been absorbed by or integrated with the local population of the Fertile Crescent without causing a major economic and social upheaval.

As it was, that mass immigration did not impede normal economic activity. The healthy transitional integration was made possible because of a profound fiscal transformation that the conquered population experienced under the new regime. State revenue was no longer administered by two different and mutually hostile imperial treasuries, the Byzantine in Constantinople and the Sāsānid in Ctesiphon. Responsibility for determining the nature of taxation—the system of collection as well as the allocation of the revenue—was taken over by one central and supreme financial institution, the *dīwān*, established by ʿUmar I (A.D. 634-644), to serve the needs of the Caliphate.[23] As for the level of taxation and the method of tax collection, the policy of the Caliphate towards the conquered population was characterized by conservative moderation.[24] It was in the matters of distribution of the accumulated wealth that the policy of the early Caliphate acquired a truly innovative character. It involved a system of fiscal benefits, administered by the *dīwān*, according to which all full-fledged members of the victorious Arab people were entitled to regular cash stipends, called *ʿaṭāʾ*, in addition to their lower taxation rates.[25] To realize the monetary implications of the *ʿaṭāʾ* system one has to point out its basic principles: according to a hierarchic order which took into account kinship with the Prophet and especially seniority as regards admission to Islam, graduated pensions were distributed to the whole Muslim population which had been displaced from its homes by the holy war (the *Muhājirūn* and *anṣār* of the early days, together with the fighting men of a later date), women, children, slaves and clients (still not numerous and not by definition foreigners), but excluding the Bedouin and others who remained, in Arabia and elsewhere, unaffected by the military expansion of Islam. The amount ranged from 200 to 12,000 silver coins, the great majority of the men receiving from 500 to 1,000 silver coins annually.[26]

---

spontanées et villes creées en Islam', *Annales de l'Institut d'Études Orientales* (Alger) 9, 1951, p. 52-75.

[23] Matti I. Moosa, 'The diwan of ʿUmar ibn al-Khaṭṭāb', *Studies in Islam*, 2, 1965, p. 67-78.

[24] D. C. Dennett, Jr., *op cit.*, p. 24 f. and *passim*.

[25] Cl. Cahen, '*ʿAṭāʾ*', *The Encyclopaedia of Islam*, new ed., i/729-730; A. S. Tritton, 'Notes on the Muslim system of pensions,' *Bulletin of the School of Oriental and African Studies*, 16, 1954, p. 170-172.

[26] Cl. Cahen, *art. cit.*, p. 729.

The implementation of a program of such fiscal magnitude could not be achieved without meeting two fundamental requirements: the adoption of a standard monetary unit which would be used for registrative and normative processes; and the availability of tremendous amounts of cash for regular mass distribution. The first requirement was met by selecting the *dirham* unit, the Arabic term for *drachma*, or the basic Sāsānid silver unit to be used in the operations of the *dīwān*. As for the required cash, it was partially obtained from huge amounts of booty which flowed into Medina during the period of rapid conquests.[27] There can hardly be any doubt, however, that the bulk of the cash was coming from tax collections, for in spite of the downfall of the Sāsānid monarchy and the expulsion of the Byzantine hierarchy the entire tax base survived virtually intact. The main reason for such development was the non-destructive character of the great conquest. Certainly, battles were fought and some cities endured prolonged sieges, but in general the dramatic takeover was accomplished without substantial losses by the tax-paying civilian population or by revenue-yielding establishments. Nor did agricultural and artisan production show any ill-effects of the imposition of the Arab regime. The conquerors did not levy any taxes in excess of what the population of the Near East had been paying for the benefit of the ousted rulers. But whereas in pre-Islamic times tax revenues had been shared by two different administrations, after the Arab invasion all of them came under the jurisdiction of the Caliphate. Furthermore, after the victory of the Arabs no center of political and administrative jurisdiction over Near Eastern territories was located outside the Near East, as had been the case of Rome and Constantinople. Consequently, none of the monies collected by the Caliphate supported an external capital and its policies, but by means of the *'aṭā'* system, all of them were retained, re-invested, diffused for the benefit of the local Near Eastern population.

With the regular financial assistance provided by the Caliphate the Arab immigrants, far from becoming an economic liability, functioned as a mechanism reactivating cash mobility. Whether members of ruling elite or the masses of ordinary warriors Arab settlers constituted a potent consumer class generating economic demand, stimulating productivity, and above all energizing the circulation of money. Hoarded coinage reappeared on the markets either because of categorical fiscal demands [28]

[27] Cl. Cahen, 'Bayt al-Māl', *The Encyclopaedia of Islam, new ed.*, i/141; E. A. Beliaev, op. cit., p. 140-141.

[28] E. Ashtor, *Les métaux précieux et la balance des payments du Proche-Orient à la basse époque*, Paris, 1971, p. 15.

or because of the prospects of profitable investments. Even so, with favorable economic trends induced by the fiscal policy of the Caliphate, the monetary demands soon exceeded the volume of specie in circulation.

This is evident from the fact that shortly after the Arab conquest various Near Eastern mints, previously inactive or shut down during the invasion, resumed their production. In Syria copper coins or the *fulūs* (sing. *fals*) were struck in imitation of Byzantine *follis* but with gradual additions of Arabic elements, epigraphic and iconographic, mostly of a religious and geographic character.[29] In Egypt purely Byzantine copper coins of one or more types of Heraclius (and of Constans II, A.D. 641-668) very likely made their reappearance coming from the mint of Alexandria.[30] In former Sāsānid provinces anonymous Arab adaptations of the *drachmas* were produced, predominantly of the popular early Khusrau II type.[31] There is no evidence that the new rulers were directly and consciously involved in this development.[32] Obviously, fresh production of coins by various widely scattered mints resulted from local initiative responding to altered market conditions. An expanding economy led to expansion of monetary activities, and consequently to a growing demand for stabilized and uniform specie.

With the continuation of Arab immigration new consumer centers were arising in previously impoverished regions of the Near East. The expansion of old towns and proliferation of new urban settlements, such as Fusṭāṭ in Egypt,[33] Ramlah in Palestine,[34] Baṣrah and Kūfah in Mesopotamia,[35] created a boom in the housing industry. The growth of the financially subsidized urban population generated a strong demand for food supplies, thus stimulating speculative agriculture and interest in acquisition of landed property.[36] Likewise, internal trade benefited from the new situation by performing economic functions between the urban and rural population.

For people with money it was a period of profitable investments and remunerative cash transactions. Prominent in this respect were the

---

[29] A. Udovitch, 'Fals', *The Encyclopaedia of Islam*, new ed., i/768; G. C. Miles, 'The early Islamic bronze coinage of Egypt,' *Centennial Volume of the American Numismatic Society*, New York, 1958, p. 471-472.

[30] G. C. Miles, *art. cit.*, p. 472.

[31] J. Walker, *A catalogue of the Arab-Sassanian coins*, London, 1941, p. 5.

[32] G. C. Miles, *art. cit.*, p. 471.

[33] J. Jomier, 'Fusṭāṭ', *The Encyclopaedia of Islam*, new ed., ii/957-959; G. T. Scanlon, 'Housing and sanitation,' *The Islamic City*, Oxford, 1970, p. 170-194.

[34] E. Reitemeyer, *op. cit.*, p. 73 f.

[35] *Ibid.*, p. 11 f.; 29 f; 46 f.

[36] Saleh A. Ali, 'Muslim estates in Hidjaz in the first century A.D.'. *Journal of the Economic and Social History of the Orient*, 2, 1959, p. 247-261.

early followers of the Prophet, obviously exploiting their political advantages and capitalistic opportunities in the Ḥijāz. Outside Medina, al-Zubayr bought al-Ghabā for 17,000 and sold it for 1,700,000 dirhams.[37] The value of al-Zubayr's property at his death was 50,000 gold coins.[38] At the death of ʿAbd al-Raḥmān ibn ʿAwf al-Zuhrī, a quarter of his property was worty 84,000 gold coins.[39] ʿAbd Allāh ibn Saʿd ibn Abī Sarḥ sent 3,000 qanāṭīr (weight measures) of gold from Ifrīqīyah to Medina; he ordered this gold to be given to the family of al-Ḥakam.[40] On the day ʿUthmān was killed, he possessed, in the hands of this treasurer, 100,000 gold coins and a million *dirhams*.[41]

Similar trends continued after the establishment of the Umayyad regime in A.D. 661, except that Syria succeeded the Ḥijāz as the most favored province of the Empire. Her inhabitants were reaping financial dividends from the location of the *dīwān* and the central treasury in Damascus. By then some fifteen mints operated in Syria [42] and over fifty others in former Sāsānid territories,[43] supplying currency for the monetary needs of an expanding economy. However, the production of all those mints, regardless of the magnitude of their total output,[44] failed to satisfy two desirable requirements. First, none of those mints issued gold coins, a preferred specie in former Byzantine provinces. The markets had to rely on the Byzantine *solidi* circulating under their Arabic name of *dīnār*. Pressure for supply of gold coins increased with the economic boom in Syria. As a matter of fact, on three occasions the Umayyads had to pay tribute to the Byzantines in gold cash,[45] adding to the rarity of the gold currency. Secondly, both the pre-conquest and the freshly manufactured currency lacked external and internal uniformity. Most of Near Eastern territories were now integrated as one

---

[37] *Ibid.*, p. 254.

[38] B. Lewis, 'On the revolutions in early Islam', *Studia Islamica*, 32, 1970, p. 222.

[29] *Supra.*

[40] E. Beliaev, *op. cit.*, p. 144.

[41] B. Lewis, *art. cit.*, p. 221.

[42] A. S. Kirkbride, 'Coins of the Byzantine-Arab transition period', *The Quarterly of the Department of Antiquities in Palestine,*' 13, 1948, p. 59-63; J. Walker, *A catalogue of the Arab-Byzantine and post-reform Umaiyad coins*. London, 1956, p. xxxiii-xxxiv. In the light of an article by Raoul Curiel, 'Monnaie de bronze d'Ahnās-Miṣr', *Revue Numismatique*, VIe série, Tome X, 1968, p. 131-137, it appears that some of the places whose names were displayed on the coins, might have served as distribution centers rather than as the actual mints.

[43] J. Walker, *A catalogue of the Arab-Sassanian coins*, London, 1941, p. cix; G. C. Miles, 'Abarqubādh, a new Umayyad mint', *The American Numismatic Society Museum Notes*, 4, 1950, p. 115-120.

[44] W. G. Andrews et al., 'Early Islamic mint output. A preliminary inquiry into the methodology and application of the "Coin-die count" method', *Journal of the Economic and Social History of the Orient*, 9, 1966, p. 212-241.

[45] G. Ostrogorsky, *Geschichte des Byzantinischen Staates*, München, 1963, p. 97, 104, 108.

common market area, but the coinage in circulation belonged to the bygone era. Residual Byzantine *solidi* must have suffered from wear and tear, besides including some debased series.[46] The post-conquest silver coins, coming from divers mints operating without any control on the part of the central government, were of unequal quality in weight, in fineness, and even in stylistic features. To add political insult to economic injury, some of the series were issued by rebel factions to disseminate anti-Umayyad propaganda.[47] Obviously, the chaotic coinage condition constituted a real impediment in many essential areas of monetary operations. It confused producers and merchants, artisans and laborers, buyers and sellers. It complicated the functions of tax assessors and collectors. It created special bookkeeping problems for the staff of the *dīwān*. To cope with this last difficulty fictitious standard money of account was used by the *dīwān*.[48] Monetary requirements of the expanding economy demanded that an end be put to that unhealthy legacy of the past.

A new era in the monetary history of the Near East opened with the full implementation of the famous coinage reform of ʿAbd al-Malik (A.D. 685-705), under whom the Umayyad state reached the zenith of its history. Enjoying the services of some dynamic governors and administrators, as well as strong economic foundations, the reform-minded ruler launched a policy of monetary reorganization. The main goals of that policy were as follows: to initiate production of gold coinage in the Muslim Empire; to reform silver coinage; to prescribe such standards of weight and fineness as to make the value of the reformed coins correspond with the ideal money of account; and, finally, to give the new coinage uniformity of style including insistence on epigraphic manifestations of the religious identity of the Arab empire. Preceded by a number of transitional series, the new standardized gold and silver coins—the Islamic *dīnārs* and *dirhams*—made their appearance in A.D. 696.7, and A.D. 698/9, respectively.[49] This event was followed by the release of non-pictorial Islamic copper coins, the earliest preserved reformed *fals* dating from A.D. 705/6; but the effect of the reform on the *fulūs* was purely epigraphic with no metrological innovations.[50]

---

[46] Ph. Grierson, 'Notes on the fineness of the Byzantine solidus', *Byzantinische Zeitschrift*, 54, 1961, p. 92.

[47] J. Walker, *A catalogue of the Arab-Sassanian coins, ed. cit.*, p. xlii.

[48] Ibn Khaldūn, *The Maqaddimah*, transl. F. Rosenthal, Princeton, 1967, ii/59.

[49] G. C. Miles, 'Dīnār', *The Encyclopaedia of Islam*, new ed., ii/297-298; *idem*, 'The earliest Arab gold coinage', *The American Numismatic Society Museum Notes*, 13, 1967, p. 205-229; Ph. Grierson, 'The monetary reform of ʿAbd al-Malik', *Journal of the Economic and Social History of the Orient*, 3, 1960, p. 241-264.

[50] A. Udovitch, *art. cit.*, ii/768.

Although the coinage reform of ʿAbd al-Malik was essentially a monetary measure, it involved a number of political, administrative, and economic problems. By reforming Near Eastern currency the Arab government recognized its responsibility in respect of the monetary exigencies of the Muslim Empire. By starting production of its own gold coinage the Arab government successfully challenged a monopoly which had traditionally been regarded as an exclusive prerogative of the Roman Empire and of its Byzantine successor. This challenge acquired especial significance considering that the standard of fineness of the *dīnār* was fixed at 96% of purity of gold alloy,[51] or equal, if not superior to that of the contemporary Byzantine *solidi*.[52] By insisting on Arabic and Islamic epigraphic features, and on independent weight standards—4.25 grams for *dīnārs*, and 2.97 g. for *dirhams*—this regime re-emphasized the arrival of the new era in the life of Near Eastern society.

The mass production of the new standardized coinage indicated that the central government asserted control over the existing mints. It also implied the availability of experienced goldsmiths and chemists capable of refining gold to the level required by the standard of *dīnārs*. Umayyad *dīnārs* were produced in Damascus,[53] in North Africa and Spain.[54] There is evidence also that a mint in Egypt [55] and another in the Ḥijāz struck *dīnārs* during that period.[56]

In implementing his reform of silver coinage ʿAbd al-Malik relied on his dynamic viceroy of Eastern provinces, al-Ḥajjāj ibn Yūsuf, who undertook the task of imposing the new type all over the former Sāsānid area. Except for the outlying Eastern provinces, where the latest of the Arab-Sāsānid coin survivals still appeared a century later,[57] all the existing mints in the Eastern part of the Umayyad kingdom were forced to adopt the reformed type of silver currency. Al-Ḥajjāj is also credited with the opening of the first mint to be built under the Arab regime.[58] Though textual sources do not specify where this event took place, numismatic data speak in favor of Kūfah as the site of its location.

---

[51] A. S. Ehrenkreutz, 'Studies in the monetary history of the Near East in the Middle Ages', *Journal of the Economic and Social History of the Orient*, 2, 1959, p. 137.

[52] Ph. Grierson, 'Notes on the fineness of the Byzantine solidus', *Byzantinische Zeitschrift*, 54, 1961, p. 92.

[53] A. S. Ehrenkreutz, *art. cit.*, p. 138.

[54] *Supra.*

[55] *Supra.*

[56] G. C. Miles, *Rare Islamic coins*, (Numismatic Notes and Monographs, 118) 1950, p. 21-22.

[57] J. Walker, *A catalogue of the Arab-Sassanian coins*, ed. cit., p. xxvi.

[58] H. Sauvaire, 'Matériaux pour servir à l'histoire de la numismatique et de la métrologie musulmanes', *Journal Asiatique*, 19, 1882, p. 281.

Other new mints were constructed in Baṣrah and Wāsiṭ.[59] By then silver coins were in demand also in former Byzantine territories, since the mints of Damascus, North Africa, and eventually of Spain, joined in production of *dirhams*.[60]

The reform of ʿAbd al-Malik would not have succeeded without sufficient stocks of precious metals. In those the Muslim Empire more than abounded. To begin with, the mints could depend on all Byzantine and Sāsānid specie, now turned obsolete, delivered for conversion into new Islamic currency. Furthermore, favorable market conditions must have attracted much bullion to the mints, to be turned into legal tender of high purchase value. Lastly, ʿAbd al-Malik's state had an easy access to various oriferous regions (e.g., Nubia, Western sudan, Ḥijāz) [61] and argentiferous regions (e.g., Armenia, Khurāsān),[62] from which gold and silver were coming as a result of natural commercial exchanges or of special tribute arrangements.[63]

Monetary problems received the attention of yet another dynamic Umayyad ruler, Hishām (A.D. 724-743). One of his measures in this respect was a great centralization of the coin production. The striking of gold became restricted to Damascus (although the operations of a mint in Egypt must not be ruled out),[64] while the coining of silver became essentially limited to a small number of centrally located mints instead of over forty which had been involved in supplying the reformed *dirhams*.[65] It is possible that the drastic decrease in the number of mints was ordered to lower the production in response to a diminishing demand on the markets which might have by then become saturated with the specie released following the reform of ʿAbd al-Malik. On the other hand, Hishām might have been concerned that in spite of the thrust of the reform of ʿAbd al-Malik the new Islamic coinage suffered from certain irregularities. For instance, Western *dīnārs* (those struck in North Africa and Spain) displayed certain epigraphic peculiarities of their own.[66] Furthermore, unlike the main center of coinage production in Damascus, the mints of Ifrīqīyah and of Andalus issued fractions of *dīnārs*, such as the half and the third *dīnārs*,[67] characterized by a great

---

59 S. Lane-Poole, *Catalogue of Oriental coins in the British Museum*, London, 1875, i/23, 27.
60 G. C. Miles, 'Dirham', *The Encyclopaedia of Islam*, new ed., ii/319.
61 Al-Hamdānī, *op. cit.*, p. 140-142.
62 *Ibid.*, p. 142 f.
63 F. Lokkegard, 'Baḳṭ', *The Encyclopaedia of Islam*, new ed., i/966.
64 A. S. Ehrenkreutz, *art. cit.*, p. 141.
65 E. von Zambaur, *Die Münzprägungen des Islams*, Wiesbaden, 1968, tables 1 and 2.
66 G. C. Miles, 'Dīnār', *The Encyclopaedia of Islam*, new ed., ii/297.
67 *Supra.*

diversity in the standard of fineness.[68] A lack of stability and of uniformity of the standard of fineness appears to have been also one of the features of the early Islamic silver coinage.[69]

As a result of Hishām's efforts production of irregular Islamic *dīnārs* was discontinued—at least down to the end of Umayyad dynasty—and the standard gold issues maintained at an excellent, 96-98%, level of fineness.[70] A similar effect was achieved in silver coinage. The overwhelming prevalence of the 99% pure *dirhams* among preserved specimens struck under Hishām points to that level as being the official standard prescribed by his administration. After the death of Hishām, the Umayyad ruling establishment quickly disintegrated to be given a *coup de grâce* in A.D. 750 by the ʿAbbāsid challengers. But even during the seven years of Umayyad agony, A.D. 743-750, Islamic *dirhams* produced by the mints of the central government possessed a stable and excellent standard of fineness.[71]

The inception, supply and perfection of standardized Islamic coinage—an indispensable ingredient of a healthy monetary economy—was one of the most enduring accomplishments of the Umayyads. Shortly after their fall the system of *ʿaṭāʾ* was abandoned, but diffusion of Islamic currency went on propelled by the dynamics of an expanding economy. Important in that process was the rise of a new ʿAbbāsid capital in Baghdād. In addition to being the capital of the Caliphate—with the usual governmental, administrative, bureaucratic and fiscal paraphernalia—Baghdād rapidly became one of the richest metropolises of Medieval World. Situated more centrally than Damascus, Baghdād, with its numerous markets and rich populace, assumed the role of the principal receiver and distributor, or the principal transmitter of money in the economic structure of the early period of the ʿAbbāsid Caliphate. A special function in this regard was discharged by the mint of Baghdād, which succeeded that of Damascus as the main supplier of Islamic gold coinage.[72] Being the first Islamic mint to strike *dīnārs* in the Eastern lands of the Caliphate the mint of the ʿAbbāsid capital decisively contributed to the popularity of gold currency in the former Sāsānid territories.

---

[68] A. S. Ehrenkreutz, *art. cit.*, p. 136.

[69] The references to the purity of *dirhams* are based on the results of the neutron activation analysis of several hundreds of Umayyad *dirhams*, carried out by Prof. A. A. Gordus at the University of Michigan. The present author is indebted to him for making the data from that important examination available for this publication.

[70] A. S. Ehrenkreutz, *art. cit.*, p. 138.

[71] Fifteen specimens, dating from that period, out of a sample of twenty *dirhams* showed a standard of 99% or more. The remaining five were 98-98.9% pure.

[72] A. S. Ehrenkreutz, *art. cit.*, p. 140.

The mint of Baghdād joined some thirty other ʿAbbāsid mints engaged in striking *dirhams.*[73] The wide geographic dispersion of those mints—from Spain in the West to Transoxania in the East—and the scale of their production resulted in two interesting internal and external monetary developments. Internally, it led to a considerable volume of silver specie floating on the markets of the Caliphate, and to a consequent drop in the value of *dirhams.* Whereas in the earlier period of Islamic administration their value had been rated at 10-12 *dirhams* to a *dīnār,* at the beginning of the ninth century the exchange rate in Iraq dropped to 20-22 to 1, to become 25 to 1 in the middle of that century.[74] It was probably this inflationary trend which brought about a sudden cessation of copper minting in the first half of the ninth century, and started the centuries-long scarcity of copper coins.[75] Externally, *dirhams* supplied by Islamic mints became an extremely effective monetary weapon in the hands of Near Eastern merchants launching a highly successful commercial expansion in quest of East European markets.[76]

The decline of the authority of the ʿAbbāsid caliphs, and the emergence of various semi-autonomous regional regimes, were bound to affect the monetary situation of the Muslim Empire. Silver mines of Spain were dominated by the Umayyads. Secessionist Idrīsids and Aghlabids controlled the routes leading to gold mines of Western Sudan, while the Ṭūlūnids monopolized the flow of gold from Nubia. Finally, the argentiferous regions of the East came under the domination of the Ṭāhirids and of their Sāmānid successors. With progressive proliferation of mints and the eventual decentralization of gold coinage—in A.D. 889 *dīnārs* were struck in nearly twenty different places[77] —uniformity of coinage could not last for long. Beginning with Hārūn al-Rashīd (A.D. 786-809) ʿAbbāsid caliphs abdicated their personal responsibility of supervising the standard of coinage.[78] The name of the caliphs continued to be included in the inscriptions on coins struck by loyal governors or by nominally submissive petty dynasts, but that propagandist tradition did not save the coinage of the Caliphate from various corrosive influences. In the tenth century commercial and banking activities of the Caliphate were reaching their peak, with the mass circulation of money being

[73] E. von Zambaur, *op. cit.*, table 2 f.

[74] E. Ashtor, *Histoire des prix et des salaires dans l'Orient Médiéval,* Paris, 1969, p. 40.

[75] A. Udovitch, *art. cit.*, ii/769.

[76] R. Kiersnowski, *Pieniądz kruszcowy w Polsce średniowiecznej,* Warszawa, 1960, p. 123 f; Th. Lewicki, 'Il commercio arabo con la Russia e con i paesi slavi d'Occidente nei secoli IX-XI', *Annali dell'Istituto Universitario Orientale di Napoli,* Nuova Serie, 8, 1959, p. 60.

[77] G. C. Miles, *The numismatic history of Rayy,* New York, 1938, p. 119.

[78] Al-Maqrīzī, *op. cit.*, p. 19.

their essential attribute. By then, however, the markets of the Near East experienced the reappearance of coins characterized by appalling instability both in their standard of weight[79] and of fineness.[80] Those were the symptoms of growing economic difficulties destined to reverse the course of Islamic monetary history.

---

[79] A. S. Ehrenkreutz, *art. cit.*, p. 146; idem, 'The standard of fineness of Western and Eastern *dinars* before the Crusades', *Journal of the Economic and Social History of the Orient*, 6, 1963, p. 243-277.

[80] A. S. Ehrenkreutz, 'Studies in the monetary history of the Near East in the Middle Ages', *Journal of the Economic and Social History of the Orient*, 2, 1959, p. 145.

III

ANOTHER ORIENTALIST'S REMARKS CONCERNING THE PIRENNE THESIS*

By now fifty years have elapsed since the initial publication of Henri Pirenne's brilliant concepts regarding the causes of the decay of the Ancient order in Western Europe [1]). His provocative contributions to Medieval European history are sufficiently influential to warrant further comments today [2]). In my view, however, the half-a-century old debate, stimulated by his controversial ideas, has suffered from two shortcomings. First, although the validity of Pirenne's thesis depended decisively on a proper understanding of the Moslem Near East and its relations with Europe in the early Middle Ages, no specialists in the field of Islamic history—three isolated instances excepting—made themselves heard on the polemical subject. And second, although the impact of the dramatic changes in the Near East on the situation in Western Europe has constituted the focal issue in the Pirennean controversy, nobody has raised the question of the immediate effect of the Arab victory upon the economic conditions in the Near East itself.

---

*) Paper presented at the Sixth Conference on Medieval Studies, May 1971, sponsored by the Medieval Institute, Western Michigan University, Kalamazoo, Michigan.

1) H. Pirenne, 'Mahomet et Charlemagne', *Revue belge de philologie et de l'histoire*, 1. 1922, p. 77-86.

2) For a summation of several opinions concerning the validity of H. Pirenne's thesis see Anne Riising, 'The Fate of Henri Pirenne's Theses on the Consequences of the Islamic Expansion,' *Classica et Medievalia*, 13, 1952, p. 87-130; also, Alfred F. Havighurst, ed., *The Pirenne Thesis, Analysis, Criticism, and Revision*, Boston, 1958.

The three exceptional instances involved the contributions of professional Orientalist scholars: Daniel C. Dennett, Jr.,[1]) Claude Cahen[2]), and more recently, Elie Ashtor[3]). Cahen's article concerned itself primarily with the methodological aspects of the role of Moslem coinage in the commercial relations between the Near East and Europe[4]). Furthermore, it concentrated on the advanced stage of Near Eastern economic expansion, rather than on the situation which had arisen shortly after the subjugation of the near East by the Caliphate. On the other hand, Dennett and Ashtor addressed themselves, even if not exclusively, to the central issue of the causal relationship between the expansion of Islam and the collapse of the traditional order in Western Europe.

Dennett rejected Pirenne's interpretation of the Near Eastern role in the European decay. According to Dennett, the profound changes in early Medieval Europe should not be attributed to adverse economic trends—especially in the sphere of trans-Mediterranean commerce—which were allegedly generated by a hostile policy of the victorious Moslem regime. To quote Dennett: "There is no evidence to prove that the Arabs either desired to close, or actually did close the Mediterranean to the commerce of the West either in the seventh or eighth centuries[5])".

1) 'Pirenne and Muhammad,' *Speculum*, 23, 1948, p. 165-190.

2) 'Quelques problèmes concernant l'expansion économique musulmane au Haut Moyen Age,' *Settimane di Studio del Centro Italiano di Studi sull'Alto Medioevo*, 12, 1965, p. 391-432.

3) 'Quelques observations d'un Orientaliste sur la thèse de Pirenne,' *Journal of the Economic and Social History of the Orient*, 13, 1970, p. 166-194; also, 'Nouvelles refléxions sur la thèse de Pirenne,' *Revue suisse d'histoire*, 20, 1970, p. 601-607.

4) The problem of the bearing of Moslem coinage on monetary developments in Western Europe was discussed by a number of 'Occidentalists', e.g. S. Bolin, 'Mohammed, Charlemagne and Ruric,' *The Scandinavian Economic History Review*, 1, 1953, p. 5-39; C. M. Cipolla, 'Sans Mahomet, Charlemagne est inconcevable,' *Annales (Économies, Sociétés, Civilisations)* 17, 1962, p. 130-136; J. Duplessy, 'La circulation des monnaies arabes en Europe occidentale du VIIIe au XIIIe siècle,' *Revue Numismatique*, Ve série, 18, 1956, p. 101-163; Ph. Grierson, 'The monetary reforms of ʿAbd al-Malik. Their metrological basis and their financial repercussions,' *Journal of the Economic and Social History of the Orient*, 3, 1960, p. 241-264; Fr. Himly, 'Y a-t-il emprise musulmane sur l'économie des Etats européens du VIIIe au Xe siècle,' *Revue suisse d'histoire*. 5, 1955, p. 31-81.

5) D. C. Dennett, Jr., *art. cit.*, p. 189.

A different position was taken by Ashtor. Having focused his observations on the problem of the Mediterranean trade in the ninth and early tenth centuries—i.e., the period of the Carolingian state in the West, and of the domination of the 'Abbāsid Caliphate in the East—he has concluded that the volume of transit trade moving across Italy and Spain was „très réduit ou même infime [1])". One of the main factors behind this decline was general maritime insecurity prevailing in the Mediterranean because of the almost incessant warfare involving Byzantine and Moslem fleets. In support of this argument, which is in agreement with the main thrust of Pirenne's thesis, Ashtor adduced evidence pointing to the rapid decadence of Syrian and Egyptian coastal towns in the wake of the victory of the Arabs [2]).

But neither Dennett, nor Cahen, nor Ashtor has ever claimed that his contribution offered all that the Orientalists could and should state on the subject of the Pirennean dispute. The current increase in interest and research in the field of Medieval Near Eastern economic history [3]) seems to portend that a more comprehensive interpretation of the historical role of Moslem Near East in the formation of Medieval Europe would soon be forthcoming.

In the meantime, however, I wish to make a few observations of my own on the Pirennean thesis in the context of Medieval Near Eastern economic history. Although based on solid heuristic foundations, my remarks, like those of Pirenne and of his supporters and adversaries, are speculative in nature. Perhaps they will not add much to the quality level of the Pirennean debate, but at least they will increase by 25% the number of Orientalists actively participating in the famous controversy.

If, as postulated by Pirenne, the alleged cessation of the Mediterranean trade had been capable of ruining Europe it would have produced similar consequences, if not even more disastrous consequences,

1) E. Ashtor, 'Quelques observations . . . ,' p. 188; also, *idem*, 'Nouvelles réflexions . . . ,' p. 602.

2) *Idem*, 'Quelques observations . . . ,' p. 170; 'Nouvelles réflexions . . . ,' p. 605.

3) *Cf.*, M. Cook, ed., *Studies in the Economic History of the Middle East from the Rise of Islam to the Present Day*, London, 1970.

for the Near Eastern economy. International commerce in the Near East gave its society important benefits from the lucrative transit trade, as well as import and export transactions which flowed across that strategic area connecting European markets with Africa, India, and Far East and South East Asia [1]). For that very reason, the economic policy of the Arabs in the conquered territories—especially their indifference to or their interference with trade—was of crucial importance to the Near East, and only secondarily to Western Europe.

Although the economic and social fate of the Near East in the Middle Ages, and by extension that of Western Europe, depended on the fundamental decisions of the Caliphate in the seventh and early eight centuries, their historical significance has not been incisively interpreted or persuasively explained. The conflicting opinions of Dennett and Ashtor may serve as an illustration. "There is no evidence to prove that the Arabs . . . desired to close . . . the Mediterranean to the commerce of the West either in the seventh or eighth centuries" stated Dennett [2]). On the contrary! There exists textual evidence explicitly proving that the Arab regime insisted on freedom of maritime trade. It consists of a separate article in the solemn fiscal decree issued between A.D. 717-720 by Caliph 'Umar II, proclaiming: "As for the sea, we hold that its way is the way of the dry land. God hath said: 'God it is Who hath subdued to you the sea that the vessels may sail thereon by His command and that ye may seek of His bounty!' Therefore He hath given permission therein that who so wills may trade thereon; and I hold that we should place no obstacle between it and any one of the people. For dry land and sea belong alike to God; He hath subdued them to His servants to seek of His bounty for themselves in both of them. How then should we intervene between God's servants and their means of livelihood [3])?"

Of course, it does not necessarily follow that the official governmental declaration in favor of the "open sea" policy constituted a

1) For a recent authoritative discussion of the significance of the Near East as transit area *see* J. Innes Miller, *The Spice Trade of the Roman Empire*, Oxford, 1969.
2) D. C. Dennett, Jr., *loc. cit.*
3) *Cf.*, H. A. R. Gibb, 'The Fiscal Rescript of 'Umar II,' *Arabica*, 2, 1955, p. 6.

guarantee of healthy trade conditions. Indeed, the fact that 'Umar made such an unequivocal statement suggests that Mediterranean trade conditions left something to be desired.

As for Ashtor's opinion regarding the responsibility of maritime insecurity for dwindling Mediterranean commerce, one is tempted to reverse the alleged causal relationship. Could it be the maritime insecurity had resulted from a lack of interest on the part of "inter-continental" business to invest their capital in trans-Mediterranean operations? With Mediterranean trade thus becoming "très réduit ou même infime [1])," Arab authorities had little motivation to commit their resources for the maintenance of strong naval forces and burdensome coastal fortresses and shipyards in Syria and Egypt. It is this factor which may well have accounted for the spread of insecurity in the Mediterranean, and which may have precipitated a rapid decline of formerly flourishing towns along the coast of Syria and Egypt.

Is it plausible to postulate that "inter-continental" commerce operating from the Near East ,or using that area as its strategic transit zone, had lost interest in the markets to the north of the Mediterranean? Very definitely so. Indeed, one of the most significant results of the Arab victory on economic history was a natural, organic redirection of commercial activities in the sensitive area of the Near East, brought about by a specific fiscal policy of the new regime, and by the ensuing emergence of lucrative markets within the borders of the Caliphate. To understand the nature of that significant evolution one has to consider the basic aspects of the economic situation arising from the Arab domination in the Near East.

Unlike their effects in the sphere of politics, religion and culture, the victories of the Arabs and the establishment of the Caliphate did not result in any drastic or revolutionary changes in the economic life of Near Eastern society. As in pre-Islamic times, agriculture, artisan production, and internal and external commerce, as well as the institution of metallic currency, continued as the basic features of the economy of the Near East. Moreover, the entire tax base survived

1) E. Ashtor, 'Quelques observations . . . ,' p. 188.

virtually intact in spite of the downfall of the Sāsānid monarchy and the expulsion of the Byzantine hierarchy. The main reason for such developments was the non-destructive character of the great conquest. Certainly, battles were fought and some cities endured prolonged siege operations, but in general the dramatic takeover was accomplished without substantial losses by the tax-paying civilian population or by revenue-yielding establishments.

A major transformation, however, occurred in the nature of the executive power structure of Near Eastern fiscal organization. State revenue was no longer administered by two different and mutually hostile imperial treasuries, the Byzantine in Constantinople and the Sāsānid in Ctesiphon. Responsibility for determining the nature of taxation, for the system of collection as well as for the allocation of the revenue, was taken over by one central and supreme financial institution, established by Caliph ʿUmar I (A.D. 634-644), to serve the needs of the Caliphate [1]). The way in which the new administration discharged its fiscal responsibility during the initial period of its existence proved to be instrumental in ushering in a new and dynamic era in the history of Near Eastern economy.

As regards the level of taxation and the method of tax collection, the policy of the Caliphate towards the conquered areas was characterized by conservative moderation. Except for minor local modifications Arab conquerors did not interfere initially with the system or systems of taxation inherited from their predecessors [2]). It was in the matters of distribution of the accumulated wealth that the policy of the early Caliphate acquired a truly innovative character. To understand the essence and implications of the drastic fiscal innovations one has to consider a demographic change which the Near East uderwent in the wake of Arab victory.

As it happened, one of the outstanding demographic problems

1) *Cf.*, Matti I. Moosa, 'The dīwān of ʿUmar ibn al-Khaṭṭāb,' *Studies in Islam*, 2, 1965, p. 67-78; Gerd-Rüdiger Puin, *Der Dīwān von ʿUmar ibn al-Ḫaṭṭāb. Ein Beitrag zur frühislamischen Verwaltungsgeschichte*, 1970.

2) *Cf.*, D. C. Dennett, Jr., *Conversion and the Poll Tax in Early Islam*, Cambridge, 1950.

of the Arab invasion was the mass immigration of the surplus population from the Arabian peninsula to the sedentarized zone of the Near East. It is true that certain segments of the Near Eastern sedentary population were displaced as a result of the Arab victory. (I refer to the Byzantine and Sāsānid ruling elite whose members were either expelled or exterminated by the Arabs). There is no doubt, however, that the number of the newcomers exceeded by far the displaced Byzantine and Sāsānid elements, for to accommodate the mass of Arab immigrants it was not enough to take over premises vacated by the ousted population. Indeed, entire new quarters had to be added to old towns, or completely new urban settlements had to be founded [1]. With the exception of a small minority, the mass of the Arab immigrants represented unskilled labor which under normal political and social conditions could hardly have been absorbed by or integrated with the local sedentary population of the Fertile Crescent without causing a major economic and social upheaval. As it was, that mass immigration did not impede normal economic activity. The healthy transitional integration was accomplished because of the introduction by the Caliphate of an unusual system of fiscal benefits, according to which all full-fledged members of the victorious Arab people were entitled to regular cash stipends, called *ʿaṭāʾ*, in addition to their lower taxation rates [2]. Because of that ingenious system, the early Arab immigrants, far from being a liability, constituted a strongly subsidized social and ethnic group capable of growing economic roots in the new territories, with little disadvantage to the local labor or artisan force.

One may argue, of course, that the operation of the system of *ʿaṭāʾ* constituted a fiscal burden on the local population. After all, the money distributed among the members of the privileged class was normally obtained from taxes imposed on the non-Arab Near Eastern

1) *Cf.*, E. Reitemeyer, *Die Städtegründungen der Araber im Islam*, Leipzig, 1912; E. Pauty, 'Villes spontanées et villes creées en Islam,' *Annales de l'Institut d'Études Orientales* (Algér), 9, 1951, p. 52-75.

2) *Cf.*, Cl. Cahen, '"Aṭāʾ,' *The Encyclopaedia of Islam*, new edition, i/729-730; A. S. Tritton, 'Notes on the Muslim System of Pensions,' *Bulletin of the School of Oriental and African Studies*, 16, 1954, p. 170-172; Gerd-Rüdiger Puin, *op. cit.*

population. But as stated above, the conquerors did not levy any taxes that the population of the Near East had not been paying for the benefit of the earlier political regimes. Like the Byzantines and the Sāsānids before, the Arab conquerors assumed responsibility for maintaining political and administrative cohesiveness in Near Eastern territories. Unlike pre-Islamic times, no center of political and administrative gravity enjoying jurisdiction over Near Eastern territories, was located outside the Near East, as had been the case of Rome and Constantinople. Consequently, none of the monies collected by the Caliphate supported an external capital and its policies, but by means of the *'aṭā'* system, all of them were retained, re-invested, diffused for the benefit of the local Near Eastern population.

It is obvious that the rise of a political and administrative power structure in the central regions of the Near East, in Syria under the Umayyads and in Mesopotamia under the 'Abbāsids, was accompanied by a powerful injection of ready cash into the Near Eastern economy. In pre-Islamic times economic production in the Mediterranean provinces of the Near East had been geared to meet the needs of huge consumer centers such as Rome, and later Constantinople. Hence the importance of the coastal towns in Egypt and Syria. But with the establishment of the Arab regime, new consumer centers arose in the Near Eastern regions themselves. Arab settlers, whether ruling elite or members of rank and file, constituted a potent consumer class. By establishing themselves in the sedentarized lands of the Near East they necessarily generated a substantial increase in economic productivity. The expansion of old towns and proliferation of new urban settlements created a boom in the housing industry. Ashtor refers to the decline of some coastal cities, but he forgets to mention the foundation and growth of Fusṭāṭ in Egypt [1]), or Ramlah in Palestine [2]), of Baṣrah, Kūfah and Wāsiṭ in Mesopotamia [3]), and of several other inland towns which came into prominence following the victory

1) *Cf.*, J. Jomier, 'Fusṭāṭ,' *The Encyclopaedia of Islam*, new edition, ii/957-959; G. T. Scanlon, 'Housing and Sanitation,' *The Islamic City*, Oxford, 1970, p. 179-194.
2) *Cf.*, E. Reitemeyer, *op. cit.*, p. 73 f.
3) *Ibid.*, p. 11f; 29f; 46f.

of the Arabs. Some wealthy residents or protectors of various towns and communities encouraged refined architectural and artistic creativity. Monumental architecture or sumptuous mosaic decorations ceased to be a monopoly of the Sāsānids or of the Byzantines. Byzantine craftsmen were now employed in the construction of Islamic shrines [1]).

Furthermore, the growth of the urban population generated a strong demand for food supplies, thus stimulating speculative agriculture and interest in acquisition of landed property [2]). Likewise, internal trade benefited from the new situation by performing economic functions between the urban and rural population [3]).

All these favorable economic trends were reflected in the concurrent monetary developments. The best known event in the monetary history of the period is the great reform of Caliph ʿAbd al-Malik (A.D. 685-715) who introduced trimetallic Arabic coinage (gold, silver, and copper, i.e. *dīnār*, *dirham*, and *fals*) to serve as the classical model for Near Eastern coinage production in the Middle Ages. Various numismatic and ideological ramifications of that reform have already received adequate scholarly attention [4]), but not its internal economic implications. Maurice Lombard, who investigated the function of gold in the economic supremacy of the Moslem world, defined that particular phase of Moslem history (8th-9th centuries) as the age of administrative reforms, marked by the return to circulation of precious metals accumulated in church treasuries [5]). He failed, however, to elaborate

---

1) O. Grabar, 'Islamic Art and Byzantium,' *Dumbarton Oaks Papers*, 1964, p. 69-88; also, H. A. R. Gibb, 'Arab-Byzantine Relations under the Umayyad Caliphate,' *Dumbarton Oaks Papers*, 12, 1958, p. 219-233.

2) *Cf.*, Saleh A. Ali, 'Muslim Estates in Hidjaz in the First Century A.D.,' *Journal of the Economic and Social History of the Orient*, 2, 1959, p. 247-261; O. Grabar, "Umayyad 'Palace' and the ʿAbbāsid 'Revolution'," *Studia Islamica*, 18, 1963, p. 5-18, esp. p. 7-8; 14-15.

3) For the importance of the Near Eastern mercantile class in that early period *see* S. D. Goitein, 'The Rise of the Near Eastern Bourgeoisie in Early Islamic Times,' *Cahiers d'histoire mondiale*, 3, 1957, p. 583-604.

4) *Cf.*, G. C. Miles, 'Dīnār,' *The Encyclopaedia of Islam*, new edition, ii/297-299; *idem*, 'Dirham,' *ibid.*, ii/319-320; A. L. Udovitch, 'Fals,' *ibid.*, ii/768-769.

5) M. Lombard, 'Les bases monétaires d'une suprématie économique. L'or musulman du VIIe au XIe siècle,' *Annales* (*Economies, Sociétés, Civilisations*), 2, 1947, p. 143-160.

on the economic justification behind the decision of the Arab administration to release vast quantities of gold, silver, and copper coins for the use of Near Eastern markets. Under normal conditions the volume of coinage in circulation represents the total value of economic activities a given society happens to be engaged in. In other words, the volume of coinage in use is regulated by the actual state of the economy. An expanding economy calls for an increase of coinage, a shrinking economy for its withdrawal, debasement or hoarding. And certainly, an indiscriminate release or oversupply of coinage, with its unavoidable inflationary consequences, is as disastrous for economy as ruthless overtaxation. In the case of early Islamic history, the monetary reform of ʿAbd al-Malik—its alleged religious or ideological background notwithstanding—must have been undertaken in response to the expanding market conditions. Although the supply of new coins assumed tremendous proportions, and although their production kept on being expanded during the early Caliphate [1]), no inflationary developments were set off by such a monetary policy [2]). General stability of prices or [3]), to be more precise, lack of source references to any drastic rise in the prices of commodities—seems to suggest that the sustained intensive output of coins in the early Caliphate bore witness to the great vitality of the Near Eastern market in that period.

All these developments could not have left the position of the intercontinental commerce unaffected. In a certain sense the political consequences of the great Arab victory had contributed to a major change in this area. With the expulsion of the Byzantines and the destruction of the Sāsānids, the political barrier which had hitherto divided the Near East into two separate blocs ceased to exist. The removal of this artificial barrier, which had been at the root of many destructive wars between the pre-Islamic powers, meant that the natural trade exchange between the western and eastern regions of

---

1) W. G. Andrews Jr., *et al.*, 'Early Islamic Mint Output,' *Journal of the Economic and Social History of the Orient*, 9, 1966, p. 212-241.
2) E. Ashtor, *Histoire des prix et des salaires dans l'Orient médiévale*, Paris, 1969, p. 40.
3) *Ibid.*, p. 453f.

the Near East could operate without harmful obstructions motivated by political considerations. Indeed, before one proceeds to consider the validity of Pirenne's allegations that the Arabs were guilty of disrupting the unity of the Mediterranean world, one should credit them with the integration of almost entire Near Eastern subcontinent into a common market area with obvious benefits to long-distance trade investors.

"L'économie marchande du Moyen Age musulman, comme celle de l'Antiquité, était surtout une économie de spéculation et d'acquisition", declared Cl. Cahen referring to the flexibility and economic adaptability of commerce in Islamic Middle Ages [1]). In view of the expanding economy of the Caliphate, in view of the emergence of large consumer centers, in view of the rapid growth of local market demand, the long-distance merchants had small need for the markets of Western Europe. Instead of crossing or circumventing the Mediterranean, the Far East trade merchants, like those of the India and Africa trade, or even the distributors of the fruits of local Near Eastern production, could meet their profit requirements by directing their shipments or caravans to Damascus, Fusṭāṭ, Baghdād or Qayrawān. Obviously, it was this natural economically motivated re-orientation of trans-continental commerce, which precipitated a catastrophic decline in trans-Mediterranean trade, deplored by Pirenne and his supporters.

And today, so far as the Pirennean debate is concerned, the time has come when more attention should be devoted to the nature and consequences of the Near Eastern economic developments in the early Middle Ages. Instead of debating the issue of the Mediterranean trade following the Arab conquest, the Pirennean polemicists should consider the position of commerce to the east of the former *mare nostrum*. Above all, they should admit the possibility that the roots of some of the issues in the Pirennean controversy may be found in the progressive and constructive economic policy of the Arab conquerors.

---

1) Cl. Cahen, 'Quelques mots sur le déclin commercial du monde musulman à la fin du moyen âge,' *Studies in the Economic History of the Middle East*, London, 1970, p. 35.

IV

BYZANTINE TETARTERA AND ISLAMIC DĪNĀRS

In the course of the second half of the tenth century, Byzantine authorities began to issue lightweight *solidi* which came to be known as *tetartèra* [1]). In discussing this monetary phenomenon Professor Philip Grierson ingeniously attempts to explain the nature of that coinage in the light of territorial acquisitions of the Byzantine Empire in Syria, during the reign of Nicephorus Phocas and his immediate successors [2]). According to Grierson, the population of that area was accustomed to the handling of lightweight Muṣlim *dīnārs*. Consequently, Byzantine authorities, desiring to conform with Syrian monetary practices, decided to produce Imperial gold coinage with a reduced weight standard.

While Mme Ahrweiler-Glykatzi has recently suggested a different interpretation of the motivation behind the monetary measure of Nicephorus Phocas [2a], I feel compelled to question the validity of another aspect of Professor Grierson's thesis. I refer here to the problem of the Fāṭimid *dīnārs* which, according to Grierson (and Ahrweiler-Glykatzi, after him) [2b], were to serve as the weight prototype of the *tetartèra* of Nicephorus Phocas. This is how this proposition is formulated:

---

1) For bibliographical references on the subject of the *tetartèron*, see Ph. Grierson, "Nomisma, tetartèron et dinar: un plaidoyer pour Nicéphore Phocas", *Revue Belge de Numismatique*, 100, 1954, p. 75-84; also, H. Ahrweiler-Glykatzi, "Nouvelle hypothèse sur le tétartéron d'or et la politique monétaire de Nicéphore Phocas", *Mélanges G. Ostrogorsky I*, (Recueil des travaux de l'Institut d'Etudes Byzantines, No. VIII), p. 1-9.

2) Ph. Grierson, *art. cit.*, p. 81-83.

2a) H. Ahrweiler, *art. cit.*, p. 8-9.

2b) *Ibid.*, p. 8.

La plupart de ces pays avaient été sous gouvernement musulman pendant près de trois siècles et étaient ainsi habitués à l'usage du dinar arabe. Celui-ci, dans la deuxième moitié du Xe siècle, était en somme le dinar fatimide, car aucun monnayage d'or n'avait plus été émis par les Abbassides depuis Al-Muqtadir (908-932) et celui des Buwayhides circulait bien plus à l'Est, en Mésopotamie et en Perse, tandis que les Hamdanides, qui gouvernaient la Syrie, ne frappaient pratiquement pas l'or. Les Fatimides, d'autre part, battaient des monnaies d'or en Égypte depuis 341 de l'Hégire (952-3 après J.-C.) et en Palestine et même en Syrie, à Tripoli et à Tyr, depuis 359 H. (969-70). Ce numéraire était émis en d'énormes quantités et durant la deuxième moitié du Xe et tout le XIe siècle il dominait la vie commerciale de la Méditerranée orientale.

Le dinar fatimide représente une diminution légère, mais bien perceptible, de l'étalon traditionnel des Ommeyades et des Abbassides. Le dinar de ces derniers, comme on peut le voir clairement d'après la liste de monnaies dans l'ouvrage de Lavoix, a été frappé au poids de 4,25 g environ, tandis que le dinar fatimide variait entre 4,05 et 4,15 g. Ceci est un poids identique à celui du tetartèron...[1])

A few of the points raised in the above statement can be easily dismissed as inaccurate generalizations. Gold coins issued in the name of the ʿAbbāsid caliphs continued to be struck after the reign of al-Muqtadir. Those produced on behalf of Caliph al-Rāḍī (A.D. 940-944) circulated in Fāṭimid territories as late as A.D. 973 [2]). Mesopotamian mints working for the benefit of the Buwayhids were situated much closer to Syria than were the North African mints of the Fāṭimids. Although the numismatic legacy of the Ḥamdānids is scanty indeed, they were reported to have been involved in the striking of excellent gold coinage. Above all, it is utterly incorrect to state that the Fāṭimids struck gold coins in Egypt since A.H. 341 (A.D. 952-953). The Fāṭimids did not establish their political and administrative control over Egypt

---

1) Ph. Grierson, *art. cit.*, p. 81-82.
2) Cf. al-Maqrīzī, *Ittiʿāẓ al-ḥunafāʾ*, 1948, p. 172.

until July of A.D. 969. A few Fāṭimid *dīnārs* which, judging by their legends, had been struck in Egypt prior to that date, constitute a puzzling and so far unsolved historical phenomenon. That no Fāṭimid coins had been struck in Egypt before the final invasion of Egypt is evident from the proclamation issued on behalf of Caliph al-Muʿizz, in which a promise was made to improve the local coinage and to raise its standard to that of the Fāṭimid coinage [1]).

It is the two main arguments underlying Grierson's thesis which call for a closer scrutiny: Was the population of northern Syria really accustomed to the use of Fāṭimid *dīnārs* at the time of its conquest by Nicephorus Phocas? Did the weight standard of Fāṭimid *dīnārs* constitute a departure from the conventional standard of ʿAbbāsid gold coinage? To answer these questions one must begin by stressing the chronological aspects of these arguments. Professor Grierson implies that the population of Syria had been accustomed to the handling of Fāṭimid *dīnārs* prior to the death of Nicephorus Phocas (12.10.969), i.e., before the eastward expansion of the Fāṭimids and their minting of gold coins in Egypt. In other words, it is implied that Syrian markets were dominated by Fāṭimid *dīnārs* struck in North African mints between A.D. 909 and 969. One could speculate that the Syrian trade balance favored such a development or that there was an intensive diffusion of Fāṭimid *dīnārs* for the purpose of Ismāʿīlī propaganda. But, other than such speculative ideas, I find no evidence suggesting widespread use of North African *dīnārs* in Syria prior to the establishment of the Fāṭimids in Egypt. On the other hand, there exists textual and numismatic evidence indicating that the Syrian population handled other than Fāṭimid *dīnārs*, struck by various regimes of Syria and of adjacent territories. One may refer here to the activities of Syrian mints such as Aleppo, Damascus, Ramlah (Filasṭīn), and Tiberias, as attested by available gold coins dating from the pre-Ikhshīdid and Ikhshīdid period (A.D. 905-935-969). While it is impossible to state how intensive their production was, the activities of these Syrian mints

1) Cf. A. S. Ehrenkreutz, "Studies in the Monetary History of the Near East in the Middle Ages. II", *JESHO*, 6, iii, 1963, p. 258.

suggest a demand for local gold coinage. Furthermore, considering the excellent intrinsic quality of Egyptian *dīnārs*, struck by the Ṭūlūnids and the Ikhshīdids [1]), it is reasonable to assume that Egyptian gold coinage enjoyed popularity in Syrian markets in the pre-Fāṭimid period. If, then, the population of Syria could depend on the supply of local coins or on that coming from neighbouring Egypt, one finds it difficult to understand how the Fāṭimid *dīnārs*, originating from distant North African mints, could assert themselves on Syrian markets prior to A.D. 969.

Finally, one must consider the problem of the weight standard of relevant types of *dīnārs*. There is no question about the weight of ʿAbbāsid *dīnārs*. As long as they were struck according to a fixed standard, their weight amounted to 4.25 grammes, representing the conventional standard adopted by ʿAbd al-Malik [2]). In the course of the tenth century a fixed standard was abandoned by ʿAbbāsid mints. A similar lack of any uniform standard of weight characterized the *dīnārs* struck in Syria for at least one century before the advent of the Fāṭimids. Ṭūlūnid, post-Ṭūlūnid, and Ikhshīdid issues in Syria weighed significantly less than 4.0 grammes [3]). The same was true of Ikhshīdid *dīnārs* of Egypt [4]). On the other hand, the Egyptian gold coinage of the Ṭūlūnids (A.D. 868-905) as well as that of the Aghlabids (A.D. 800-909), the predecessors of the Fāṭimids in North Africa, was characterized by a stable and uniform standard of weight. It appears, however, that there existed a definite difference in the weight standard of the *dīnārs* of the two dynasties. By applying the frequency distribution method, one can see that the majority of Aghlabid specimens [5]) fall

1) Cf. *Idem*, "Studies in the Monetary History of the Near East in the Middle Ages", *JESHO*, 2, ii, 1959, p. 149-150, 152-153.

2) Cf. Ph. Grierson, "The Monetary Reforms of ʿAbd al-Malik", *JESHO*, 3, 1960, p. 253f.

3) Cf. O. Grabar, *The Coinage of the Ṭūlūnids*, (*Numismatic Notes and Monographs*, no. 139), 1957, p. 76 *and passim*; P. Balog, "Table de références des monnaies ikhchidites", *RBN*, 103, 1957, p. 110.

4) *Ibid.*

5) In tabulating these statistics I have considered the undamaged specimens in the collection of the American Numismatic Society. I have also consulted the

within the weight category of 4.16-4.2 grammes. The average weight of specimens in that category amounts to 4.183 grammes. Adding 1.5 per cent to compensate for loss due to wear [1]), one obtains the weight of 4.245 grammes, which almost exactly corresponds to the classical standard of Islamic *dīnārs*. The majority of Ṭūlūnid specimens fall within the weight class of 4.11-4.15 grammes. The average weight of specimens in this category is 4.132 grammes, which, after the "wear" adjustment, produces the figure 4.193. The second highest number of Ṭūlūnid specimens fall within even lower weight brackets. On the basis of this analysis one may submit that Egyptian Ṭūlūnid *dīnārs* were characterized by a light standard of weight, in distinction from regular Umayyad, ʿAbbāsid, or Aghlabid gold coinage.

TABLE I

(a) *Dīnārs* of the	(b) Number of Specimens	(c) Frequency Peak (Wgt. in g.)	(d) Number of Spec. in (c)	(e) Ave. Wgt. of Spec. in (c)	(f) Adjusted Ave. Wgt. of Spec. in (c)
Aghlabids (A.D. 800-909)	105	4.16-4.2	31	4.183	4.245
Ṭūlūnids (Egypt only) (A.D. 868-905)	167	i) 4.11-4.15	45	4.132	4.193
		ii) 4.06-4.1	33	4.091	4.152 [2])

In inquiring into the nature of the weight standard of Fāṭimid gold

---

following numismatic catalogues: S. Lane-Poole, *Catalogue of Oriental Coins in the British Museum*; H. Lavoix, *Catalogue des monnaies musulmanes de la Bibliothèque Nationale*; G. C. Miles, *Fāṭimid Coins in the Collection of the University Museum, Philadelphia, and the American Numismatic Society*. For Ṭūlūnid *dīnārs* I have also consulted the files of Professor O. Grabar, which served for his publication of *The Coinage of the Ṭūlūnids*. Of the Fāṭimid *dīnārs* those of al-Mustaʿlī (A.D. 1094-1101) have not been considered because of an inadequate number of available specimens.

1) Cf. G. C. Miles, "Byzantine Miliaresion and Arab Dirhem: Some Notes on Their Relationship", *The American Numismatic Society Museum Notes*, 9, 1960, p. 214.

2) It is interesting to observe that in the case of these two types of lighter *dīnārs*, the difference between their respective weight and that of the conventional *dīnār* amounts to about one *ḥabbah* (or 1/72 of a *dīnār*) in the case of the former, and to about 1/2 *qīrāṭ* (or 1/48 of a *dīnār*) in the case of the latter. Such lighter *dīnārs* are frequently referred to in the ninth Egyptian papyri. Cf. A. Grohmann, *Einführung und Chrestomathie zur arabischen Papyruskunde*, 1954, p. 187-188.

coinage for the purpose of the present discussion, one must distinguish two phases. During the early pre-Egyptian period Fāṭimid *dīnārs* were struck in North African mints. It was the weight standard of the North African Fāṭimid *dīnārs* which allegedly served as the prototype of the *tetartèra* of Nicephorus Phocas. During the second period, extending from the conquest of Egypt to the reign of al-Āmir (A.D. 1101-1130), Fāṭimid *dīnārs* produced in Egyptian mints asserted their monetary preponderance because of the excellent stability of their weight standard and high intrinsic quality [1]). Consequently, by studying the weight of *dīnārs* dating from the second period, one would be justified in drawing conclusions about the weight standard of Fāṭimid gold coinage in general.

As may be seen from the following table, the pre-Egyptian or North African *dīnārs* of the Fāṭimids do not show any decrease in standard of weight.

TABLE II

(a) Fāṭimid *Dīnārs*	(b) Number of Specimens	(c) Frequency Peak (Wgt. in g.)	(d) Number of Spec. in (c)	(e) Ave. Wgt. of Spec. in (c)	(f) Adjusted Ave. Wgt. of Spec. in (c)
North African, prior to A.D. 969-970	34	4.16-4.2	11	4.19	4.25
Egyptian, of:					
al-Muʿizz (A.D. 952-975)	35	i) 4.06-4.1	9	4.088	4.149
		ii) 4.11-4.15	8	4.133	4.194
		iii) 4.16-4.2	8	4.173	4.235
al-ʿAzīz (A.D. 975-996)	41	4.11-4.15	24	4.128	4.189
al-Ḥākim (A.D. 996-1021)	51	4.16-4.2	19	4.188	4.25
al-Ẓāhir (A.D. 1021-1036)	21	i) 4.16-4.2	5	4.178	4.24
		ii) 4.21-4.25	5	4.232	4.295
al-Mustanṣir (A.D. 1036-1094)	135	4.21-4.25	24	4.229	4.292
al-Āmir (A.D. 1101-1130)	101	4.16-4.2	15	4.186	4.252

1) Cf. A. S. Ehrenkreutz, "Studies in the Monetary History...II", *JESHO*, 6, iii, 1963, p. 257f.

The average weight of specimens in the peak frequency category of 4.16-4.2 amounts to 4.19, which after the "wear" adjustment produces the exact figure of 4.25. Thus, there seems to be little doubt that as regards their gold minting policy the Fāṭimids continued the traditions of the Aghlabids [1]). And since the Fāṭimid *dīnārs* prior to A.D. 969 were not of a light standard of weight, they could not influence the weight standard of the *tetartèra* of Nicephorus Phocas.

Upon the establishment of the Fāṭimids in Egypt the weight standard of their Egyptian *dīnārs* seems to have undergone an interesting evolution. One can definitely detect a decrease in the weight standard of *dīnārs* of al-Mu'izz (d. A.D. 975). The adjusted average weight of specimens in the highest frequency group amounts to 4.149 grammes. The second highest frequency group consists of specimens with an adjusted average weight of 4.194. The number of specimens in this group is equaled, however, by specimens with an adjusted average weight of 4.235. One should emphasize immediately that the striking of such lightweight *dīnārs* did not constitute an innovation in Egyptian monetary history. It is enough to glance at the weight standard of Ṭūlūnid *dīnārs*, as compiled in Table I, to notice a weight relationship between them and the *dīnārs* of al-Mu'izz. It is quite probable that in restoring monetary stability after the Ikhshīdid disorganization, al-Mu 'izz adopted the weight standard of the excellent gold coins of the Ṭūlūnids. Consequently, if one admits this possibility, one is bound to conclude that Egyptian Ṭūlūnid *dīnārs* rather than Fāṭimid gold coinage influenced the weight standard of the *tetartèra*.

At any rate, the striking of such lightweight *dīnārs* by the Fāṭimids was of short duration. They were still produced under al-'Azīz (d. A.D. 996). Beginning with the reign of al-Ḥākim (d. A.D. 1021) the regular standard of c. 4.25 seems to have prevailed again. The standard of *dīnārs* of al-Ẓāhir (d. A.D. 1036) and al-Mustanṣir (d. A.D. 1094) appears to have exceeded that level. On the other hand, the specimens issued during the reign of al-Āmir (d. A.D. 1130), who is known to have

1) Cf. *Ibid.*, p. 256-257.

proceeded with special investigations in the production of gold coinage [1]), indicate the prevalence of the regular 4.25 standard. Finally, the two highest frequency concentrations among all Egyptian specimens of the Fāṭimids are represented by *dīnārs* falling within the weight brackets of 4.11-4.15 and 4.16-4.2. The adjusted average of specimens in the former is 4.24; that in the latter amounts to 4.246. It thus appears to me that these findings are conclusive enough to dispel any notions about the light weight standard of Fāṭimid *dīnārs*.

1) Cf. A. S. Ehrenkreutz, "The Standard of Fineness of Gold Coins Circulating in Egypt at the Time of the Crusades", *JAOS*, 74, iii, 1954, p. 165.

V

NUMISMATICS RE-MONETIZED*

In 1956 Jean Duplessy, in his article "La circulation des monnaies arabes en Europe occidentale du VIIIe au XIIIe siecle,"[1] boldly challenged the validity of numismatic evidence hitherto adduced in support of various theories pertaining to the relations between Western Europe and the Near East in the Middle Ages. As adequate evidence for far-reaching generalizations, the modest number of Muslim coins (241 whole and fractionary *dīnārs,* 153 whole and fractionary *dirhams,* 1 *fals*) originating from thirty-six West European treasure troves could hardly be regarded as sufficient. Furthermore, maintained Duplessy, these meager numismatic resources were neither properly analyzed nor correlated with pertinent textual evidence. He emphasized that before any definitive and categorical conclusions could be formulated many more studies must be undertaken, such as "étude critique des textes arabes, dépouillement complet et classement par régions des chartes et documents divers de l'Europe occidentale; recherches sur les raisons de chacun des enfouissements connus, sur le pouvoir d'achat des monnaies d'or, sur les relations commerciales et les produits échangés."[2]

Although Duplessy's conclusions were made in the context of West European history they could apply to the way numismatic evidence has been treated, at least until recently, by research studies dealing with economic—and more especially with monetary—developments in the Medieval Near East. This is not to say that specialists in medieval Near Eastern history have not recognized numismatics as a productive "ancilla" of their discipline. Quite the contrary. For many centuries Islamic coins have attracted the attention of historians and chroniclers. As early as the

*In its original form this paper was presented at the XXIXth International Congress of Orientalists held in 1973 in Paris.

[1]*Revue Numismatique,* V^{e} serie, 18, 1956, pp. 101-163.

[2]*Ibid.,* p. 119.

fifteenth century, al-Maqrīzī (A.D. 1364-1422) composed his *Shudhūr al-'uqūd fī dhikr al-nuqūd*[3] in which he attempted to reconstruct the history of Islamic coinage with heavy reliance on numismatic evidence. Indeed, a myriad of typological variants characterizing Islamic coinage produced by an incredibly high number of mints elevated the field of Muslim numismatics from its ancillary level to a quasi-sovereign position attracting to its own service a whole range of auxiliary and subsidiary disciplines. Metallurgy and metrology helped to ascertain the physical category of examined specimens. Paleography, epigraphy and philology assisted in reading and interpreting religious and political allusions, while onomastics and diplomatics explained or confirmed the structure and hierarchic value of titles appearing in the inscriptions on coins. The services of heraldry and cryptography were required to understand coats of arms and cryptic symbols imprinted on the coins. Chronology was helpful in dating the specimens, while toponymics and geography were essential in identifying and locating the mints whose names were included in the inscriptions. Above all, familiarity with history was indispensable for undertaking even preliminary steps in providing critical descriptions of coins.

Services rendered by those or other disciplines and techniques were richly rewarded. Muslim numismatics supplied valuable information to historians and experts in ancillary and auxiliary sciences. Epigraphers and paleographers have learned stylistic variations of the *kūfī* and *naskhī* script. Philologists have encountered interesting lexicographic expressions. Students of diplomatics and heraldics have added to their knowledge about protocol and blazons, as well as about hierarchic relationship between various princes, sultans and the caliphate. And those interested in political and administrative history have found answers concerning distribution of dynastic capitals and provincial centers of power.

To a large degree experts consulting numismatic evidence were seeking information pertaining to the identity and political status of the people in whose names the examined coins appeared to have been struck. Interestingly enough, such an approach corresponded with the secondary function of Islamic coinage—that of

[3]Ed. by L. A. Mayer, Alexandria, 1933; also by Muḥammad Baḥr al-'Ulūm, al-Najaf, 1967.

spreading religious and political propaganda, of disseminating news about the acquisition of power by individuals or by dynastic establishments, and of popularizing their status and prestige.

However the primary function of Islamic coinage was not to serve as means of public propaganda. Nor were Muslim coins struck to supply exciting research materials for the use of modern numismatists, or to satisfy passionate desires of numismatic collectors. The initial appearance of Islamic coinage came about in response to economic requirements prevailing in the Near East following the Arab invasion. The motivation behind the inception of Islamic coinage was in absolute harmony with the monetary traditions of Near Eastern economy. From that time on Muslim coins were to constitute an extremely significant and sensitive instrument in the highly monetized life of Medieval Near Eastern society. Their external characteristics might have been influenced by some socio-political factors, but their intrinsic value or exchange rate was as a rule determined by economic circumstances prevailing on the markets at the time of their production and circulation. Consequently, the institution of Islamic coinage should be treated primarily in the context of medieval Near Eastern economy—or more specifically, in the context of its monetary phenomenology.

Surviving specimens of Islamic coinage were once treated merely as a small part of medieval economic or monetary history. Today they constitute an extremely important body of tangible, unintentional relics or traces, or source materials. Once these Islamic numismatic relics become heuristically re-monetized they acquire the status of key sources of information about the economic problems of Near Eastern society in the Middle Ages.

Many of the important questions arising from the study of Islamic numismatic sources have been perceived and rigorously treated by several generations of outstanding specialists.[4] For

[4] L. A. Mayer, *Bibliography of Moslem Numismatics,* London, 1954; A. Kmietowicz, 'Supplements to L. Mayer's "Bibliography of Moslem Numismatics," ' *Folia Orientalia,* 2, 1960, pp. 259-275; G. C. Miles, 'Islamic and Sasanian Numismatics: Retrospect and Prospect,' *Congrès International de Numismatique,* Paris, 1953, Tome Premier, *Rapports,* Paris, 1953, pp. 129-144; *idem,* 'Islamic Numismatics: a Progress Report,' *Congresso Internazionale di Numismatica,* Roma, 1961, vol. I. *Relazioni,* Roma, 1961, pp. 181-192; Helen W. Mitchell Brown, 'Islamic Near East,' in *A Survey of*

instance, we have by now a very good idea about the location and the periods of operation of most of the mints involved in medieval production of Islamic coins.[5] Related to this problem were investigations into the nature of jurisdictional authority and responsibility for production, as well as into the very character—centralized versus decentralized—of the system of Islamic mints. We also know a good deal about the preference of various areas in different periods as regards their choice between gold and silver coinage. And we have learned the basic weight standards of different categories of Islamic coinage, as well as the fact that at certain times production or circulation of some of the categories appears to have been suspended—for example, that of the *fulūs* during the first half of the ninth century A.D.[6] or that of the *dirhams* around A.D. 1000.[7]

Economic historians have welcomed rigorous, meticulous rules by which modern numismatists determine the circumstances of appearance and of acquisition of each numismatic specimen. Although heaps of heterogenous coins preserved in old shoe-boxes in some antique shops in fashionable tourist zones of the Near East have hardly merited this kind of treatment, hoards of Islamic coins surfacing in different regions of Africa, Asia and Europe—not only in the lands of the former *Dār al-Islām* but to the south, east and north of the territories of the caliphate—all these coins, if properly and systematically analyzed and recorded, could shed some light on the range of the circulation of Islamic coinage. A detailed typological examination of the contents of each hoard might lead to the determination of the geographic and chronological distance separating the place and date of the "birth" of each

Numismatic Research, 1966-1971, ed. by Jacques Yvon and Helen W. Mitchell Brown, New York, 1973, ii/319-334.

[5]E. von Zambaur, *Die Münzprägungen des Islams zeitlich und örtlich geordnet.* I Band: *Der Westen und Osten bis zum Indus, mit synoptischen Tabellen.* Edited by P. Jaeckel, Wiesbaden, 1968; G. C. Miles, 'Additions to Zambaur's *Münzprägungen des Islams,' The American Numismatic Society Museum Notes,* 17, 1971, pp. 229-233.

[6]A. L. Udovitch, 'Fals,' *Encyclopaedia of Islam,* new edition, ii/769.

[7]R. P. Blake, 'The Circulation of Silver in the Moslem East down to the Mongol Epoch,' *Harvard Journal of Asiatic Studies,* 2, 1937, pp. 211 f. Blake's thesis merits a re-examination in the light of more recently published textual and numismatic evidence.

specimen in the hoard from the *locus* and *terminus post quem* of its burial. This consideration is of particular consequence in the case of a trove of primary character, consisting of coins homogeneous as to place and date of issue, and pointing to the magnitude and mobility of capital invested in commercial transactions.[8]

Although all questions concerning the economic status and behavior of coinage circulating on medieval Near Eastern markets may never be answered satisfactorily, research in recent decades has advanced considerably in determining the monetary essence or the real monetary identity of numismatic specimens. Systematic correlation of the metallic features of examined specimens with the price and wage data derived from textual sources would obviously contribute to a better understanding of divers monetary patterns. Most promising in this respect has been the study of the coin alloys. Starting with the application of the specific gravity method to gold coinage,[9] and the subsequent use of

[8] R. Kiersnowski, *Pieniądz kruszcowy w Polsce średniowiecznej,* Warszawa, 1962, p. 76. The same book (p. 58, n. 17) contains a very useful bibliography of significant contributions pertaining to Oriental treasure troves in Central, Northern and Eastern Europe. It consists of about sixty items published in Czech, Danish, English, Finnish, German, Hungarian, Icelandic, Latvian, Norwegian, Polish, Russian, Slovakian and Swedish. For a survey of more recent Russian contributions on the subject, see T. Lewicki, 'Nouveaux travaux russes concernant les trésors de monnaies musulmanes trouvés en Europe orientale et en Asie Centrale (1959-1963),' *Journal of the Economic and Social History of the Orient,* 8, 1965, pp. 81-90; also see, *idem,* 'Il commercio arabo con la Russia e con i paesi slavi d'Occidente nei secoli IX-XI,' *Annali dell' Instituto Universitario Orientale di Napoli,* Nuova Serie, 8, 1959, pp. 47-61; also, Fr. Kmietowicz, 'Drogi napływu srebra arabskiego na południowe wybrzeże Bałtyku i przynależność etniczna,' *Wiadomości Numizmatyczne,* 12, 1968, pp. 65-86 (English summary); also Ph. Grierson, 'The Interpretation of Coin Finds,' *The Numismatic Chronicle,* Seventh Series, 5, 1965, pp. i-xvi; also, A Matuszewski and J. Wielowiejski, 'Statistical Method of Investigating the Structure of Currency Circulation from Coin Finds,' *Wiadomości Numizmatyczne,* 17, 1973, pp. 17-25.

[9] A. S. Ehrenkreutz, 'The Standard of Fineness of Gold Coins Circulating in Egypt at the Time of the Crusades,' *Journal of the American Oriental Society,* 74, 1954, pp. 162-166; *idem,* 'Studies in the Monetary History of the Near East in the Middle Ages,' *Journal of the Economic and Social History of the Orient,* 2, 1959, pp. 128-161; 6, 1963, pp. 1-35; E. R. Caley, 'Validity of the Specific Gravity Method for the Determination of the Fineness of Gold Objects,' *Ohio Journal of Science,* 49, 1949, pp. 73-82; *idem,* 'Estimation of Composition of Ancient Metal Objects: Utility of Specific Gravity Measurements,' *Analytical Chemistry,* 24, 1952, pp. 676-681.

spectrography,[10] we now have recourse to the latest in numismatic technology: the non-destructive neutron activation analysis.[11]

The most significant and direct heuristic advantage of using the NAA (neutron activation analysis) method is accurate ascertainment of the metallic fineness of examined coins. This information constitutes an important key to a number of essential problems. For instance, by correlating information about the intrinsic quality of the coins with textual data we may arrive at plausible solutions concerning identification of monetary units or types otherwise known only from incidental references in medieval documents. Also by possessing information concerning large samples of *dīnārs, dirhams* and even *fulūs* which were struck over a long period of time, it is possible to reconstruct various trends in the quality of coinage in circulation. This in turn should contribute to a better understanding of recorded fluctuations of wages and prices as well as of the reasons underlying the rates of exchange between divers monetary types.

Besides revealing the identity and percentage of principal metals in the alloys of coins, the NAA method permits detection of minute traces of various organic impurities (for example, copper, tin, arsenic, antimony, zinc, or even gold in the case of silver and vice versa), the presence of which could neither be discovered nor eliminated by means of medieval refining processes.[12] This opens up yet another research dimension, especially in the case of coins or jewels or similar preciosa delivered to the mint. Thus, after learning about the nature and percentage of impurities

[10] Ph. Grierson, 'Trace Elements in Byzantine Copper Coins of the 6th and 7th centuries,' *Dona Numismatica Walter Hāvernick zum 23. Januar 1965 dargebracht*, Hamburg, 1965, p. 31; S. Young, 'An Analysis of Chinese Blue-and-White,' *Oriental Art*, 2, 1956, pp. 43-47.

[11] J. L. Bacharach, 'History, Science and Coins,' *Michigan Technic*, 82, 1964, pp. 24-26; J. L. Bacharach and A. A. Gordus, 'Studies on the Fineness of Silver Coins,' *Journal of the Economic and Social History of the Orient*, 11, 1968, pp. 298-317; A. K. Craig, 'Neutrons and Numismatics,' *The Numismatist*, 76, 1963, pp. 1085-1086; A. A. Gordus, 'Activation Analysis, Artefacts and Art,' *New Scientist*, 17 October 1968, pp. 128-132; D. Shoenberg and D. J. Roaf, 'The Fermi Surfaces of Copper, Silver and Gold. I. The de Haas-van Alphen Effect. II. Calculation of the Fermi Surfaces.' *Philosophical Transactions of the Royal Society of London*, Series A. *Mathematical and Physical Sciences*, No. 1052, vol. 255, 1962, pp. 85-152.

[12] J. L. Bacharach and A. A. Gordus, *op. cit.*, p. 300.

appearing in "primary" *dīnārs* and *dirhams* one can link these coins with oriferous or argentiferous regions, the mine products of which happen to be characterized by the same organic elements.[13] This in turn allows one to trace the routes of the movement of precious metals between the mines and the mints, and of their subsequent dispersion in the shape of coins. There is little doubt that control over those economically strategic routes constituted an important factor in the shaping of Near Eastern history.[14]

Modern treatment of numismatic evidence demands a most meticulous scrutiny of the minutest weight characteristics of examined specimens. A precise study of the weight characteristics of a particular coin series, when correlated with other information, may furnish answers concerning the exact nature of monetary reforms undertaken by medieval regimes.[15] It may also help us to reconstruct the system and function of divers Islamic weight units and standards.[16]

It is evident that Islamic numismatic materials, when treated rigorously and exhaustively, can supply a great deal of interesting

[13] R. A. Messier, 'The Almoravids. West African Gold and the Gold Currency of the Mediterranean Basin,' *Journal of the Economic and Social History of the Orient,* 17, 1974, p. 37.

[14] *Ibid.,* p. 41.

[15] J. L. Bacharach, 'The Dinar versus the Ducat,' *International Journal of Middle East Studies,* 4, 1973, pp. 77-96.

[16] *Idem,* 'Circassian Monetary Policy: Silver,' *The Numismatic Chronicle,* Seventh Series, 11, 1971, pp. 267-281; P. Balog, 'The Ayyubid Glass Jetons and Their Use,' *Journal of the Economic and Social History of the Orient,* 9, 1966, pp. 242-256; Ph. Grierson, 'Weight and Coinage,' *The Numismatic Chronicle,* Seventh Series, 4, 1964, pp. iii-xxiii; *idem.* 'Visigothic Metrology,' *The Numismatic Chronicle,* Sixth Series, 13, 1953, pp. 74-87; W. Kubiak, 'Zagadnienie "odważników handlowych" u Ibrāhīma ibn Ja'kūba,' *Slavia Antiqua,* 5, pp. 368-376; A. Launois, 'Estampilles, poids, étalons monetaires et autres disques musulmans en verre,' *Bulletin d'Études Orientales* 22, 1969, pp. 69-127; G. C. Miles, 'Contributions to Arabic Metrology' (*Numismatic Notes and Monographs,* 141, 1958; 150, 1963); idem, 'Byzantine Miliaresion and Arab Dirhem: Some Notes on Their Relationship,' *The American Numismatic Society Museum Notes,* 9, 1960, pp. 189-218; *idem,* 'On the Varieties and Accuracy of Eight Century Arab Coin Weights,' *Eretz-Israel* (L. A. Mayer Memorial Volume) 7, 1963, pp. 78-87; J. Štěpkova, 'Ueber das Wesen und die Funktion der Dirhamen Bruchstuecke,' *Charisteria Orientalis praecipue ad Persiam pertinentia,* Praha, 1956, pp. 329-337; Ch. Toll, 'Einige metrologische und metallurgische Termini im Arabischen,' *Orientalia Suecana,* 18, 1969, pp. 142-152.

information pertaining to a whole range of aspects of Medieval Near Eastern monetary history. It is fairly easy to establish when, where and by whom these or other types of coinage were produced, to indicate their standard of weight and fineness, and in consequence to explain their purchasing power and rate of exchange. Nor is it impossible–under certain propitious conditions–to suggest the provenience of precious metals involved in the manufacture of the coins, or to speculate on the range of their circulation. There still remains one problem not unimportant for the progress of our reconstruction of medieval economic developments, namely the problem of the volume of coinage in circulation, or at least of the volume of coinage produced annually by individual mints.[17] In view of a deplorable lack of explicit or even implicit textual information is it realistic to expect anything from numismatic evidence on this problem? The answer is "yes" *if our expectations do not reach beyond some general impressions about the level of production of Islamic mints* in given years or periods. Obviously, it is plausible to assume that twenty mints operating in A.D. 889 were likely to produce a larger quantity of *dīnārs* than three mints performing the same function on behalf of Hārūn al-Rashīd (A.D. 786-809).[18] Likewise, a drastic reduction of the number of mints by Hishām (A.D. 724-743) probably resulted in a drop in the volume of silver coins released for circulation–a cooling-off process following an intensive production of *dirhams* necessitated by the reform of 'Abd al-Malik (A.D. 685-705).[19] Neither is it unreasonable to believe–and to look for affirmation in numismatic evidence–that reported monetary reforms, like those undertaken by the Fāṭimid caliph al-Āmir (A.D. 495-524) and by the Ayyūbid sultan al-Kāmil (A.D. 615-635) involved an increase in the output of coins.[20]

[17] A. S. Ehrenkreutz, 'Monetary Aspects of Medieval Near Eastern Economic History,' *Studies in the Economic History of the Middle East*, ed. by M. A. Cook, London, 1970, p. 47.

[18] G. C. Miles, *The Numismatic History of Rayy*, New York, 1950, p. 119.

[19] This point is discussed by the present author in his article on 'Money' to appear in the *Wirtschaftsgeschichte des Vorderen Orients zu islamischer Zeit*, published by E. J. Brill.

[20] A. S. Ehrenkreutz, 'Contributions to the Knowledge of the Fiscal Administration of Egypt in the Middle Ages,' *Bulletin of the School of Oriental and African Studies,'* 16, 1954, p. 504; 508.

Another approach, involving the "coin-die count" method offers means of speculative comparison of the annual output by different mints at different periods. This method calls for precise identification of coin-dies responsible for the design imprinted or impressed on the obverse and reverse of each single coin. This identification allows determination of the number of detectable dies employed in the production of examined coins belonging to one and the same mint-and-year series. Accurate identification and classification of coin-dies—the particular characteristics of which cannot sometimes be discerned without microscopic inspection—should be regarded as a normal descriptive procedure. To an historian the number of coin-dies in a homogeneous sample constitutes a better criterion of the level of production than assumptions based on the total number of specimens contained in such a sample. This point may be illustrated by means of the following hypothetical example. Let us assume that a tabulation of all surviving *dīnārs* specimens struck in A.H. 300 has revealed that there are 1,000 specimens from Baghdād and only 10 from Egypt. A close scrutiny of the Baghdādī specimens reveals that all of them were struck by only one and the same set of coin-dies. On the other hand the ten Egyptian specimens turn out to have been produced by ten different dies. In the light of this evidence one may postulate that in A.H. 300 the production of *dīnārs* by the mint of Egypt exceeded that of the mint of Baghdād.

As far as I know only three attempts have been made so far to determine the number of dies involved in the manufacture of Islamic coin series. Dr. George C. Miles examined 685 *dirhams* struck in A.H. 400 by the mint of Cordoba and produced some interesting statistics.[21] A seminar group at the University of Michigan carried out a preliminary inquiry using for that purpose catalog reproductions of silver and gold coins struck in pre-'Abbāsid period.[22] Intrigued by the results yielded by that limited venture the same group embarked on a more ambitious research project involving the task of photographing and re-examining about 2,000 *dīnārs* struck by pre-Mamlūk rulers of Egypt, and available in

[21] G. C. Miles, 'The Year 400 A. H./1009-1010 A.D. at the Mint of Cordoba,' *Numisma*, 17, 1967, pp. 9-25.

[22] 'Early Islamic Mint Output,' *Journal of the Economic and Social History of the Orient*, 9, 1966, pp. 212-241.

major numismatic collections of New York, London, Oxford, Copenhagen, Paris, Milan, Istanbul and Tunis.[23]

Detailed results of this inquiry will appear in a separate report; at this stage let me share some of the preliminary conclusions. Statistically speaking, duplicate specimens–that is, *dīnārs* produced by the same set of dies–appear in samples consisting of four coins. In other words, samples of 1 to 3 coins tend to show an equal ratio of coins to the detectable sets of dies, but samples of four specimens as a rule include a pair of coins produced by one and the same set of dies. In that case the ratio of original coin-dies to actual coin specimens decreases, to be 3:4. The larger the sample the greater the disproportion is likely to be. The assumption is that if one keeps on accumulating specimens belonging to the same mint-and-year series one may eventually reach a point at which the number of identified coin-dies would become stationary and would not be affected by further additions to the sample. The figure emerging could then be regarded as representing the total number of coin-dies used in the annual production.

Unfortunately, we are far from having approached such a desirable situation,[24] and because of the small size of examined samples it is difficult to speak of any consistent patterns emerging from our study. For instance, samples dating from A.H. 359 and 366, consisting of seven specimens, appear to have been produced by seven different dies each, but a larger sample, dating from A.H. 364 and containing nine *dīnārs,* involves only four different dies, resulting in a ratio of 4:9.

On the other hand, one can see a relationship between the number of coin-dies and certain events reported in the chronicles. This is particularly evident during the periods of monetary reforms. One such reform, undertaken by al-Āmir in the second decade of the sixth century A.H., stepped up production of *dīnārs* by Egyptian mints in order to compensate for the loss of Syrian mints resulting from the invasion by the Crusaders.[25] A study of

[23]The members of the seminar are indebted to scholarly officials in charge of the respective collections, for their kind cooperation and professional assistance in carrying out this task.

[24]It is my hope that this situation will be attained with the examination of the abundant numismatic resources of the Museum of Islamic Art in Cairo.

[25]A. S. Ehrenkreutz, 'Contributions . . . ,' *op. cit.*, pp. 507-508.

dinars issued by the mint of Miṣr during that period reveals a larger than average proportion of original coin-dies in the annual samples as can be seen from the following table:

Number of original coin-dies in samples from A.H.

Mint	514	515	516	517	518
Miṣr	5(5)*	9(10)	10(10)	4(4)	
al-Qāhirah					8(9)

*Figures in brackets indicate the total number of specimens in each sample.

A similar trend can be established in the samples corresponding chronologically with the efforts of al-Kāmil to increase production of coinage in the capital of Egypt.[26]

Number of original coin-dies in samples from A.H.

Mint	625	626	627	628	629	630	631	632	634
al-Qāhirah	3(6)	6(10)	7(14)	6(14)	2(6)	2(6)	2(6)	1(4)	2(5)

The main lesson derived from this coin-die count project is that, although its findings lend themselves to all sorts of statistical permutations and speculations, the annual mint samples should be substantially increased before valid historical inferences can be made.

The validity of the coin-die method of calculation has already been questioned by Professor A. Udovitch. According to him it suffers from inherent shortcomings such as total dependence on extant coins with no knowledge of their relationship to the coin types originally issued. Nor is it possible to establish whether each die was used for the maximum number of strikes, or even

[26] *Ibid.*, p. 508.

anything close to it.[27] With regard to the second point, I wish to submit that one would not be guilty of a major interpretative error by assuming that under normal circumstances most dies—the manufacture of which is said to have constituted a very involved preoccupation of specialist engravers on the staff of medieval Islamic mints[28]—were probably used for the maximum number of strikes, or at least close to it. As for the first weakness, its specter overshadows any argument depending exclusively on numismatic evidence. All "numismatic" conclusions—tentative, speculative or definitive—are based only on extant coins, and like any other processes of reconstruction of historical phenomenology are subject to revisions in the light of new divergent or contradictory evidence.

[27] A. L. Udovitch, 'Introductory Remarks,' *Studies in the Economic History of the Middle East,* ed. by M. A. Cook, London, 1970, p. 6.

[28] A. S. Ehrenkreutz, 'Contributions . . . ,'' *op. cit.,* p. 512.

VI

STUDIES IN THE MONETARY HISTORY OF THE NEAR EAST IN THE MIDDLE AGES

The Standard of Fineness of Some Types of Dinars*

The Mediaeval Islamic *dinar* has received an uneven treatment by Western economic historians. For example, it did not fare too well with Prof. R. S. Lopez who has claimed the monetary supremacy in the Middle Ages for the Byzantine *solidus* or *nomisma*.[1]) Prof. C. M. Cipolla, on the other hand, treated it with respect. According to this prominent scholar "through the centuries of the Middel Ages there were many types of "dollars"[2]) . . . the Byzantine *nomisma*, the Moslem *dinar*, the *fiorino* of Florence, and the *ducato* of Venice."[3]) Elaborating his interpretation of this aspect of monetary developments in the Middle Ages, Prof. Cipolla stressed the problem of the intrinsic stability which, in his opinion, has been one of the reasons for the "international" reputation of these currencies. Whether one considers the case of the *solidus* or that of the *fiorino* and the *ducato*, all them displayed a remarkable intrinsic stability for a long time following their first issue.[4]) As for the Moslem *dinar*, remarked Prof. Cipolla "We can easily see that it too

---

*) I wish to acknowledge the help of the authorities of the University of Michigan who, by providing me with the grants from the Charles L. Freer Research and Publication Fund and from the Faculty Research Fund enables me to carry out the examination of numismatic material at the Museum of the American Numismatic Society in New York.

1) R. S. Lopez, 'The Dollar of the Middle Ages,' *Journal of Economic History*, 11, 1951, p. 209-234.

2) C. M. Cipolla, *Money, Prices, and Civilization in the Mediterranean world*, Princeton, 1956, chapt. on "the Dollars of the Middle Ages", p. 13.

3) *op. cit.*, p. 21.

4) *op. cit.*, p. 23.

maintained intrinsic stability in the first two centuries of its existence. This is true for the *dinars* struck in the East. It also seems to be true for the *dinars* struck in Spain. It was only in the eleventh century that the Spanish *dinar* began to be seriously debased."[1])

Although presented as evidence in support of another idea which was the main thesis of his study, the obiter dicta of Prof. Cipolla about the *dinar* are interesting enough to justify an investigation concerning the *bonitas intrinseca* of mediaeval *dinars*. For in spite of the availability of a wealth of numismatic and textual sources the ideas of Orientalist historians and numismatists concerning the problem in question are yet to be crystallized. Such an investigation, however, cannot be undertaken without settling one fundamental question, namely: what is really meant by the term *Moslem dinar* in a discussion of this kind. Even in the above quotation from the study of Prof. Cipolla there is a reference to two types of Moslem *dinars* at least: *dinars* struck in the East, and those struck in Spain, or Spanish *dinars*. The specification in this instance is based on the difference in the place of issuance of these *dinars*. Indeed the striking of *dinars* in a number of places constituted one of the characteristic features of the minting production of Mediaeval Islam. This was carried out in several mints scattered all over the Near East. Even during the earliest period of Moslem minting production the coining of gold was accomplished in at least four areas: Egypt,[2]) Syria, North Africa, and Spain.[3]) It is true that beginning with Hishām (A.D. 724-743) the Umayyad caliphs seem to have centralized the minting of gold issues[4]), but this monopoly of the caliphs was abandoned by the 'Abbāsids. The striking of *dinars* by the governors of Egypt,[5]) and of North Africa[6]) was the first break in the shortlived monopoly of the central government. Further decentralization followed apace. Instead

1) *Supra*. For the authority concerning the Spanish *dinars* Prof. Cipolla refers to G. C. Miles, *The Coinage of Umayyads of Spain*, New York, 1950, p. 90.

2) Cf. A. Grohmann, *Einführung und Chrestomathie zur arabischen Papyruskunde*, Praha, 1954, p. 186.

3) Cf. J. Walker, *A catalogue of the Arab-Byzantine and postreform Umaiyad coins*, London, 1956, p. lv-lix.

4) *ibid.*, p. lix.

5) Cf. A. Grohmann, *op. cit.*, p. 193.

6) Cf. H. Lavoix, *Catalogue des monnaies musulmanes de la Bibliothèque Nationale*, Paris, 1887-94, iii/345.

of three *dinar* issuing mints (Baghdād, Egypt, Ifriqīyah) under Hārūn al-Rashīd (A.D. 786-809), the number of such mints in A.D. 889 amounted to about twenty.[1])

Had all the mints stuck to a uniform type of *dinars* there would have been no ground for any distinction between the issues of different provenience. In reality, however, the gold series of particular mints often differed from one another, not only from the point of view of external characteristics but also on account of their intrinsic quality. This was the result of a custom prevailing in Mediaeval Islam according to which the standard of fineness of the official coinage was arbitrarily fixed by the ruler,[2]) or even by a special official appointed to supervise the minting production.[3]) With the shrinking of the authority of the caliphs of Baghdād it was no longer possible to maintain an effective centralized control over the mints operating in politically and administratively emancipated areas. Consequently, instead of one supreme authority responsible for decisions in the matters of gold coinage there were many rulers who determined the standard of *dinars* according to their particular needs or means. Thus in Mediaeval Near East there were in circulation several types of *dinars* with different standards of fineness. The number of different types in circulation was further multiplied by the fact that the standard of gold issues often varied over the centuries within one and the same political area. Political or economic changes frequently led to the issuance of new types of *dinars* which were usually called by the name of the rulers or officials responsible for such measures. Some of the types were held in great esteem because of their intrinsic value. Among the 'Abbāsid *dinars* those struck during the reigns of al-Mā'mūn (A.D. 813-833) and al-Wāthiq (A.D. 842-847) were famous for their excellent standard of fineness.[4]) The standard establish-

---

1) Cf. G. C. Miles, *The numismatic history of Rayy*, New York, 1950, p. 119.

2) Cf. Ibn Khaldūn, *Les Prolégomènes*, transl. par M. de Slane, Paris, 1863-68, i/460; ii/55, 60; see also A. S. Ehrenkreutz, "Contributions to the knowledge of the fiscal administration of Egypt in the Middel Ages", *BSOAS*, 16, iii, 1954, p. 510 n. 3.

3) Such was the office of *nāẓir as-sikka* established by Hārūn ar-Rashīd. Cf. al-Maqrizi, *Shudhūr al-'uqūd*, ed. L. A. Mayer, Alexandria, 1933, p. 8; transl. of A. I. S. de Sacy, *Traité des monnoies musulmanes,* Paris, 1797, p. 30-31.

4) Cf., A. Grohmann, *op. cit.*, p. 193.

ed by al-Sindī, the supervisor of coinage under Hārūn al-Rashīd, was also very high and was still aspired to by minters of the tenth century.[1]) In Egypt the standard of *Aḥmadī dinars* (so called after Aḥmed ibn Ṭūlūn, the governor of Egypt between A.D. 868-884) was said to have equalled that of al-Sindī.[2]) Excellent were also the *dinars* of the Fāṭimid caliph al-Āmir (A.D. 1101-1130).[3]) The latter ordered an investigation of the operations of his mints, which resulted in the raising of the standard of gold issues.[4]) The *Āmirī* standard was reached if not excelled by that prescribed by the great Ayyūbid sultan al-Kāmil (A.D. 1218-1238), whose *dinars* were called al-Kāmilī al-Āmirī.[5]) Among the *dinars* struck in western Islamic territories the issues of the Almoravids, called al-Murābitīyah[6]) did not enjoy too high a reputation.[7]) On the other hand those of the Almohades, called al-Ya'qūbī, were known to be struck of very fine gold.[8])

Certainly, all these *dinars* were produced in Moslem territories by Moslem authorities, and as such they may rightly be called Moslem *dinars* in much the same sense as one might refer to the *solidi*, *floreens* and *ducats* as Christian coins. But if in discussing the intrinsic value of mediaeval gold coins one makes a differentiation between various types struck in Christian countries, then a similar treatment should be given to the coinage of the Moslems. It is only by treating separately the issues of different Moslem minting areas that one may arrive at a better understanding of monetary developments in the Mediterranean area in the Middle Ages. Again, the remarks of Prof. Cipolla may serve here to

---

1) Cf., al-Maqrīzī, *Shudhūr al-'uqūd*, *ed. cit.*, p. 8; transl. of A. I. S. de Sacy, *ed. cit.* p. 32. Also aṣ-*Ṣūlī*, *Akhbār ar-Rāḍī billāh wa'l-Muttaqī billāh*, transl. by M. Canard, Alger, 1946, ii/57.

2) For a list of relevant authorities see O. Grabar, *The coinage of the Ṭūlūnids*, New York, 1957, p. 59, n. 3. The standard of the *dinars* of the 'Abbāsid caliph al-Mu'taṣim (A. D. 833-842) was accordingly called *al-Mu'taṣimī*.

3) Cf. al-Maqrīzī in H. Sauvaire, "Matériaux pour servir à l'histoire de la numismatique et de la métrologie musulmanes", *JA*, VII série, 19, 1882, p. 102.

4) Cf., A. S. Ehrenkreutz, *art. cit.*, p. 508.

5) Cf., A. S., Ehrenkreutz, "The standard of fineness of gold coins circulating in Egypt at the time of the Crusades", *JAOS*, 74, iii, 1954, p. 164.

6) Cf., H. Sauvaire, *art. cit.* *JA*, VII s6rie, 19, 1882, p. 41-42.

7) Cf., A. S. Ehrenkreutz, *art. cit.* p. 163.

8) Cf., *ibid.*

illustrate the point. When he writes about the debasement of the Byzantine *solidi* in the eleventh century there can hardly be any doubt concerning the identity of coins he refers to. But it is by no means clear what he has in mind by referring to the *dinars* struck in the East. Does he mean the *dinars* struck in Baghdād, i.e. in the capital of the 'Abbāsid caliphate? Or does he refer to the issues of the Buwayhids (A.D. 932-A.D. 1048) struck in Baghdād or perhaps in Shirāz? Or perhaps to the issues of the Seljūks, of the Isfahān mint? Are the Egyptian *dinars* included in the consideration of the *dinars* struck in the East? Unless the scope of the term *Eastern dinars* is defined, the comparison of their intrinsic value with that of the *solidi* is not very revealing. Still less acceptable for this kind of discussion is the use of the general term *Moslem dinar*. Not that the term in question has no application in the technical nomenclature pertaining to the Moslem monetary system. But in a technical sense the term *Moslem dinar* is applicable only to the legal *dinar*, i.e. a gold unit whose standards of weight and fineness were formulated by Moslem jurists, and which also served as the standard money of account. The need for such standard accounting unit arose with Islamic conquests. The circulation of a great number of different monetary types in the conquered territories led to the adoption of fixed units of account in order to facilitate pecuniary transactions. If one is to accept the view of Ibn Khaldūn (A.D. 1332-1406) it was this problem of *dinars* of account that constituted one of the reasons for the famous reform of 'Abd al-Malik (A.D. 685-705). In introducing a new type of *dinars* (and of *dirhams*) that great Arabic administrator supplied the markets with new coins based on the legal standards of the ideal money of account.[1]) In the light of this information it appears that the standard of the reformed *dinars* of 'Abd al-Malik corresponded to that of the legal Moslem *dinar*. Consequently, by examining the standard of the *dinars* of 'Abd al-Malik one might infer the prescribed standard of the legal Moslem *dinar*. Unfortunately, as Ibn Khaldūn recorded it himself, the reform of 'Abd al-Malik had limited consequences for monetary development, because "those in charge of the production of coins[2]) chose to depart from the legal standards assigned to the *dinar* and *dirham*, so

1) Cf. Ibn Khaldūn, *op. cit.*, p. 60.

2) "*ahl as-sikka*", cf., Ibn Khaldūn, *Muqaddima*, Cairo, al-Maktaba al-tijārīya, n. d., p. 263.

that they (i.e. the standards) became different in each region and country. And so the people returned to their original custom of using fictitious legal standards."[1]) Thus, even if the nature of the standard of fineness of the legal *dinar* were assertained, it would not have much bearing on the knowledge of the intrinsic value of various types of gold coins which circulated in the Near East during the Middle Ages. As a result and in order to arrive at some general conclusions concerning the intrinsic value of Moslem gold coinage, one has to proceed with a systematic reconstruction of the standards of fineness of particular types of mediaeval *dinars*.

Apart from its importance for comparative studies of 'international' monetary developments such a reconstruction should contribute towards a better understanding of the economic life in mediaeval Moslem world. It is true that mediaeval texts containing references to pecuniary matters do not always list specific types of currency beyond the basic distinction between *dinar* (gold coin), *dirham* (silver coin) and fractions thereof. These unspecified monetary formulations seem to refer to the legal money of account. This is quite normal, considering that in the Moslem Near East not only prices or salaries, but even entire state fiscal assessments were evaluated in terms of such units of account.[2]) But the actual transactions, payments, purchases or sales, were carried out by means of local types of real money, issued in various areas in different periods, and whose purchasing power and exchange value depended on their particular intrinsic quality.[3])

Although Prof. Cipolla does not mention his authority for the remarks concerning the intrinsic stability of the Moslem *dinar*[4]) there seems to be little doubt that he relied on Vazquez Queipo for the point in question.[5])

---

1) *Ibid.*, p. 253-264.

2) E.g. in Egypt of the Ayyūbids. Cf., C. Cahen, "Le régime des impôts dans le Fayyum ayyūbide", *Arabica*, 3, i, p. 12.

3) Cf., C. Cahen, "Quelques problèmes économiques et fiscaux de l'Iraq bouyide d'après un traité de mathématiques, "*Annales de l'Institut d'Études Orientales d'Alger*, 10, 1952, p. 338f.

4) Except for his remark about the *dinars* struck in Spain, cf. above, p. 131, n. 5.

5) V. Vazquez Queipo, *Essai sur les systèmes métriques et monétaires des anciens peuples depuis les premiers temps historiques jusqu'à la fin du Khalifat d'Orient*, Paris, 1859.

As correct as Queipo's findings might be, the scope of his analysis of the intrinsic value of *dinars* cannot be regarded as sufficient evidence for drawing any far reaching conclusions. For the research of Queipo was limited to the examination of one Umayyad *dinar* of A.H. 104, two 'Abbāsid *dinars* of A.H. 193 and 361 respectively; two *dinars* of the Fāṭimids of A.H. 416 and 445 respectively; and about twenty *dinars* struck over a period of some 500 years by different Moslem rulers of Spain. Thus the knowledge of the standard of fineness of so few specimens, selected at random and originating among so many different areas and periods, does not prove at all that "Non seulement le poids du dinar fut constant pendant les deux premiers siècles et jusqu'à la moitié du troisième de l'hégire, mais aussi le titre en a été presque fin, ou, du moins, autant que le permettait alors l'état de la science."[1])

To improve the state of our knowledge of the standard of fineness of gold coins struck in Moslem territories during the Middle Ages the present writer has undertaken a task of measuring the specific gravity of some 450 specimens available in the collections of the American Numismatic Society.[2]) The examination was limited to the undamaged *dinars* consisting of the following main categories: the 'mintless' *dinars*, *dinars* struck in Baghdād and Samārrā, and *dinars* struck in Pre-Fāṭimid Egypt. A few additional specimens from certain provincial mints have also been included in the investigation. The choice of the Baghdad (and Samārrā) and Egyptian issues was determined by two considerations: a) the availability of a great number of specimens from these areas; and b) speculation that a confrontation of the Baghdādī and Egyptian issues may help to establish the official standard prescribed by the 'Abbāsid caliphs. Although the method of measuring the specific gravity suffers from certain limitations[3]), it nevertheless permits one to draw interesting conclusions concerning the standard of fineness of the

---

1) *Ibid.*, ii/395.

2) I wish to acknowledge the kindness of Dr. G. C. Miles of the American Numismatic Society Museum in New York for allowing me to examine the coins under his curatorship.

3) Cf., E. R. Caley, "Estimation of Composition of Ancient Metal Objects". *Analytical Chemistry*, 24, 1952, p. 677; also F. C. Thompson, "The use of the microscope in numismatic studies," *Numismatic Chronicle*, 6th ser., 16, 1956, p. 337.

examined specimens. Furthermore, the available number of specimens belonging to the same methodically classified categories offers statistical opportunities to validate more general conclusions.

UMAYYAD REFORMED DINARS

The first group of specimens submitted to the examination consisted of the reformed *dinars* struck during the period of the Umayyads (A.D. 696/7 – the year of the appearance of the new *dinars* –, to A.D. 750 – as the year of the fall of the dynasty). With the exception of three specimens (2 from Spain, bearing the mint name *al-Andalus*, and one with the mint name *al-Ḥijāz*,[1]) all examined *dinars* in this group were the 'mintless' *dinars*.[2]) Along with such mintless Umayyad specimens, nineteen fractions of *dinars*, also mintless but characterized by 'Western legends'[3]), have been considered in this investigation.

The standard of the Umayyad specimens may be presented by means of the following distribution table. (Spanish specimens are distinguished by means of round brackets; 'Western legend' fractions by means of square brackets; the Ḥijāz issue is symbolized by letter H).

TABLE I

Distribution of the examined Umayyad specimens according to their standard of fineness

	Below 89%	89%	90%	91%	92%	93%	94%	95%	96%	97%	98%	99%	100%
Number of Specimens	[2]	1+[1]	–	1+[4]	1	1	1+[5]	3+[2]	40+[4]	22+(1)+H	22	3+(1)	–

As appears from the above table a considerable majority of the available Umayyad *dinars* possesses a degree of fineness of 96%. This group constitutes 37.9% of the total of the examined specimens of the

1) For a discussion concerning the location of that mint see G. C. Miles, *Rare Islamic Coins*, in *Numismatic Notes and Monographs*, 118, 1950, p. 21-22.

2) The striking of "anonymous" and "mintless" *dinars* constituted a characteristic feature of early Islamic minting production. It was abandoned during the reign of the 'Abbāsid caliph al-Hādī (A.D. 785-786) when for the first time personal names appeared on issues of gold. Under Hārūn ar-Rashīd (A. D. 786-809) the name of the ruling sovereign made its appearance on *dinars*. Beginnng with the time of al-Mā'mūn (A. D. 813-833) also the mint names appeared on gold issues.

3) Cf., J. Walker, *op. cit.*, p. lvii-lix.

post-reform Umayyad period. If one excluded the fractions of *dinars*, the percentage of this high quality *dinars* would rise to 41.6% of the total number. The high and stable standard of Umayyad *dinars* becomes even more conspicuous when one considers that the next two best categories fall in the 97% and 98% classes, with 24 and 22 specimens respectively. If one excludes fractionary units, the number of *dinars* falling in these three standard classes represents an impressive 89% of the examined lot of the Umayyad period.

As far as the three specimens with mint names are concerned, the two Spanish *dinars* display the standard of 96% and 99%, respectively; the Ḥijāz specimen has 97% degree of fineness. Such isolated specimens do not permit to draw any conclusions concerning the standard of *dinars* struck in Spanish mints in the Umayyad period. On the other hand, the available number of fractionary specimens originating from the West seems to be adequate for such consideration. The distribution of relatively even groups of specimens over a number of finess categories ranging from 'below 89%' (1 specimen of 65%, 1 specimen of 89%) to 96%, seems to suggest that as far as the fractions of *dinars* were concerned they were not struck according to any fixed standard of fineness.

To what extent, however, was the standard of 96% of fineness respected during the reign of different Umayyad rulers? The following frequency distribution table may help to answer this question. (Excluded from this table are fractions of *dinars*).

TABLE II

Distribution of the examined specimens according to their standard of fineness and arranged by successive Umayyad rulers

Name of the ruler (Dates in A.H.)*	*Below* 89%	89%	90%	91%	92%	93%	94%	95%	96%	97%	98%	99%	100%
'Abd al-Malik (65-86)	–	–	–	–	–	–	1	1	9	8	4	1	–
al-Walīd (86-96)	–	–	–	1	–	–	–	1	13	5	–	1	–
Sulaymān (96-99)	–	1	–	–	–	–	–	–	2	4	–	–	–
'Umar (99-101)	–	–	–	–	–	–	–	–	1	–	1	–	–
Yazīd II (101-105)	–	–	–	–	–	–	–	–	1	1+(1)	–	(1)	–
Hishām (105-125)	–	–	–	–	–	–	–	–	11	3+Ḥ	11	1	–
al-Walīd II-Yazīd III (125-126)	–	–	–	–	–	–	–	–	3	–	–	–	–
Marwān II	–	–	–	–	–	–	–	1	–	1	2	–	–

*) Since these early *dinars* were anonymous, it is impossible to establish to whom should precisely be assigned the specimens which bear the date of the year of a change of rulers.

The consistency with which the specimens of 96% fineness dominate over other specimens during a half of a century of the Umayyad era is quite conspicuous. This may be best recognized by indicating the high proportion of such *dinars* among the examined specimens.

Ruler	*Total number of specimens*	*Number of specimens in the best three fineness groups*		
		96%	97%	98%
ʻAbd al-Malik	24	9 (or 37.5%)	8 (or 33.3%)	4 (or 16.6%)
al-Walīd	21	13 (or 61.9%)	5 (or 23.8%)	
Hishām	28	11 (or 39.2%)	4 (or 14.2%)	11 (or 39.2%)

The tabulation of the standards of specimens struck in the same calendar years further confirms this remarkable stability of the Umayyad *dinars*. This is indicated on the following diagram.

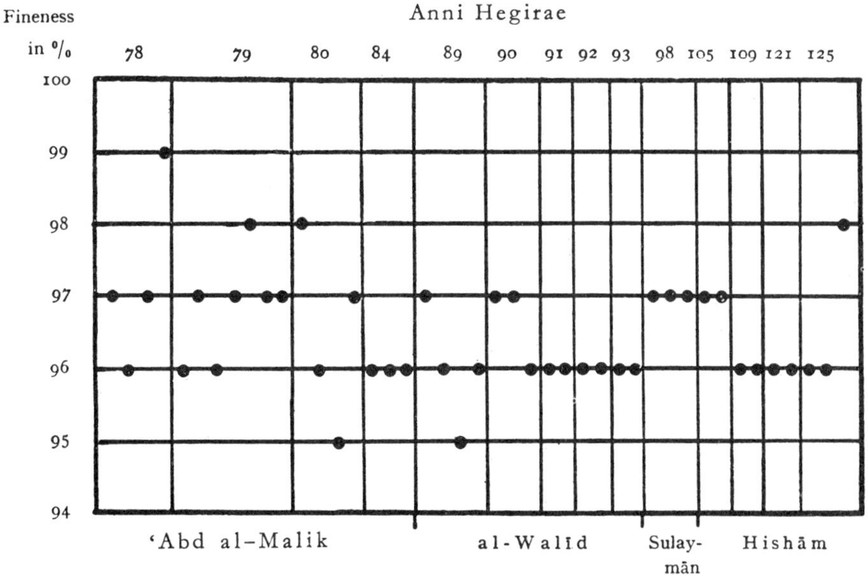

Diagram I

On the basis of the examination of the Umayyad specimens it appears that the standard of the reformed *dinars* of ʻAbd al-Malik was fixed at 96% degree of fineness. The incidence of a few specimens with the intrinsic value lower than the standard of 96%, probably constitutes an exception to the rule.[1])

An interesting problem is posed by the specimens with 98% of fineness. Prior to the series of dinars of al-Hishām, the occurrence of this standard is rather exceptional (only 5 specimens out of 57 pre-Hishām specimens). But this situation changes radically with the *dinars* of al-Hishām as well as those of his successors. The 98% fine *dinars* make up the largest group of the specimens of al-Hishām, which is equalled only by 96% fine *dinars*. Similar *dinars* occur among the specimens of Marwān II, and also among the early specimens of the 'Abbāsids. Could this diochotomy in the standard of fineness of *dinars* of that period be interpreted as an indication of the existence of a mint issuing gold coins with that specific standard of fineness? There is no doubt that prior to the reign of al-Hishām gold coins were struck in Damascus,[2]), North Africa (Ifrīqīyah),[3]) Spain,[4]) and Egypt.[5]) Centralizing policy of al-Hishām might have resulted in the suspension of the minting of gold in the West[6]) and at the same time in an increase of the production of a more centrally located mint whose issues were characterized by the high standard of 98% of fineness.[7])

---

1) The question arises, however, as to the minimal differential to cause the necessity of distuinguishing between the standards of fineness. As far as the minting authorities were concerned, they differentiated between the gold coins whose standards of fineness differed by as little as 2.5 % (Cf., A. S. Ehrenkreutz, "The standard of fineness of gold coins circulating in Egypt at the time of the Crusades", *JAOS*, 74, iii, 1954, p. 163). Special qualitative and quantitative tests were practised to determine the standard of gold coins with utmost accuracy (Cf., A. S. Ehrenkreutz, "Extracts from the technical manual on the Ayyūbid mint in Cairo", *BSOAS*, 15, iii, 1953, p. 433-435). Certainly, a difference of 2 % in the standard of fineness would hardly affect the purchasing and exchange value of single *dinars* in retail transactions. But one must remember that gold coins were used for large scale financial operations, and with large quantities of *dinars* even the difference of 2 % could not be overlooked.

2) Cf., al-Balādhurī, *Futūh al-buldān*, Cairo, 1932, p. 452.

3) Cf., J. Walker, *op. cit.*, p. lv.

4) *Supra.*

5) Cf., A. Grohmann, *op. cit.*, p. 186.

6)Cf., J. Walker, *op. cit.*, p. lix. For the fiscal policy of al-Hishām, see F. Gabrieli, *Il Califfato di Hishâm, Studi di Storia Omayyade, Alexandrie*, 1935, p. 123f.

7) See discussion below, p. 141.

'ABBĀSID DINARS

The 'Abbāsid specimens examined may be divided in the following groups: 1) 'mintless' *dinars*; 2) *dinars* struck in the capital of the 'Abbāsid caliphate (Baghdād, and also Sāmarrā); 3) 'Abāsid Egyptian pre-Ṭūlūnid *dinars*; 5) 'Abbāsid Egyptian pre-Ikhshīdid *dinars*; 6) Ikhshīdid *dinars*.

TABLE III

*Distribution of the examined 'Abbāsid 'mintless' dinars according to their standard of fineness.**)

	Below 89%	89%	90%	91%	92%	93%	94%	95%	96%	97%	98%	99%	100%
Number of specimens	4	3	3	5	4	3	16	15	36	17	13	1	1

*) Excluded from this table are the "mintless" specimens which have been identified as the issues of the Egyptian mint.

As was the case with the Umayyad *dinars*, a great majority of the mintless 'Abbāsid specimens reveal a standard of 96% of fineness. Of the 121 *dinars* examined 36 or 29.7% fall in that significant category. The next highest group falls into the 96% group, and consists of 17 specimens, or 14% of the total. The consistency with which the standard of 96% of fineness appears among the mintless *dinars* during that phase of the 'Abbasid minting production is evident in the following table.

TABLE IV

'Abbāsid mintless dinars
Frequency distribution according to standard of fineness

Name of the ruler (dates in A.H.)	*Number of specimens* *Below* 89%	89%	90%	91%	92%	93%	94%	95%	96 %	97%	98%	99%	100%
al-Saffāḥ (132-136)	–	–	–	–	–	–	1	–	1	2	1	–	–
al-Manṣūr (136-158)	–	–	–	2	2	–	4	4	10	5	5	–	–
al-Mahdī (158-169)	–	–	1	–	1	1	4	5	8	–	1	–	–
al-Hādī (169-170)	–	–	–	–	–	1	2	–	1	–	–	–	–
Hārūn al-Rashīd (170-193)	2	2	1	–	–	1	3	4	12	5	5	–	–
al-Amīn (193-198)	–	–	–	–	–	–	1	1	4	1	–	–	–
al-Mā'mūn	2	1	1	3	1	–	1	1	–	4	1	1	1
Total	4	3	3	5	4	3	16	15	36	17	13	1	1

This conspicuous concentration of mintless 'Abbāsid specimens in 96% class may be further substantiated by means of the following tabulation.

TABLE V

	Total number of specimens	Number of specimens with 96% fineness	Number of specimens in the second largest group: % of fineness	Number of specimens in the second largest group: number of specimens
al-Manṣūr	32	10 (or 31.2%)	97 ; 98	5 (or 15%) each
al-Mahdī	21	8 (or 38%)	95	5 (or 23.3%)
Hārūn al-Rashīd	35	12 (or 34.2%)	97 ; 98	5 (or 14.2%) each

Along with the specimens with 96% of fineness, there are many specimens displaying both higher and inferior standards of fineness. Close scrutiny of the frequency of specimens with different standards of fineness permits one to make a few interesting observations. One may begin with the problem of the standard of 98% fineness. The number of times this standard occurs among the early mintless specimens of the 'Abbāsids is really conspicuous. Of the 15 examines *dinars* struck between A.H. 132-146, six are 98%, and five 97% fine. Only two specimens show the standard of 96%, and one is 91% fine. But the high standard disappears in the specimens struck between A.H. 145-170 (except for a *dinar* of A.H. 163 which has the standard of 98% of fineness). Now, both these years, A.H. 146 and 170, consitute significant dates in the monetary history of the 'Abbāsid caliphate. The first one is associated with the activity of the mint of the newly established capital of the 'Abbāsids-Baghdād or Madīnat al-Salām. The earliest available coins struck by that mint date from A.H. 146 (A.D. 763/64).[1]) The second date, A.H. 170 is significant because it was in that year that gold coins appeared showing the name of Egyptian governors,[2]) permitting one to identify the mint of otherwise undistinguishable *dinars*. Of the six such Egyptian specimens 2 are 98% fine, 2 are 97% fine, 1 has the standard of 96%, and another one that of 95%. Two slightly clipped specimens with the names of Egyptian governors have the standard of 98% and

1) Cf., S. Lane-Poole, *Catalogue of Oriental Coins in the British Museum*, London, 1875-1888, i/47.

2) Cf., A. Grohmann, *op. cit.*, p. 194.

96%, respectively.[1]) In addition there is yet another specimen which could possibly be attributed to the Egyptian mint because of certain epigraphic characteristics.[2]) Its fineness is 99%. If one takes into account all these Egyptian specimens the standard of fineness characteristic of the Egyptian *dinars* appears to be 98%. Should one assume that the mintless *dinars* with 98% of fineness were of Egyptian origin, then such an hypothesis would lead to the following observation about the early production of reformed gold coins of the early Caliphate. Originally the minting of reformed gold coins was accomplished in Damascus, Spain, North Africa and Egypt. The issues of the mint of Egypt were characterised by a high standard of fineness. As stated above,[3]) the centralizing tendencies of Hishām resulted in the closing of the mints in the West. The reduction in the output of gold coins caused by the suspension of Western mints was compensated for by intensified operations of the mint of Egypt, whose issues continued to possess a very high intrinsic value. The victory and the establishment of the 'Abbāsid regime did not at first produce any substantial changes as far as the organization of minting production was concerned. Egypt continued to issue gold coins, possibly Damascus also. A change came with the establishment of the new capital in Baghdād in A.H. 145. A new mint, that of the capital, began its operations in A.H. 146. The opening of the mint of the capital was accompanied by the loss of significance, if not by a total suspension of the production of gold coins by the mints of Egypt and of Damascus. But about a quarter of a century later the mint of Egypt resumed its normal production of gold coins.

Naturally, all these observations are purely hypothetical. An examination of more *dinars* from that period, possibly also a spectroscopic analysis, may either confirm these conjectures, or perhaps reject them completely.

Another problem is posed by the intrinsic value of *dinars* struck during the period of several successive supervisors of coinage, an institution set up by Hārūn al-Rashīd.[4]) A list of these officials may be

---

1) Cf., items UM 70, and UM 71 in the appended list.

2) Cf., G. C. Miles, "Some early Arab dinars", *Museum Notes*, The American Numismatic Society, 3, p. 108, item ANS/68.

3) See above p. 138.

4) See above p. 131, n. 1.

reconstructed on the basis of information derived from al-Maqrīzī[1]) as well as from numismatic evidence:

Supervisor	Dates in A.H.	Caliph
Jaʿ far ibn Yaḥyā	177—187	Hārūn al-Rashīd
al-Sindī ibn Yaḥyā al-Harashī	187—193	,,
al-Faḍl ibn al-Rabīʿ	193—196	al-Amīn

The examination of specimens struck during the period of these three supervisors of coinage reveals that the establishment of that office did not affect the intrinsic value of gold coins whose standards resembled that of the earlier *dinars*. This may be realized by tabulating comparative data pertaining to the standard of fineness of gold coins struck before and during the period of the three supervisors.

					Total	Standard of fineness		
						96%	97%	99%
Number of the ʿAbbāsid specimens	struck	before and during	the period of the supervisors		53	20 (or 37.7%)	3 (or 5.6%)	2 (or 3.7%)
					38	14 (or 36.8%)	5 (or 13.1%)	4 (or 10.5%)

Nor can one trace anything special about the standard of fineness of eleven specimens struck during the office of al-Sindī. It is true that three such specimens have the standard of 98%, but these might have originated in Egypt. Besides, there are three specimens in the 96% class, two in the 95% class, and two debased coins as well. Thus the precise reason for the excellent reputation of the *dinars* of al-Sindi, recorded in mediaeval sources,[2]) has yet to be solved.[3])

The earliest symptoms of a debasement in the standard of fineness may be observed among the specimens issued during the twenty years following the death of Hārūn al-Rashīd. It was, of course, a period of great political instability brought on by the civil war between al-Amīn and al-Māʾmūn, and its revolutionary aftermath. The coins issued during the period of the fratricidal conflict may be divided into two groups: those struck in the name of al-Amīn, and those issued in the name of al-Māʾmūn. For obvious reasons the coins of al-Māʾmūn must have been

---

1) *Ibid.*
2) See above p. 131, n. 15.
3) Cf., O. Grabar, *op. cit.*, p. 59, n. 3.

issued by a mint (or mints) situated outside the control of the ruling caliph. The operations of this mint could have continued for some time after the death of al-Amīn (A.H. 198/A.D. 813), considering that al-Mā'mūn decided to transfer his court to Baghdād only in A.H. 204 (A.D. 819). The difference in the standard of fineness between the two groups is quite apparent. While the seven specimens of al-Amīn show a considerable stability, the coins issued in the name of al-Mā'mūn (during the life of al-Amīn, and prior to al-Mā'mūn's entry in Baghdād) suffer not only from instability but also from an obvious deterioration in the standard of fineness. This situation is illustrated by means of the following graph correlating the numismatic data with the main political events of the period.

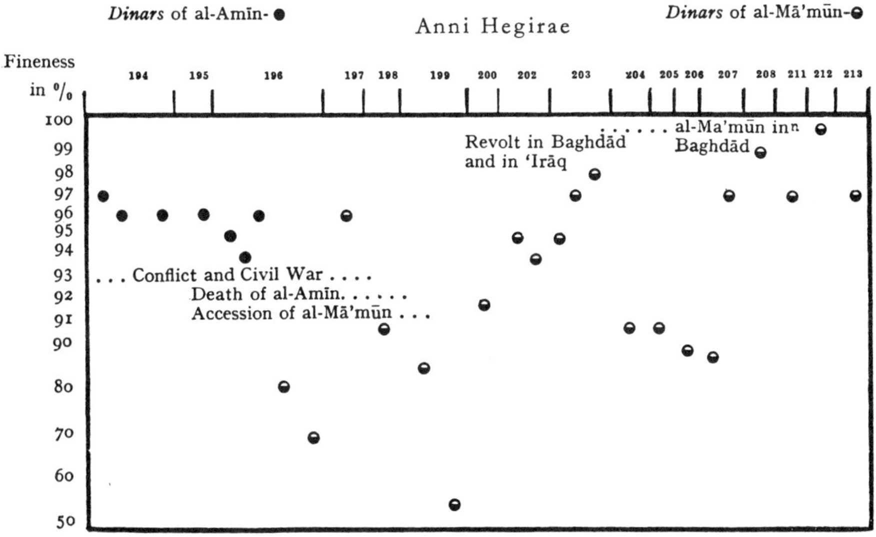

Diagram II

As one can also see from the above graph the last five specimens of al-Mā'mūn present an excellent standard of fineness. It is very likely that the intrinsic quality of later series of al-Mā'mūn's coinage contributed to the high reputation enjoyed by the *dinars* of that caliph.)[1]

---

1) See above p. 130, n. 4.

DINARS STRUCK IN THE CAPITAL OF THE 'ABBĀSID CALIPHATE (BAGHDĀD AND SĀMARRĀ)

Beginning with the reign of al-Mā'mūn mintnames were included in the inscription of the *dinars*, permitting thus a differentiation between the series of various origins. Unfortunately the total number of specimens from the capital for the entire period of over 400 years amounted to 35 *dinars*. Even so, one may observe a few interesting features, especially with regard to the final period of the activities of the 'Abbāsid mint in Baghdād.

The specimens issued during the period extending from the rule of al-Mu'taṣim (A.H. 218-227/A.D. 833-842) to that of al-Mu'tamid (A.H. 256-279/A.D. 870-892) do not differ in standard from those struck under normal conditions in the preceding periods:

Dinar of	*A.H.*	*Mint*	*Standard of fineness*
al-Mu'taṣim	222	Baghdād	96 %
,,	226	Sāmarrā	98 %
al-Wāthiq	227	Baghdād	98 %
,,	231	,,	98 %
al-Muntaṣir	247 (248?)	Sāmarrā	76 %
al-Mu 'tamid	258	Baghdād	94 %
,,	261	Sāmarrā	96 %
,,	263	,,	96 %

As may be seen from the above table the examined issues of al-Mu'taṣim and al-Wāthiq confirm the reputation enjoyed by the *dinars* of these two caliphs.[1]) And the two coins of al-Mu'tamid have the regular standard of 96%.

The isolated issues struck in Baghdād during the first half of the tenth century are still of good quality (those of al-Rāḍī: 97%; 94%; those of the Ḥamdānid Amīr al-Umarā', Nāṣir al-Dawlah, 97%; 94%; 95%;) although some of them are of an inferior standard (A.H. 288 - 90%; 305 - 85%; 307 - 90%).

A critical deterioration in standard has been established in the speci-

1) *Ibid.*

mens struck by the Buwayhid masters of Baghdād. Their standard of fineness is as follows:

Dinar of	*A.H.*	*Standard of fineness*
Rukn al-Dawlah	365	89 %
'Aḍud al-Dawlah	366	93 %
Bahā' al-Dawlah	404	56 %
Sulṭān al-Dawlah	409	62 %

Even if the number of these specimens is limited, their examination confirms textual reports concerning the poor quality of the coinage under the regime of the Buwayhids.[1]) Whether this crisis was caused by administrative inexperience of that regime or by general monetary difficulties caused by the acute shortage of silver which afflicted the Near East towards the end of the tenth century,[2]) is a question worthy of a separate investigation.

The last group of available Baghdādī *dinars* consisted of thirteen specimens struck during the last half of a century of the 'Abbāsid dynasty.[3]) The standard of fineness of these specimens is presented on the following table.

TABLE VI

Distribution of the examined specimens struck between A.H. 611—656 / *A.D.* 1214—1258, *according to their standard of fineness*

Name of the ruler (Dates in A.H.)	90 %	91 %	92 %	93 %	94 %	95 %	96 %
al-Nāṣir (575—622)	1	2	–	3	–	–	–
al-Mustanṣir (623—640)	–	–	–	–	–	–	1
al-Musta 'ṣim (640—656)	–	2	2	1	1	–	–

If one may use the evidence obtained from this number of specimens, it appears that during the final phase of the 'Abbāsid Caliphate the gold issues of Baghdād possessed a lower standard of fineness. By contrast with the early mintless Umayyad and 'Abbāsid *dinars*, the standard of

1) Cf., A. Grohmann, *op. cit.*, p. 193; also, G. C. Miles, *The Numismatic History of Rayy*, (*Numismatic Studies*, No. 2), New York, 1938, p. 176-177.

2) Cf., R. P. Blake, "The circulation of silver in the Moslem East down to the Mongol epoch," *Harvard Journal of Asiatic Studies*, 2, 1937, p. 291.

3) For the two examined Saljūqid specimens see Appendix, *Madīnat al-Salām*, A. H. 492 and 494.

96% is represented in the last group by only one specimen. It also constitutes the finest specimen of the entire group of the latest Baghdādī *dinars* .The rest of the specimens are distributed between the 90%-94% classes of fineness. On the other hand there are no specimens in this group with the extremely bad standard of fineness like that of the available Buwayhid specimens.

It is interesting to compare this debasement in the standard of fineness of late Baghdādī *dinars* with a similar deterioration in the standard of weight. The weight frequency distribution of Baghdādī *dinars* issued during two distinct phases appears on the following diagram:

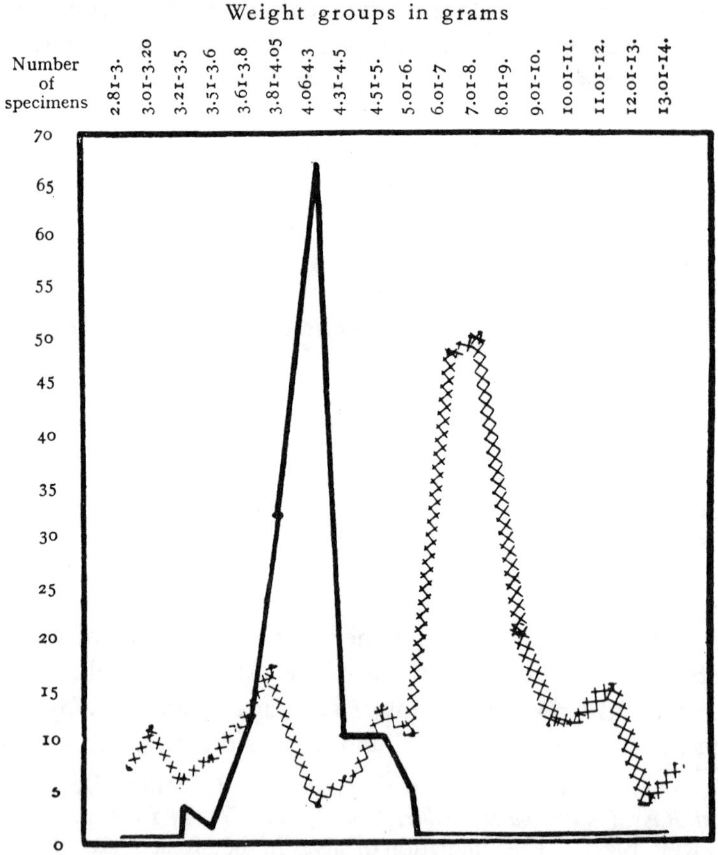

Dinars struck during the period of { al-Mā'mūn — al-Muṭī' (A.D. 813-974) ▬ ; al-Ṭā'i' — al-Musta'ṣim (A.D. 974-1258) XXX }

Diagram III

As one can see from the above diagram[1]) gold coins struck in Baghdād (and in Sāmarrā) during the early period possessed a relatively stable standard of fineness. But this situation drastically changed in the following period extending from the reign of al-Ṭā'i' to the sack of Baghdād by the Mongols. As far as the *dinars* of that period are concerned it is not possible to establish any distinct weight standard, for along with very light, or rather underweight *dinars*, there were extremely heavy coins.

On the basis of such a comparison it appears that the quality of Baghdādī *dinars* greatly deteriorated towards the end of the tenth century. The Buwayhid domination seems to have been the crucial period in that development. Uniformity in weight standard disappeared completely and the alloy was debased. During the final phase of the activities of

---

1) The composition of this table is based on the material compiled from the following works:

J. Allan, "Unpublished Coins of the Caliphate", *Numismatic Chronicle*, 4th ser., 19, 1919, p. 194-198.

O. Codrington, *Some rare and unedited Arabic and Persian coins, some in the collection of Dr. J. Gerson da Cunha, and some in the writer's own cabinet*, Hertford, Austin and Sons, 1889.

J. Gerson da Cunha, *Catalogue of the Coins in the Numismatic Cabinet belonging to J. Gerson da Cunha*, Bombay, 1888-89.

S. Lane-Poole, *op. cit.*

Idem, *Catalogue of the collection of Arabic Coins preserved in the Khedivial Library at Cairo*, London, 1897.

H. Lavoix, *op. cit.*

D. S. Margoliouth, "A gold coin (dinar) of Mustanjid", *JRAS*, 1927.

al-Naqshabandī, *ad-Dīnār al-Islāmī fī al-Matḥaf al-'Irāqī*, Baghdād, vol. 1, 1953.

H. Nützel, *Katalog der orientalischen Münzen. Königliche Museen zu Berlin*, Berlin, vol. 1, 1898.

J. Østrup, *Catalogue des monnaies arabes et turques du Cabinet Royal des Médailles du Musée National de Copenhague*, Copenhagen, 1938.

E. T. Rogers Bey, "Catalogue of the collection of Mohammadan Coins", *Numismatic Chronicle*, 3rd ser., 3, 1883, p. 202-260.

D. Sourdel, *Inventaire des monnaies musulmanes anciennes du Musée de Caboul*, (Institut Français de Damas), Damascus, 1953.

E. von Zambaur, "Nouvelles contributions à la numismatique orientale," *Numismatische Zeitschrift*, 47, 1914, p. 115-190.

the mint of Baghdād, the standard of fineness was more or less stabilized, although it never reached the high degree which had characterised the issues of the pre-Buwayhid era. There was no improvement, however, in the standard of weight.

'ABBĀSID EGYPTIAN PRE-ṬŪLŪNID DINARS

Beginning with the reign of al-Mā'mūn the identity of Egyptian *dinars* cannot be questioned since, apart from a few early exceptions, all of them show the mint of their origin. The intrinsic quality of the examined specimens is presented in the following distribution table:

TABLE VII

Distribution of the examined pre-Ṭūlūnid Egyptian specimens according to their standard of fineness

Ruler (Dates in A.H.)	*Below* 89%	89%	90%	91%	92%	93%	94%	95%	96%	97%	98%	99%	100%
al-Mā'mūn (198-218)	–	–	–	1	–	–	2	1	2	1	5	1	–
al-Mu'taṣim (218-227)	–	–	–	–	–	–	–	–	–	–	1	1	1
al-Wāthiq (227-232)	–	–	–	–	–	–	–	–	–	–	1	–	–
al-Mutawakkil (232-247)	–	–	–	–	–	–	–	–	1	6	4	–	2
al-Musta'īn (248-252)	–	–	–	–	–	–	–	–	–	3	–	–	1
al-Mu'tazz (252-255)	–	–	–	–	–	–	–	–	–	–	2	1	–
al-Mu'tamid (256-279)	1	–	–	–	–	–	–	–	–	1	3	4	–
Total	1	–	–	1	–	–	2	1	3	11	16	7	4

The stability and the high degree of fineness of the Egyptian *dinars* of that period is quite impressive. Of the 46 specimens only 5 (or 10.8%) have a standard lower than 96%. One must stress that four of these five 'inferior' *dinars* (A.H. 201 - 95%; 204 - 94%; 209 - 94%; 210 - 91%) were issued during the troubled years of the initial phase of al-Mā'mūn's reign. It is very likely that this unusual deterioration in the quality of Egyptian issues was produced by the slackening of the administrative preponderance of Baghdād over Egypt, as well as by the very difficult economic circumstances of that time. On the one hand the struggle between Arab factions[1]) and the resulting interruption of trade routes between Egypt and Nubia[2]), must have hampered the supply of the gold ore from the South[3]). On the other hand Egyptian trade activities and, consequently the normal circulation of gold in Egypt, must have suffered from the invasion of the Andalusians, whose longlasting pitatelike activities were brought to an end only in A.H. 212.[4])

Whether or not one includes these early 'debased' *dinars*, a statistical evaluation shows the prevalence of the standard of 98% of fineness among the Egyptian specimens of that period. Of the total number of 46 specimens, 16 (or 34.7%) have the standard of 98% of fineness. The frequency with which this standard is met with the Egyptian issues corroborates the hypothetical identification of the mintless *dinars* with a similar degree of fineness as being a product of the Egyptian mint.

ṬŪLŪNID DINARS

TABLE VIII

Distribution of Ṭūlūnid specimens according to their standard of fineness

Name of the Ruler (Dates in A.H.)	*Below* 89%	89%	90%	91%	92%	93%	94%	95%	96%	97%	98%	99%	100%
Aḥmād ibn Ṭūlūn (266-270)	1	–	–	–	–	–	–	–	–	–	2	2	1
Khumarawayh (270-282)	–	–	–	–	–	–	4	1	2	4	2	1	–
Jaysh (282-283)	–	–	–	–	–	–	–	–	–	1	2	–	–
Hārūn (283-292)	–	–	–	–	–	–	3	1	3	2	2	–	–
Total	1	–	–	–	–	–	7	2	5	7	8	3	1

The study of this group of *dinars* is particularly important since it was in that period that the mint of Egypt was emancipated from the control of the capital of the Caliphate. This development resulted from the political achievements of Aḥmad ibn Ṭūlūn.[5]) Prof. O. Grabar has recently discussed the bearing of the various stages of the career of this

1) Cf., S. Lane-Poole, *A history of Egypt in the Middle Ages*, London, 1925, p. 35.

2) Cf., *History of the Patriarchs of the Coptic Church of Alexandria*, ed. and transl. by B. Evetts, Paris, iv/426-427.

3) For gold in Nubia see al-Ya'qubī, *Les Pays*, transl. G. Wiet, Cairo, 1937, p. 190, and n. 1 on that page.

4) S. Lane-Poole, *op. cit.*, p. 35-36.

5) O. Grabar, *The coinage of the Ṭūlūnids*, New York, 1957.

colorful figure on the history of Egyptian coinage. Nevertheless it seems necessary to repeat here that Aḥmad ibn Ṭūlūn is said to have shown personal interest in the minting production of his state, and that the standard of his dinars reportedly equalled that of al-Sindī.[1]) Although it has not proved possible to establish what was really the nature of the standard of al-Sindī, one can easily state that as far as the standard of fineness is concerned, the *dinars* of Aḥmad ibn Ṭūlūn correspond to the finest Baghdādī and Egyptian issues of the pre-Ṭūlūnid era. Whether because of his political ambitions, or because of general economic prosperity prevailing in Egypt under his regime, it appears that Aḥmad ibn Ṭūlūn succeeded in maintaining the same high standard which had characterised the Egyptian issues of his predecessors.

But with the issues of Ibn Ṭūlūn's successors one may detect symptoms of a slight debasement. Along with some specimens of 96%-99% of fineness, *dinars* with 94%-95% degree of purity appear. Consequently, while the largest single group of the Ṭūlūnid *dinars* (8 out of 34, or 23,5%) falls in the class of 98% of fineness, seven specimens (or 20.5%) have the standard of 94%. But a majority of the Ṭūlūnid specimens (24, or 64.6%) still falls between the 96%-100% limits.

As for a few provincial Ṭūlūnid *dinars*, they display the following standard of fineness:

Mint	*A.H.*	%
Al-Rāfiqah	274	92
,,	277	95
,,	278	88
Antākiyah	278	92
Filasṭīn	282	96
Ḥimṣ	285	88

'ABBĀSID EGYPTIAN PRE-IKHSHĪDID DINARS (A.H. 292-329/A.D. 905-940)

The examination of available specimens from this period reveals that the reestablishment of the control of Baghdād over Egypt did not stop the gradual deterioration in the standard of fineness, which was notice-

1) Cf., above, p. 131, n. 2.

able with the later Ṭūlūnid *dinars*. The following table plainly demonstrates the full extent of the debasement.

TABLE IX

ʿAbbāsid pre-Ikhshīdid specimens

Name of the Ruler (Dates in A.H.)	*Below* 89%	89%	90%	91%	92%	93%	94%	95%	96%	97%	98%	99%	100%
al-Muktafī (298-295)	1	–	–	–	–	–	–	–	1	–	–	1	–
al-Muqtadir (295-320)	1	1	1	2	1	5	6	2	4	1	–	–	–
al-Rāḍī (322-329)	10	1	–	–	–	–	–	–	–	–	–	–	–
Total	12	2	1	2	1	5	6	2	5	1	–	1	–

In sharp contrast to the preceding periods of Egyptian minting history only a few specimens show a high standard of fineness. Out of 38 *dinars* examined only 7 (or 18.4%) fall between 96%-99% limits, whereas there were only 5 specimens having a 96% degree of fineness. On the other hand there are among these specimens as many as 12 (or 31.5%) *dinars* whose standard falls below the 89% limit. Total number of specimens below the 96% limit consists of an overwhelming majority of 31 (or 81.5%) *dinars*. A crucial date in this process of debasement seems to have been the year 915 (A.H. 304). The following diagram may illustrate the difference in the standard of *dinars* before and after that date.

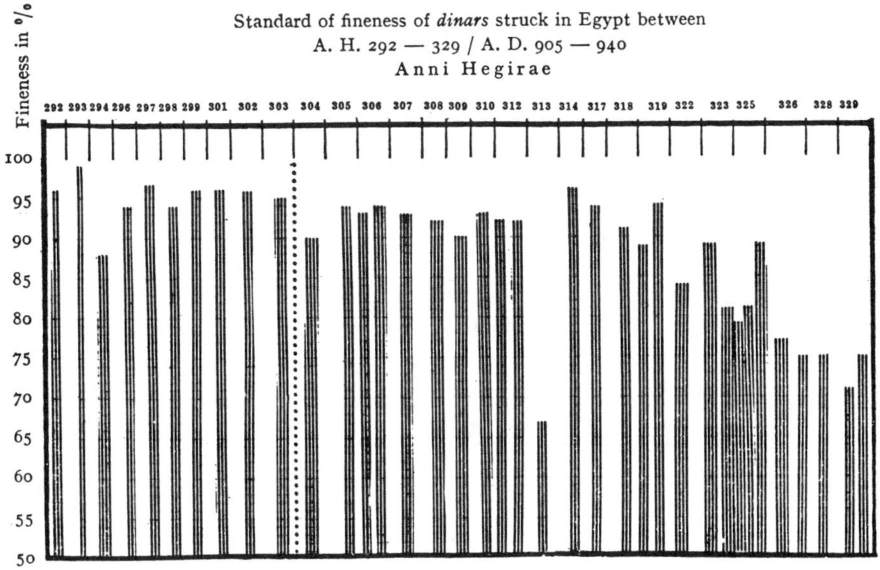

Diagram IV

This sharp decline in the quality of Egyptian *dinars* coincides with the opening of the Fāṭimid pressure against Egypt. It is very likely that the 'Abbāsid authorities were forced to proceed with a debasement of gold coins because of the rising costs of the maintenance of strong military forces to withstand the invasions of the Fāṭimids. Moreover, the influx the West African gold ore must have been reduced because of the domination of the Fāṭimids over North African trade routes. The worst phase in the debasement in question occured during the reign of al-Rāḍī.[1] This was an obvious consequence of grave internal disorders which afflicted Egypt in the years immediately preceding the rise of Muḥammad ibn Ṭughj al-Ikhshīd.[2]

As for the provincial issues of that period, they display the following intrinsic quality:

Mint	*A.H.*	%
al-Rāfiqah	294	89
,,	295	90
Damascus	295	97
,,	297	96
al-Mawṣil	293	98
Filasṭīn	291	94
,,	293	95
,,	308	93
,,	319	90

IKHSHĪDID DINARS

The quality of the specimens struck in Egypt during the shortlived regime of the Ikhshīdids (A.H. 323-357/A.D. 935-969), plainly illustrates the importance of stable political government for the maintenance of sound coinage. The consolidation of the power of Muḥammad ibn Ṭughj al-Ikhshīd in Egypt, his emancipation from any effective control of Baghdād, a temporary relaxation of the pressure of the

1) Cf., G. Wiet, *L'Égypte Arabe*, in G. Hanotaux', *Histoire de la Nation Égyptienne*, Paris, iv/121.

2) *Ibid.*, p. 126-127.

Fāṭimids, the reestablishment of internal peace and security for members of different religious communities,[1]) and an active interest of the ruler in the matters of gold coinage,[2]) all contributed to a revival of economic prosperity in the country of the Nile. That prosperity is reflected in the standard of the Egyptian *dinars* of that period.

TABLE X

Distribution of Ikhshīdid specimens according to their standard of fineness

Name of the ruler (Dates in A.H.)	96 %	97 %	98 %	99 %
Muḥammad ibn Ṭughj (322—334)	–	1	–	1
Unūjur (334—349)	1	–	3	2
ʿAlī (349—355)	–	1	1	2
Kafūr (355—357)	–	–	2	–
Total	1	2	6	5

The intrinsic quality of the available Ikhshīdid pieces not only differs from that of the preceding period, but resembles closely the standard of Egyptian *dinars* of the former centuries. Out of the total number of 14 specimens, 5 (or 35.7%) have the standard of 99%. Six (or 42.8%) *dinars* have the 'regular' Egyptian standard of 98%. Two others have the standard of 97%, and one of 96% of fineness. No specimens with a standard inferior to 96% were found in the examined lot.[3])

The only provincial issues of the Ikhshīdids available for examination were seven *dinars* from Palestine, whose standard of fineness is as follows:

A.H.	%	*A.H.*	%
331	93	353	89
335	91	355	92
337	95	358	93
341	93		

---

1) *Ibid.*, p. 135.

2) Cf., A. S. Ehrenkreutz, "Contributions to the knowledge of the fiscal administration of Egypt in the Middle Ages", *BSOAS*, 16, iii, 1954, p. 510, n. 3.

3) It must be noted that although Muḥammad ibn Ṭughj governed Egypt since A. H. 323—A. D. 935, the earliest available *dinars* issued in his name date from A. H. 331. Cf., P. Balog, "Tables de références des monnaies ikhchidites", *Revue belge de Numismatique*, 103, p. 1957, p. 108-109, 120. It is the latter that have been considered as the Ikhshīdid *dinars* in the present study.

CONCLUSIONS

In summing up the results of this investigation one may list the following observations concerning the standard of fineness of the examined series of *dinars*:

1) The standard of fineness of reformed mintless *dinars* was maintained at 96% and 98%. The duality in standard could have been produced by the striking of gold in two different mints.

2) The standard of mintless 'Abbāsid *dinars* did not differ from the standard of the Umayyad *dinars*.

3) The standard of the mintless *dinars* with the names of Egyptian governors excelled that of other mintless *dinars*.

4) A temporary debasement in the standard of fineness of the mintless *dinars* took place in the beginning of the 9th century during and immediately after the civil war between al-Amīn and al-Mā'mūn.

5) Between A.D. 836-942 the issues of the mint of Baghdād possessed a high degree of fineness of 96% and above, although towards the end of that period inferior *dinars* were issued for circulation.

6) A critical deterioration in the standard of Baghdād *dinars* took place during the period of the Buwayhids (A.D. 946-1055).

7) In the final decades of the activity of the 'Abbāsid mint of Baghdād the standard of fineness fluctuated between 91%-94%. Although it was superior to that of the Buwayhid issues it never reached the quality of early Baghdādī *dinars*.

8) The standard of fineness of Egyptian *dinars* down to the second half of the tenth centruy was better than that of the Baghdādī issues. It was maintained at 98%. Slightly inferior *dinars* were struck by the successors of Aḥmad ibn Ṭūlūn. A temporary serious debasement occured during the period of 'Abbāsid restoration in Egypt after the fall of the Ṭūlūnids. But the usual excellent standard of Egyptian gold coinage was reestablished by the Ikhshīdids.

9) The standard of *dinars* struck in Palestine during the first half of the tenth century was set at 93% of fineness.

The above conclusions are illustrated on the following and final diagram.

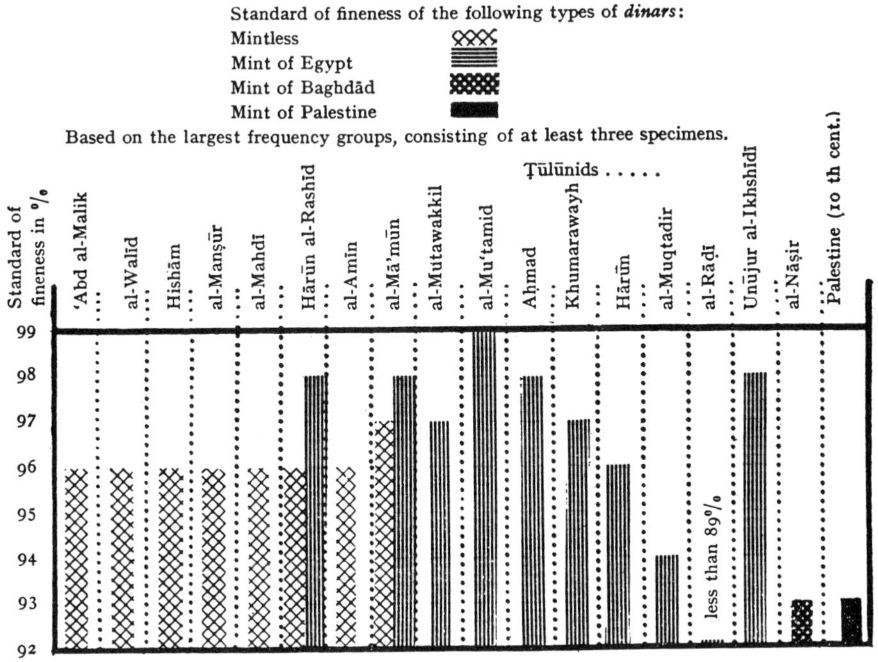

Diagram V

APPENDIX

List of examined specimens

Reference and rulers (dynasties)	A.H.	Fineness of gold in %	Reference and rulers (dynasties)	A.H.	Fineness of gold in %
Umayyads			Umayyads		
UM 1	—	94	HSA 7/539	78	99
UM 2	77	96	ANS 9	79	96
ANS 4	78	97	ANS 10	79	97
UM 3	78	96	ANS 11	79	96
HSA 6/537	78	97	UM 8	79	97

HSA 12/536	79	98
HSA 13/538	79	97
HSA 14/544	79	97
ANS 16	80	98
HSA 17/540	80	96
HSA 18/541	80	95
HSA 19/542	80	97
ANS 21	81	97
UM 22	82	96
Um 24	84	96
UM 25	84	96
HSA 25/543	84	96
UM 26	85	98
UM 27	86	96
UM 28	86	91
UM 31	88	97
UM 30	88	96
UM 33	89	97
UM 34	89	96
UM 32	89	95
HSA 57/105	89	96
UM 37	90	97
UM 36	90	97
UM 35	90	96
UM 40	91	96
UM 38	91	96
UM 41 (*niṣf*)	91	94
UM 43 (*thulth*)	91	92
UM 45	92	96
UM 44	92	96
UM 47 (*thulth*)	92	94
n.n.	93	96
UM 48	93	96
HSA 51/13157	94	97
HSA 57/107	94	96
UM 49	94	99
UM 50 (*niṣf*)	94	94
UM 52 (*thulth*)	94	96
UM 53 (*thulth*)	94	89
UM 54	95	96
UM 55	96	96
UM 57 (*niṣf*)	96	85
UM 59 (*thulth*)	96	65
UM 60	97	97
HSA 61/13158	97	96
n.n.	98	97
HSA 57/108	98	97
UM 63	98	97
UM 64 (*thulth*)	99	95
UM 65 (*thulth*)	99	93
n.n. (*thulth*)	99	91
HSA 57/109	99	96
UM 66	100	98
UM 68 (*thulth*)	100	96
n.n. (*thulth*)	100	94
n.n. (*thulth*)	101	98
HSA 72/13159	102	97
HSA 72/13161 (*niṣf*)	102	95
n.n. (*thulth*)	102	91
HSA 74/13212 (*thulth*)	102	91
UM 76	103	97
HSA 77/14067	103	93
HSA 78/13211	103	99
UM 79 (*thulth*)	103	91
UM 80 (*thulth*)	103	96
UM 81 (*thulth*)	103	96
UM 83	105	97
UM 84 (al-Ḥijāz)	105	97
UM 85	106	99
UM 87	107	96
UM 86	107	98
UM 88	108	97
HSA 57/106	108	98
UM 90	109	96
UM 89	109	96
UM 92	110	89
UM 91	110	98
UM 93	111	98
UM 94	112	96
UM 95	113	96
UM 96	114	98
UM 97	115	96
UM 98	116	98
UM 99	117	98
UM 102	119	98
UM 101	119	96
UM 104	120	98
UM 103	120	96

ANS	121	96
HSA 106/10625	121	96
ANS 108	122	96
UM 107	122	98
UM 109	123	97
ANS 111	124	98
ANS 113	125	96
UM 112	125	96
HSA 114/10626	125	98
UM 115	126	96
UM 116	128	98
UM 117	129	97
UM 118	130	98
UM 120	132	95
ʿAbbāsids		
UM 1	132	96
UM 2	133	94
ANS 4	134	97
UM 3	134	98
UM 5	135	97
ANS 7	136	98
UM 6	136	91
UM 9	138	98
ANS 11	139	97
UM 10	139	98
UM 13	141	98
UM 14	142	97
UM 15	143	97
UM 16	144	96
UM 17	144	98
UM 19	146	94
ANS 20	146	96
UM 21	147	96
UM 22	148	95
UM 23	149	96
UM 24	150	96
ANS 25	150	97
ANS 26	151	95
ANS 28	152	96
ANS 29	152	96
UM 27	152	95
ANS 31	153	92
ANS 32	153	97
UM 30	153	94
UM 33	154	96
UM 34	155	94
ANS 36	156	96
ANS 48/70	156	94
UM 37	157	96
ANS 38	157	95
ANS 39	157	92
HSA 57/110	157	91
ANS 41	158	96
UM 40	158	92
UM 42	159	95
UM 43	160	96
UM 44	161	96
ANS 45	161	95
UM 46	162	94
ANS 47	162	96
ANS 49	163	95
UM 48	163	98
ANS 57	164	96
UM 52	165	96
ANS 53	165	94
ANS 55	166	93
UM 56	167	96
ANS 52/125	167	94
UM 57	167	95
UM 58	167	90
ANS 60	168	94
UM 59	168	95
ANS 61	161	96
ANS 64	169	96
UM 62	169	94
ANS 65	169	93
UM 63	169	94
ANS 68	170	99
UM 66	170	89
UM 67 (ʿAlī)	170	98
UM 70 (Mūsā) (clipped)	171	96
UM 71 (Mūsā) (clipped)	172	98
UM 72	172	96
UM 73 (ʿUmar)	172	96
ANS 74 (ʿUmar)	173	95
ANS 75	173	98

UM 76 ('Umar)	174	98
UM 77 (Dāwūd)	174	97
UM 78 (Mūsā)	175	97
UM 79	175	96
UM 80	177	97
ANS 82	177	96
ANS 83	177	61
UM 81	177	96
UM 84	178	96
UM 85	178	96
ANS 87	179	95
UM 86	179	96
UM 88	179	97
UM 89	180	96
UM 90	181	98
UM 92	182	97
UM 93	183	97
ANS 94	183	89
UM 95	184	96
UM 96	184	94
UM 97	184	94
UM 98	185	95
ANS 100	185	94
ANS 103	186	90
UM 104	187	98
UM 105	187	95
UM 106	187	87
UM 107	188	95
UM 109	190	96
UM 111	190	93
ANS 110	190	97
UM 112	191	96
UM 113	192	96
UM 114	192	98
UM 115	193	98
al-Amīn		
UM 116	194	97
UM 117	194	96
ANS 118	194	96
UM 119	195	96
UM 122	196	95
ANS 123	196	94
UM 124	196	96
UM 125 (al-Mā'mūn)	196	81
UM 126 (al-Mā'mūn)	196	70
UM 127 (al-Mā'mūn)	197	96
ANS 129	198	91
al-Mā'mūn		
UM 128 (al-Mā'mūn, al-Muṭṭalib)	198	96
ANS 130 (al-'Irāq)	199	85
ANS 131 (al-Mā'mūn)	199	55
UM 133 (Miṣr)	199	96
UM 134	200	92
UM 135 (Miṣr)	200	96
ANS 137a (Miṣr)	201	97
UM 137 (Miṣr)	201	95
UM 138	202	95
UM 139	202	94
UM 140 (al-'Irāq)	203	95
UM 142	203	97
UM 144 (Miṣr)	203	98
ANS 141	203	98
ANS 143	203	91
ANS 146 (Miṣr)	204	94
ANS 148	205	91
UM 149	206	90
UM 150	207	89
UM 151	207	97
UM 152	208	99
UM 153 (Miṣr)	209	94
UM 154 (Miṣr)	210	91
ANS 155	211	97
UM 156	212	100
UM 157	213	97
UM 158 (Miṣr)	214	98
UM 159 "	215	98
UM 160 "	216	99
ANS 161 (Miṣr)	217	98
UM 162 (Miṣr)	218	98
al-Mu'taṣim		
ANS (Miṣr)	220	100
UM (Miṣr)	221	99
ANS (Madīnat as-Salām)	222	96
UM (Miṣr)	224	98
UM RIC 140 (Surra man-ra'ā)	226	98

al-Wāthiq		
ANS 141 (Madīnat as-Salām)	227	98
UM (Miṣr)	231	98
UM RIC 144 (Madīnat as-Salām)	231	98
al-Mutawakkil		
UM (Miṣr)	233	97
UM ,,	234	98
ANS ,,	234	97
UM ,,	235	97
ANS ,,	235	100
UM ,,	238	97
ANS 56-159 (Miṣr)	239	98
UM ,,	241	96
UM ,,	242	97
ANS (Miṣr)	243	98
ANS ,,	245	97
UM ,,	245	100
UM RIC 146 (Miṣr)	247	98
al-Muntaṣir		
ANS 147 (Surra man-ra'a)	—	76
al-Musta'īn		
UM (Miṣr)	248	100
UM ,,	249	97
ANS ,,	249	97
UM ,,	250	97
al-Mu'tazz		
UM (Miṣr)	252	99
ANS 56-159 (Miṣr)	254	98
UM RIC 150 (Miṣr)	255	98
al-Mu'tamid		
UM RIC 152 (Miṣr)	257	98
ANS 153 (Miṣr)	257	87
UM RIC 154 (Miṣr)	258	99
UM RIC 155 ,,	258	98
ANS (Madīnat as-Salām)	258	94
ANS (Miṣr)	259	99
UM ,,	260	97
ANS (Surra man ra'ā)	261	96
ANS ,,	263	96
ANS (Miṣr)	263	99
ANS 41-19 (Miṣr)	263	98
UM (Miṣr)	263	99
al-Mu'taḍid		
ANS (Madīnat as-Salām)	288	90
al-Muktafī		
UM RIC 163 (Filasṭīn)	291	94
UM (Miṣr)	292	96
UM RIC 167 (Filasṭīn)	293	95
UM (Miṣr)	293	99
ANS (al-Mawṣil)	293	98
UM RIC 169 (al-Rāfiqah)	294	89
UM (Miṣr)	294	88
ANS 171 (Damascus)	295	97
UM RIC 172 (al-Rāfiqah)	295	90
al-Muqtadir		
UM (Miṣr)	296	94
UM RIC 174 (Damascus)	297	96
ANS (Miṣr)	297	97
UM ,,	298	94
UM Ric 178 (Miṣr)	299	96
UM (Miṣr)	301	96
UM ,,	302	96
UM RIC 180 (Miṣr)	303	95
ANS 51-104 (Miṣr)	303	95
ANS (Miṣr)	304	90
UM (Madīnat as-Salām)	305	85
UM (Miṣr)	305	94
ANS ,,	306	93
UM ,,	306	94
UM ,,	307	93
ANS (Madīnat as-Salām)	307	90
ANS 55-68 (Filasṭīn)	308	93
UM (Miṣr)	308	92
UM ,,	309	91
UM ,,	310	93
ANS ,,	312	93

UM „	312	93
UM RIC/187 (Miṣr)	313	67
UM RIC/189 „	314	96
UM (Miṣr)	317	94
UM „	318	91
UM RIC/193 (Filasṭīn)	319	90
UM RIC/194 (Miṣr)	319	89
UM RIC/195 „	319	94
ar-Rāḍī		
UM RIC/201 (Miṣr)	322	84
UM „	323	89
ANS „	323	81
UM „	325	79
ANS 41-19 „	325	81
UM „	325	85
ANS „	326	77
UM „	326	75
ANS (Madīnat as-Salām)	326	97
UM (Miṣr)	328	75
UM „	329	71
UM „	329	67
UM RIC/205 (Madīnat as-Salām)	329	94
al-Ḥamdānids		
Nāṣir ad-Dawlah		
ANS (Madīnat as-Salām)	331	97
ANS (Madīnat as-Salām)	331	94
ANS (Madīnat as-Salām)	331	95
Buyids (Buwayhids)		
Rukn ad-Dawlah		
ANS (Madīnat as-Salām)	365	89
ʻAḍud ad-Dawlah		
ANS (Madīnat as-Salām)	366	93
Bahā'ad-Dawlah		
ANS (Madīnat as-Salām)	404	56
Sulṭān ad-Dawlah		
ANS (Madīnat as-Salām)	409	62
Seljuks		
Barkiyaruq		
ANS (Madīnat ad-Salām)	492	96
ANS (Madīnat as-Salām)	494	90
ʻAbbāsids		
an-Nāṣir		
ANS (Madīnat as-Salām)	611	91
UM RIC/205 (Madīnat as-Salām)	612	90
UM RIC 206 (Madīnat as-Salām)	613	93
ANS Madīnat as-Salām)	613	93
Um RIC 209 (Madīnat as-Salām)	620	93
ANS)Madīnat as-Salām)	622	91
al-Mustanṣir		
ANS (Madīnat as-Salām)	638	96
al-Mustaʻṣim		
ANS (Madīnat as-Salām)	641	94
ANS (Madīnat as-Salām)	642	91
UM RIC 215 (Madīnat as-Salām)	643	91
ANS (Madīnat as-Salām)	645	92
ANS (Madīnat as-Salām)	654	93
UM (Madīnat as-Salām)	656	92
Ṭūlūnids		
Aḥmad ibn Ṭūlūn		
ANS (Mṣr)	266	99
UM (Miṣr)	268	82
ANS „	268	100
UM „	269	98

UM ,,	270	99
ANS ,,	270	98
Khumarawayh		
UM (Miṣr)	271	99
UM ,,	272	94
ANS 44/163 (Miṣr)	272	98
UM (Miṣr)	273	94
ANS 51/146 (Miṣr)	273	96
UM (Miṣr)	274	96
ANS 55/68 (ar-Rāfiqah)	274	92
UM (Miṣr)	276	98
UM ,,	277	94
ANS ,,	277	95
ANS 55/68 (ar-Rāfiqah)	277	95
ANS (ar-Rāfiqah)	278	88
UM (Miṣr)	278	94
ANS (Anṭākiyah)	278	92
UM (Miṣr)	279	97
ANS ,,	279	97
UM ,,	282	97
ANS 54/119 (Filasṭīn)	282	96
Jaysh ibn Khumarawayh		
UM (Miṣr	283	98
ANS 51/146 (Miṣr)	284	97
Um (Miṣr)	284	98
Hārūn ibn Khumarawayh		
ANS (Ḥimṣ)	285	88
UM (Miṣr)	285	96
ANS ,,	285	96
UM ,,	286	98
ANS ,,	287	94
UM ,,	287	98
UM ,,	287	97
UM ,,	288	95
ANS ,,	288	97
UM ,,	289	96

UM ,,	289	94
UM ,,	291	94
Ikhshīdids		
Muḥammad ibn Ṭughj		
ANS 57/82 (Filasṭīn)	331	93
UM (Miṣr)	333	99
ANS ,,	333	97
Unūjur		
ANS 57/82 (Filasṭīn)	335	91
UM (Miṣr)	337	98
ANS 57/82 (Filasṭīn)	337	95
ANS 55/57 (Miṣr)	339	99
UM (Miṣr)	341	99
ANS 57/82 (Filasṭīn)	341	93
UM (Miṣr)	342	96
ANS 55/57 (Miṣr)	344	98
ANS 41/19 ,,	345	98
'Alì		
UM (Miṣr)	350	97
ANS ,,	351	99
ANS 57/99 (Miṣr)	353	98
ANS 57/82 (Filasṭīn)	353	89
UM (Miṣr)	354	99
UM (Kafūr) (Miṣr)	355	98
UM (Kafūr) ,,	355	98
ANS 57/82 Kafūr) (Filasṭīn)	355	92
Aḥmad ibn 'Alī		
ANS 57/99 (Filasṭīn)	358	93
ANS 57/99 ,,	358	93

Abbreviations used in the above list refer to the following collections available in the Museum of the American Numismatic Society:

ANS – American Numismatic Society
HSA – Hispanic Society of America
UM – University of Pennsylvania Museum

VII

STUDIES IN THE MONETARY HISTORY OF THE NEAR EAST IN THE MIDDLE AGES

II

THE STANDARD OF FINENESS OF WESTERN AND EASTERN *DĪNĀRS* BEFORE THE CRUSADES*

> *. . . il serait á souhaiter, pour les progrès de la numismatique orientale, que les grands cabinets de medailles de Londres, Paris, Saint-Pétersbourg, etc., sacrifiassent quelques-uns de leurs doubles pour les faire analyser et en déterminer le titre. Ce serait un grand service rendu à la science.* H. Sauvaire, 'Matériaux . . .', *JA*, VII série, 19, 1882, p. 111.

About ten years ago I carried out my first examination of numismatic evidence, aiming at the elucidation of the problem of the intrinsic value of Medieval Near Eastern gold coins. Since that time I have engaged in a series of similar projects involving analysis of a considerable number of such coins. Although numismatic materials covered by my research predominantly consisted of specimens existing in the American Numismatic Museum [1]), I have also been fortunate in securing additional information concerning coins from other collections [2]).

*) I wish to acknowledge the help of the Center for Near and Middle Eastern Studies of the University of Michigan, whose financial assistance enabled me to carry out the examination of numismatic materials at the Museum of the American Numismatic Society in New York.

1) I wish to reiterate my academic indebtedness to Dr. G. C. Miles of the American Numismatic Society Museum, for kindly allowing me to examine the coins under his curatorship.

2) I wish to thank Dr. John Walker, Keeper of the Department of Coins and Medals in the British Museum, Dr. A. D. H. Bivar, formerly at the Ashmolean Museum, Oxford, and Professor Ph. Grierson of Gonville and Caius College, Cambridge for providing me with interesting data concerning the standard of fineness of some Muslim *dīnārs* accessible to them.

The data obtained through these investigations have been included in, or served as the basis for, a number of my publications in the field of Medieval Near Eastern monetary history [1]). The present article pursues the same type of treatment. Considering, however, the number of years elapsed since my first investigation, it seems advisable at this stage of my heuristic endeavors to provide this article with a methodological introduction. *Noblesse oblige*! And while I do not wish to claim the status of an authority on that subject, I think that a whole decade of research activities imposes an obligation on me to sum up my observations concerning the nature of the fineness of Islamic gold coins.

Terminology

By the "standard of fineness" we mean the principle determining the metallic composition of coins [2]). The fineness of gold coins depends on the quantitative ratio of the precious metal to other inclusions in their alloy [3]).

In Medieval Arabic terminology, the term used with reference to the standard of fineness was *'iyār* [4]). Medieval Near Eastern gold coins were called *dīnārs*. Apart from this generic term of classical origin [5]),

---

1) These publications will be referred to in the present article by means of the following abbreviations:

'Extracts' = 'Extracts from a technical manual on the Ayyūbid mint of Cairo', *BSOAS*, 15, 1953.

'Contributions' = 'Contributions to the monetary history of Egypt in the Middle Ages', *BSOAS*, 16, 1954.

'The standard of fineness' = 'The standard of fineness of gold coins circulating in Egypt at the time of the Crusades', *JAOS*, 74, 1954.

'The crisis of *dīnār*' = 'The crisis of *dīnār* in the Egypt of Saladin', *JAOS*, 76, 1956.

'Studies' = 'Studies of the monetary history of the Near East in the Middle Ages', *JESHO*, 2, 1959.

2) French — *titre*, German — *Feingehalt*, *Korn* (in the Middle Ages: *Witte*, *Brand*, *Gelöt*, *Albedo*), Italian — *titolo*, Swedish — *halt*. Cf., A. R. Frey, *Dictionary of numismatic names*, 1947; also A. Luschin von Ebengreuth, *Allgemeine Münzkunde und Geldgeschichte des Mittelalters und der Neueren Zeit*, 1926, p. 197.

3) Cf., Fr. Frhr. von Schrötter, *Wörterbuch der Münzkunde*, 1930, p. 190.

4) Cf., E. W. Lane, *Arabic-English Lexicon*, I, 5, p. 2209; also R. Dozy, *Supplément aux dictionnaires arabes*, ii/194.

5) Cf., G. C. Miles, 'Dīnār', *EI* (new ed.), ii/297.

dīnārs were also called by more specific names derived from the mint places, e.g., *dīnār dimishqī* [1]), *dīnār miṣrī* [2]), or from the names of rulers or officials responsible for the issuance of the coins, e.g., *dīnār aḥmadī* [3]), *dīnār rāḍī* [4]). Although smaller denominations, such as half and quarter *dīnārs* were also struck, I have concentrated my attention on the whole *dīnārs* as constituting the regular, official type of gold coinage.

The problem of the standard of fineness

The significance of the problem of the *ʿiyār* arises from the fact that the different types or series of *dīnārs* were not uniform—as regards their standard of fineness. This fact appears clearly from textual evidence. It was an obvious consequence of the many economic and administrative changes and upheavals which the Muslim Empire underwent during the long centuries of its existence. Various areas at various times benefited from the availability of *dīnārs* of a very high standard of fineness. There were others, however, which suffered from the circulation of debased gold coinage. Certain authorities and regimes were conscious of the need to maintain or even to improve the purity of their gold coins, but there were also administrations either indifferent to such monetary matters or incapable of maintaining a stable standard of *dīnārs*. This diversity or lack of uniformity in the standard of fineness of Medieval Near Eastern *dīnārs* necessarily affected the rate of exchange between the different categories of *dīnārs*, between the gold, silver and copper coinage, as well as between the Islamic and non-Islamic gold coins.

These various details concerning the *ʿiyār* problem were directly or indirectly referred to by Medieval historians. Some of them referred

1) i.e. *dīnār* of Damascus, cf., H. Sauvaire, 'Matériaux pour servir à l'histoire de la numismatique et de la métrologie musulmanes' (thereafter, Sauvaire, 'Matériaux'), *JA*, VII ser., 15, 1880, p. 448-449.

2) i.e. *dīnār* of Miṣr (Egypt), cf., Sauvaire, 'Matériaux', *JA*, VII ser., 19, 1882, p. 45-47.

3) i.e. *dīnār* of Aḥmad (ibn Ṭūlūn, governor of Egypt, (A. H. 254-270/A. D. 868-884) cf., Sauvaire, 'Matériaux', *JA*, VII sér., 15, 1880, p. 271-272.

4) i. e. *dīnār* of al-Rāḍī (ʿAbbāsid caliph , A. H. 322-329/A. H. 934-940) cf., Sauvaire, 'Matériaux', *JA*, VII ser., 15, 1880, p. 449.

to certain standards of fineness by special names, such, for instance, as *al-ʿiyār al-sindī* [1]), or *al-ʿiyār al-āmirī* [2]), both of which were of excellent quality [3]). There exist also Medieval professional manuals of technological, mathematical and administrative character, which contain chapters discussing the adjustment of gold alloys for the striking of *dīnārs* according to desired standards of fineness [4]).

There is one basic piece of information which so far has not been found in Medieval textual sources, and this is the exact specification of the precise nature of at least one *ʿiyār* of the *dīnārs*. Truly, we read that some *dīnārs* had a very good standard of fineness, and that others were superb, while yet others were quite debased. In spite of these details, we fail to learn what the exact nature of any of these standards was. What we would like to know would consist of a precise indication, something like: that *ʿiyār* A was of X % of gold, of Y % of silver and Z % of copper. If we had such specifications with reference to at least one *ʿiyār* then perhaps we could attempt to reconstruct the whole pattern of differences between various classes of *dīnārs*. This in turn would permit us to understand the principles underlying the nature of exchange rates between various types of coins. Without the solution of the problem it is difficult to arrive at a historically pragmatic interpretation of the price and salary pattern which is so vital for our comprehension of Medieval Near Eastern economic history. Thus, to supplement our limited knowledge concerning the problem of *ʿiyār*, which is based on textual evidence, we have to turn to numismatic materials.

It is hardly possible to overestimate the importance of numismatic studies in research activities dealing with Medieval Near Eastern

---

1) I. e. the *ʿiyār* of al-Sindī (superintendent of coinage in Baghdād, A. H. 187-193 A. D. 802-808), cf., 'Studies', p. 131.

2) i. e. the *ʿiyār of al-Āmir* (Fāṭimid caliph, A. H. 495-523 A. D. 1101-1130) cf., 'Studies', p. 131; 'The standard of fineness', p. 164.

3) *Supra*.

4) e. g. Ibn Baʿrah, *Kitāb fī kashf al-asrār al-ʿilmīyah bi-dār al-ḍarb al-miṣrīyah* (cf, 'Extracts', p. 435-436): *Kitāb al-ḥāwī* (cf. Sauvaire, 'Matériaux', JA, VII sér., 19, 1882. p. 101-102) al-Karajī, *Kitāb al-kāfī fī al-ḥisāb*, transl. by A. Hochheim, 1878-80, iii/22.

history [1]). In this respect there exists a rich body of professional literature produced by several generations of outstanding Orientalists [2]) whose treatment of numismatic specimens has been characterised by a rigorous and exhaustive, or rather *almost* exhaustive, consideration of external and internal evidence. My hesitation in making the above statement is caused by the fact that the usual standard procedure of examination of numismatic specimens has not included an inquiry into the *exact*, *precise* nature of their alloy. And yet, fundamental principles of external criticism demand more than mere specifications such as *aurum*, *argentum* or *aes*, with which numismatists seem to be contented. To satisfy the needs of modern economic historians an examination of numismatic materials should try to establish the exact metallic composition of examined coins. The importance of this methodological principle becomes apparent when one considers that so many issues in the monetary history of Medieval Near East depended directly on the intrinsic quality of the coins.

The preceding remarks must not be regarded as a condemnation of the accomplishments of Orientalist numismatists. They are postulated here as a plea for a more analytical treatment of numismatic sources. Let us assume, for the sake of argument, that it is possible to *exactly identify* the metallic contents of *dīnārs*. A study of data yielded by this kind of absolutely accurate identification would throw an interesting light on various areas of Near Eastern economic history. It would for instance, be possible to establish the provenance and circulation of gold reaching different mints. It would also be possible to trace chemical processes used in the refining and adjusting of the alloy. It would further become feasible to classify *dīnārs* according to their standards of fineness, and to correlate such a classification with corresponding

1) For the role of numismatics in historical studies see Ph. Grierson, *Numismatics and history*, London, 1951.

2) Cf., L. A. *Bibliography of Moslem numismatics*, London, 1954. also, A. Kmietowicz, "Supplements to L. Mayer's 'Bibliography of Moslem Numismatics' ", *Folia Orientalia*, 2, ii, 1960, p. 259-275. For a recent report on the present state of Islamic numismatics see G. C. Miles, 'Islamic numismatics": a progress report,' *Congresso Internazionale di Numismatica*, Roma, 1961, i/181-192.

data derived from textual sources. Finally, it would facilitate a reconstruction of the pattern of exchange rates, prices and salaries. Whether such an absolute, precise analytical identification is technologically feasible or not, there is no doubt that Islamic gold coins preserved in numismatic collections hold the key to the knowledge about the standard of fineness of Medieval Near Eastern *dīnārs*.

Examination of the alloy of dīnārs

There are several ways of analysing the alloys of metallic objects. Not all of them, however, can be applied to numismatic source materials. Thus, for instance, one can hardly apply the classical quantitative chemical analysis to specimens treasured in numismatic collections because this method entails a partial destruction of an irreplaceable source [1]). Nor does the modern method of semiquantitative spectrochemical analysis leave the examined objects intact [2]). Under these circumstances, in order to establish the metallic quality of *dīnār* specimens, one has to rely on the Archimedean method of measuring specific gravity. The value of this method in respect of numismatic materials has been analytically discussed by Earle R. Caley, "Estimation of composition of ancient metal objects. Utility of specific gravity measurements", *Analytical Chemistry*, 24, iv. April, 1952, p. 676-681. This method has been used by Ph. Grierson in a series of investigations whose results were published in his articles "Visigothic metrology", *Numismatic Chronicle*, Sixth Series, 13, 1953, p. 74-87; "The debasement of the bezant in the eleventh century", *Byzantinische Zeitschrift*, 47, 1954, p. 379-394; "Notes on the fineness of the Byzantine solidus", *Byzantinische Zeitschrift*, 54, 1961, pp. 91-97. It is also this method that I have relied upon in my research dealing with the standard of fineness of Medieval *dīnārs*.

Specific gravity measurements

In discussing the S. G. (specific gravity) measurements I wish to

1) Cf., R. J. Gettens and Cl. L. Waring, 'The composition of some ancient Persian and other Near Eastern silver objects', *Ars Orientalis*, 2, 1957, p. 83.
2) *Ibid.*, p. 82-83.

begin by emphasizing that the results obtained by this method fall short of the postulated metallic identification of the alloys of *dīnārs*. The establishment of the S. G. does not reveal the number and quantity of different metallic elements possibly admixed in the alloy of a coin. Nor does it indicate the origin of the ore. All one can expect from such an examination is a rather accurate establishment of the S. G. of coins, which can serve as a basis for an approximate estimation of their standard of fineness. This limited character of the evaluation of the standard of fineness results from the fact that the S. G. of gold varies according to the nature of metallic admixtures. "The presence of foreign inclusions in the metal, or worse yet the presence of hidden cavities, may cause serious error. Another serious source of error may be a lack of knowledge of the particular metals alloyed with the gold" [1]). Fortunately this source of error is not very serious for alloys of very high gold content, but it becomes increasingly serious with decrease in gold content [2]).

What is then the value of my undertakings? Or, in other words, to what extent is information derived from the measurements of S. G. of *dīnārs* valid enough to be utilised in historical research? The answer to this question is that considering the lack of other suitable methods, the establishment of the standard of fineness of *dīnārs* on the basis of the S. G. measurements constitutes a valid source of historical information, provided that such an examination has the character of a *mass observation*. The examination of isolated specimens, as it was done by Vazquez Queipo [3]), is meaningless. It can reveal the S.G. of particular *dīnārs* but it does not establish the purity of gold alloy, nor does it even hint at the relative significance of its standard of fineness. Quite different results are produced by a mass observation. One may still be ignorant of the particular inclusions in the metallic composition of *dīnārs*. One may still err concerning the exact degree of purity of their alloy. But

1) Earle R. Caley, *art. cit.*, p. 677.

2) *Supra*, also, *idem*, 'Validity of the specific gravity method for the determination of the fineness of gold objects', *Ohio Journal of Science*, 49, 1949, p. 73-74, 79.

3) V. Vazquez Queipo, *Essai sur les systèmes métriques et monétaires des anciens peuples depuis les premiers temps historiques jusqu'à la fin du Khalifat d'Orient*, Paris, 1859.

one can easily discern excellent or good quality *dīnārs* from inferior and adulterated ones. Consequently, by consistently applying the same steps in the process of measuring, as well as the *same interpretative criteria*, to a substantial number of *dīnārs* grouped according to certain categories (chronological, geographical, dynastic), one should be able to establish certain patterns in the intrinsic quality of the examined specimens. The message read from such data becomes particularly meaningful when it is correlated with textual evidence.

In summing up these few methodological observations chiefly based on my personal reflections, I wish to reiterate that in discussing the standard of fineness of Medieval Near Eastern *dīnārs* I do not claim to provide absolutely accurate figures concerning each single *dīnār* included in my inquiries. I merely attempt to arrive at such conclusions which the limited method of S.G. measurements allows one to reach. In my calculations I assume that as a rule, the alloy of examined *dīnārs* consists of gold and silver [1]). Since the regular medieval *dīnārs* contained a high degree of gold, possible errors in my calculations are of insignificant nature. Certainly, the range of errors becomes significant in the case of low quality *dīnārs* whose metallic composition may include silver or copper, or both, or even other admixtures. In this case, however, the very occurrence of such low quality *dīnārs* is significant, no matter whether their degree of fineness is e.g. 65 % or 67 % pure. In the light of these reservations, the lists of *dīnārs*, with which my publications are provided, should not be regarded as registers of the standard of fineness of examined specimens, but as registers of conclusions based on S. G. measurements. As to the ultimate value of this highly prosaic research, my hope is that my 'labors' will arouse interest and desire to improve our research methods in the important field of monetary and economic history of Medieval Near East.

The standard of fineness of Aghlabid dīnārs

The spectacular internal and external achievements of the Aghlabid dynasty (A.H. 184-296/A. D. 800-909), which held Ifrīqīyah in the

1) Cf., information contained in the treatise of Ibn Baʿrah ('Extracts,' p. 433-434).

name of the ʿAbbāsid caliphs and reigned at al-Qayrawān, could not have been accomplished without solid economic foundations [1]). One of the important economic assets of the Aghlabids was their adequate supply of gold ore of West African [2]) or even European provenance [3]). It was undoubtedly this factor which permitted the Aghlabids to challenge their suzerains of Baghdād in the sphere of monetary production, by issuing gold coinage of their own. This measure by itself constituted an infringement on the minting prerogatives of the Muslim Caliphate whose production of *dīnārs* had hitherto been highly centralized [4]). The full significance of this challenge may be grasped when one realizes the intrinsic integrity of Aghlabid *dīnārs*. An examination of the S. G. of forty five such specimens available in the collection of the American Numismatic Society has revealed that they are characterised by an excellent standard of fineness. Only one specimen appears to be debased (83 % of purity), six pieces fall within the 95 %-97 % limits of purity, twenty-two of them are 98 % pure, thirteen are 99 % fine, while three reach 100 % standard. The distribution of these high quality *dīnārs* spreads evenly over the entire period of Aghlabid domination, as can be seen from Table I.

On the basis of the above evidence one may conclude that the standard of fineness of Aghlabid *dīnārs* was set at 98-99 % degree of purity of gold. This excellent and stable standard of fineness established the Aghlabid *dīnārs* in a highly competitive position in respect to contemporary ʿIrāqī or Egyptian gold coinage [5]).

---

1) Cf., G. Marçais, ʿAghlabids', *EI* (new ed.) i/248.

2) For a discussion of the importance of West African gold regions and their relations with North African provinces in ancient times, see J. Dahse, 'Ein zweites Goldland Salomos. Vorstudien zur Geschichte Westafricas', *Zeitschrift fur Ethnologie*, 43, 1911, p. 1-79, and in respect of the Middle Ages, J. Heers, 'Le Sahara et le commerce méditerranéen à la fin du Moyen-Age', *Annales de l'Institut d'Etudes Orientales*, 16. 1958, p. 249-255.

3) If one is to accept the thesis formulated by Ph. Grierson in 'The monetary reforms of 'Abd al-Malik', *JESHO*, 3, 1960, p. 241-264, the Aghlabid state must have played an important role in the movement of gold stocks from Europe to the metropolitan areas of the Caliphate in the early Middle Ages.

4) Cf., 'Studies', p. 129.

5) Concerning the intrinsic quality of these types of coinage, see 'Studies', p. 154.

TABLE I

Distribution of the examined Aghlabid *dīnārs* according to their standard of fineness

Name of the ruler (Dates in A. H./A. D.)	Below 90 %	95 %	96 %	97 %	98 %	99 %	100 %
ʿAbd Allāh I (197-201/812-817)	—	—	—	—	1	—	—
Ziyādat Allāh I (201-223/817-838)	1	1	1	2	7	7	—
Muḥammad I (226-244/841-856)	—	—	—	—	3	1	1
Aḥmad ibn Muḥammad (242-249/856-863)	—	—	1	—	4	2	1
Muḥammad II (250-261/863-875)	—	—	—	—	4	1	—
Ibrāhīm II (261-289/875-902)	—	—	—	1	2	2	1
Ziyādat Allāh III (290-296/903-909)	—	—	—	—	1	—	—
Total	1	1	2	3	22	13	3

Sāmānid and Ghaznawid dīnārs

The process of decentralisation of gold coins production, which began with the striking of *dīnārs* by Egyptian governors and the Aghlabids, reached its maturity around A.D. 900 [1]). Instead of three *dīnār* issuing mints (Madīnat al-Salām, Miṣr, Ifrīqīyah) under Hārūn al-Rashīd (A. H. 170-193/A. D. 786-809), the number of such mints in A. H. 276/A.D. 889 amounted to about twenty [2]). Several of these mints operated in the eastern provinces of the ʿAbbāsid Caliphate, during the domination of the Sāmānid (A. H. 279-395/A. D. 892-1004) and Ghaznawid (A. H. 351-582/A. D. 962-1186) dynasties.
The rulers of these prominent dynasties had their gold coinage struck not only in the political centres of their power, but in provincial mints as well. Unfortunately, with the exception of Naysābūrī *dīnārs*, only a

1) Cf., 'Studies', p. 129.
2) *Ibid.*, p. 130.

limited number of Sāmānid and Ghaznawid gold specimens is available in the collection of the American Numismatic Society. All but two of these show a very debased standard of fineness as can be seen from the following list.

Dynasty and ruler (Dates in A. H./A. D.) Sāmānids	Mint	A. H.	Standard of fineness in %
Ismāʿīl ibn Aḥmad	Samarqand	289	84
(279-295‡892-907)	”		
Naṣr II ibn Aḥmad	”	310	97
(301-331/913-943)			
”	al-Muḥammadīyah	320	87
”	”	324	79
”	”	329	79
Nūḥ ibn Naṣr	Āmul	343	98
(331-343/943-954)			
Ghaznawids Maḥmūd	Harāt	396	75
(389-421/999-1030	”	399	75
	”	419	68
Mawdūd	Ghaznah	434	69
(433-440/1041-1048)			
Ibrāhīm	no mint [1])	no date [2])	less than 50
(451-492/1059-1999)	no mint	”	” ”

There is however in the same collection an interesting series of *dīnārs* struck by the mint of Naysābūr during the domination of the dynasties in question as well as in the subsequent period [3]). The results of the examination of such Sāmānid and Ghaznawid specimens, to which a Simjūrid dīnār has also been added, have been tabulated below, (see Table II).

It appears from the above table that the two largest groups, consisting of nine specimens each, display 94 % and 96 % degree of purity. One group of five specimens shows a standard of 93 %, while four *dīnārs* are 95 % fine. As far as the group with 96 % of fineness is con-

1) Inscriptions on coins classed as 'no mint' do not include mint names.
2) Inscriptions on coins classed as 'no date' do not include any dates.
3) See, *infra*, Saljūqid *dīnārs*, p. 262.

TABLE II

Distribution of the examined Naysābūrī *dīnārs* struck under the Sāmānids, Simjūrids and Ghaznawids, according to their standard of fineness

Dynasty and ruler (Dates in A. H./A. D.)	Below 80%	90%	91%	92%	93%	94%	95%	96%	97%	98%	99%
Sāmānids											
Naṣr II Ibn Aḥmad (301-331/913-943)	—	—	—	—	1	1	—	—	—	—	—
ʿAbd al-Malik ibn Nūḥ (343-350/954-961)	—	—	—	—	—	—	—	1	—	—	—
Manṣūr ibn Nūḥ 350-365/961-976)	—	—	—	—	—	—	1	1	—	—	—
Nūḥ ibn Manṣūr (365-387/976-997)	—	—	—	—	—	—	—	—	—	1	—
Total (Sāmānid)	—	—	—	—	1	1	1	2	—	1	—
Simjūrids											
Abū ʿAlī Muḥammad (374-377/984-987)	—	—	—	—	—	—	—	1	—	—	—
Ghaznawids											
Maḥmūd (389-421/999-1030)	1	—	2	2	4	7	3	3	—	—	—
Masʿūd (421-432/1030-1041)	—	1	—	—	—	1	—	3	1	—	1
Total (Ghaznawid)	1	1	2	2	4	8	3	6	1	—	1
Grand total	1	1	2	2	5	9	4	9	1	1	1

cerned, their alloy corresponds to the official standard of the ʿAbbāsid *dīnārs* of Baghdād [1]). One should note, however, that this group of Naysābūrī *dīnārs*, together with three superior specimens, constitutes only one third of the examined Naysābūrī lot. A great majority (24 out of 36) of the Naysābūrī specimens is characterised by a standard lower than 96 %. On the other hand, the largest concentration of examined coins (27 out of 36) falls within the 93-96 % limit. It is, however, remarkable

1) Cf., 'Studies', p. 154.

that only two specimens (or 5.5 % of the whole lot) show a standard inferior to 90 % of fineness.

In commenting on the standard of the *dīnārs* struck by the mint of Naysābūr, one should remember that in spite of being the seat of the Governor of Khurāsān administering all the territories to the south of the Oxus river [1]), Naysābūr was not the capital of any of these or of the subsequent Saljūqid dynasties. Thus its mint ranked, at least from the vantage point of its geographic situation, as a provincial one not only in relation to the mint of the capital of the ʿAbbāsid caliphate but in respect of the mint of Samarqand or of Ghaznah as well. A further point worth considering is the question of gold supplies on which the mint of Naysābūr relied for its production of *dīnārs*. Intensive trade operations for which that area was famous during the period in question must have necessarily caused an influx of gold bullion to Naysābūr. The outflow of silver produced by the large scale exploitation of Transoxanian mines [2]), must also have been responsible for the presence of gold stocks of external origin.

It is also possible that the mint of Naysābūr relied on deliveries from important gold deposits situated between that town and Mashhad, whose existence has been attested by modern geological surveys [3]).

In considering the chronological distribution of the examined specimens one may observe the following pattern. Down to A. H. 397/A. D. 1006/7, the mint of Naysābūr maintained a relatively stable standard of fineness of 94 % and above, for its gold issues. A light deterioration in the intrinsic quality of Naysābūrī *dīnārs* occurred between A. H. 399-419/A. D. 1008-1028. This period was notorious for the ruinous economic squeeze applied by Maḥmūd of Ghaznah [4]). However, with the accession of Masʿūd in A. H. 421/A. D. 1030, the intrinsic quality of Naysābūrī *dīnārs* was restored to its earlier level.

---

1) Cf., W. Barthold, *Turkestan down to the Mongol invasion*, London, 1958, p. 229.
2) For a discussion of the significance of Transoxanian mines see S. Bolin, 'Mohammed, Charlemagne and Ruric', *Scandinavian Economic History Review*, 1, 1953, p. 5-39.
3) Cf. R. J. Forbes, *Metallurgy in Antiquity*, 1950, p. 150.
4) Cf. W. Barthold, *op. cit.*, p. 287-288.

Buwayhid *dīnārs*

A critical debasement of gold coins struck in Baghdād, which took place during the Buwayhid period (A. H. 320-447/A. D. 932-1055) [1]), can be detected in *dīnārs* struck by the mints of Baghdād and of other cities. Here is a list of Buwayhid specimens from the collection of the American Numismatic Society, whose standards of fineness attest the deplorable coinage conditions prevailing in the metropolitan areas of the ʿAbbāsid Caliphate during the period in question.

Name of ruler	Mint		Standard of fineness in %
Rukn al-Dawlah	al-Muḥammadīyah	341	97
Rukn al-Dawlah	Sawah	346	94
Muʿizz al-Dawlah	Madīnat al-Salām	349	90
Rukn al-Dawlah	Madīnat al-Salām	356	89
ʿAḍud al-Dawlah	Madīnat al-Salām	366	93
Bahā' al-Dawlah	Sūq al-Ahwāz	397(9)	less than 50
Bahā' al-Dawlah	Sūq al-Ahwāz	397	less than 50
Bahā' al-Dawlah	Sūq al-Ahwāz	397	less than 50
Bahā' al-Dawlah	Sūq al-Ahwāz	398	less than 50
Bahā' al-Dawlah	Madīnat al-Salām	409	56
Sulṭān al-Dawlah	Madīnat al-Salām	409	62

Fāṭimid dīnārs

a) *Dīnārs* struck before the conquest of Egypt.

While the markets of the ʿAbbāsid Caliphate in the 4/10 century experienced the circulation of *dīnārs* of questionable quality, the rising dynasty of the Fāṭimids was supplying the western regions of the Muslim Empire with excellent gold coinage. In this respect the Fāṭimids appear to have continued the best monetary traditions of their Aghlabid predecessors in North Africa (see Table III). Only two of thirty Fāṭimid specimens of that period have a standard inferior to 98 %, but they are nonetheless better than 90 % fine. On the other hand, twenty-eight of these specimens display a standard of fineness of 98-100 %. Their intrinsic resemblance to Aghlabid *dīnārs* may be

1) Cf., 'Studies', p. 144-148.

TABLE III

Distribution of the examined Fāṭimid *dīnārs*, struck between A. H. 297-358/A. D. 909-969 (i.e. before the conquest of Egypt), according to their standard of fineness

Name of ruler (Dates in A. H./A. D.)	Mint	92%	94%	98%	99%	100%
al-Mahdī	al-Qayrawān	—	—	1	6	1
297-322/909-934)	No mint	—	—	—	—	1
	al-Mahdīyah	1	—	3	1	—
al-Manṣūr	al-Mahdīyah	—	—	—	—	1
(334-341/946-953)	al-Manṣūrīyah	—	—	—	1	—
al-Muʿizz	al-Manṣūrīyah	—	—	2	4	5
(341-356/953-975)	No mint	—	1	—	1	2
Total	al-Qayrawān	—	—	1	6	—
	al-Mahdīyah	1	—	3	1	1
	al-Manṣūriyah	—	—	2	5	5
	No mint	—	1	—	1	3
Grand total		1	1	6	13	9

appreciated by means of the following table (see Table IV). The frequency of *dīnārs* with a standard of fineness of 98 % and above is overwhelming in both groups of specimens. Thirty-eight (or 84.5 %) of Aghlabid, and twenty-eight (or 93.4 %) of Fāṭimid *dīnārs* show this degree of fineness, indicating that the major political change-over resulting from the emergence of Fāṭimid power did not affect the quality of North African gold coinage.

TABLE IV

Distribution of the examined Aghlabid and Fāṭimid *dīnārs* struck before the conquest of Egypt, according to their standard of fineness.

	Below 90%	92%	94%	95%	96%	97%	98%	99%	100%
Aghlabid *dīnārs*	1	—	—	1	2	3	22.	13	3
Fāṭimid *dīnārs*	—	1	1	—	—	—	6	13	9

b) *Dīnārs* struck after the conquest of Egypt.

Judging by numismatic evidence alone, gold coinage of Egypt struck by the Ikhshīdids was characterised by a very good standard of fineness [1]). However, according to textual evidence, Egyptian markets on the eve of Fāṭimid invasion were afflicted by monetary complications [2]). It is quite possible that some monetary instability in Egypt was caused by the circulation of low quality 'Abbāsid *dīnārs* of 'Irāqī or Syrian provenance. It is further possible that the declining Ikhshīdid administration, suffering from ever increasing economic, political and military difficulties, was ultimately forced to debase Egyptian *dīnārs* which were subsequently absorbed by Fāṭimid mints. At any rate, the problem of Egyptian coinage difficulties must have been a serious one since it was raised in the surrender negotations between the Egyptian delegation and Jawhar al-Ṣaqlabī, the commander of the invading Fāṭimid army. Following the conclusion of these negotations, a special proclamation was addressed to the people of Egypt in Sha'bān 358/ July 969, on behalf of the Fāṭimid caliph al-Mu'izz (A. H. 341-356/A. D. 953-975), announcing the political 'program' of the victorious regime. As far as monetary problems were concerned the following measures were promised: improvement of coinage, adjustment of its intrinsic quality to the Fāṭimid standard; elimination of debased coins from circulation [3]).

The new regime in Egypt did not fail to implement the pledged monetary reforms. Shortly after Jawhar's entry to the capital of Egypt, its mint began to issue *dīnārs* in the name of the Fāṭimid caliph [4]). The striking of Fāṭimid *dīnārs* in Egypt was accompanied by a series of administrative measures aiming at the withdrawal of other types of gold coins from circulation [5]). A substantial number of Fāṭimid *dīnārs* struck after the conquest of Egypt (available in the collection of the American Numismatic Society), has made it possible to ascertain to

---

1) *Ibid.*, p. 153.

2) Cf., a recent discussion by E. Ashtor, 'Essai sur les prix et les salaires dans l'empire califien', *RSO*, 36, 1961, p. 35.

3) Cf., Ibn Ḥammād, *Akhbār mulūk bānī 'Ubayd*, 1927, p. 42 (Arabic text), p. 65 (French transl.); also, al-Maqrizi, *Itti'āẓ al-ḥunafā'*, 1948, p. 150.

4) Cf., al-Maqrīzī, op. cit., p. 165.

5) Cf., *Ibid.*, p. 172, 183, 199.

TABLE V

Distribution of the examined Fāṭimid *dīnārs*, struck between A. H. 358-487/A. D. 969-1094 in North Africa and Egypt, according to their standard of fineness.

Name of ruler (Dates in A. H./A. D.)	Mint	Below 90%	94%	95%	96%	97%	98%	99%	100%
al-Muʿizz (341-365/953-975)	al-Manṣūrīyah	—	—	—	—	—	—	3	2
	No mint	—	1	—	—	—	—	—	—
	Miṣr	—	—	—	—	—	1	14	4
al-ʿAzīz (365-386/976-996)	al-Manṣūrīyah	—	—	—	—	—	—	1	1
	al-Mahdīyah	—	—	—	—	—	2	2	2
al-Ḥākim (386-411/996-1021)	Miṣr	—	—	1	1	1	17	4	—
al-Ẓāhir (411-427/1021-1036)	al-Manṣūrīyah	—	—	—	1	—	—	1	—
	al-Mahdīyah	—	—	—	—	—	1	1	—
	Miṣr	—	—	—	1	—	1	9	—
al-Mustanṣir (427-487/1036-1094)	al-Manṣūrīyah	—	—	—	—	—	1	1	—
	al-Mahdīyah	—	—	—	1	—	—	—	—
	Miṣr	2	—	—	2	8	23	16	3
	al-Iskandarīyah	1	—	—	2	2	10	3	—
Total by mints	al-Manṣūrīyah	—	—	—	1	—	1	6	3
	al-Mahdīyah	—	—	—	1	—	3	3	2
	Miṣr	2	—	—	4	9	43	49	16
	al-Iskandarīyah	1	—	—	2	2	10	3	—
	No mint	—	1	—	—	—	—	—	—

what extent the victory of the Fāṭimids resulted in an intrinsic improvement of the gold coinage in the conquered provinces (see Table V).

The results yielded by this investigation, presented in Table VI, permit us to assess the significance of Fāṭimid reforms in the sphere of the standard of fineness of Egyptian *dīnārs*. Of 139 examined specimens, 121 (or 87.8 %) show a standard of fineness of 98 % and above. It thus appears that the Fāṭimids, by fixing the fineness of Egyptian *dīnārs* at 98-99 %, adjusted their standard to the level of their North African gold coinage. Table VI serves to illustrate the comparison between the North African and Egyptian Fāṭimid *dīnārs* (see Table VI).

TABLE VI

Distribution of the examined North African and Egyptian Fāṭimid *dīnārs*, struck prior to A. H. 487/A. D. 1094

	Below 90%	92%	94%	95%	96%	97%	98%	99%	100%
North African *dīnārs* struck before the conquest of Egypt	—	1	1	—	—	—	6	13	9
North African *dīnārs* struck after the conquest of Egypt	—	—	—	—	2	—	4	9	5
Total	—	1	1	—	2	—	10	22	14
Egyptian *dīnārs*	3	—	—	1	6	11	53	52	16
Grand total	3	1	1	1	8	11	63	74	30

c) Fāṭimid *dīnārs* struck in Syria.

Effective intrinsic improvement has also been detected in Fāṭimid *dīnārs* struck by various mints of Syria. An examination of 43 such specimens has yielded the results presented in Table VII. As one can see from this table, the three largest frequency groups are formed by the standards of 98 %-15 specimens (or 34.8 % of the whole lot), of 97 %-8 specimens (or 18.6 %), and that of 96 %-7 specimens (or

TABLE VII

Distribution of the examined Fāṭimid *dīnārs* struck between A. H. 358-487 /A. D. 969-1094 in Syria, according to their standard of fineness.

Mint	90%	94%	95%	96%	97%	98%	99%
ʿAkkā	—	—	—	—	—	1	—
Dimishq	—	—	1	—	—	—	—
Filaṣṭīn	1	1	—	2	—	5	4
Ḥalab	—	1	—	—	—	—	—
Ṣūr	—	—	2	3	4	4	—
Ṭabarīyah	—	1	—	—	—	2	—
Ṭarābulus	—	—	1	2	4	3	1
Total	1	3	4	7	8	15	5

16.2 %). Thirty-five *dīnārs* (or 81.3 % of the examined lot) fall within a standard of 96-98 %. This high intrinsic quality of Fāṭimid Syrian *dīnārs* sharply contrasts with Syrian gold coinage struck prior to the Fāṭimid invasion. The largest group in the lot of sixteen pre-Fāṭimid *dīnārs* examined, is formed by four specimens displaying a standard of 93 % of fineness. While no specimen is better than 97 % fine, eleven (or 68.7 %) of them are below 95 % fine. This intrinsic difference between the pre-Fāṭimid and Fāṭimid Syrian *dīnārs* can easily be grasped by means of Table VIII.

TABLE VIII

Distribution of the examined Syrian *dīnārs*, struck before and after the Fāṭimid expansion in Syria, according to their standard of fineness.

Syrian *dīnārs* between A. H. 278/358/A. D. 891-969 Mint	Below 90%	90%	91%	92%	93%	94%	95%	96%	97%	98%	99%
Anṭākiyah	—	—	—	1	—	—	—	—	—	—	—
Dimishq	—	—	—	—	—	—	—	1	1	—	—
Filasṭīn	1	1	1	1	4	1	2	1	—	—	—
Ḥimṣ	1	—	—	—	—	—	—	—	—	—	—
Total	2	1	1	2	4	1	2	2	1		
Total of Syrian *dīnārs* struck between A. H. 358-487/A. D. 969-1094	—	1	—	—	—	3	4	7	8	15	5

d) Fāṭimid *dīnārs* before the Crusades [1]).

All these data (see Table IX), based on the examination of numismatic evidence, clearly demonstrate the success of the Fāṭimids in the sphere of gold coinage production. It is obvious that by ruling over the entire length of the North African coastal area, the Fāṭimids benefited from

1) For a discussion of Fāṭimid *dīnārs* struck during the period of the Crusades, see 'The standard of fineness', p. 164; also, 'The crisis of *dīnār*', p. 178 f.

TABLE IX

Distribution of Fāṭimid *dīnārs*, struck between A. H. 297-487/A. D. 909-1094, according to their standard of fineness and irrespectively of their mint provenance

Below 90%	90%	92%	94%	95%	96%	97%	98%	99%	100%
3	1	1	4	5	15	19	78	79	30

gold imports coming from West African and Nubian oriferous regions. The fact, however, that they succeeded in maintaining such a remarkable stability of their gold coins must be attributed to their efficient minting organisation [1]). A fixed weight standard [2]), and a superb degree of fineness of 98 % and above, which characterised Fāṭimid *dīnārs*, continued to the invasion of the Crusades [3]). This long stability of gold coinage appears not to have been affected by the terrible economic upheavals of the reign of al-Mustanṣir (A. H. 427-487/A. D. 1036-1094). There is no doubt that the excellent quality of Fāṭimid *dīnārs* reflected the great economic prosperity which Egypt enjoyed prior to the Crusades.

Saljūqid *dīnārs*

A reinvigoration of the political, religious and economic structure of the ʿAbbāsid Caliphate following the establishment of the Saljūqid regime in the middle of the 5/11th century, found its expression in the intrinsic quality of eastern *dīnārs* (see Table X).

Although the examined specimens, belonging to the collection of the American Numismatic Society, come from different mints of the eastern Caliphate, they display a rather uniform standard of fineness. The largest frequency group consists of specimens with 95 % degree of fineness. Indeed, the total of 48 specimens, twenty-nine pieces (or 60 % of the examined lot) show a standard of 95 % and above. Nineteen specimens (or 40 %) are inferior to 95 % of fineness. Four *dīnārs* (or 8.3 %) are worse than 90 %. The standard of 95 % appears to have prevailed

1) Cf., 'Contributions', p. 510-511.
2) Cf., 'The crisis of *dīnār*, p. 178-180.
3) Cf., *Ibid.*, p. 180; 'Contributions', p. 507-508.

TABLE X

Distribution of the examined Saljūqid *dīnārs* according to their standard of fineness

Name of ruler (Dates in A. H./A. D.)	Mint	Below 90%	90%	91%	92%	93%	94%	95%	96%	97%	98%
Tughril Beg	al-Rayy	1	—	—	—	—	1	1	2	3	1
(d. 455/1063)	Naysābūr	—	—	—	1	2	4	5	3	3	2
Alp Arslān	al-Rayy	—	—	—	1	—	—	—	—	—	1
(455-465/1063-1072)	Iṣfahān	—	—	—	—	—	—	—	2	—	1
Malik Shāh	al-Rayy	1	—	—	—	—	—	2	—	1	—
(465-485/1072-1092)	Iṣfahān	1	—	2	—	—	—	12	—	—	—
	Naysābūr	—	—	—	2	1	—	—	—	—	—
	Farah	1	—	—	—	—	—	—	—	—	—
Barkiyārūq (487-498/1094-1104)	Madīnat al-Salām	—	1	—	—	—	—	—	1	—	—
Total by mints	al-Rayy	2	—	—	1	—	1	3	2	42	2
	Naysābūr	—	—	—	3	3	4	5	3	3	2
	Iṣfahān	1	—	2	—	—	—	1	2	—	1
	Farah	1	—	—	—	—	—	—	—	—	—
	Madīnat al-Salām	—	1	—	—	—	—	—	—	—	—
Grand total		4	1	2	4	3	5	9	8	7	5

TABLE XI

Distribution of the examined *dīnārs* struck in Madīnat al-Salām, al-Rayy (al-Muḥammadīyah) and Naysābūr under different dynasties, according to their standard of fineness

Mint	Domination of the	Below 90%	90%	91%	92%	93%	94%	95%	96%	97%	98%	99%
Madīnat al-Salām	Buwayhids	3	1	—	—	1	—	—	—	—	—	—
	Saljūqids	—	1	—	—	—	—	—	1	—	—	—
al-Rayy	Sāmānids	3	—	—	—	—	—	—	—	—	—	—
	Buwayhids	—	—	—	—	—	—	—	—	1	—	—
	Saljūqids	2	—	—	1	—	1	3	2	4	2	—
Naysābūr	Sāmānids	—	—	—	—	1	1	1	2	—	1	—
	Simjūrids	—	—	—	—	—	—	—	1	—	—	—
	Ghaznawids	2	—	2	2	4	8	3	6	1	—	1
	Saljūqids	—	—	—	3	3	4	5	3	3	2	—

among the Naysābūrī *dīnārs* of that period. It is perhaps worth while to investigate to what extent the succession of different political regimes affected the standard of fineness of *dīnārs* struck by the mint of Naysābūr (see Table XI).

While the mints of Madīnat al-Salām and that of al-Rayy are not adequately represented in the above table, the 59 examined specimens struck by the mint of Naysābūr under different dynasties permit the following observations. It appears that in spite of political changes, the mint of Naysābūr maintained a relatively stable standard of fineness of their *dīnārs*. Whether under the domination of the Sāmānids, Simjūrids, Ghaznawids or the Saljūqids, *dīnārs* struck by the mint of Naysābūr were as a rule characterised by a standard of 94-96 % of fineness.

Dīnārs of Western and Eastern dynasties.

In order to appreciate the nature of intrinsic difference between *dīnārs* struck by Western and Eastern dynasties of Medieval Muslim Empire, the following table has been prepared, based on the examination of 450 specimens (see Table XII).

The data tabulated above are almost self-expressive. The difference in the intrinsic quality between the Western and Eastern *dīnārs* becomes even more apparent in the following compilation:

	Dīnārs Eastern	Western
Total number of examined specimens	109	341
Number of spec's in the largest standard group	23 spec's or 21.1%	114 spec's or 33.4%
Largest standard group	Below 90%	98%
Number of spec's in the second largest standard group	17 spec's or 15.5%	100 spec's or 29.3%
Second largest standard group	96%	99%
Number and % of spec's falling within the standard of:		
below 90%	23 or 21.1%	8 or 2.3%
below 96%	74 or 67%	38 or 11.1%
96% and above	35 or 32%	303 or 89.1%
100%	0	34 or 9.9%

In the light of all this evidence, it conclusively appears that in addition to their superiority on account of a fixed weight standard [1]), Western *dīnārs* excelled their Eastern counterparts from the point of view of the standard of fineness. This monetary situation continued down to the end of the 5/11th century, when the activities of the Crusaders undermined the stability of Syrian and Egyptian *dīnārs* [2]).

TABLE XII

Distribution of the examined *dīnārs* struck under Western and Eastern dynasties, according to their standard of fineness

Western Dynasties	Below 90%	90%	91%	92%	93%	94%	95%	96%	97%	98%	99%	100%
Aghlabids	1	—	—	—	—	—	1	2	3	22	13	3
Ṭūlūnids (Egypt)	3					7	2	5	7	8	3	1
Ṭūlūnids (Provinces)	2	—	—	2	—	—	1	1	—	—	—	—
Ikhshīdids (Egypt)	—	—	—	—	—	—	—	1	2	6	5	—
Ikhshīdids (Provinces)	1	—	1	1	3	—	1	—	—	—	—	—
Fāṭimids (Prior to A. H. 487/A. D. 1094)												
(Egypt)	3	—	—	—	—	—	1	6	11	53	52	16
(N. Africa, Syria)	—	1	—	1	—	4	4	9	8	25	27	14
Eastern Dynasties												
Sāmānids	4	—	—	—	1	2	2	2	1	2	—	—
Simjūrids	—	—	—	—	—	—	—	1	—	—	—	—
Buwayhids	7	1	—	—	1	1	—	—	1	—	—	—
Ghaznawids	8	—	2	2	4	8	3	6	1	—	1	—
Saljūqids	4	1	2	4	3	5	9	8	7	5	—	—
Total												
Western Dynasties	8	1	1	4	3	11	10	24	31	114	100	34
Eastern Dynasties	23	2	4	6	9	16	14	17	10	7	1	—

1) See above, p. 262, n. 2.
2) Cf., 'Contributions', p. 507-508.

APPENDIX

REGISTER OF EXAMINED COINS

Reference	Dynasty and ruler (Dates in A. H./A. D.)	Mint	A. H.	Fineness of gold in %
UM	Aghlabids ʿAbd Allāh I (197-201/812-817)		200	98
UM	Ziyādat Allāh (201-223/816-838)		202	99
UM	,, ,,		203	99
UM	,, ,,		204	99
UM	,, ,,		204	98
ANS/1951	,, ,,		205	99
UM	,, ,,		205	95
UM	,, ,,		206	98
UM	,, ,,		207	99
ANS 58.183	,, ,,		211	83
UM	,, ,,		212	98
UM	,, ,,		212	97
UM	,, ,,		214	97
UM	,, ,,		215	98
UM	,, ,,		217	96
UM	,, ,,		218	99
UM	,, ,,		219	98
UM	,, ,,		220	99
ANS 59. 92	,, ,,		221	98
UM	,, ,,		222	98
UM	Muḥammad I (226-244/841-856)		227	98
ANS Newell Coll.	,,		228	98
UM	,,		229	99
UM	,,		232	100
UM	,,		232	98
UM	Aḥmad ibn Muḥammad (242-249/856-863)		243(?)	100
ANS 56-159	,, ,, ,,		244	98
ANS 50.73	,, ,, ,,		245	96
UM	,, ,, ,,		245	99
UM	,, ,, ,,		246	98
ANS 58 183	,, ,, ,,		246	98
UM	,, ,, ,,		248	99
UM248UM	,, ,, ,,		249	98
UM	Muḥammad II (250-261/863-875)		250	98
ANS Newell Coll.	,,		254	98

Reference	Dynasty and ruler (Dates in A. H./A. D.)	Mint	A. H.	Fineness of gold in %
UM	Muḥammad II (250-261/863-875		255	98
UM	"		256	99
ANS 58 183	"		258	98
HSA	Ibrāhīm II (261-289/875-902)		261	98
UM	"		263	99
UM	"		267	100
ANS Newell Coll.	"		284	98
ANS 56.100	"		285	97
UM	"		286	99
ANS 58 183	Ziyādat Allāh III (290-296/903-909)		291	98
	Sāmānids			
ANS	Ismāʿīl ibn Aḥmad (279-295/892-907)	Samarqand	289	84
ANS	Naṣr II ibn Aḥmad (301-331/913-943)	Samarqand	310	97
ANS	" " "	al-Muḥammadīyah	320	87
ANS	" " "	"	324	79
ANS Miles	" " "	"	329	79
ANS	" " "	Naysābūr	315	93
ANS	" " "	"	323	94
ANS Miles	Nūḥ ibn Naṣr (331-343/943-954)	"	333?	94
ANS	" " "	"	334	95
ANS	" " "	Amul	343	98
ANS	ʿAbd al-Malik ibn Nūḥ (343-350/954-961)	Naysābūr	346	96
ANS	Manṣūr ibn Nūḥ (350-365/961-976)	"	359	96
ANS	" " "	"	361	95
ANS	Nūḥ ibn Manṣūr (365-387/976-997)	"	377	98
	Simjūrids			
ANS	Abū ʿAlī Muḥammad (374-377/984-987)	Naysābūr	383	96
	Ghaznawids			
ANS	Maḥmūd (389-421/999-1030)	Naysābūr "	385	96
ANS	"	"	385	95
ANS	"	"	387	91
ANS	"	"	390	65
ANS	"	"	391	94

Reference	Dynasty and ruler (Dates in A. H./A. D.)	Mint	A. H.	Fineness of gold in %
ANS	Maḥmūd (389-421/999-1030)	Naysābūr	394	96
ANS	”	”	397	96
ANS	”	”	399	94
ANS	”	”	401	94
ANS	”	”	402	94
ANS	”	”	406	93
ANS	”	”	406	95
ANS	”	”	407	93
ANS	”	”	407	95
ANS	”	”	410	94
ANS	”	”	412	94
ANS	”	”	415	93
ANS	”	”	417	92
ANS	”	”	418	92
ANS	”	”	418	91
ANS	”	”	418	93
ANS	”	”	419	94
ANS	”	Harāt	396	75
ANS	”	”	399	75
ANS	”	”	419	68
ANS	Masʿūd (421-432/1030-1041)	Naysābūr	422	97
ANS	”	”	423?	96
ANS	”	”	424	96
ANS	”	”	424	96
ANS	”	”	427	99
ANS	”	”	429	80
ANS	”	”	431	94
ANS	Mawdūd (433-440/1041-1048)	Ghaznah	434	69
ANS	Ibrāhīm (451-492ṭ1059-1099)	no mint	no date	less than 50
ANS	”	” ”	” ”	less than 50
	Buwayhids			
ANS 62-128	Rukn al-Dawlah	al-Muḥammadīyah	341	97
ANS	” ” ”	Sawah	346	94
ANS 62-126	Muʿizz al-Dawlah	Madīnat al-Salām	349	90
ANS	Rukn al-Dawlah	” ” ”	356	89
ANS	ʿAḍud al-Dawlah	” ” ”	366	93
ANS	Bahāʿ al-Dawlah	Sūq al-Ahwāz	397(9)	less than 50
ANS	” ” ”	” ” ”	397	less than 50
ANS	” ” ”	” ” ”	397	less than 50
ANS	” ” ”	” ” ”	398	less than 50

Reference	Dynasty and ruler (Dates in A. H./A. D.)	Mint	A. H.	Fineness of gold in %
ANS	Bahā' al-Dawlah	Madīnat al-Salām	404	566
ANS	Sulṭān al-Dawlah	,, ,, ,,	409	62
	Fāṭimids			
ANS	al-Mahdī (297-322/909-934)	al-Qayrawān	300	99
ANS	,, ,,		301	99
Miles 1	,, ,,	,, ,,	303	99
ANS	,, ,,	,, ,,	304	99
ANS	,, ,,	,, ,,	305	99
ANS	,, ,,	,, ,,	307	98
ANS	,, ,,	,, ,,	309	99
ANS	,, ,,	al-Mahdīyah	311	92
Miles 3	,, ,,	no mint	314	100
ANS	,, ,,	al-Mahdīyah	314	98
ANS	,, ,,	,, ,,	318	98
ANS	,, ,,	,, ,,	318	98
ANS	,, ,,	,, ,,	31?	99
Miles 13	al-Manṣūr (334-341/946-953)	al-Manṣūrīyah	341	99
Miles 14	,, ,,	al-Mahdīyah	337	100
Miles 28	al-Mu'izz (341-365/953-975)	Filasṭīn	359	99
ANS	,, ,,	,,	364	99
Miles 29	,, ,,	Miṣr	358	100
Miles 30	,, ,,	,,	359	99
Miles 31	,, ,,	,,	359	98
Miles 32	,, ,,	,,	359	99
Miles 33	,, ,,	,,	360	99
Miles 34	,, ,,	,,	361	99
Miles 35	,, ,,	,,	361	99
Miles 36	,, ,,	,,	361	99
Miles 37	,, ,,	,,	361	99
Miles 38	,, ,,	,,	362	99
Miles 39	,, ,,	,,	362	99
Miles 40	,, ,,	,,	362	99
Miles 41	,, ,,	,,	362	99
Miles 42	,, ,,	,,	363	100
Miles 43	,, ,,	,,	363	100
Miles 44	,, ,,	,,	364	99
Miles 45	,, ,,	,,	364	99
Miles 46	,, ,,	,,	364	100
Miles 47	,, ,,	,,	365	99
Miles 48	,, ,,	al-Manṣūrīyah	342	99
ANS 62-126	,, ,,	,, ,,	344	98

Reference	Dynasty and ruler (Dates in A. H./A. D.)	Mint	A. H.	Fineness of gold in %
Miles 49	al-Muʿizz (341-365/953-975	al-Manṣūrīyah	346	98
Miles 50	,, ,,	,, ,,	347	100
Miles 53	,, ,,	,, ,,	353	100
Miles 54	,, ,,	,, ,,	357	100
Miles 56	,, ,,	,, ,,	360	99
Miles 57	,, ,,	,, ,,	360	100
Miles 58	,, ,,	,, ,,	361	99
Miles 60	,, ,,	,, ,,	361	99
Miles 61	,, ,,	,, ,,	362	100
ANS	,, ,,	no mint	342	100
ANS	,, ,,	,, ,,	348	100
ANS	,, ,,	,, ,,	35?	99
ANS	,, ,,	,, ,,	362	94
Miles 78	al-ʿAzīz (365-386/976-996)	Filasṭīn	370	98
Miles 79	,, ,,	,,	370	99
Miles 80	,, ,,	,,	371	99
Miles 81	,, ,,	,,	371	98
Miles 83	,, ,,	,,	375	98
Miles 84	,, ,,	,,	376	98
Miles 85	,, ,,	,,	378	98
Miles 86	,, ,,	Miṣr	365	100
Miles 87	,, ,,	,,	366	100
Miles 88	,, ,,	,,	366	99
Miles 89	,, ,,	,,	367	99
Miles 90	,, ,,	,,	368	100
Miles 91	,, ,,	,,	369	100
Miles 92	,, ,,	,,	369	99
Miles 93	,, ,,	,,	370	99
Miles 95	,, ,,	,,	371	100
Miles 96	,, ,,	,,	372	99
Miles 98	,, ,,	,,	374	99
Miles 99	,, ,,	,,	375	99
Miles 100	,, ,,	,,	376	99
Miles 101	,, ,,	,,	377	99
Miles 102	,, ,,	,,	378	100
Miles 103	,, ,,	,,	380	99
Miles 104	,, ,,	,,	382	98
Miles 105	,, ,,	,,	382	100
Miles 106	,, ,,	,,	384	100
Miles 107	,, ,,	,,	385	100
Miles 109	,, ,,	al-Manṣūrīyah	375	99
Miles 110	,, ,,	,, ,,	385	100

Reference	Dynasty and ruler (Dates in A. H./A. D.)	Mint	A. H.	Fineness of gold in %
Miles 111	al-ʿAzīz	al-Mahdīyah	370	99
Miles 112	,, ,,	,, ,,	370	98
Miles 113	,, ,,	,, ,,	371	98
ANS	,, ,,	,, ,,	374	100
Miles 114	,, ,,	,, ,,	381	100
Miles 115	,, ,,	,, ,,	383	99
Miles 135	al-Ḥākim (386-411/996-1021)	Miṣr	386	99
Miles 136	,, ,,	,,	387	98
Miles 137	,, ,,	,,		99
Miles 138	,, ,,	,,	388	98
Miles 140	,, ,,	,,	390	98
Miles 141	,, ,,	,,	392	98
Miles 142	,, ,,	,,	392	98
Miles 144	,, ,,	,,	393	98
Miles 145	,, ,,	,,	394	95
Miles 146	,, ,,	,,	397	97
Miles 147	,, ,,	,,	398	96
Miles 148	,, ,,	,,	399	98
Miles 149	,, ,,	,,	400	98
Miles 150	,, ,,	,,	403	98
Miles 151	,, ,,	,,	403	99
Miles 153	,, ,,	,,	405	98
Miles 154	,, ,,	,,	406	99
ANS	,, ,,	,,	406	98
Miles 156	,, ,,	,,	407	98
Miles 157	,, ,,	,,	408	98
Miles 158	,, ,,	,,	409	98
Miles 159	,, ,,	,,	410	98
Miles 160	,, ,,	,,	410	98
Miles 161	,, ,,	,,	411	98
Miles 212	al-Ẓāhir (411-427/1021-1036)	Ṣūr	424	98
Miles 213	,, ,,	Miṣr	413	99
ANS	,, ,,	,,	414	99
Miles 214	,, ,,	,,	414	96
Miles 216	,, ,,	,,	418	99
Miles 220	,, ,,	,,	419	98
Miles 222	,, ,,	,,	422	99
Miles 223	,, ,,	,,	422	99
Miles 224	,, ,,	,,	423	99
Miles 225	,, ,,	,,	425	99
Miles 227	,, ,,	,,	427	99
Miles 430	,, ,,	al-Manṣūrīyah	420	96

Reference	Dynasty and ruler (Dates in A. H./A. D.)	Mint	A. H.	Fineness of gold in %
Miles 239	al-Ẓāhir	al-Manṣūrīah	no date	99
Miles 245	„ „	al-Mahdīyah	419	99
Miles 246	„ „	„ „	420	98
Miles 259	al-Mustanṣir (427-487/1036-1094)	al-Iskandarīyah	425	81
Miles 260	„ „	„ „	465	98
Miles 261	„ „	„ „	471	96
Miles 262	„ „	„ „	472	96
Miles 263	„ „	„ „	473	98
Miles 264	„ „	„ „	474	97
Miles 265	„ „	„	474	98
Miles 266	„ „	„ „	475	99
Miles 267	„ „	„ „	477?	98
Miles 268	„ „	„ „	478	99
Miles 269	„ „	„ „	479	98
Miles 271	„ „	„ „	483	99
Miles 272	„ „	„ „	483	97
Miles 273	„ „	„ „	484	98
Miles 274	„ „	„ „	485	98
HSA 62-107	„ „	„ „	485	98
Miles 275	„ „	„ „	486	98
Miles 276	„ „	„ „	487	98
Miles 277	„ „	Ḥalab	446	94
Miles 278	„ „	Dimishq	437	95
Miles 280	„ „	„	447	93
Miles 288	„ „	Sūr	434	98
Miles 289	„ „	„	435	97
Miles 290	„ „	„	437	98
Miles 291	„ „	„	439	98
Miles 292	„ „	„	441	96
Miles 293	„ „	„	442	97
Miles 294	„ „	„	443	97
Miles 295	„ „	„	444	96
Miles 296	„ „	„	446	95
Miles 297	„ „	„	447	97
Miles 298	„ „	„	450	96
ANS	„ „	„	458	95
Miles 300	„ „	Ṭabarīyah	439	98
ANS 62-126	„ „	„	441	94
Miles 301	„ „	„	447	98
Miles 302	„ „	Ṭarabulus	431	99
Miles 303	„ „	„	436	95
Miles 304	„ „	„	439	97
Miles 305	„ „	„	440	97

Reference	Dynasty and ruler (Dates in A. H./A. D.)	Mint Mint	A. H. A. H.	Fineness of gold in %
ANS	al-Mustanṣir	Ṭarabulus	442	97
Miles 306	,, ,,	,,	444	96
Miles 307	,, ,,	,,	446	96
Miles 308	,, ,,	,,	449	97
ANS	,, ,,	,,	463	98
ANS	,, ,,	,,	468	98
Miles 310	,, ,,	,,	471	98
Miles 311	,, ,,	ʿAkkā	472	98
Miles 312	,, ,,	Filasṭīn	438	96
Miles 313	,, ,,	,,	438	96
Miles 314	,, ,,	,,	443	94
Miles 345	,, ,,	,,	444	90
Miles 316	,, ,,	Miṣr	427	99
Miles 317	,, ,,	,,	428	100
Miles 318	,, ,,	,,	428	97
Miles 319	,, ,,	,,	429	98
Miles 321	,, ,,	,,	431	98
Miles 322	,, ,,	,,	431	98
Miles 324	,, ,,	,,	433	98
Miles 325	,, ,,	,,	434	100
Miles 326	,, ,,	,,	434	92
Miles 327	,, ,,	,,	435	99
Miles 328	,, ,,	,,	435	98
Miles 329	,, ,,	,,	436	99
Miles 330	,, ,,	,,	437	79
Miles 331	,, ,,	,,	438	99
Miles 332	,, ,,	,,	439	99
Miles 335	,, ,,	,,	440	97
Miles 337	,, ,,	,,	441	99
Miles 338	,, ,,	,,	442	99
Miles 339	,, ,,	,,	442	98
Miles 340	,, ,,	,,	443	98
Miles 341	,, ,,	,,	443	99
Miles 342	,, ,,	,,	444	98
Miles 344	,, ,,	,,	445	99
Miles 345	,, ,,	,,	446	97
Miles 348	,, ,,	,,	447	99
Miles 349	,, ,,	,,	448	98
Miles 351	,, ,,	,,	450	99
Miles 352	,, ,,	,,	450	98
Miles 354	,, ,,	,,	451	98
Miles 355	,, ,,	,,	452	98
Miles 356	,, ,,	,,	453	98
Miles 357	,, ,,	,,	454	98

Reference	Dynasty and ruler (Dates in A. H./A. D.)	Mint	A. H.	Fineness of gold in %
Miles 358	al-Mustanṣir	Miṣr	454	99
Miles 359	,, ,,	,,	455	99
Miles 360	,, ,,	,,	456	99
Miles 361	,, ,,	,,	457	82
Miles 362	,, ,,	,,	458	98
Miles 365	,, ,,	,,	464	99
Miles 366	,, ,,	,,	466	97
Miles 367	,, ,,	,,	469	98
Miles 368	,, ,,	,,	470	98
ANS	,, ,,	,,	471	98
Miles 369	,, ,,	,,	472	97
Miles 370	,, ,,	,,	473	97
Miles 371	,, ,,	,,	474	98
ANS	,, ,,	,,	475	100
Miles	,, ,,	,,	478	98
Miles 373	,, ,,	,,	479	98
Miles 376	,, ,,	,,	481	97
Miles 377	,, ,,	,,	482	98
Miles 378	,, ,,	,,	483	97
Miles 379	,, ,,	,,	485	98
Miles 380	,, ,,	,,	486	99
ANS	,, ,,	al-Manṣūrīyah	429	98
Miles 62-126	,, ,,	,, ,,	431	99
Miles 382	,, ,,	al-Mahdīyah	455	96
	ʿAbbāsids			
UM RIC 163	al-Muktafī (289-295/902-908)	Filasṭīn	291	94
UM RIC 167	,, ,,	,,	293	95
ANS 171	,, ,,	Dimishq	295	97
UM RIC 174	al-Muqtadir (295-320/908-932)	,,	297	96
ANS 55-68	,, ,,	Filasṭīn	308	93
UM RIC 193	,, ,,	,,	319	90
	Saljūqids			
ANS	Ṭughril Beg (d. 455/1063)	al-Rayy	434	97
ANS	,, ,,	,, ,,	435	97
ANS	,, ,,	,, ,,	440	96
ANS	,, ,,	,, ,,	440	98
ANS	,, ,,	,, ,,	444	94
ANS	,, ,,	,, ,,	445	95
ANS	,, ,,	,, ,,	447	97
ANS	,, ,,	,, ,,	452	96
ANS	,, ,,	,, ,,	453	89

Reference	Dynasty and ruler (Dates in A. H./A. D.)	Mint	A. H.	Fineness of gold in %
ANS	Ṭughril Beg (d. 455/1063)	Naysābūr	432	94
ANS	,, ,,	,,	433	92
ANS	,, ,,	,,	434	93
ANS	,, ,,	,,	434	95
ANS	,, ,,	,,	435	97
ANS	,, ,,	,,	435	98
ANS	,, ,,	,,	437	93
ANS	,, ,,	,,	438	98
ANS	,, ,,	,,	439	95
ANS	,, ,,	,,	440	96
ANS	,, ,,	,,	440	94
ANS	,, ,,	,,	441	96
ANS	,, ,,	,,	441	94
ANS	,, ,,	,,	442	95
ANS	,, ,,	,,	443	95
ANS	,, ,,	,,	444	95
ANS	,, ,,	,,	445	94
ANS	,, ,,	,,	447	97
ANS	,, ,,	,,	448	97
ANS	,, ,,	,,	449	96
ANS	Alp Arslān (455-465/1063-1072)	al-Rayy	457	98
ANS	,, ,,	,, ,,	461	92
ANS	,, ,,	Iṣfahān	457?	98
ANS	,, ,,	,,	457	96
ANS	,, ,,	,,	(46)3	96
ANS	Malik Shāh (465-485/1072-1092)	al-Rayy	477	89
ANS	,, ,,	,, ,,	480	95
ANS	,, ,,	,, ,,	481	97
ANS	,, ,,	,, ,,	484	95
ANS	,, ,,	Naysābūr	471	92
ANS	,, ,,	,,	474	92
ANS	,, ,,	,,	4(75)	93
ANS	,, ,,	Iṣfahān	473	91
ANS	,, ,,	,,	475	91
ANS	,, ,,	,,	476	89
ANS	,, ,,	,,	485	95
ANS	,, ,,	Farah	475	89
	Ṭūlūnids			
ANS	Aḥmad ibn Ṭūlūn (254-270/868-884)	Miṣr	266	99
ANS	,, ,,	,,	268	82

Reference	Dynasty and ruler (Dates in A. H./A. D.)	Mint	A. H.	Fineness of gold in %
UM	Aḥmad ibn Ṭūlūn	Miṣr	269	98
UM	,, ,, ,,	,,	270	99
ANS	,, ,, ,,	,,	270	98
UM	Khumarawayh (270-282/884-895)	,,	271	99
UM	,,	,,	272	94
ANS 44/163	,,	,,	272	98
UM	,,	,,	273	94
ANS 51/146	,,	,,	273	96
UM	,,	,,	274	96
ANS	,,	al-Rāfiqah	274	92
UM	,,	Miṣr	276	98
UM	,,	,,	277	94
ANS	,,	,,	277	95
ANS	,,	al-Rāfiqah	277	95
ANS	,,	,, ,,	278	88
UM 55/68	,,	Miṣr	278	94
ANS	,,	Anṭākiyah	278	92
UM	,,	Miṣr	279	97
ANS	,,	,,	279	97
UM	,,	,,	282	97
ANS 54/119	,,	Filasṭīn	282	96
UM	Jaysh ibn Khumarawayh (282-284/895-897)	Miṣr	283	98
ANS 51/146	,, ,,	,,	284	97
UM	,, ,, ,,	,,	284	98
ANS	Hārūn ibn Khumarawayh	Ḥimṣ	285	88
UM	,, ,, ,,	Miṣr	285	96
ANS	,, ,, ,,	,,	285	96
UM	,, ,, ,,	,,	286	98
ANS	Hārūn ibn Khumarawayh	Miṣr	287	94
UM	,, ,, ,,	,,	287	98
UM	,, ,, ,,	,,	287	97
UM	,, ,, ,,	,,	288	95
ANS	,, ,, ,,	,,	288	97
UM	,, ,, ,,	,,	289	96
UM	,, ,, ,,	,,	289	94
UM	,, ,, ,,	,,	291	94
	Ikhshīdids			
ANS 57/82	Muḥammad ibn Ṭughj (323-334/935-946)	Filasṭīn	331	93
UM	,, ,, ,,	Miṣr	333	99
ANS	,, ,, ,,	,,	333	97

Reference	Dynasty and ruler (Dates in A. H./A. D.)	Mint	A. H.	Fineness of gold in %
ANS 57/82	Unūjur (334-349/946-960)	Filasṭīn	335	93
UM	,,	Miṣr	337	98
ANS 57/82	,,	Filasṭīn	337	95
ANS 55/57	,,	Miṣr	339	99
ANS 57/82	,,	Filasṭīn	341	93
UM	,,	Miṣr	342	96
ANS 55/57	,,	,,	344	98
ANS 41/19	,,	,,	345	98
UM	ʿAlī (349-355/960-966)	,,	350	97
ANS	,,	,,	351	99
ANS 57/99	,,	,,	353	98
ANS 57/82	,,	Filasṭīn	353	89
UM	,,	Miṣr	354	99
UM	Kafūr (355-357/966-968)	,,	355	98
UM	,,	,,	355	98
ANS 57/82	,,	Filasṭīn	355	92
ANS 57/99	Aḥmad ibn ʿAlī (357-358/968-969)	Filasṭīn	358	93
ANS 57/99	,, ,, ,,	,,	358	93

Abbreviations used in the above list refer to the following collections or publications of *dīnārs*:

ANS — American Numismatic Society
HSA — Hispanic Society of America
Miles — G. C. Miles, *Fāṭimid coins*, 1951
UM — University Museum in Philadelphia

VIII

EARLY ISLAMIC MINT OUTPUT

A preliminary inquiry into the methodology and application of the "Coin-die count" method

PREPARED BY A SEMINAR

at

THE UNIVERSITY OF MICHIGAN

PART I

In the spring term of 1966 the members of a seminar dealing with medieval Muslim numismatics, offered by the Department of Near Eastern Languages and Literatures of the University of Michigan [1]), decided to carry out a research project which would involve the utilization of numismatic source materials for the study of medieval Near Eastern economic history. It was also decided that the project should be so devised as to require the application of electronic computers, providing the members of the seminar with an opportunity to practice the use of modern technological devices in historical heuristic processes. In the light of such seminar desiderata, the problem of the quantitative character of medieval Islamic coinage production appeared to lend itself appropriately to such an undertaking. The present paper has been prepared by the members of the seminar [2]) in order to report on their methodological procedures and the findings resulting from their inquiry.

The Subject of Research

The project undertaken by the seminar consisted of an inquiry into the output of gold and silver coins by the mints of the Muslim Near

---

1) The members of the seminar are indebted to the Department for supporting financially the project in question.

2) The team in question consisted of the following researchers: Walter G. Andrews Jr., Jere L. Bacharach, Ellen C. Colingsworth, Andrew S. Ehrenkreutz and William E. Gohlman, all of whom are jointly responsible for this contribution.

East in the Middle Ages. The significance of any information pertaining to this problem can hardly be overestimated. To begin with, the ascertainment of such information would add to the knowledge of the actual operations of such an important economic institution as the medieval Islamic mint. The knowledge of the annual coinage production of individual mints would also shed interesting light on the circulation of precious metals, as well as on the monetary policy of the caliphate or various regional or dynastic regimes at different times in medieval history. Above all, a statistical survey of minting productivity would contribute significantly to the study of medieval Near Eastern economic history. Since the economy of the medieval Muslim empire depended on a sophisticated monetary system employing gold and silver as its official standard currency, the supply or availability of coins in circulation necessarily affected economic activities of the Near Eastern population at various levels of its social organization. The supply of coinage was of special consequence in the sphere of prices and wages, a subject particularly relevant to the study of economic history.

Whether one is concerned with production or consumption, commerce, banking or remunerable services, he must regard prices and wages as an instrumental guideline in tracing the history of economic developments. This very subject has recently attracted the attention of Orientalist historians, especially that of Professor E. Ashtor, who has devoted a series of articles to the study of prices and wages. In them he has offered interesting interpretations of their fluctuations, relying on information derived from textual evidence [1]).

1) Cf. Ashtor, "Prix et salaires à l'époque des Mameloukes", *REI*, 1950, pp. 56-71; also, "Le coût de la vie dans l'Égypte médiévale", *JESHO*, 3, 1960, pp. 56-77; "Corrections et additions", *JESHO*, 3, 1960, p. 240; also, "Essai sur les prix et les salaires dans l'empire califien", *RSO*, 36, 1961, pp. 19-69; also, "Le coût de la vie dans la Syrie Médiévale", *Arabica*, 8, 1961, pp. 59-73; also, "Le coût de la vie en Palestine au Moyen Age", *Eretz-Israel*, 7, 1963, pp. 154-64; also, "La recherche des prix dans l'Orient Médiéval. Sources, methodes et problèmes", *Studia Islamica*, 21, 1964, pp. 101-144. Also extremely relevant for the point in question is S. D. Goitein, "The exchange rate of gold and silver money in Fāṭimid and Ayyūbid times", *JESHO*, 8, 1965, pp. 1-46.

Fundamental as these contributions are, our understanding of the problem of medieval Near Eastern prices and wages will not be advanced without an inquiry into the quantitative nature of coin production. Without resorting to sophisticated equations defining the relationship between the prices and the volume of coins in circulation [1]), one may state that one of the major factors conditioning the price and wage situation in the medieval Near East was the volume of coins available for the needs of its society. One of the salient features of the monetary system of the medieval caliphate was that it depended on its own mints for coinage supply. For this reason the problem of Islamic coinage production acquires a significant status in the field of economic history. If properly investigated, it may turn out to be a tool revealing or even explaining some of the causes underlying the main currents of medieval Near Eastern economic developments. Hence, in the light of these arguments, an inquiry into the productivity of Islamic mints is fully warranted.

Problem of Sources

One of the basic difficulties of launching such an inquiry is the lack of textual information regarding the output of Islamic mints. Archival documents containing statistical registers covering minting activities of the early Islamic period are yet to be discovered. Some information pertaining to this problem can perhaps be extracted—albeit with a considerable stretch of speculative interpretation—from specialized, administrative or technological treatises. Thus, for instance, al-Nābulusī, in his *Lumaʿ al-qawānīn al-muḍīyah fī dawāwīn al-diyār al-miṣrīyah* [1]),

1) For a recent discussion of the application of economic equation formulas for the study of medieval monetary developments, see R. Kiersnowski, *Pieniądz kruszcowy w Polsce średniowiecznej*, 1960, p. 428 f. (e.g., Marx' equation as interpreted by S. Tabaczyński, "Rozwój stosunków towarowo-pieniężnych...", *Pierwsza Sesja Archeologiczna Instytutu Historii Kultury Materialnej P.A.N.*, Warszawa-Wroclaw, 1957; Fisher's equation as applied by C. Cipolla, "Encore Mohamet et Charlemagne... Déflation monétaire", *Annales (Économies — Sociétés — Civilisations)* 4, 1949.

2) Edited by Cl. Cahen, *BEO*, (l'Institut Français de Damas) 16, 1958-60, pp. 119-134; Arabic text pp. 1-78.

stressed the fact that the operations of the mint of Cairo yielded during the two years H. 636 and 637 over 80, 000 dīnārs [1]). At the time of the writing of the treatise, i.e., A. H. 637-647, the revenue of the mint declined to less than 100 dīnārs per month [2]), or 1200 a year. On the other hand, Ibn Baʿrah, writing between A.H. 615-622 [3]), stated that in his days charges levied by the sultan on gold coined in the Cairo mint were fixed at 5 p.c. By correlating the information furnished by the two authors, one is tempted to infer that the output of the mint of Cairo during the period of the Ayyūbids fluctuated between c. 800, 000 dīnārs [4]) at the peak of minting production in A.H. 636 and 637, and c. 24, 000 dīnārs in the waning days of that regime.

It is obvious that such reasoning is extremely tenuous in character, even with regard to the specific case of the output of the Ayyūbid mint of Cairo. Under no circumstances can the scanty data pertaining to the Ayyūbid coin output be applied to the production of mints operating in other regions and periods [5]).

In spite of the deplorable lack of textual source materials, an inquiry into the productivity of Islamic mints can be undertaken by resorting to numismatic evidence. Islamic numismatic sources are extremely significant because of the tremendous quantities of preserved specimens and the wealth of information which can be extracted from them. This last attribute of Islamic numismatic source materials arises from

---

1) *Supra*, p. 52 (Arab. Text)
2) *Loc. cit.*
3) Cf. A. S. Ehrenkreutz, "Extracts from the technical manual on the Ayyūbid mint in Cairo", *BSOAS*, 15, 1953, p. 423.
4) This inference is corroborated by another passage in *Kitāb lumaʿ al-qawānīn* (*ed. cit.*, p. 54 of Arab. text) according to which the minters could make a profit of as much as 600 dīnārs in three or four days. This would produce a figure of c. 531, 000 — 708, 000 dīnārs minted in a Hijrah year of 354 days.
5) The case of the mints of Kūfah, Baghdād, Samarrā, Wāsiṭ and Baṣrah, operating for the benefit of the ʿAbbāsid Caliphate, may serve as an illustration of the point in question. While the revenue yielded by these establishments in A. H. 306 has been recorded for posterity (cf., A. von Kremer, "Über das Einnahmebudget des Abbasiden-Reiches vom Jahre 306 H. (918-919)", Denkschriften der Akademie der Wissenschaften in Vienna, Phil. Hist. Klasse, 36, 1888, p. 307) it is not known what percentage of the total output of dīnārs the given amount represents.

the fact that as, a rule, gold and silver coinage dating from the classical period of the Caliphate displayed registrative inscriptions such as the nominal value of the coins, the year and the place of their issue, one or several religious quotations, usually Qur'ānic, the name of the sovereign ruler, the name of the heir apparent, the name of the local ruler or governor, and sometimes the name of the officials in charge of minting production.

Because several generations of outstanding specialists have contributed a considerable volume of pertinent numismatic literature, a copious amount of valuable information has been placed at the disposal of scholars studying medieval Near Eastern history. In the sphere of monetary history, for instance, the establishment and registration of mint names displayed by Islamic coin specimens has permitted scholars to draw general conclusions concerning the chronological and geographic evolution of medieval Near Eastern mint production. Thus it has been established that down to the rule of Hārūn al-Rashīd (A.D. 786-809) there were only three mints issuing gold coins, but by A.D. 889 (A.H. 276) the number of such mints rose to about twenty [1]). This evidence suggests that in the ninth century of the Christian era, there took place a decentralization and probably intensification of gold coinage production in the Muslim Empire.

Unfortunately, in spite of the availability of valuable numismatic sources, no attempt has been made to exploit them for a more specific and analytical study of medieval Near Eastern minting production. That a great deal can be achieved in this respect has been demonstrated by the project undertaken by the members of this seminar, who decided to utilize Islamic numismatic source materials for the application of the "coin-die count" method.

The "Coin-die Count" Method

In recent years quite a number of monetary historians have approached the problem of the estimation of ancient and medieval European coinage production by means of the "coin-die count" method. Roughly

1) Cf., G. C. Miles, *The numismatic history of Rayy*, 1950, p. 119.

speaking, this method involves two basic phases: (I) The estimation of the number of dies (*V*) [1]) employed in the production of a coinage series, and (II) the estimation of the quantity of coins (*b*) which the dies were capable of producing. The product of *V* x *b* would indicate the quantity (Q) of coins manufactured in the series in question.

Phase (I) calls for the discernment of traces of coin die variants in a random sample of specimens belonging to a series. The ratio of coin die variants to the number of random samples has been accepted as a basis for calculations aiming at a statistical estimate of the actual number of dies involved in the production of the series [2]).

Phase (II) involves the multiplication of the total of estimated dies by the average number of coins which these dies were capable of producing. However, the problem of estimating the capacity or longevity of coin dies can hardly, if at all, be resolved. "We have no means of calculating the length of life of a die in ancient times", G. F. Hill observed pessimistically [3]). According to S. Suchodolski, coin dies used in the tenth and eleventh century European mints produced around 3, 000 coins [4]). To quote D. M. Metcalf: "... numismatists have not yet resolved their differences of opinion, although there is now a much better consensus than there was even as recently as five years ago. It seems that in the fourteenth century an upper, or reverse, die (which was the one that wore out more quickly) might be used to produce as many as 10, 000 coins; and recent experiments in the manufacture and use of dies similar to those produced in a medieval mint have gone far to confirm such a figure" [5]).

---

1) These symbols are borrowed from L. Brunetti, "Die Höchstwahrscheinlichkeit bei statistischen Problemen der Numismatik", *Jahrbuch für Numismatik und Geldgeschichte*, 15, 1965, p. 53.

2) D. M. Metcalf, "How large was the the Anglo-Saxon Currency?", *The Economic History Review*, 18, iii, 1965, pp. 476-477.

3) G. F. Hill, "Ancient methods of coining", *NC*, 5th ser., 2, 1922, p. 23.

4) S. Suchodolski, "Z badań nad techniką bicia monet we Wczesnym Średniowieczu", *Wiadomości numizmatyczne*, 3, 1959, p. 38.

5) D. M. Metcalf, art. cit., p. 477. Yet another formula was proposed by L. Brunetti, "Über eine Formel zur Berechnung der ungefähren Stempel-Schlagzahl", *Jahrbuch für Numismatik und Geldgeschichte*, 15, 1965, pp. 65-74. The fallacy of that

The "Coin-die Count" Method as Applied by the Seminar

Although the members of the seminar have considered the various aspects of the "coin-die count" method, the focus of their present research has been on phase I, i.e., the establishment of the number of dies employed in Islamic mint production. In carrying out this task, the seminar did not attempt to go beyond the detection of die variants traceable in examined coin specimens. Appealing though they may be, statistical computative reconstructions were not resorted to. Apart from certain difficulties of a practical nature, these procedures were rejected on the grounds of their being somewhat incompatible with the principles of moderation which modern historians should try to adhere to in their research activities. Because of the wide dispersion of existing Islamic coin specimens, it was impossible for a research group, operating from a university campus, to survey a large number of samples belonging to a single homogeneous series required for the application of statistical formulas. However, analytical descriptions or photographic reproductions of a selective body of Islamic coins, found in various museum catalogues or relevant numismatic literature, have made it possible to estimate coin-die variations without speculative calculation.

Obviously, with such limitations the project in question could not produce conclusions concerning the total number of dies, but it could definitely assert the at least such-and-such number of dies had been in use, as demonstrated and proven by available evidence. This cautious procedure is of great significance from the point of view of its consequences for immediate inquiry into the productivity of Islamic mints, as well as for other related interpretative inquiries pertaining to monetary developments. Thus, instead of furnishing a body of conclu-

---

pseudo-scientific formula has been demonstrated by D. G. Sellwood, "Some experiments in Greek minting technique", *Numismatic Chronicle*, 7th ser. 3, 1963, pp. 218 and 229-230. For the most recent discussion of the problem of various formulae for establishing die totals see Ph. Grierson, "Byzantine coinage as source material", Thirteenth International Congress of Byzantine Studies, Oxford, 1966, *Main Papers*, X, pp. 1-17.

sions resting on speculative, quicksand foundations, this research has aimed at compiling informative data based on the solid ground of historical evidence. Additional data may reduce or expand the size of this base, but it won't affect a bit its testimonial integrity.

By studying die variants discernible on coins produced by the same mints over longer periods of time, one can readily establish trends in mint production. For example, a decrease or increase in the number of die variants, as evidenced by available coin specimens struck by the mint of Damascus or Wāsiṭ over a period of several decades or centuries, may be regarded as an indication of a decrease of increase in the mint output of Damascus or Wāsiṭ. Such a method falls short of compiling the totals of mint production, but it is more informative than generalizations based on the number of mints in operation [1]).

This attitude of methodological wariness has influenced the seminar in its consideration of phase II, i.e., the estimation of the longevity or productivity of coin-dies. As mentioned above [2]), this problem is determined by the average number of coins struck by coin-dies (symbolized by *b*). In the case of this seminar's interests the question is: How many coins were struck by medieval Islamic dies? How many by the reverse, how many by the obverse dies? The figure of 10, 000 coins advocated by Metcalf may be plausible, but it refers to Anglo-Saxon coinage production [3]). Since nothing is known about the longevity of Near Eastern dies, the application of the formula $V \times b$ proves to be impossible.

Description of Seminar Procedures

Although it is hoped that this inquiry will be continued to eventually cover the entire scope of medieval Near Eastern monetary production, the present research has been concerned with the initial phase of its history, beginning with transitional Arab-Byzantine and Arab-Sasanian issues, and ending with the last Umayyad coins of A. H. 132. Further-

1) See above, p. 216.
2) See above, p. 217.
3) See above, p. 217.

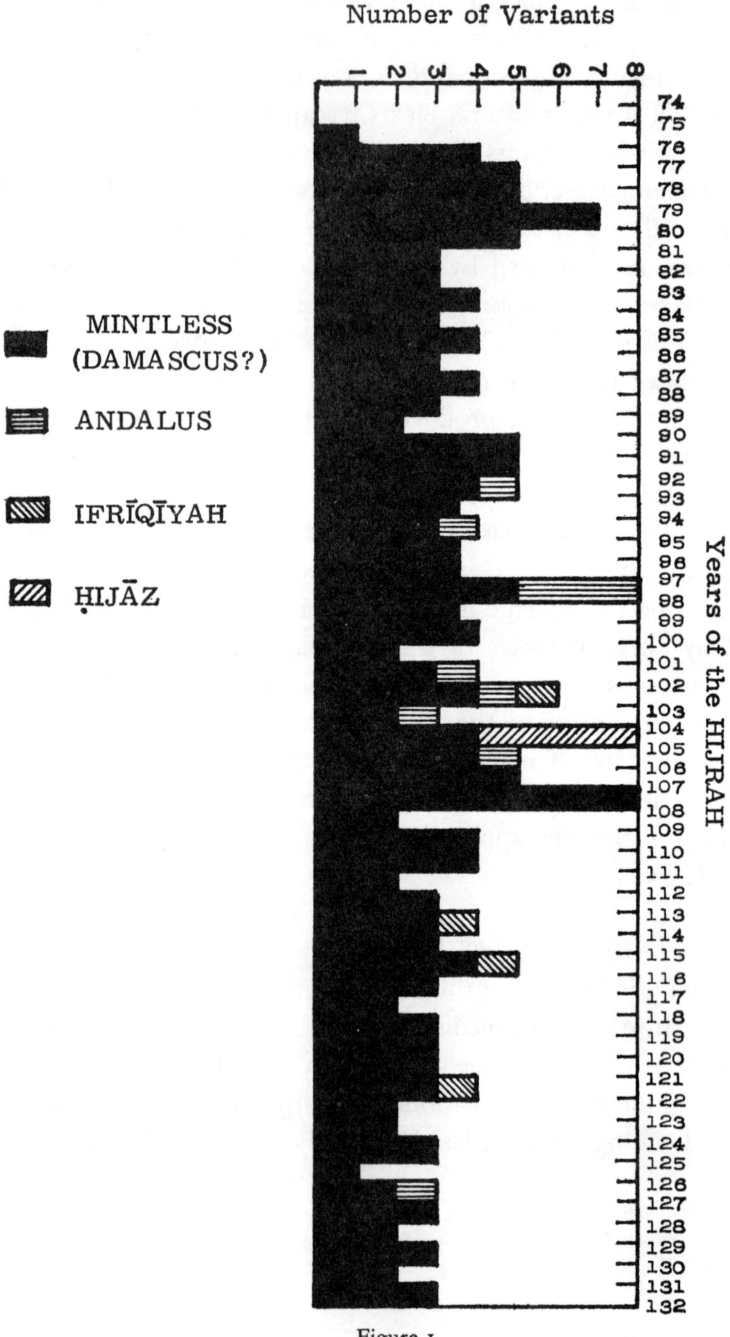
Number of Variants
1
2
3
4
5
6
7
8
MINTLESS (DAMASCUS?)
ANDALUS
IFRĪQĪYAH
ḤIJĀZ
Years of the HIJRAH
74
75
76
77
78
79
80
81
82
83
84
85
86
87
88
89
90
91
92
93
94
95
96
97
98
99
100
101
102
103
104
105
106
107
108
109
110
111
112
113
114
115
116
117
118
119
120
121
122
123
124
125
126
127
128
129
130
131
132

Figure 1

more, this investigation has been limited to the official coinage, i.e., gold coins or *dīnārs* and silver coins or *dirhams*. Except for some specimens from the collection of the Kelsey Museum of Archaeology of The University of Michigan [1]), the entire body of numismatic materials has been examined by means of published information found mainly in the contributions of the late John Walker, George C. Miles, and ʿAbd al-Raḥmān Fahmī [2]). Two teams made up of members of the seminar alternated in two three-hour sessions a week, scrutinizing these materials in an attempt to detect every possible trace of coin die variations. Certain basic variations could easily be established because of registrative inscriptions such as personal names appearing on transitional coins, the mint names shown by reformed Umayyad dirhams, and the date listings displayed by both the reformed dirhams and dīnārs of the pre-ʿAbbāsid period. The difficulty consisted of trying to discern die variants in coins belonging to the same metallic, denominational, mint and date categories. Certainly, some characteristic marks of distinction are pointed out in the literature consulted. Unfortunately, in the case of apparently identical coins, the authors of the materials under study have frequently failed to indicated or to notice any evidence of difference between dies responsible for the production of such specimens [3]).

In studying these materials, the researchers have quickly learned not to trust coin descriptions consisting of summary "*like* . . ." or "*as*. . ." statements referring to earlier prototypes [4]). Far from being satisfied

---

1) The seminar members wish to express their gratitude to the staff of the museum, for many instances of cooperation and of cordial encouragement.

2) For the complete bibliographical list and abbreviations concerning the published materials utilized in this research, see below, p. 240.

3) This remark should not be understood as an accusation of carelessness or inaptitude levelled against the established authorities in the field of Islamic numismatics. The blame rests with scholars studying monetary and economic developments of Islamic Near East, who have failed to utilize or to insist upon the supply of more detailed and analytical information pertaining to numismatic source materials.

4) A typical example of such a summary treatment is found in *Fahmī*, where descriptions of hundreds of obverses of reformed Umayyad dīnārs are dispensed with by means of a reference to the obverse description of the first Umayyad dīnār

with such a perfunctory treatment of coin descriptions, the members of the seminar decided to scrutinize available reproductions of relevant coins in order to establish die variants other than the ones indicated by the authors of the consulted materials. This method involved a meticulous inspection of each available reproduction by means of the naked eye, the magnifying glass and the screen projector. A special plastic transparent gadget, facetiously referred to as the "numolabe", and based on the inscription distribution dial devised by Walker [1]), was used to detect the minutest epigraphical deviations in the inscriptions of seemingly identical coins. Only upon the most detailed analysis of all relevant aspects were coins declared as identical or diverse.

Each coin betraying traces of an original die (obverse, reverse, or both) was carefully registered on a numbered index card. The specifications recorded referred to the metallic type (*dīnār* or *dirham*), monetary denomination (full, half, third or quarter *dīnār* or *dirham*), the name of the caliph (or countercaliph, e.g., ʿAbd Allāh ibn al-Zubayr) and that of the governor (if appearing on coins), the province, mint and the date of striking, the uniqueness of the obverse and reverse of the coin (for the purpose of recording consistency the side with the date notation has been treated as the reverse of a coin), and finally the bibliographical reference. The total number of index cards produced by this research has reached 1, 440. The total number of die variants recorded for the period A.H. 31-132 amounts to 2, 440.

It is obvious that with the great diversity of the basic categories of marshalled evidence (*dīnārs*, *dirhams*, their denominational subunits, different mints, and, above all, over one hundred years of annual

---

specimen listed in that catalogue. The following table based on the contribution of Dr. Fahmī (pp. 309-323) may serve as a relevant illustration:

	Catalogued dīnārs, Islamic Museum Cairo								
A.H.	111	112	113	114	115	116	117	118	119
Holdings	36	18	16	33	32	39	64	44	39
Photographs or Detailed Descriptions	2	1	1	1	2	1	1	1	2

1) *Cf.*, Walker II, p. 84.

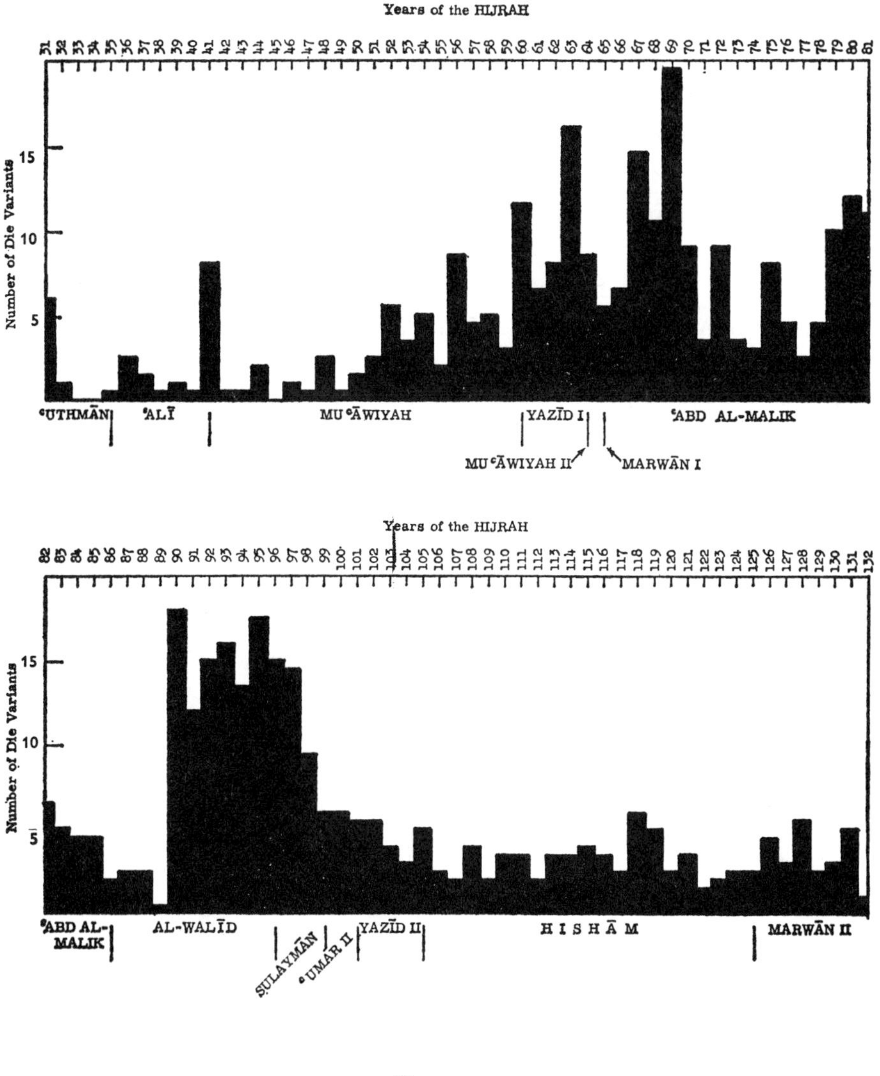
Years of the HIJRAH
Number of Die Variants
ᶜUTHMĀN
ᶜALĪ
MUᶜĀWIYAH
YAZĪD I
ᶜABD AL-MALIK
MUᶜĀWIYAH II
MARWĀN I
Years of the HIJRAH
Number of Die Variants
ᶜABD AL-MALIK
AL-WALĪD
SULAYMĀN
ᶜUMAR II
YAZĪD II
HISHĀM
MARWĀN II

Figure 2

differentiation) the task of processing these data for purposes of historical interpretation would have presented an enormous task if undertaken by ordinary means of tabulation. However, as mentioned above [1]), the seminar members resorted to electronic computers to carry out this tedious task. The results obtained from this experiment proved to be extremely rewarding. It is true that preparatory activities were time consuming. A special numerical code had to be devised into which the data from the index cards had to be converted [2]). The codified body of these data was recorded on working computer sheets. These sheets were then turned over to professional key punch typists who produced special computer punch cards. Once these punched cards were ready, the computer programming phase followed [3]). The culminating moment came with feeding the computer with punch cards which were processed in accordance with the arranged programming. It took only 1 minute 20. 7 seconds to process and type data consisting of 2,756 lines presented on 53 pages [4]). These results speak for themselves. The value of computers in historical research, whenever large volumes of data are involved, can hardly be disputed.

Part II

The preliminary step in the surveying of the following data consisted of the definition of the die heads themselves. The obverse die is the one which produces the obverse of a coin and the reverse die is responsible for the reverse of a coin. But which is the obverse and reverse face in Islamic coinage? Numismatists of the Classical Period have esta-

---

1) See above, p. 221.

2) In working on this phase of the research the seminar members have greatly depended on a valuable study of Jeanette Wakin, *The Coinage of the Ayyūbids*, 1963, examining the application of electronic computers for the treatment of numismatic materials. This extremely important contribution produced in the course of the annual seminar at the American Numismatic Society has not yet appeared in a published form.

3) We wish to thank Mr. Robert Blue for carrying out the difficult task of programming our data.

4) Special thanks are recorded herewith, to the Office of Academic Research and the Computing Center of the University of Michigan for allowing and financing all the computer and editing operations involved in this research.

blished which side is the obverse side, but Islamic numismatists have not. Traditionally they have defined the face with "lā ilāh illā Allāh. . ." in the center as the obverse [1]). According to this convention the mint and date specification, if registered, of the Umayyad gold appear on the reverse, while those of the Post-Reform Umayyad silver are displayed on the obverse. Using Umayyad gold as a starting point it has been decided to regard the dated side of the coins as the reverse and the dateless side as the obverse, rather than to rely on the traditional definition [2]).

The position of the die affects its life as the bottom die is held in place in a block to give it support. Also the top die receives the full force of the hammer blow while the bottom die is protected from the direct hammer blow by the coin flan. This protected position of the bottom die has led numismatists to estimate that the comparative lives of a top die to a bottom die is 2 : 1 [3]).

As mentioned it has been assumed that the dated side of the Umayyad coinage was the reverse and as such, it had to be produced by the top die. The reasoning behind this assumption is that for every new Muslim year, at least one new die had to be cut with the new date on it. This means that if we had at least one dīnār for every year from A.H. 76 to 132 and no other information, we would have had a minimum of 57 reverse or top and one obverse or bottom die variants. Consequently, for the production of the reverses the less durable or the top die was probably used.

---

1) Even this general rule is not always true as the recent catalogue of Dr. Paul Balog, *The Coinage of Mamlūk Egypt and Syria*, A.N.S. Studies # 12, New York, 1964, where he defines the obverse as the side with the name of the ruler.

2) If one was to follow the traditional definition the date would appear on reverse of the dīnārs and the obverses of the dirhams until the reign of the ʿAbbāsid caliph al-Muʿtaṣim (A. H. 218-227/A.D. 833-842) when the mint and date appear on the traditional obverse for both dīnārs and dirhams.

3) *Cf.*, D. G. Sellwood, "Some experiments in Greek minting technique," *Numismatic Chronicle*, 7th ser., 3, 1963, p. 230.

Table I: Summary of Totals

	Number of coins examined	Obverse die variants	Reverse die variants
Gold	248	164	240
Silver	1192	958	1078
Totals	1140	1122	1318

As can be seen from Table I, it has been possible to identify 1318 reverse and 1122 obverse die variants out of a total sample of 1140 pre-Umayyad and Umayyad Islamic coins. Unfortunately, the data compiled in this tabulation is not sufficient to test the hypothesis concerning the identification of the upper and the bottom dies. This shortcoming derives from the fact that consulted catalogues and articles do not treat both sides of the coins equally, giving very brief descriptions of the obverses and even fewer photographs. It is not unusual to have photographs of unique reverses, which are known to be different, and none of the obverses, which are listed as "similar to above" [1]).

Consequently, the apparent discrepancy between the reverse and obverse die variants revealed by our research should not be attributed to a lesser frequency of the obverses but to a lesser number of obverse specimens available for examination. It is hoped that future research will encompass more evidence to allow the testing of our working hypothesis.

What this research has demonstrated is the very existence of a considerable number of die variations. This conclusion is important for our understanding of medieval minting techniques, more particularly of the method in which the dies were manufactured. If the dies were cast from a master mold as P. Balog suggested [2]), then we should have had only 57 reverse die variants for the mintless dīnārs from A.H. 76 to 132, plus a few from North Africa and Spain, rather than the 240 variants recorded. The project reveals that dies from the

1) See above, p. 218.

2) *Cf.*, P. Balog, "Notes on Ancient and Medieval minting technique", *Numismatic Chronicle*, 6th ser., 16, 1955, p. 196.

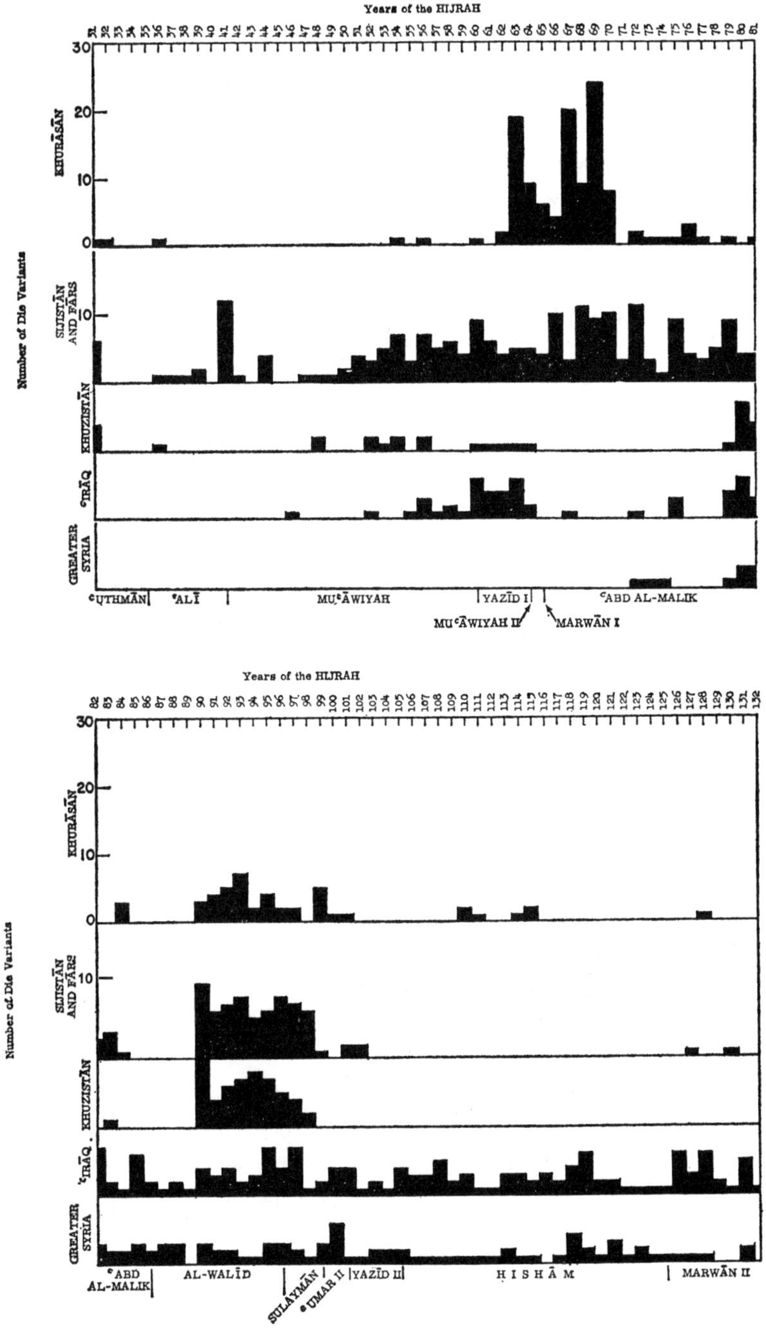
Years of the HIJRAH
Number of Die Variants
KHURĀSĀN
SIJISTĀN AND FĀRS
KHUZISTĀN
ʿIRĀQ
GREATER SYRIA
ʿUTHMĀN
ʿALĪ
MUʿĀWIYAH
YAZĪD I
ʿABD AL-MALIK
MUʿĀWIYAH II
MARWĀN I
ʿABD AL-MALIK
AL-WALĪD
SULAYMĀN
ʿUMAR II
YAZĪD II
HISHĀM
MARWĀN II

Figure 3

same mint and year are different and therefore each of them must have been cut independently from one another.

Of the 248 gold coins for which there was enough information available to determine whether they were prototypes, 216 were dīnārs, 8 were half-dīnārs, 20 were third-dīnārs and 4 were of an odd weight class [1]). These totals set the absolute limitations on the number of die variants for each category. Disregarding the last group the number of die variants found were as follows:

Table II Gold Die Variants, A.H. 76-132

	Sample Size	*Obverses*	*Reverses*
Dīnār	216	136	208
Half-dinār	8	8	8
Third-dīnār	20	16	20
Totals	244	150	236

If we consider the number of reverse die variants as a percentage of the number of coins in each category, the reverse die variants represent the following percentages: dīnārs—91.6%; half-dīnārs—100%; third-dīnārs—100%; and the total reverse variants—96.7%. The half-dīnārs and third-dīnārs were minted in North Africa and Spain between A.H. 90 and 106 [2]). For a study of die variations it is important to note that in the case of these fractional dīnārs the number of reverse variants is maximal. The total of 208 whole dīnār variants or 91.6% of the total reflects the great variety of die production. The ultimate aim of this type of study from a methodological point of view is to obtain a sample so large that the percentage of die variants to the total drops to the point where it can be assumed that most of the die variants have been examined.

The 208 dīnār reverse variants include 190 mintless dīnārs, probably minted in Damascus, and 18 from the Ḥijāz, North Africa and Spain. Four of the latter group are from "Maʿdin Amīr al-Muʾminīn bi'l-

---

1) Miles, *RIC*, no. 54. Lane-Poole, ix, nos. 73, 74, 75.
2) Walker, ii, pl lvii.

Ḥijāz" (The Mine of the Commander of the Faithful in the Ḥijāz) and are dated A.H. 105. The rest are from the mints "Ifrīqīyah" and "al-Andalus" and were minted between A.H. 93 and 127 [1]).

The following bar graph represents the total number of reverse die variants for gold by years with the variants for Ḥijāz, North Africa and Spain indicated. (See Figure I.).

The most obvious trend is the relative consistency of the graph which is characterized by very few high or low points. If the reverse variants of the mintless dīnārs were evenly distributed, each year would have a little over three variants. The long period after A.H. 81 when the number of variants fluctuates between two and four (A.H. 91, 92, 98, 107, 108, and 126 excepting) shows an even distribution. Unlike the silver die variants below there is no sharp decline in the late 80's nor a major rise in the 90's. It would be tempting to conclude that with such a centralized production the output of gold during the Umayyad period was consistent, and unaffected by political and economic changes. But does this chart represent the real mint output as a function of die variants? Unfortunately, the limited nature of the published sources available for this research does not allow us to answer this question [2]).

Dirham Die Variants

As can be seen from Table I, the total sample of Islamic silver coins struck during the pre-Umayyad and Umayyad period consisted of 1192 specimens. The year of the issue of 42 of these coins could not be established. In addition one coin, struck in Baṣrah in A.H. 81, represented a rather unusual half dirham specimen. The remaining 1149 coins revealed 919 obverse and 1039 reverse die variants. Adopting always the higher number for statistical purposes, one may state that the total of 1039 reverse die variants constitutes 90. 4% of the considered silver coins. The distribution of these variants is presented in the following table:

---

1) "Ifrīqīyah": A.H. 103, 114, 117, 122. "al-Andalus": A.H. 93, 95, 98 (3 variants), 102, 103, 104, 106, 127.

2) See above, p. 220.

Table III Distribution of Dirham Die Variants

	Gd. Tot.	Pre-Umayyad A.H. 31-41	Umayyad Total	Umayyad A.H. 42-80*	Umayyad A.H. 81-132**
obverse	919	40	879	424	455
reverse	1039	40	999	425	574

* Before the reform of ʿAbd al-Malik
** After the reform

Upon studying the distribution of these die variants one notices an interesting pattern. The examined dirhams from the first decade of the Muslim mint activities revealed 40 obverse and 40 reverse die variants. The specimens produced during the nine decades of the Umayyad period yielded 879 obverses and 999 reverses, or an average of 97.6 and 111 variants respectively per decade. The obverse average is over twice as large as that of the pre-Umayyad decade, and the reverse average is almost three times as high.

A comparison of the average number of die variants shows no discrepancy between the pre-reform and post-reform Umayyad specimens. Using the reverses as our sample one can observe that 425 variants belong to the four pre-reform decades, and 574 to the subsequent five decades, or an average of about 110 and 112 variants per decade respectively. This statistical comparison appears to indicate that the great coinage reform of ʿAbd al-Malik did not produce any detectable increase in the number of dies used in mint production. Unless a more durable material was introduced for the manufacturing of the dies, one may infer on the basis of this sample that the output of the Islamic mints did not increase as a result of the otherwise dramatic reform.

In spite of the apparent stability which these totals suggest, a detailed scrutiny of these samples, on a year to year basis, reveals significant fluctuations in their annual distribution. Thus the number of the die variants coming from the first 20 years of the Muslim mint production (A.H. 31-50) is very low, the highest frequency group consisting of one variant only. In spite of this low number of die variants the overall totals for the first decade amount to 40. This is caused by the fact that as many as 12 die variants have been established in the coins struck in

A.H. 31, and 16 in those produced in A.H. 41, or the year of the end of the orthodox and the beginning of the Umayyad caliphate.

On the other hand, a high number of dies has been detected in the group of coins struck during the period extending from A.H. 56-71. In that period the lowest number of die variants for a single year is 6 (A.H. 59) and the highest 39 (A.H. 69). The coins struck in A.H. 61 and 66 revealed 13 die variants for each year; those issued in A.H. 56 and 64 yielded 17 specimens each. The number of die variants in the remaining coins from that period fluctuated from 9 to 31 a year. A similar high level period extended from A.H. 78-85. The lowest number of die variants detected in the silver coinage of that period amounted to 9, occurring three times, in A.H. 78, 84, 85. The specimens struck in A.H. 79, 80, 81 showed successively 20, 24, and 22 variants. It is appropriate to mention that the period of A.H. 78-85 corresponds to the years of the implementation of the great coinage reform of ʿAbd al-Malik. Even more significant is the fact that the number of dirhams struck during the following Hijrah years 86-89, during which the reform must have come into effect, drastically contrasts with those of the preceding period. There were four die variants in A.H. 86 (the year of transition from ʿAbd al-Malik to al-Walīd), 5 each for A.H. 87 and 88, and one, one single die variant for A.H. 89.

Beginning with the dirhams of A.H. 90 a new high is revealed, which extends through the dirhams of A.H. 105. The minimum group of less than 10 die variants occurs only twice, in A.H. 100 (8 variants) and 104 (6 variants). A group of 10 die variants is represented by A.H. 105 dirhams. All other years of this period are represented by more than 10 die variants, 5 different years showing groups belonging to a category containing 11-20 variants, and 8 years with over 20 die variants each. The peak in this period is represented by the coins of A.H. 90 (36 variants) which open an unusually high series: A.H. 91—24; 92—30; 93—32; 94—27; 95—35; 96—30; 97—29; 98—29.

Finally the coinage struck during the remaining phase of the Umayyad regime (A.H. 106-132) shows a steady series of smaller die variant groups. The minimum group is constituted by one variant (A.H. 126)

the year of rapid changes in the office of the caliphate (al-Walīd II, Yazīd III, Ibrāhīm). The largest group consists of 12 variants (A.H. 118), followed by that of 11 (A.H. 128), 10 (A.H. 119 and 131). The size of the remaining groups fluctuates from 2 to 9 die specimens, the most frequent groups consisting of 7 (A.H. 110, 111, 113, 114, 116, 121) and 5 die variants (A.H. 106, 117, 120, 124, 125, 128). The fluctuations in the number of die variants during the entire period are illustrated by means of the following graph:
(See Figure II)

Geographic Distribution of Established Die Variants

As was to be expected, an overwhelming majority of geographically identifiable dirhams comes from the Eastern regions of the caliphate. Of the total of 921 obverse and 1049 reverse die variants only 104 or 11. 2% obverses and 138 or 13. 1% reverses were produced outside the former Sasanid areas. Western regions (Spain and North Africa) are represented by 29 obverse and 51 reverse die variants, or 3. 1% of 4. 8% respectively of the total sample. Central regions (Egypt, Greater Syria, Ḥijāz and Yaman) account for 75 or 8. 1% of the obverse and 87 or 8. 3% of the reverse die variants. With the exception of six specimens produced in Greater Syria between A.H. 72-80, all of these non-Eastern die variants belong to the post-reform Umayyad period. Considering that the bulk of the die variants consists of the "Eastern" specimens the pattern of mint production in those broad geographic areas parallels the trends discussed in the preceding section.

Some interesting observations can be made, however, upon studying the distribution of the die variants according to more specific provincial criteria. Thus five provincial areas may be singled out because of a considerable number of their die variants. They are: Sijistān and Fārs with 302, ʿIrāq with 183, Khurāsān with 147, Greater Syria with 86, and Khuzistān with 83 die variants. Of those, Khurāsām, Khuzistān, Sijistān and Fārs are represented by die variant specimens dating from the very beginning of Islamic mint production, i.e., A.H. 31. However, the die variants from Khurāsān and Khuzistān in the pre-

Umayyad period constitute rather rare phenomena. A continuous series from Khurāsān begins only with A.H. 62 and ends with A.H. 70. This period is characterized by an unusually high frequency of the Khurā sānian die variants: 2 in A.H. 62; 19 in 63; 9 in 64; 6 in 65; 4 in 66; 20 in 67; 9 in 68; 24 in 69; and 8 in A.H. 70. Another concentration of the die variants from that province spreads over the years A.H. 90-97. In A.H. 90—3 die variants; 91—4; 92—5; 93—7;94—2;95—4; 96—2; 97—2. With the conclusion of that phase the die variants from Khurāsān hardly ever occur. Only 11 obverses and 14 reverses belong to the entire period of the last 35 years of the Umayyad regime. As for the specimens from Khuzistān, they show two series of die variant concentrations. There is a brief spell of three years: A.H. 79 with one variant; 80 with 7; and A.H. 81 with 4 die variants A longer one, stretching from A.H. 90-98, is represented by the following numbers of die specimens: A.H. 90—10; 91—4; 92—6; 93—7; 94—8; 95—7; 96—5; 97—4; 98—2. The die variants from A.H. 98 constitute the last Umayyad specimens from Khuzistān.

In contrast with Khurāsān and Khuzistān, the specimens from the Sijistān and Fārs area show a long uninterrupted series of die variants spreading over a long period of 38 years, from A.H. 47 to A.H. 84. The highest frequency group is made up of four specimens, occurring eight times in A.H. 51, 59, 62, 65, 76, 80, 81, 83. The largest number of die variants in one year consists of 11 specimens, occurring twice in A.H. 68 and 72. Single die variants occur only five times, twice at the beginning (A.H. 47, 48, 49) and twice toward the end (A.H. 74, 84) of that series. Another concentration of die variants is shown by the years A.H. 90-98. This series runs as follows: A.H. 90—11 die variants; 91—7; 92—8; 93—9; 94—6; 95—7; 96—9; 97—7; 98—7. In spite of the sharp difference in the total numbers the chronological distribution of the die variants from the three areas shows two common characteristics. Thus no specimens from either Sijistān and Fārs or Khurāsān and Khuzistān occur between A.H. 85-89. (In the case of Khurāsān that pause includes A.H. 84 as well). Furthermore, the occurrence of the die variants from those provinces ceases with A.H. 100.

Isolated specimens that belong to the last 32 years of the Umayyad dynasty constitute exceptions to the rule.

It is precisely in this respect that the die variants from Greater Syria and ʿIrāq differ from those of the above discussed areas. The first established dirhams from ʿIrāq date from A.H. 46, the Syrian ones come from A.H. 72. A continuous series of the die variants from ʿIrāq begins in A.H. 80 and runs through A.H. 132. That from Greater Syria opens in A.H. 79 and continues till the end of the Umayyad regime, except for A.H. 89, 116, 129, 130, and 132. One can see then that whereas the Eastern provincial areas are not represented in the last three decades of the Umayyad regime, this situation does not apply to ʿIrāq and Greater Syria.

As for the interesting period between A.H. 85-89, i.e., the period almost immediately following the reform of ʿAbd al-Malik, characterized by the lack of die variant specimens from Eastern provinces, one can observe the following trend in the distribution of the samples from Greater Syria and ʿIrāq. The die variants from Greater Syria occur at their usual low level of frequency (one to three die variants) in every one of the significant years, with the exception of A.H. 89 which is not represented by a single specimen. As for ʿIrāq, this period is preceded by a relatively high level series: A.H. 79—4 die variants; 80—6; 81—3; 82—7. This is followed by a drop to two die variants in A.H. 83, and to one in A.H. 84. A.H. 85 is marked by six obverse and four reverse specimens. Beginning with A.H. 86 and ending with A.H. 89 there occurs another decline: A.H. 86—2; 87—1; 88—2; 89—1 die variant. Significantly enough, as in the case of the Eastern specimens, the occurrence of ʿIrāq die variants picks up beginning with A.H. 90. All these trends are illustrated by means of the following graph. (See Figure III.).

Distribution of Coinage by Mint and Governor

During the period A.H. 31-80, coin production seems to be characterized by marked fluctuations in output over relatively short intervals of time. While totals indicated an average of more than nine die variants (obverse or reverse) per year from 34 mints, most of them located in the eastern provinces, totals in certain ten-year periods rise to an average of as much as 19 variants per year. The production totals of individual mints show the same significant fluctuations. No single mint produces with any consistency throughout this time and while Dārābjird, Nahr-Tīrā and Bishāpūr are responsible for about 50% of die variants examined even these mints seem to have had periods of very high and very low levels of production.

In this respect it is significant to note that in this period some 80% of coins appearing in the totals bear the names of provincial governors representing factions supporting either the Umayyad Caliphate or the Counter-caliphate of ʿAbd Allāh ibn al-Zubayr. It is, therefore, possible to assert that political pressures and conflicts may have been responsible for the uneven pattern of coinage production during this time, since high levels of production coincide with periods of intense competition in the eastern provinces.

One such high point occurring in the period A.H. 60-71 serves as an example of the effects of competition on coinage production. During this time Salm ibn Ziyād's governorship in Kurāsān was threatened by partisans of the rebel Ibn al-Zubayr and all but ended (A.H. 64) by Ibn Khāzim who governed the province until A.H. 71 in the name of the counter-caliphate. As a result of the appearance of coinage issued bearing the names of both rival governors the average number of die variants rises to approximately 19 as compared to nine for the whole period.

During the period A.H. 78-84 minting activity was relatively high, with 30 mints in operation. The most prolific mints were those in Damascus and Baṣrah, while the total number of die variants for this period is 93 obverse and 107 reverse, or approximately 13 obverse and 15 reverse per year. The next period, A.H. 85-89, shows a drastic reduction in output, with only five mints in operation. The locus of operations also shifted from such mints as Nahr-Tīrā, Bishāpūr, and Dārābjird to Damascus and Wāsiṭ, the two Umayyad administrative centers, which together produced more than 80% of the samples

Table IV

				Mu'awiyah II, Marwān I										
		*		Yazīd I		**		*				'Abd al-Malik		
		60	61	62	63	64	65	66	67	68	69	70	71	72
Dārābjird	obv	0	0	1	2	1	3	1	0	6	3	0	1	6
	rev	2	0	1	2	2	4	3	0	6	2	0	1	2
Nahr-Tīrā	obv	1	0	1	11	6	4	4	3	1	17	6	0	2
	rev	1	0	1	6	5	2	2	4	1	6	6	0	8
Abrashahr	obv	1	0	0	1	2	2	0	2	1	2	0	0	0
	rev	1	0	0	1	2	1	0	2	1	1	0	0	0
Bishāpūr	obv	4	3	2	1	1	0	1	3	3	2	6	2	0
	rev	3	2	2	1	1	0	1	1	3	3	4	2	0
Khurāsān	obv	2	0	2	19	9	6	4	20	9	24	8	0	2
	rev	2	0	2	13	8	3	2	18	8	12	7	0	2
Abdallah ibn Khāzim	obv	0	0	0	4	1	4	4	10	8	19	5	0	2
	rev	0	0	0	3	1	2	2	9	7	9	5	0	2
Salm ibn Ziyād	obv	0	0	1	16	8	2	0	8	1	5	3	0	0
	rev	0	0	1	11	7	1	0	7	1	3	2	0	0

Table V

								'Abd al-Malik						
		77	78	79	80	81	82	83	84	85	86	87	88	89
Al-Baṣrah	obv	0	0	1	2	3	3	0	0	0	0	0	0	0
	rev	0	0	1	2	3	5	0	0	0	0	0	0	0
Dimishq	obv	0	0	1	2	3	3	1	2	2	2	3	3	0
	rev	0	0	1	2	3	2	2	1	3	1	3	2	0
Nahr-Tīrā	obv	0	0	1	1	1	0	0	2	0	0	0	0	0
	rev	0	0	1	1	1	0	0	2	0	0	0	0	0
Wāsit	obv	0	0	0	0	0	0	0	1	6	1	1	2	1
	rev	0	0	0	0	0	0	0	1	4	2	1	1	1

analyzed, or 21 of 24 obverse and 18 of 22 reverse. The overall rate of production was five obverse and four reverse per year. The following table shows the fluctuations in the production of Baṣrah, Nahr-Tīrā, and Wāsiṭ, and the relatively steady production of Damascus during the period just prior to and at the time of the coinage reforms of ʿAbd al-Malik, A.H. 78-89.

In the period A.H. 90-101 mint activity increased sharply, reaching the highest overall rate of production during the Umayyad Caliphate. Not only was the total production high—235 obverse and 296 reverse, or 20 obverse and 25 reverse per year—but the number of mints in operation, 38, was the greatest of any period analyzed. Damascus and Wāsiṭ were leaders in production, as was Nahr-Tīrā, which returned to production along with many other mints in the eastern region of the Umayyad Caliphate. The following table shows the production of Baṣrah, Damascus, Nahr-Tīrā, and Wāsiṭ during this period:

Table VI

			Al-Walīd I				*Sulaymān			*Umar II		*
		90	91	92	93	94	95	96	97	98	99	100	101
Al-Baṣrah													
	obv	0	0	0	0	1	0	0	0	0	0	2	2
	rev	0	0	0	0	1	0	0	0	0	0	3	2
Dimishq													
	obv	2	2	1	0	0	2	3	2	1	3	6	1
	rev	3	2	2	1	1	3	3	2	1	2	5	1
Nahr-Tīrā													
	obv	4	1	2	2	2	1	2	1	0	1	1	1
	rev	2	1	3	3	2	2	2	2	0	3	1	1
Wāsiṭ													
	obv	1	3	4	1	2	3	2	1	1	1	0	1
	rev	2	2	3	1	1	4	2	1	1	2	0	1

In the last period, A.H. 102-132, production was lower than in the one immediately preceding, totalling 150 obverse and 203 reverse, or 5 and 7 per year, respectively. In addition to the lower total production the number of mints in operation declined to 13, with Damascus and Wāsiṭ together accounting for almost 50% of the production of this period. The following table shows the steady production of Damascus and Wāsiṭ and the very meager production of Baṣrah and Nahr-Tīrā.

Table VII

		Yazīd II			*					Hishām		
Al-Baṣrah		102	103	104	105	106	107	108	109	110	111	112
	obv	0	0	0	0	0	0	0	0	0	0	0
	rev	0	0	0	0	0	0	0	0	0	0	0
Dimishq												
	obv	1	1	1	2	1	0	1	1	1	1	1
	rev	1	2	2	1	1	1	1	1	1	1	1
Nahr-Tīrā												
	obv	0	0	0	0	0	0	0	0	2	0	0
	rev	0	0	0	0	0	0	0	0	2	0	0
Wāsiṭ												
	obv	0	2	1	4	3	2	2	2	2	1	1
	rev	0	2	1	2	1	1	3	1	1	1	1

Table VII (continued)

		Hishām										
Al-Baṣrah		113	114	115	116	117	118	119	120	121	122	123
	obv	0	0	0	0	0	0	0	0	0	0	0
	rev	0	0	0	0	0	0	0	0	0	0	0
Dimishq												
	obv	2	0	0	0	1	3	2	0	1	1	2
	rev	2	1	1	0	1	4	2	1	3	1	1
Nahr-Tīrā												
	obv	3	3	0	0	0	0	0	0	0	0	0
	rev	3	3	0	0	0	0	0	0	0	0	0
Wāsiṭ												
	obv	0	0	2	2	1	2	2	2	2	1	1
	rev	0	0	2	3	1	2	2	2	2	1	1

Coin Production and the Umayyads

As can be seen from the preceding discussion the tabulations of die variants confirm prevailing notions about the role of the Umayyad regime in the inception and expansion of Islamic coin production. The reigns of ʿAbd al-Malik (A.D. 685—705), al-Walīd (A.D. 705—715) and of Hishām (A.D. 724—743) appear to have particularly sig-

Table VII (continued)

		Al-Walid II, Yazid III, Ibrāhim								
		Hishām		*	**	*		Marwān II		*
Al-Baṣrah		124	125	126	127	128	129	130	131	132
	obv	0	0	0	0	1	0	0	0	0
	rev	0	0	0	0	1	0	0	0	0
Dimishq										
	obv	1	1	0	0	0	0	0	1	0
	rev	1	1	1	1	1	0	0	2	0
Nahr-Tīrā										
	obv	0	0	0	0	0	0	0	0	0
	rev	0	0	0	0	0	0	0	0	0
Wāsiṭ										
	obv	1	1	3	2	2	2	1	2	1
	rev	1	1	6	2	2	1	2	3	1

nificant in that development. ʿAbd al-Malik's rule is best remembered for the inception of purely Islamic coinage (A.H. 74-77/A.D. 693-697), an innovation dramatized by the striking of gold coinage in defiance of the hitherto respected monopoly of the Byzantine Empire. It is probably in connection with the implementation of that reform that the mint of Damascus opened regular operations. One should notice, however, that in spite of the initial surge the production of the reformed silver coinage ran into some impediments in the last years of that caliph's reign reaching its lowest level in the early years of al-Walīd. Apart from its slow start the reign of al-Walīd stands out as the most intensive period in the history of Umayyad coinage. No doubt this increase in the output of coins was accomplished by the opening of new mints. Finally, the reign of Hishām was characterized by the restriction of coin production to the mints operating in the areas remaining under the strict control of the Umayyad administration (Syria, ʿIrāq) to the exclusion of the mints in the Eastern provinces. This centralizing policy is associated with a marked decline of silver coin output.

Final Remarks Apart from the above sample results made on the basis of a preliminary analysis of early Islamic coin-die variants, one can postulate the following general conclusions:

1) Because coin-dies used for the striking of Umayyad dīnārs and dirhams were engraved separately and not passed from a single matrix, a study of die variants traceable in preserved numismatic specimens permits one to secure valid information concerning the number of dies employed in the annual production of Islamic mints.

2) To achieve meaningful results a research of this kind should encompass the largest possible number of variants in every typological, geographic, chronological and dynastic category of investigated coinage.

3) Interpretative control of data yielded by mass observation of die variants may be expediently accomplished by using electronic computers.

4) The application of the viable "coin die" method will advance our knowledge of medieval Near Eastern coinage production beyond the fallacious generalizations based solely on the total numbers and geo-chronological distribution of survived numismatic specimens.

Unfortunately, standard numismatic catalogs and publications do not provide references to every die variant traceable in the described coins. Consequently, historians interested in studying medieval coin production have either to postpone the realization of their projects until the advent of more informative and rigorous numismatic literature, or to take upon themselves the task of a direct analysis of the numismatic resources preserved in public and private collections.

BIBLIOGRAPHY AND ABBREVIATIONS

ʿAbd al-Raḥmān Fahmī, *Fajr al-sikkah al-ʿarabīyah*, al-Qāhirah, 1965. (abbr. Fahmī).

S. Lane-Poole, *Catalogue of Oriental Coins in the British Museum*, London, 1875-1888. (abbr. Lane-Poole).

H. Lavoix, *Catalogue des monnaies musulmanes de la Bibliothèque Nationale*, Paris, 1887-1894.

L. A. Mayer, "A hoard of Umayyad dinars from el Lajjūn", *The Quarterlv of the Department of Antiquities in Palestine*, 4, 1935, pp. 100-102.

G. C. Miles, "Abarqubādh, a new Umayyad mint", *Museum Notes* (The American Numismatic Society) 4, 1950, pp. 115-120.

——, *The Coinage of the Umayyads of Spain* (Hispanic Numismatic Series, Monograph # 1, part 1), New York, 1950.

——, *Excavation Coins from the Persepolis Region* (Numismatic Notes and Monographs, # 143), New York, 1959.

——, "The Iconography of Umayyad Coinage", *Ars Orientalis*, 3, 1959, pp. 207-213.

——, *Rare Islamic Coins* (Numismatic Notes and Monographs, # 118), New York, 1950. (abbr. Miles, *RIC*).
——, "Some Arab Dīnārs", *Museum Notes* (ANS) 3, 1948, pp. 93-114.
——, "Some Arab-Sasanian and Related Coins", *Museum Notes* (ANS) 7. 1957, pp. 187-209.
——, "Some New Light on the History of Kirmān in the First Century of the Hijrah", *The World of Islam. Studies in Honour of Philip K. Hitti*, London & New York, 1959, pp. 85-98.
Nasir Nakshabandi, "The Zakho Treasure", *Sumer*, 6, ii, 1950, pp. 177-188.
J. Walker, *A Catalogue of the Muhammadan Coins in the British Museum*, Vol. 1, *A Catalogue of the Arab-Sassanian Coins* (abbr. Walker, I).
——, Vol. 2. *A Catalogue of the Arab-Byzantine and Post-reform Umayyad Coins*. London, 1941-1956. (abbr. Walker, II).
——, "Oriental Coins", *British Museum Quarterly*, 21/ii, 1957, pp. 46-48.
——, "Some New Arab-Sassanian Coins", *Numismatic Chronicle*, 6th ser., 11, 1952, pp. 106-110.

IX

NUMISMATO-STATISTICAL REFLECTIONS ON THE ANNUAL GOLD COINAGE PRODUCTION OF THE ṬŪLŪNID MINT IN EGYPT*

This paper constitutes an addendum to my contribution presented at the XXIX International Congress of Orientalists in Paris [1]). I refer here to my preliminary remarks concerning a research project involving the use of the coin-die count as a method of inquiring into the annual output of Islamic mints in the Middle Ages. Among other things I stated that "the main lesson derived from this coin-die count project is that although its findings lend themselves to all sorts of statistical permutations and speculations, the annual mint samples should be substantially increased before valid historical inferences can be made" [2]). By now the number of dīnār specimens, photographed and examined for the purpose of this inquiry, has considerably increased. To the previously reported specimens from the renowned collections of New York, London, Oxford, Copenhagen, Paris, Milan, Istanbul, and Tunis, there have now been added those from the National Museum of Antiquities in Damascus, from the Th. & O. Horovitz Collection (Geneva), from a "Private French Collection", and especially from the Museum of Islamic Art in

*) An abbreviated version of this article was presented at the 30th International Congress of Human Sciences in Asia and North Africa (August, 1976, Mexico City). In collecting and interpreting the numismatic data I relied on the assistance of several of my younger colleagues, especially on Drs. W. Andrews Jr., J. L. Bacharach, W. Gohlman, A. Messier, S. Moment-Atis and L. Obler, as well as on that of my graduate students: S. Ballard, Z. Fadil, E. Heck, N. McKenzie and Lois Aroian.

1) 'Numismatics re-monetized,' *Michigan Oriental Studies in honor of George G. Cameron*, Ann Arbor, Mich., 1976, p. 207-218.

2) *Ibid.*, p. 217.

Cairo [3]). Although it would be difficult to argue that the samples of dīnārs belonging to the same mint-and-year series have reached a point at which the number of identified dies would not be affected by further additions to the sample [4]), they constitute a considerable body of numismatic evidence to warrant new methodological discussion. Furthermore, the results of my inquiry, based on an examination of Ṭūlūnid samples, seem to point to one conclusion: that under normal economic circumstances a rather limited number of dies was used for the production of gold coinage by the Ṭūlūnid mint of Egypt.

I shall begin this discussion with a consideration of two articles offering coin die statistics based on examination of two separate aggregations of Islamic silver coinage. One of them, contributed by N. M. Lowick, deals with a large number of dirhams contained in an early tenth century hoard from Isfahan [5]). The author examined the coins for die-links, or duplicate dirhams, wherever a particular mint/date combination was represented by more than one specimen. The results of his examination were tabulated as follows:

Illustration 1.

Die-links in an early Tenth Century hoard from Iṣfahān

Die-links, obverse and reverse: 53 (17 ʿAbbāsid, 36 Sāmānid)
Die-links, obverse only: 47 (16 ʿAbbāsid, 2 Ṣaffārid, 29 Sāmānid)
Die-links, reverse only: 28 (12 ʿAbbāsid, 2 Ṣaffārid, 14 Sāmānid)
Total number of coins checked for die-links: ʿAbbāsid 192, Ṣaffārid 8, Sāmānid 198, Būyid 6.

(N. M. Lowick, "An early tenth century hoard from Isfahan", *The Numismatic Chronicle*, Seventh Series, 15, 1975, p. 117)

Unfortunately the results of this analysis were disappointing as regards the possibility of considering the number of dies involved in the

3) I wish to reiterate the expressions of my gratitude to scholarly officials in charge of the respective collections, for their kind cooperation and professional assistance in carrying out the tasks in collecting my evidence. Special thanks are registered here in respect of Prof. Hassanein Rabie who was instrumental in making specimens from the Museum of Islamic Art in Cairo accessible to me.

4) "Numismatics re-monetized", p. 216.

5) N. M. Lowick, "An early tenth century hoard from Isfahan", *The Numismatic Chronicle*, Seventh Series, 15, 1975, p. 110-154.

annual production, "No consistent ratio was observed between the number of coins of a particular mint/date variety and the number of die-links in that group, doubtless because the number of specimens present was far too small to reflect the number of dies used. Die-links were found, naturally enough, to be commonest among coins of heavily represented mints: Isbahān and Shīrāz of the ʿAbbāsid mints, Samarqand and al-Shāsh of the Sāmānid mints. However, the seventy-eight Baghdad coins yielded only one die-linked pair . . . a pointer to what must have been the truly enormous output of the ʿAbbāsid capital" [6]).

On the other hand, the late George C. Miles carried out a very laborious and meticulous die examination of no less than 685 dirhams struck in A.H. 400 = A.D. 1009/1010 by the mint of Cordoba [7]). Quantitative results of his inquiry he tabulated as follows:

Illustration 2.

The production of dirham dies in Spain in the year 400 H.

Mint	Ruler	Days	No. of recorded specimens	Min. no. obv. dies	Min. no. rev. dies	Min. total no. of dies
Al-Andalus	Muhammad II 1st reign	76	264	38	43	72
Al-Andalus	Sulayman	ca. 88	237	31	14	45
Madinat al-Zahra'	Sulayman	ca. 108	160	22	14	36
Al-Andalus	Hisham II		23	4	4	8
Madinat al-Zahra'	Hisham II	21	1	1	1	2
Totals		293	685	96	67	163

(George C. Miles, "The year 400 A.H./1009-1010 A.D. at the Mint of Cordoba", *Numisma*, Año XVII, Núms. 84-89, 1967, p. 22).

The figures yielded by Miles' investigation are extremely impressive. However, as he stressed in his comments, the year of A.H. 400 had been notorious for rapid political changes involving three successions of ephemeral regimes [8]). Under those circumstances the production of the

6) *Ibid.*, p. 118.

7) George C. Miles, "The year 400 A.H./1009-1010 A.D. at the Mint of Cordoba", *Numisma*, Año XVII, Núms. 84-89, 1967, p. 9-25.

8) *Ibid.*, p. 10.

mint must have been abnormally high since its operations were dictated rather by diplomatic and political considerations than by the needs of the market. For this reason, unless by way of contrast, the output of the mint of Cordoba in the year in question cannot serve as a suitable example of the annual production of a Muslim mint in the Middle Ages. In spite of this reservation, the data compiled by Miles lend themselves to comparative estimates of the output of dirhams in Spain in A.H. 400. Bearing in mind that the number of different dies must have been far in excess of known specimens [9]), and assuming that all pairs of dies were capable of producing up to 10,000 silver coins [10]), then one may suggest that in the light of adduced numismatic evidence the volume of dirhams struck in A.H. 400 in Spain appears to have surpassed 670,000 coins.

The volume of over half a million dirhams loses a lot of its grandeur when its value is converted into gold units—i.e., into contemporary dīnārs. Even by adopting a rather low exchange rate of 1 dīnār to 17 dirhams [11]), one would find that the market value of 670,000 Spanish dirhams amounted to ca. 39,410 dīnārs. To produce this quantity of gold coins a mint would not require more than four pairs of dies.

This point is made in order to emphasize a great difference between the volume of gold and of silver coins in circulation in the medieval Near East. An excessive presence of gold coinage on the markets would unavoidably lead to its cheapening. This in turn could undermine the function of dīnārs as the standard money to which the value of dirhams (at least in pre-Mamlūk times) was related, causing harmful effects on wages, prices, and pecuniary transactions generally [12]). It is also likely

---

9) *Ibid.*, p. 22.

10) For an exhaustive, critical discussion of the merits of various methods of estimation of the capacity of medieval coin dies, see Philip Grierson, "The volume of Anglo-Saxon coinage", *Economic History Review*, 20, 1967, p. 153-160; also, S. Suchodolski, "The organisation of minting in 11th- and 12th-century Poland", *Polish Numismatic News*, 2, 1973 (Special issue for the International Numismatic Congress in New York and Washington, 10-16 September 1973) p. 75 f.

11) S. D. Goitein, *A Mediterranean Society*, 1967, i/370.

12) *Ibid.*, p. 491.

that the owners of gold bullion were reluctant to have it coined or re-coined, fearing the risk of arbitrary governmental confiscations [13]).

The sharp contrast between the volume of gold and of silver coinage produced by medieval Islamic mints is the main reason why modern historians handling numismatic evidence generally find a huge disproportion between the survived gold and silver specimens. It also explains why samples of gold coins belonging to the same mint/date combination reveal a number of dies which is much lower than that found in silver coin samples.

The fact that average annual production of dīnārs was carried out with the use of a small number of dies is confirmed by a study of a sample of gold coins struck in Egypt during the initial years of Fāṭimid domination—i.e., from 17th Sha'bān 358 till the end of A.H. 362 [14]). One should stress that the conqueror of Egypt, Jawhar, brought with him considerable quantities of bullion [15]), that he promised to improve the quality of Egyptian coinage [16]), and that a mass circulation of Fāṭimid dīnārs produced in Egypt would have helped to disseminate the news about the Shī'ite victory. However, an analysis of 36 gold specimens dating from those years has revealed only 19 pairs of dies, the proportion of dies to die-links in A.H. 361 being 2:7. Their small number notwithstanding, the 19 pairs of dies, if used to full capacity, could have produced ca. 190,000 dīnārs which at the exchange rate of 1:18 [17]) would correspond to 3,420,000 dirhams, producing an annual average of 684,000.

---

13) Cf. G. Hennequin, "Points de vue sur l'histoire monétaire de l'Égypte musulmane au Moyen Âge", *Annales Islamologiques*, 12, 1974, p. 13.

14) The problem of the production of dīnārs during these years will be treated by me in a separate article.

15) Cf. M. Canard, "L'impérialisme des Fatimides et leur propagande", *Annales de l'Institut des Études Orientales*, 6, 1942-47, p. 178, n. 82.

16) Th. Bianquis, "La prise du pouvoir par les Fatimides en Égypte (357-363/968-974)", *Annales Islamologiques*, 11, 1972, p. 69, 78.

17) This was a rather low exchange rate, imposed in A.H. 397 by al-Ḥākim. Cf. al-Maqrīzī, *Ighāthat al-ummah*, al-Qāhirah, 1940, p. 16. Jawhar wanted to impose an exchange rate of 1:25½ for the dīnārs of al-Mu'izz, and 1:15 for those of the 'Abbāsid caliph al-Rāḍī. Cf. Th. Bianquis, *art. cit.*, p. 79.

So far I have dealt with the difference between the number of dies used in the production of gold and silver coins in medieval Near East. I wish now to present the results of a die count inquiry applied to Ṭūlūnid dīnārs struck by the mint of Egypt (Miṣr). One has to begin this survey by referring to the total number of specimens involved in the investigation. The most comprehensive catalog of Ṭūlūnid coinage, contributed in 1957 by Oleg Grabar [18]), lists 449 published and unpublished specimens from Miṣr, known to have belonged to various collections. The sample investigated in this present inquiry consisted of 204 specimens or 45 % of Grabar's total. Each specimen was meticulously examined; whenever a die variant was revealed the photograph of such specimen was enlarged and included in a corpus of Ṭūlūnid coin dies [19]).

The total sample, covering the entire period of Ṭūlūnid gold coinage production in Egypt—i.e., from A.H. 266 to A.H. 292—contained 105 obverse and 113 reverse dies [20]). However, for the purpose of this investigation only those years were taken into account where at least six specimens are available. These conditions were met by eighteen annual samples: four of them consisting of 6 specimens (A.H. 280, 281, 283, 291); five consisting of 7 specimens (A.H. 267, 269, 274, 288, 289); three of 8 (A.H. 276, 278, 279); and the samples of A.H. 266, 268, 272, 273, 287 represented by 9, 13, 16, 31, and 11 specimens respectively. The total of 171 specimens constitutes c. 50 % of the total of 338 listed by Grabar for the corresponding years. The above data, as well as the number of dies and die-links in the obverses and reverses, have been presented in the following table.

---

18) *The Coinage of the Ṭūlūnids* (Numismatic Notes and Monographs No. 139), hereafter referred to as CT.

19) The thorough reexamination of Ṭūlūnid gold specimens from Misṛ has revealed a larger number of die variants used in one and the same year than that implied by the typological differentiation offered by Grabar.

20) By reverse is meant here the part of a pair of dies, which produces the dated face of dīnār. Cf. Al-Hamdânî, *Kitâb al-Gauharatain*, herausgegeben und übersetzt von Christopher Toll, (Acta Universitatis Upsaliensis. Studia Semitica Upsaliensia 1) 1968, p. 344/345.

Illustration 3.

Statistical distribution of dies and die-links in the annual dīnār samples from Ṭūlūnid Egypt.

A.H.	CT total	No. of examined specimens	Obverses dies	Obverses die-links	Reverses dies	Reverses die-links
266	13	9	5	4	6	3
267	20	7	5	2	5	2
268	14	13	10	3	10	3
269	12	7	5	2	5	2
270	27	8	4	4	4	4
272	19	16	5	11	5	9 *)
273	27	31	8	22 **)	10	21
274	19	7	3	4	3	4
276	8	8	5	4 ***)	5	3
278	21	8	3	5	3	5
279	16	8	5	3	5	3
280	10	6	2	4	2	4
281	10	6	4	2	4	2
283	24	6	4	2	4	2
287	29	11	6	5	6	5
288	23	7	4	3	4	3
289	23	7	4	3	6	1
291	23	6	3	3	3	3

*) Two pictures of reverses were unavailable for examination.
**) Picture of one obverse was unavailable for examination.
***) One obverse links with a die of A.H. 272.

The quantitative relationship among the number of examined specimens, dies and die-links in the annual samples is illustrated in the following graph.

When compared with the size of silver coinage samples, and with the number of dies counted in such samples, the figures involved in the present inquiry may appear deficient. Doubtless, they would have been more convincing had this inquiry encompassed the remaining 50 % of specimens listed in CT. In spite of this limitation the obtained data permit a few interesting conclusions. The first and obvious one is that we have now established what was the minimum number of dies employed annually for the striking of dīnārs in Ṭūlūnid Egypt—i.e., one can now state that in a given year at least so and so many obverse and

Illustration 4.

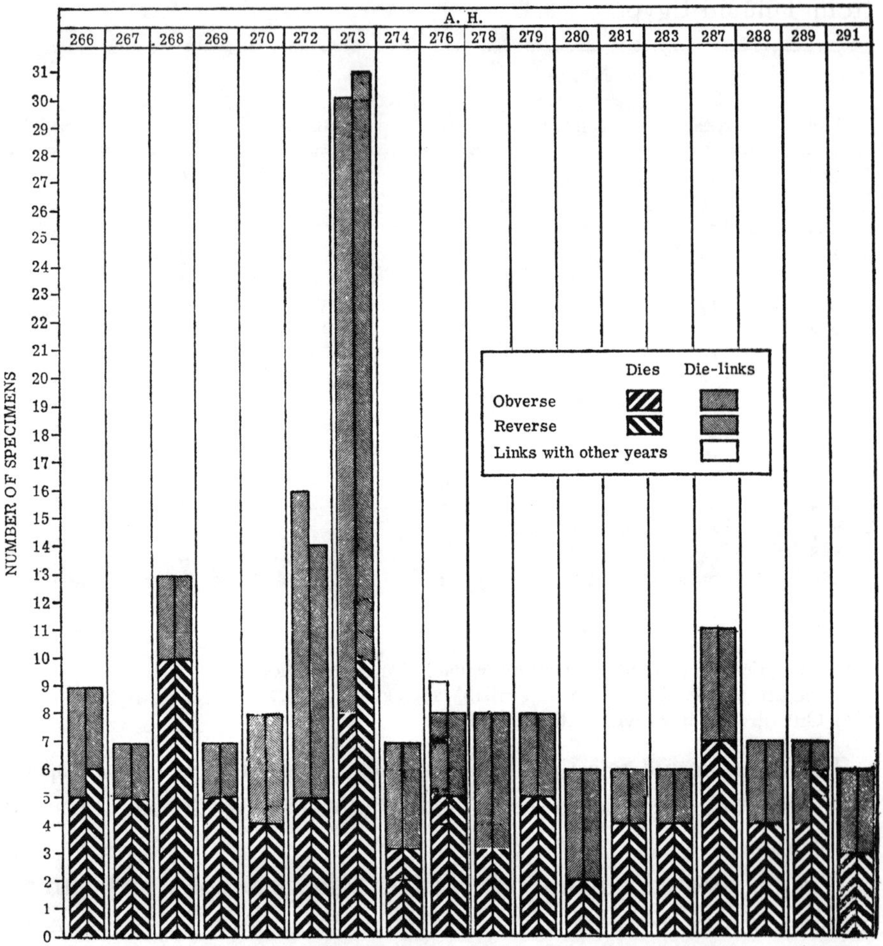

4. Dies and die-links in the annual dīnār samples from Ṭūlūnid Egypt

reverse dies were used for striking Ṭūlūnid dīnārs in Egypt, which offers a better clue to the level of production than speculations based on the total numbers of survived specimens [21]). While it is impossible to estimate the actual quantity of dies used in the production, one is tempted to conclude that their number was not too high. One arrives at this conclusion by studying the ratio of dies to die-links in individual samples. It is true that in the case of A.H. 267, 268 and 269 the ratio of dies (obverse and reverse) to die-links is 5:2, 10:3 and 5:2 respectively. The exceptionally high ratio of 6:1, found in the sample of A.H. 289, applied to reverses only and can easily be explained by the fact of the death of caliph al-Muʿtaḍid and the necessity of using a new reverse die with the name of his successor, al-Muktafī. In an analogous situation, occurring in A.H. 279 because of the death of al-Muʿtamid and the accession of al-Muʿtaḍid, the ratio of reverse dies to die-links is 5:3. In all other samples the ratio is quite low. The most revealing, however, are the samples of A.H. 272 and 273. The former consists of 16 obverse and 14 reverse specimens, or only 3 and 5 less respectively than the total in CT, but the ratio of obverse dies to die-links is 5:11, and that of reverse dies to die-links is 5:9. The size of the other sample is larger by 3 obverses and 4 reverses than that in CT. In this case the obverses show as many as 22 die-links and only 8 dies, while the reverses count 21 die-links and 10 dies. Considering the size of the last sample one may assume that in this instance the number of detected dies approximates the number of dies actually used in A.H. 273 production of dīnārs. Would the use ± 10 dies indicate a high, average or low level of operations as regards the output of dīnārs in Egypt under the Ṭūlūnids?

Unfortunately, textual sources provide no clues concerning the volume of coins produced in this period by the Egyptian mint. On the other hand, there exists evidence pertaining to its output in the final phase of the Ayyūbid regime. According to al-Nābulusī (d. A.H. 660/1261 A.D.), an authority on fiscal administration, "the mint [of Cairo]

---

21) Cf. A. S. Ehrenkreutz, *art. cit.*, p. 215.

under good management issued close to 3,000 dīnārs per month until it produced in the years of 636 and 637 a total of ca. 80,000 dīnārs" [22]). In other words, in the period of al-Nābulusī normal production of gold coins by the main mint of Egypt amounted to ca. 36-40,000 dīnārs per year, a volume which could be struck with the use of 4 pairs of dies. If this was the case in the waning decades of Egypt's age of gold, why wouldn't a similar situation obtain at its beginning? Should such assumption prove correct one could state that the figure of ± 10 dies, as suggested by the study of numismatic evidence, appears to be reasonable with reference to Ṭūlūnid production of dīnārs in Egypt.

The present inquiry also suggests an answer to the question whether coin dies were used "for the maximum number of strikes, or even anything close to it" [23]). An answer to this question, at least for the Ṭūlūnid period, is offered by our data. It seems likely that if the obverse dies had not been used to capacity—i.e., if they had not been worn out through continuous striking in a given year—they would have been used in the subsequent year. In the event of such practice, die-links found in one annual series would have been found in the following year or years. As it is, except for one specimen, the 181 obverses include no further die-links for the two different years. Since the exceptional die-link involves A.H. 272 and 276, it seems that it was occasioned by negligent misplacement of the die and its accidental recovery four years later, rather than by its earlier under-use. As for the reverse dies, they had to be discarded with the lapse of each year because of the date in their inscriptions. Also, as upper or trussel dies they deteriorated faster than the lower or anvil dies. Under those circumstances they could not result in any trans-annual die-links. The fact that in three instances (A.H. 266, 273, 289) the reverse dies outnumber the obverse dies in our sample suggests that they were not under-used.

By adopting the figure of ca. 10,000 of dīnārs per each pair of dies,

---

22) *Kitāb luma' al-qawānīn al-muḍiyya*, édition préparée par C. Becker et mise au point par Claude Cahen, Extrait du *Bulletin d'Études Orientales*, 16, 1958-1960, p. 52. Ayyūbid gold production will be treated by me in a separate article.

23) A. Udovitch, "Introductory remarks", *Studies in the Economic History of the Middle East*, 1970, p. 6.

one can speculate that the annual production of the Ṭūlūnid mint in Egypt did not exceed 100,000 dīnārs. Such quantitatively low but qualitatively high level of production might well have met the prevailing demand for new dīnārs [24]). One should bear in mind, that the mint of Egypt had been producing dīnārs long before the rise of Aḥmad ibn Ṭūlūn and his dynasty. Secondly, the markets of Egypt were wide open to the circulation of gold coins produced in other mints of the caliphate, especially those of Baghdād and of Ifrīqīyah. Furthermore, the production of Ṭūlūnid gold coins was carried out in several provincial mints such as that of Aleppo, Antioch, Damascus, Filasṭīn, Ḥarrān, Ḥimṣ and Rāfiqah.

Nor did Egypt seem to have suffered from any particular drain of gold coins. When in A.H. 279 Khumārawayh committed his regime to annual payments of 300,000 dīnārs to the capital of the Caliphate, that sum did not even amount to 7 % of the revenue from the Egyptian land tax [25]). Furthermore, one is not certain whether either sum actually involved gold coinage or silver coinage evaluated and reported in gold currency. There is no question about Ibn Ṭūlūn's heavy expenditures: the cost of his army and fleet and of his campaigns in Syria, in addition to all the money spent on the construction of his famous mosque, a sumptuous palace, a hospital, and aquaeduct. But if it is true that in spite of huge expenses Aḥmad ibn Ṭūlūn filled his treasury with 10,000,000 dīnārs, then it is obvious that there was no special pressure for new gold coinage to be struck in Egypt. Finally, when the value of 100,000 dīnārs, at the then prevailing exchange rate of 1:24 [26]), amounted to 2,400,000 dirhams, one is inclined to accept the conclusion about the low output of dīnārs by the Ṭūlūnid mint of Egypt, suggested by the results of the coin-die investigation.

---

24) A. S. Ehrenkreutz, "Studies in the monetary history of the Near East in the Middle Ages", *Journal of the Economic and Social History of the Orient*, 2, 1959, p. 149-150.

25) Zaky Mohamed Hassan, *Les Tulunides*, 1933, p. 245.

26) According to a quotation for A.H. 260, cf. K. W. Hofmeier, "Beiträge zur arabischen Papyrusforschung. I. Das System arabischer Steuerverrechnung im 9. Jahrhundert n. Chr.", *Der Islam*, 4, 1913, p. 100.

APPENDIX

List of examined dīnārs

List of abbreviations

AMİ, Artuk	=	Arkeoloji Müzesi İstanbul (Ibrahim Artuk accession no.).
ANS, unp.	=	American Numismatic Society Collection, unpublished specimen.
B.M., unp.	=	British Museum, London; unpublished specimen.
B.M., II,	=	S. Lane-Poole, *Catalogue of Oriental Coins in the British Museum*, vol. II.
B.M., IX,	=	S. Lane-Poole, *op. cit.*, vol. IX.
BN, unp.	=	Bibliothèque Nationale, Paris; unpublished specimen.
F/i,	=	Abdel Rahman Fahmy, *Fağr as-Sikka al-ʿArabīya*, vol. I.
Milan, no.	=	The Castello Sforzesco Collection in Milan.
MNdC	=	Musée Nationale de Copenhague.
OU,	=	Ashmolean Museum Collection, Oxford Museum.
Paris, III,	=	H. Lavoix, *Catalogue des Monnaies Musulmanes de la Bibliothèque Nationale*: III, *Egypte et Syrie*, (Paris, 1896).
PFC	=	Private French Collection.
RCT	=	Rogers Bey, Edward Thomas, *The International Numismata Orientalia*. Part IV. *The coins of the Ṭúlúni dynasty*. London, Trubner & Co., 1877.
Schul.	=	Schulman, Hans M. F., auction catalogues.
YvKB	=	Yapı ve Kredi Bankası Collection, Istanbul.

A.H.	*Obverse*	*Reverse*
266	RCT, photo 4 = AMI, Artuk 595	RCT, photo 4 = AMI, Artuk 595 = F/i, 2905
	ANS, unp. = YvKB, T/1/2	ANS, unp. = YvKB, T/1/2
	B.M., II, no. 218	B.M., II, no. 218
	Paris, III, no. 6 = F/i, 2905	Paris, III, no. 6
	ANS, unp. = Paris, III, no. 5	ANS, unp.
		Paris, III, no. 5
267	Paris, III, no. 7 = AMI, Artuk 596	Paris, III, no. 7 = AMI, Artuk 596 = F/i, 2906
	B.M., II, 219	B.M., II, 219
	OU, unp.	OU, unp.
	ANS, unp.	ANS, unp.
	Paris, III, no. 8 = F/i, 2906	Paris, III, no. 8
268	ANS, unp. = F/i, 2910	ANS, unp. = F/i, 2910
	ANS, unp.	ANS, unp.
	YvKB, T/1/3	YvKB, T/1/3
	AMI, Artuk 597	AMI, Artuk 597 = F/i, 2908
	Paris, III, no. 9	Paris, III, no. 9 = F/i, 2909
	Paris, III, no. 10	Paris, III, no. 10
	Paris, III, no. 10 bis	Paris, III, no. 10 bis

A.H.	*Obverse*	*Reverse*
	B.M., II, no. 219 b = F/i, 2908 = F/i, 2909	B.M., II, no. 219 b
	F/i, 2907	F/i, 2907
	F/i, 2911	F/i, 2911
269	B.M., II, no. 220	B.M., II, no. 220
	BN, unp. = F/i, 2912	BN, unp.
	ANS, no. 8	ANS, no. 8
	AMI, Artuk 598	AMI, Artuk 598
	PFC = YvKB, T/1/6	PFC = F/i, 2912 = YvKB, T/1/6
270	B.M., II, no. 220 b = F/i, 2914, 2916, 2917	B.M., II, no. 220 b = F/i, 2916, 2917
	Paris, III, no. 11 = F/i, 2915	Paris, III, no. 11 = F/i, 2914, 2915
	ANS, unp.	ANS, unp.
	ANS, unp.	ANS, unp.
272	ANS, unp. = MNdC, no. 1933 A.H. 276	ANS, unp. = F/i, 2932
	ANS, unp. = AMI, Artuk 603 = AMI, Artuk 603 = F/i, 2928 (A.H. 271), 2932, 2938	ANS, unp. = AMI, Artuk 603 = F/i, 293
	Paris, III, no. 25 = B.M., IX, no. 220 e = B.M., unp. = F/i, 2931, 2935, 2936, 2937	Paris, III, no. 25 = B.M., IX, no. 220 e = B.M., unp. = F/i, 2931, 2935, 2936, 2937
	F/i, 2933	F/i, 2933
	F/i, 2934	F/i, 2934
273	B.M., II, no. 222 = YvKB, T/2/2 = PFC = F/i, 2958, 2960, 2961, 2966	B.M., II, no. 222 = YvKB, T/2/2 = PFC = F/i, 2958, 2960, 2961, 2966
	ANS, unp. = ANS, unp. = F/i, 2942, 2949, 2952, 2955 (?), 2959	ANS, unp. = ANS, unp. = F/i, 2942, 2952, 2955, 2959
		F/i, 2949
	Paris, III, no. 26 = F/i, 2940, 2950, 2953, 2954, 2969	Paris, III, no. 26 = F/i, 2940, 2950, 2953, 2954, 2963, 2968
		F/i, 2969
	YvKB, T/2/3 = F/i, 2956, 2962, 2965	YvKB, T/2/3
		F/i, 2956 = F/i, 2962, 2965
	F/i, 2939	F/i, 2939
	F/i, 2967 = F/i, 2951, 2957	F/i, 2967 = F/i, 2951, 2957
	F/i, 2963	
	F/i, 2964	F/i, 2964
274	ANS, unp. = B.M., IX, no. 222 e = AMI, Artuk 604	ANS, unp. = B.M., IX, no. 222 e = AMI, Artuk 604
	BN, unp. = B.M., IX, 171.222^{c} = F/i, 2976	BN, unp. = B.M., IX, 171.222^{c} = F/i, 2976
	F/i, 2977 or 2978	F/i, 2977 or 2978

A.H.	*Obverse*	*Reverse*
276	B.M., unp. = AMI, Artuk 605 = F/i, 2980 = PFC	B.M., unp. = AMI, Artuk 605 = F/i, 2980 = PFC
	Paris, III, no. 28	Paris, III, no. 28
	ANS, unp.	ANS, unp.
	PFC	PFC
	MNdC, no. 1933 = ANS, unp.	MNdC, no. 1933
	A.H. 272	
278	ANS, unp. = YvKB, T/2/6 = PFC	ANS, unp. = YvKB, T/2/6 = PFC
	Paris, III, no. 30 bis = Paris, III, no. 30 = B.M., IX, no. 224 e	Paris, III, no. 30 bis = Paris, III, no. 30 = B.M., IX, no. 224 e
	OU, unp. = YvKB, T/2/5	OU, unp. = YvKB, T/2/5
279	F/i, 2984	F/i, 2984
	YvKB, T/2/8 = F/i, 2981	YvKB, T/2/8 = F/i, 2981
	F/i, 2985 = B.M., unp.	F/i, 2985 = B.M., unp.
	Paris, III, no. 31 = YvKB, T/2/9	Paris, III, no. 31 = YvKB, T/2/9
	RC, no. 10	RC, no. 10
280	OU, unp. = B.M., IX, no. 224 h = F/i, 2986	OU, unp. = B.M., IX, no. 224 h = F/i, 2986
	Milan, no. 437 = F/i, 2987	Milan, no. 437 = F/i, 2987
281	Paris, III, no. 33 bis	Paris, III, no. 33 bis
	B.M., unp.	B.M., unp.
	Paris, III, no. 33 = F/i, 2989	Paris, III, no. 33 = F/i, 2989
	B.M., IX, no. 224 K = F/i, 2988	B.M., no. 224 K = F/i, 2988
283	Paris, III, no. 37 = RC, no. 12 = AMI, Artuk 610	Paris, III, no. 37 = RC, no. 12 = AMI, Artuk 610
	Paris, III, no. 38	Paris, III, no. 38
	B.M., II, no. 226	B.M., II, no. 226
	RC, no. 13	RC, no. 13
287	ANS, unp. = ANS, unp. = YvKB, T/4/2 = F/i, 3000, 3006	ANS, unp. = ANS, unp. = YvKB T/4/2 = F/i, 3000, 3006
	ANS, unp.	ANS, unp.
	ANS, unp. = Paris, III, no. 42	ANS, unp. = Paris, III, no. 42
	Paris, III, no. 45	Paris, III, no. 45
	Schul., 4/6-8/67, no. 223	Schul., 4/6-8/67, no. 223
	F/i, 3007	F/i, 3007
288	Paris, III, no. 43 bis = F/i, 3009	Paris, III, no. 43 = F/i, 3008 = B.M., II, no. 229
	Paris, III, no. 43 = F/i, 3008 = B.M., II, no. 229	Paris, III, no. 43 = F/i, 3009
	ANS, unp.	ANS, unp.
	ANS, unp.	ANS, unp.

A.H.	*Obverse*	*Reverse*
289	AMI, Artuk 613	AMI, Artuk 613
	B.M., IX, no. 229 c = ANS, unp. = ANS, unp. = Paris, III, no. 44	B.M., IX, no. 229 c ANS, unp. ANS, unp. = Paris, III, no. 44
	RC, no. 14	RC, no. 14
	F/i, 3010	F/i, 3010
291	ANS, unp. = AMI, Artuk 614 = OU, unp. = B.M., II, no. 230	ANS, unp. = AMI, Artuk 614 = OU, unp. = B.M., II, no. 230
	Paris, III, no. 47	Paris, III, no. 47
	Paris, III, no. 47 bis	Paris, III, no. 47 bis

X

The Fatimids in Palestine — the Unwitting Promoters of the Crusades

The nature of this presentation may best be introduced by a reference to the relations between the Byzantines and the Crusaders. As it is well known, in A.D. 1204, the allied forces of the Venetians and the Crusaders sacked Constantinople, inflicting a blow from which the Greek Empire was never to recover. This catastrophe came in the wake of a series of incidents and explosive frictions between the Byzantines and the Crusaders ever since their first contacts on Greek territory. Paradoxically enough, this arrival of the first hosts of the armed "pelegrini Christi" i.e., of the First Crusade, in the waning years of the eleventh century, was to a large extent brought about by the efforts of Byzantine diplomacy seeking military assistance against the Saljuqid foe in Asia Minor.

In a similar way, one can easily establish a connection between the operations of the Crusaders in Syria and the downfall of the Fatimid Caliphate (A.D. 909-1171). What I propose to demonstrate is that the Fatimids themselves were, to a large extent, responsible for generating and tolerating certain specific social and economic trends in Palestine and Egypt, trends that facilitated — and even virtually invited — West European intervention in the form of a Crusade.

Obviously, when in the late spring of 1099 the Crusaders penetrated Palestine — a sensitive area in assuring Egypt's external security — the conflict between the forces of Western Christendom and the Ismā'īlī Fatimid establishment became inevitable. It must be stressed, however, that during most of the eleventh century, Fatimid policy towards the world of Christendom was far from actively antagonistic. Except for the aberrant behavior of Caliph al-Ḥākim (A.D. 996-1021), the Ismā'īlī Caliphate pursued a policy of coexistence with the Greek Empire and maintained a businesslike policy toward the ever-growing numbers of European merchants and pilgrims converging on the Syro-Egyptian coast to visit the Holy Land.

Had the confrontation between the West European invaders and the Fatimids been limited to the issue of the domination over the Holy Land, or to an ideological showdown between the forces of Christendom and of Islam, then the demise of the Fatimids would have merely constituted a transient episode in Syrian-Egyptian history. After all, the downfall of the Fatimids was neither the first nor the last dynastic change in Medieval Egypt. And, as for the Crusader challenge to Muslim domination over the Holy Land, eighty-eight years after its inception the Latin Kingdom of Jerusalem barely survived the onslaught of Ṣalāḥ al-Dīn's armies only to be totally eliminated from the Near Eastern mainland by the end of the thirteenth century by the systematic offensives of the Mamluk Sultans. It is because of the relatively localized nature of military activities and because of the ultimate military triumph of Islam that Muslim chroniclers, unlike their West European counterparts, viewed the subject of the Crusades in a less emotional and glorified perspective, regarding it as one of many episodes in the long story of military and dynastic rivalries involving Palestine.

In my opinion, the direct military confrontation between West European Christians and the Muslims in Egypt and Syria constituted but a spectacular aspect of the more profound conflict which both preceded and transcended the frame of the Crusades and which produced decisive and lasting effects in the relations between Western Europe and the Near East. In this context, Fatimid policy towards the Christians of Europe and towards their presence in Palestine prior to the launching of the First Crusade deserves an interpretational discussion.

★ ★ ★

The rise of the Fatimid Caliphate in the tenth century A.D. coincided with the beginnings of certain new trends in Western Europe, which ultimately contributed to the launching of the First Crusade and the establishment of the Latin Kingdom of Jerusalem. The Fatimid Caliphate was founded in A.D. 909 in North Africa; in A.D. 969 it took over Egypt and by the end of the tenth century its dominions stretched from the coast of the Atlantic Ocean in the West to Southern Syria (including Palestine) in the East. In Western Europe, in A.D. 911, the Abbey of Cluny was founded, to initiate an era of Church reforms which culminated in the revival of the political power of the Holy See. In Germany, during the period of the Saxon Dynasty many new towns sprang up which were at once religious centers and merchant settlements.[1] During the sixty-six years from the accession of Otto the Great to the death of Otto III (A.D. 936-1002), twenty-nine new markets were created by imperial privileges.[2] Commercial demands generated by the proliferation of these markets

1 Latouche, Robert, *The Birth of Western Economy*, New York, 1961, p. 253.
2 *Ibid.*, p. 255.

stimulated expansionist activities of the nascent Italian mercantile republics. Before the end of the tenth century, Venice secured commercial privileges from the Byzantines (March, 992),[3] and the Amalfitans from the Fatimids (A.D. 978).[4] In the military sphere, in A.D. 961 the Byzantines recovered Crete, in A.D. 963 they acquired Cyprus and in A.D. 969 they captured the key North-Syrian town of Antioch. Some daring raids carried out in Southern Syria and Northern Palestine by Byzantine contingents during the rule of Emperor John Tzimiskes (A.D. 969-975) rekindled Christian hopes of retrieving the Holy City of Jerusalem from Muslim domination.

During that period Fatimid propaganda reiterated the obligations and duties of the Ismā'īlī Imāms with respect to the safety of the world of Islam, the *Dār al-Islām*.[5] However, although the duty of the Holy War (the *jihād*) figured high on the list of their ideological priorities,[6] the Fatimid leaders did not object to truce agreements with Constantinople, as in A.D. 957/58,[7] and in 967,[8] nor to diplomatic deals involving the surrender of important territory such as the island of Crete in A.D. 961.[9]

It is quite likely that such a flexible Fatimid policy toward the Byzantines was dictated by the requirements of their eastward drive aiming at the conquest of Egypt, a necessary military objective in their supreme anti-Abbasid strategy. In that pursuit they did not mind availing themselves of the naval support of the Amalfitans.[10] But following the submission of Egypt in A.D. 969, this attitude of restraint and of diplomatic flexibility in respect to the Infidels did not change. Moreover, contrary to their supreme ideological goal of supplanting the Caliphate of the Abbasids, the Fatimids adjusted their policy to conform with the traditional Egyptian "raisons d'état." These involved the establishment of internal stability, external security, and the creation of optimal social and administrative conditions to enhance agricultural, industrial and commercial activities for the people of Egypt. Conscious of the economic dividends yielded by such a "Nilocentric" policy, the Fatimids not only abandoned the implementation of a

3 Schaube, Adolf, *Handelsgeschichte der Romanischen Völker des Mittelmeergebiets bis zum Ende der Kreuzzüge*, München, 1906, p. 18.

4 Citarella, Armand O., 'Patterns in Medieval Trade: The Commerce of Amalfi before the Crusades,' *The Journal of Economic History*, 28, 1968, p. 544.

5 Vatikiotis, Panayiotis J., *The Fatimid Theory of State*, Lahore, 1957, p. 113.

6 *Ibid.*, p. 99; Sivan, Emmanuel, *L'Islam et la Croisade*, Paris, 1968, p. 12-13.

7 Stern, S. M., 'An Embassy of the Byzantine Emperor to the Fāṭimid Caliph al-Mu'izz,' *Byzantion*, 20, 1950, p. 243.

8 Dölger, Franz, *Corpus der griechischen Urkinden des Mittelalters und der neueren Zeit*, Regesten, 1, Teil, Berlin, 1924, no. 708, p. 91.

9 Hamdani, Abbas, 'A Possible Fāṭimid Background to the Battle of Manzikert,' *Ankara Üniv. D.T.C. Falkültesi Tarih Araştırmaları Dergisi*, Cilt VI., Cilt VI., Sayı 10-11 den ayrıbasım, 1968, p. 17.

10 Citarella, Armand O., *art. cit.*, p. 545.

showdown with the Abbasid Caliphate of Baghdad, but became less and less concerned about their fundamental duty to prosecute the *jihād* against those who threatened the security of the *Dār al-Islām*. Typical in this regard was their policy towards the Byzantines best defined in a formula attributed to the great Fatimid statesman and vizir, Ya'qūb ibn Killis, who advised Caliph al-'Azīz to "keep peace with the Byzantines whenever they keep peace with you."[11]

A similar attitude characterized the policies of the Fatimids in the eleventh century in spite of some portentous changes in the power relationship between Western Christendom and Islam. One could hardly expect the Fatimids to be aware of the fact that as a result of the Cluniac remedial influence, the papacy was becoming a real factor in West European politics. Nor could they necessarily be aware of the negotiations between the Byzantine Emperor Constantine X Dukas and Pope Honorius II in A.D. 1063, aiming at the liberation of the Church of the Holy Sepulcher,[12] or of the diplomatic initiatives of Pope Gregory VII in 1074, for the purpose of assisting the Byzantines against the pressure of the Saljuqids in Asia Minor.[13] But the Fatimids were certainly aware of the resurgence of the naval power of the Italians, who resorted to military force in order to enhance their commercial activities in Muslim territories. Likewise, in the Western Mediterranean the naval power of Pisa and Genoa allowed the Christians to pass to the offensive. After driving the Muslims away from Sardinia, the Pisans and Genoese carried out devastating naval raids against Bona (A.D. 1034), Palermo (A.D. 1063), and the former capital of the Fatimids, al-Mahdīya (A.D. 1087). In this last instance, besides carrying home enormous booty, the Christian invaders enforced on the vanquished Zīrīd enemy advantageous commercial concessions for the benefit of Pisan and Genoese merchants, much to the detriment of the indigenous trade community. Even more significant were the military exploits of the Norman leaders of Southern Italy, who, between A.D. 1061 and 1072, had captured all of Sicily. In subsequent years they deployed their expansionist energies in an eastern direction by capturing, in A.D. 1082, the Byzantine fortress of Durazzo on the Dalmatian coast.

By that time the Fatimids were neither interested in nor capable of defending the *Dār al-Islām*, especially against the Italian and Norman attacks in the Western Mediterranean. Besides having lost their sway over their North African provinces the Fatimid regime experienced a prolonged socio-economic crisis in Egypt (A.D. 1054-1074), aggravated by the eruption into Syria of Saljuqid and related Turcoman forces. Consequently, in the last thirty years of the eleventh century the Fatimids concentrated on

11 Ibn Khallikān, *Wafayāt al-A'yān*, Cairo, 1948, vi/31.
12 Dölgers, Franz, *op. cit.*, 2. Teil, 1925, no. 952, p. 15.
13 Setton, Kenneth M., Ed., *A History of the Crusades*, Vol. I, Philadelphia, 1958, p. 223.

protecting Egypt from Turcoman peril. It is for that reason that they dispatched diplomatic missions to the Byzantines to secure their cooperation against the common Saljuqid enemy.[14]

While the Fatimid concern about the presence of the Turcomans in Palestine was quite warranted, their lack of precautionary measures against the growing presence of Italian merchants in the Eastern Mediterranean was bound to bring about — sooner or later — developments similar to those which had already taken place in the West. Although the Fatimids were in an excellent bargaining position because of their control over the rich Egyptian deposits of alum — a mineral in great demand for the nascent Italian textile industry[15] — they nonetheless allowed European merchants to spread their commercial influence in Egypt and Syria. By the second half of the eleventh century the Amalfitans, Genoese and Pisans not only frequented Egyptian and Syrian ports but were allowed to hold annual market days and to build churches and hostels in Jerusalem.[16] "There are few Muslim theologians (*'ulamā'*) (in Jerusalem) but many arrogant Christians. . . Christians and Jews constitute a majority," complained a contemporary geographer, al-Muqaddasī (d. ca. A.D. 990).[17] Indeed, the Fatimids not only tolerated but tried to protect an ever increasing traffic of West European pilgrims to Jerusalem and to other religious sites in Palestine.[18] Obviously, they underestimated the role of these pilgrims as disseminators of divers news about the situation in the Holy Land. Upon their return home, some of them must have told tales of the wealth and the much higher living standards enjoyed by Syrian society. Others who had experienced some adversities, or even been prevented from reaching Jerusalem because of the internal struggles waged by different Saljuqid factions or by Arab Bedouins, lamented the predicament of the Holy City and the plight of Christian minorities in Syria. Some of them, as in the case of Peter the Hermit, propagandized the need of European intervention to liberate the Holy Land from Muslim domination.

This mounting development resulted from a marked difference between the European and Egyptian perception of Palestine. To the Christians, West European and Byzantine alike, the religious aura of Jerusalem meant much more than it did to the ruling regimes of Egypt. The Byzantine emotional attitude towards Jerusalem was demonstrated as early as A.D. 631, when Heraclius had restored the Holy Cross to Jerusalem upon his

14 Hamdani, Abbas, *art. cit.*, p. 29-30.

15 al-Bakrī, *Kitāb al-masālik wa'l-mamālik*, ed. de Slane, Paris, 1913, p. 341; Cahen, Claude, 'Alun avant Phocée,' *Revue d'Histoire Économique et Sociale*, 41, 1963, p. 440.

16 Schaube, Adolf, *op. cit.*, p. 36-37.

17 al-Muqaddasī, *Aḥsan at-Taqāsīm fī Ma'rifat al-Aqālīm*, trad. par André Miquel, Damas, 1963, p. 182.

18 Brundage, James A., *The Crusades, A Documentary Survey*, Milwaukee, 1962, p. 7; Goitein, S. D., *A Mediterranean Society*, Vol. II, Berkeley, 1971, p. 370.

victory over the Sasanids. In the tenth century, the warlike emperors Nicephorus Phokas and John Tzimiskes while waging their wars in Syria, invoked the ideal of the holy war of liberation of Jerusalem. The rise of religious feeling around the end of the first Christian millennium likewise reinforced this interest in the cause of the Holy Cross. In 1095, the attitude of West European Christians was best summed up by Pope Urban II who declared in his historic oration of Clermont: "Jerusalem is the navel of the world. . . This royal city, situated in the middle of the world, is now held captive by His enemies and is made a servant, by those who know not God, for the ceremonies of the heathen. It looks and hopes for freedom; it begs unceasingly that you will come to its aid. It looks for help from you. . ."[19] In contrast, to the Fatimids of Egypt Jerusalem was only one venerable city along with Mecca, Medina, Karbala, and Najaf. However, their concern for Palestine rested not on emotional or religious but on strategic grounds. Palestine constituted a buffer zone interposed between Egypt and potential invaders from Northern Syria and Mesopotamia. Likewise, Palestinian coastal towns played an important part in East Mediterranean maritime trade and the lowlands of Palestine abounded in arable farms and orchards. Jerusalem's venerable status notwithstanding, prior to the Crusades, it had not generated emotional interest among the Fatimids and their contemporaries, comparable to that prevailing in the world of Christendom. One would look in vain for the *Faḍā'il* type of texts, extolling the merits of Jerusalem, prior to the coming of the Crusaders.[20] It was Ramle, not Jerusalem, which served as Fatimid provincial capital of Palestine; and it was in Ramle, Tiberias, and Acre, not in Jerusalem, that Fatimid gold coinage of Palestine happened to be produced.[21] The issue of a *jihād* for Jerusalem's sake could hardly arise before the period of the Crusades, but even during the period of the Crusades, Muslim successors of the Fatimids bargained off the Holy City to the Christians in return for Egypt's security.[22]

In the last quarter of the eleventh century, the Fatimids hardly exercised effective authority over Palestine. After two unsuccessful expeditions (A.D. 1078/9; 1085/6) aimed at the recovery of Jerusalem, they withdrew behind the newly constructed, powerful walls of Cairo. With Fatimid prestige undermined by an internal ideological split caused by the rise and secession of the Nizārīya sect (the "Assassins"), the Ismā'īlī Caliphate appeared to abdicate its responsibility towards Palestine. Syria, including Palestine, was divided up among various Turcoman (mainly Saljuqid) petty

19 Brundage, James A., *op. cit.*, p. 19.

20 Cf. Sivan, Emmanuel, 'The Beginnings of the Faḍā'il al-Quds Literature,' *Israel Oriental Studies*, I, 1971.

21 Cf. Shammā, Samīr, *al-Nuqūd al-Islāmīya Allatī Ḍuribat Fī Filasṭīn*, 1980, p. 143-151.

22 On February 18, A.D. 1229, al-Kāmi, and in the summer of A.D. 1241 al-Sāliḥ Ayyūb.

rulers and local Arab chieftains who asserted their authority over small districts and semi-autonomous towns.[23] The whole area thus stood open to a foreign aggression. That aggression became a reality with the arrival of the "pelegrini Christi", whose determination to liberate the Holy Land proved as decisive as their weaponry in defeating separate Muslim contingents and town garrisons, and in founding the Latin Kingdom of Jerusalem in the political vacuum created by the withdrawal of the Fatimids.

An instrumental part in the rapid expansion of the Christian Kingdom along the coast of Palestine and Syria was played by Italian fleets. After having benefited from attractive trade opportunities extended to them by the Fatimids, the Italians succeeded in exploiting the striking power of the Crusaders to pursue their strategy of establishing commercial hegemony over the outlets of Near Eastern transit routes.[24] This commercial domination gained by the Italians outlived the presence of the Crusaders in Palestine and was decisive in pushing the *Dār al-Islām* along the road of lasting societal and economic decline.

And yet, during the course of the First Crusade, there was a crisis which might have resulted in total failure of that West European adventure. After several months of painful siege operations at the impregnable fortress of Antioch, the forces of the Crusaders reached the brink of exhaustion. It was at that moment, in March of 1098, that the Fatimids appeared on the scene, not as an army bringing relief to the besieged Muslim garrison but as a diplomatic mission proposing a deal to the Crusaders, involving a partition of Syria at the expense of the Saljuqid foe. The failure of the Fatimids to join in a naval or land operation to protect the *Dār al-Islām* made easier the acquisition of the key fortress by the Crusaders. And with the Christian victory at Antioch the road to Palestine lay invitingly open. The Fatimid awakening late in the summer of 1098, came too late to reverse the progress and decisive success of the West European invasion which the Fatimids had earlier unwittingly promoted.

23 Cf. Ashtor, Eliyahu, 'Republiques urbaines dans le Proche Orient à l'époque des Croisades?' *Cahiers de Civilisation Médiévale*, 18, 1975, p. 117-131.

24 For a discussion of the evolution in Italian trade expansion, see Ehrenkreutz, Andrew S., 'Strategic Implications of the Slave Trade between Genoa and Mamlūk Egypt in the Second Half of the 13th Century,' *Islamic Middle East, 700-1900: Studies in Economic and Social History*, Princeton, N.J., 1981, p. 335-345.

XI

ADDITIONAL EVIDENCE OF THE FĀṬIMID USE OF DĪNĀRS FOR PROPAGANDA PURPOSES

ANDREW S. EHRENKREUTZ AND GENE W. HECK

In their persistent attempts to conquer Egypt, the Fāṭimids relied on subversive propaganda disseminated both by secret missionaries as well as through special dīnār issues. The use of coins as propaganda instruments – though not an innovation – was probably most effective and widespread among medieval Arab dynasties.[1] According to numismatic evidence, the Fāṭimids issued dīnārs with inscriptions listing the name of Caliph al-Muʿizz (A.H. 341–365), the mint of Egypt (Miṣr) as the place, and the years A.H. 341, 343, and 353 as the dates of their striking.[2] The fact that these alleged Fāṭimid dīnārs, ostensibly struck in Miṣr, preceded the A.H. 358 Ismāʿīlī conquest of the country of the Nile, has attracted the attention of a number of scholars. S. Lane-Poole speculated that since there was no evidence of a Fāṭimid attack on Egypt in A.H. 341, the surviving specimens might represent a minting error, or an issue struck in anticipation of forthcoming victory.[3] ʿAbd al-Raḥmān Fahmī contends that this dīnār may have been one of many struck in the name of al-Muʿizz for intended distribution to Ismāʿīlī supporters in Ikhshīdid Egypt, and suggests that there are also examples of Egyptian tapestry bearing the name of the Ismāʿīlī caliph, antedating the conquest of Egypt by several years.[4] One can add to this statement a reference to a preserved tombstone bearing an Ismāʿīlī engraving,[5] as well as to a piece of Egyptian *ṭirāz* showing an embroidered inscription which invokes the name of al-Mu–izz, "the assistance of God and the forthcoming conquest."[6] Muḥammad Bāqir al-Ḥusaynī describes at length the use of Fāṭimid dīnārs as propaganda weapons,[7]

[1] See Muḥammad Bāqir al-Ḥusaynī, "Dirāsa Taḥlīliya Islāmiya ʿan Nuqūd al-Diʿāya wa al-Aʿlām wa al-Munāsibāt," *al-Maskūkāt*, no. 6 (1975), pp. 9–16, *passim*.

[2] George Miles, *Fāṭimid Coins in the Collection of the University Museum, Philadelphia, and the American Numismatic Society* (Numismatic Notes and Monographs, No. 121) (New York, 1951), p. 51.

[3] S. Lane Poole, *History of Egypt in the Middle Ages* (London, 1901), pp. 98–99.

[4] ʿAbd al-Raḥmān Fahmī, *Al-Nuqūd al-ʿArabīya, Maḍīyuhā wa Ḥāḍiruhā* (Cairo, 1964), p. 67.

[5] *Répertoire Chronologique d'Epigraphie Arabe* (1933), IV, 127, no. 1460.

[6] *Ibid.*, (1934), V, 11, no. 1622.

[7] Al-Ḥusaynī, *passim*.

while Muḥammad al-ʿUshsh states explicitly that these coins are part of a larger quantity struck by the Fāṭimids specifically for their psychological value in the "ongoing battle for Egypt."[8]

In the light of numismatic evidence it is possible to submit that the propagandistic use of coins did not cease following the subjugation of Egypt, especially during the initial five years of the new administration under the leadership of the victorious Fāṭimid commander, Jawhar al-Ṣiqillī. The latter wasted no time in opening the mint of Miṣr[9] to implement the currency reform that he had promised to the people of Egypt in the solemn Treaty of Surrender.[10] The extant dīnārs resulting from this reform are all distinguished by several noteworthy features. Their inscriptions list the name of al-Muʿizz and are provided with the standard Shīʿī religious invocations. A neutron activation analysis (NAA) applied to some of the specimens under consideration has revealed that these dīnārs are of excellent intrinsic quality emulating or even surpassing the standard of fineness of the best medieval gold coins.[11] Still more interesting is that some of the dīnārs struck in Egypt during Jawhar's administration, i.e. from Shaʿbān A.H. 358 through Shaʿbān A.H. 362, display an epigraphic phenomenon unprecedented in the history of medieval Egyptian gold coinage. In addition to the traditional specification of the year in which they were struck (*ḍuriba hadhā al-dīnār . . . fī sana . . .*), they also list the name of the particular month (e.g. *ḍuriba hadhā al-dīnār bi-Miṣr fī Muḥarram sana . . .*). Although such "monthly datings" had appeared on rare occasions in earlier North African dīnārs,[12] their unusual frequency throughout the period of the Jawhar administration makes them an anomaly worthy of investigation.

In order to carry out this investigation, we assembled exhaustive data involving as many as 70 Fāṭimid dīnārs, struck by the mint of Miṣr between A.H. 358 and A.H. 362.[13] Of these, 17 specimens identify the date of production by years only – 10 in A.H. 358 (i.e., during the second half of that

[8] Muḥammad al-ʿUshsh, "Miṣr: Al-Qāhira ʿalā al-Nuqūd al-ʿArabīya al-Islāmīya, in *Abḥāth al-Nadwa al-Duwalīya li-Tārīkh al-Qāhira* (Cairo, 1971), II, 911–912.

[9] Al-Maqrīzī, *Ittiʿāẓ al-Ḥunafā'* (Cairo, 1948), pp. 165–66.

[10] *Ibid.*, p. 150.

[11] See W. Oddy: "The Gold Content of Fāṭimid Coins Reconsidered," *Metallurgy in Numismatics*, 1 (1980), 99–188, *passim.*

[12] We find, for instance, gold dīnārs bearing the name of the Fāṭimid caliph al-Manṣūr (father of al-Muʿizz) for the month of Dhū al-Qaʿda in A.H. 336 and A.H. 337, and quarter dīnārs for the months of Ṣafar in A.H. 338 and al-Muḥarram in A.H. 341, in S. Lane Poole's *Catalogue of Oriental Coins in the British Museum* (London, 1879), IV, 6–8; and dīnārs for the months of Muḥarram in A.H. 337 and Jumādā II in A.H. 338, in George Miles, p. 6.

[13] We wish to express our deepest gratitude and appreciation to Drs. Paul Balog, Arlette

year); 4 in A.H. 359; 2 in A.H. 361 and 1 in A.H. 362. On the other hand, 53 specimens specify not only the year but also the month in which they were issued. Moreover, in the process of accumulating these dīnārs it has become obvious that the same months have consistently reappeared in their inscriptions, while others have remained conspicuous by their absence. As illustrated below, the A.H. 358 sample consists of 10 "monthless" dīnārs; in A.H. 359, we have 4 monthless dīnārs, as well as specimens struck in Ṣafar, Dhū al-Qaʿda, and the consecutive months of Jumādā II, Rajab, Shaʿbān and Ramaḍān. In A.H. 360, there are coins representing Muḥarram and the sequential months of Jumādā I, Jumādā II and Rajab; while in A.H. 361 only the month of Jumādā I is shown in the dīnārs of that type. Similarly, the practice of monthly coin dating appears in Muḥarram, Ṣafar and Jumādā II in A.H. 362, only to vanish altogether for the remainder of Jawhar's administration (i.e., since the arrival of al-Muʿizz in Shaʿbān of A.H. 362) and for the remainder of the Fāṭimid era.

What can this seemingly systematic pattern of occurrence in the monthly dating mean? At the onset, we cannot discount the possibility that the particular distribution of our specimens may reflect nothing more than the mere circumstance of survival. That is, our sample, albeit very large for so short a period, is unrepresentative due to its being incomplete – it does not depict the full 12 month cycle of actual mint operation. Its relative size, however, combined with the occurrence of numerous specimens for certain months, to the exclusion of others, tends to discredit such a skeptical interpretation.

If the particular dīnārs within our sample are not a mere accident of survival, then we may assume that the lunar characteristics are the result of a deliberate policy. In our opinion, a strong case can be made for the argument that these truly unorthodox dīnārs were struck at Jawhar's order to propagandize Ismāʿīlī hagiographic lore by means of inscriptional references to those months

Nègre, and N. D. Nicol, and Ms. Marcia Sharabani for their counsel and assistance in the researching of this article; and to the curators and staffs of the following libraries and museums for making their collections available for our analysis:

American Numismatic Society, New York;
British Museum, London;
Bibliothèque Nationale, Paris;
Damascus National Museum, Damascus;
Department of Antiquities Museum, Jerusalem;
Milan Collection, Milan;
Musée National de Copenhague;
Münzkabinet des Kunsthistorischen Museums, Wien;
The Private Collection of Dr. Enrico Leuthold, Milano.

which were memorable in Fāṭimid history. This would be in conformity with Jawhar's liturgical innovations, such as, for instance, the changing of the text of the adhān or call to prayer from a Sunnī to Shīʿī formula.[14]

Accordingly, while the listing of the month of Muḥarram could have been intended to celebrate the beginning of the year, it also might have marked the rites of the mourning of "ʿĀshūrā" – the martyrdom of the third Ismāʿīlī Imām, Ḥusayn, son of ʿAlī and Fāṭimah and grandson of Prophet Muḥammad. Ḥusayn's birth, on the other hand, was in the month of Shaʿbān. Similarly, Jumādā II witnessed the birth of Fāṭimah, daughter of the Prophet, and for whom the Fāṭimid dynasty was named, while Jumādā I marks the month of her death. Rajab was the month of Fāṭimah and ʿAlī's marriage. In that month also, Muḥammad began his historic mission. The month of Ramaḍān was equally prominent in Ismāʿīlī history. It witnessed the death of ʿAlī, the birth of his son and second Imām, Ḥassan, as well as the birth of the Fāṭimid Caliph, al-Muʿizz, who was the ruling Imām throughout the entire period we have analyzed.

Two months, Ṣafar and Dhū al-Qaʿda, however, cannot be so easily explained. The appearance of Ṣafar in the inscriptions on the dīnārs could invoke the memory of the Nahrawān massacre in A.H. 39, to serve notice to anti-Ismāʿīlī opponents of the way the first Imām suppressed some of the Khārijite dissidents. Dhū al-Qaʿda, on the other hand, was the month in which construction began on the first Fāṭimid capital, al-Mahdīyah, in North Africa,[15] also marking the month of al-Muʿizz's accession.[16] Indeed, ʿAbd al-Raḥmān Fahmī regards the fact of dīnārs being struck in the year of al-Muʿizz's accession, A.H. 341, and bearing the inscription of the Miṣr mint, as more than mere coincidence.[17]

Future findings of Fāṭimid dīnārs, struck between A.H. 358–362, may test the validity of our hypothesis about the selectiveness and propagandistic function of specimens with lunar references. One thing appears obvious. The arrival of al-Muʿizz in Cairo in Shaʿbān of A.H. 362, and the placing of Yaʿqūb ibn Killis – an old hand in pre-Fāṭimid Egyptian administrative matters – in charge of the Ismāʿīlī treasury, terminated Jawhar's responsibility in the area of Egyptian coinage. This transition of fiscal power coincided with the disappearance of lunar references from the inscriptions on Egyptian Fāṭimid dīnārs.

[14] Al-Maqrīzī, p. 169.

[15] *Ibid.*, p. 101.

[16] E. Zambaur, *Manuel de généalogie et de chronologie pour l'histoire de l'Islam* (Hanovre, 1927), p. 94.

[17] Fahmī, p. 67.

KEY OF ABBREVIATIONS

"Balog Coll." = Private Collection of Dr. Paul Balog, Rome.
"BM" = S. Lane Poole, *Catalogue of Oriental Coins in the British Museum*, IV (1879).
"BM unp." = British Museum, London; unpublished specimen.
"D" = Damascus National Museum, Damascus, Syria.
"DAJ" = Rockefeller Museum, Department of Antiquities, Jerusalem, Israel.
"DeC" = R. Cottevieille-Giraudet, "La Collection de Courdemanche", (Monnaies musulmanes au Cabinet des Médailles), *Revue Numismatique*, 4e Serie, 37 (1934).
"FC" = G. Miles, *Fāṭimid Coins in the Collection of the University Museum, Philadelphia, and the American Numismatic Society* (Numismatic Notes and Monographs, No. 121) (New York, 1951).
"Kh." = Khedivial Collection, Cairo.
"Leuthold Coll." = Private Collection of Dr. Enrico Leuthold, Milan.
"Mil." = Milan Collection (Castello Sforzesco).
"MNdC" = Musée National de Copenhague.
"OU" = Ashmolean Collection, Oxford Museum.
"P" = Bibliothèque Nationale, Paris.
"PFC" = Private French Collection (Nègre).
"S.A. Cat." = Stephen Album Catalogue.
"Wien" = Münzkabinet des Kunsthistorischen Museums, Wien.

LIST OF THE 70 FĀṬIMID DĪNĀRS ANALYZED, A.H. 358–A.H. 362, INCLUSIVE.

COIN	DATE
1. BM IV, 29	358 (monthless)
2. DAJ 282	358 "
3. DAJ 283	358 "
4. DAJ 284	358 "
5. DeC. 5, Pl II (1935)	358 "
6. FC 29	358 "
7. Kh. 966	358 "
8. Kh. 967	358 "
9. Kh. 968	358 "
10. P 99 bis (III)	358 "
11. Balog Coll.	359 Ṣafar
12. Leuthold Coll.	359 "
13. Leuthold Coll.	359 Jumādā II
14. BM (unp.)	359 Rajab

15.	FC 30	359 "
16.	P 1036.7 (1974)	359 "
17.	BM IX, 30a (No. 318)	359 Shaʿbān
18.	D 48874	359 "
19.	DAJ 281	359 "
20.	FC 31	359 "
21.	Kh. 969	359 "
22.	Leuthold Coll.	359 "
23.	P 99 ter	359 "
24.	FC 32	359 Ramaḍān
25.	Kh. 970	359 "
26.	P 1335 (1972)	359 "
27.	Balog Coll.	359 Dhū al-Qaʿda
28.	DAJ 285	359 "
29.	BM IV, 30	359 (monthless)
30.	D 40081	359 "
31.	DeC. 254 (1935)	359 "
32.	Kh. (unenumerated)	359 "
33.	Kh. 975	360 Muḥarram
34.	Leuthold Coll.	360 "
35.	Mil. 446	360 "
36.	DAJ 280	360 Jumādā I
37.	PFC (unenumerated)	360 "
38.	Wien 7409	360 "
39.	BM IV, 31	360 Jumādā II
40.	D 4373	360 "
41.	FC 33	360 "
42.	Balog Coll.	360 Rajab
43.	BM IV, 34	361 Jumādā I
44.	FC 34	361 "
45.	FC 35	361 "
46.	FC 36	361 "
47.	Kh. 978	361 "
48.	Kh. 979	361 "
49.	MNdC, unenumerated (1942)	361 "
50.	P 100m	361 "
51.	PFC 361	361 "
52.	FC 37	361 (monthless)
53.	Kh. 977	361 "

54.	BM IV, 36	362 Muḥarram
55.	FC 38	362 "
56.	FC 39	362 "
57.	P 39 (1974)	362 "
58.	P 40 (1974)	362 "
59.	S.A.–Cat. 24–36	362 "
60.	S.A.–Cat. 25–21	362 "
61.	S.A.–Cat. 39	362 "
62.	Leuthold Coll.	362 Ṣafar
63.	BM IV, 37	362 Jumādā II
64.	FC 40	362 "
65.	Kh. 982	362 "
66.	Mil. 449	362 "
67.	OU, unpublished	362 "
68.	P 101 ter	362 "
69.	PFC 362	362 "
70.	FC 41	362 (monthless)

DISTRIBUTION OF PRODUCTION, ANNUAL AND MONTHLY BASIS,
MIṢR MINT,
A.H. 358–362

YEAR	Monthless	Muḥarram	Ṣafar	Rabīʿ I	Rabīʿ II	Jumādā I	Jumādā II	Rajab	Shaʿbān	Ramaḍān	Shawwāl	Dhū al-Qaʿda	Dhū al-Ḥijja	TOTAL
A.H. 358	ooo ooo ooo o													10
A.H. 359	ooo o		oo				o	ooo	ooo ooo o	ooo		oo		22
A.H. 360		ooo				ooo	ooo	o						10
A.H. 361	oo					ooo ooo ooo								11
A.H. 362	o	ooo ooo oo	o				ooo ooo o							17

TOTAL SAMPLE 70

XII

THE KURR SYSTEM IN MEDIEVAL IRAQ*

The purpose of this note is to analyze the contents of an interesting chapter from the work of Abū al-Wafā' al-Būzajānī (A. H. 328-381/A. D. 939-997), known as *Kitāb al-manāzil fī mā yaḥtāju ilayhi al-kuttāb wa al-'ummāl min ṣinā'at al-ḥisāb.* [1]) Because of its mathematical contents the treatise in question, as well as many other contributions of the author, have attracted the attention of scholars interested in the problems of Muslim scientific achievements. Thus, as early as 1855, F. Woepcke discussed the *Kitāb al-manāzil,* [2]) producing even a translation of a list of contents taken from a manuscript copy of the treatise, located in the collection of the library of the University of Leyden. [3]) More recently, P. Luckey in „Beiträge zur Erforschung der islamischen Mathematick", *Orientalia,* 22, 1953, p. 176 f.; O. Skirmer in "Die muslimische Lehre von der Vermessung ('ilm al-misāḥa)", *Jahresbericht* 1956/57 *der Oberrealschule mit Knabenmittelschule Bayreuth,* p. 17-50; and B. A. Rozenfeld and A. P. IUshkevich in „Matematika stran Blizhnego i Srednego Vostoka v srednie veka", *Sovetskoe Vostokovedenie,* 1958, iii, p. 101-108, have all referred to or discussed the *Kitāb al-manāzil.* [4])

All these contributions have one thing in common. They all concentrate on the mathematical and geometrical aspects of Abū al-Wafā''s treatise. Secondly, they all rely—directly or indirectly—on the Leyden manuscript. It was Cl. Cahen, however, who stressed another aspect of Abū al-Wafā''s contribution. In his article dealing with „Quelques problèmes économiques et fiscaux de l'Iraq Buyide d'après un traité de mathématiques," *Annales de l'Institut d'Etudes Orientales,* 10, 1952, pp. 326-363, Cahen referred to the economic and fiscal problems raised by Abū al-Wafā'. But Cahen's treatment was necessarily very limited because he had no access to any manuscripts except the Leyden copy. Since the latter is deficient anyhow, consisting only of three initial chapters as against the seven that are specified in the introductory list of contents, Cl. Cahen utilized the contribution of Woepcke, questioning, nevertheless, the reliability of some of his renderings of Abū al-Wafā''s text. [5]) This was, for instance, particularly true of Chapter One of the Fifth Section, rendered by Woepcke as „Des differents troupeaux de chameaux et de leur échange dans le territoire de Baçrah et Qoûfah, et dans les provinces environnantes . . ." [6]).

---

*) In its original version this paper was read at the annual meeting of the American Oriental Society, held in Cambridge, Massachusetts, on April 3-5, 1962.

1) For basic bio-bibliographical details, see *GAL,* i/223 S, i/400. Also, F. Woepcke, „Recherches sur l'histoire des sciences mathématiques chez les orientaux, d'apres des traités inédits arabes et persans," *JA,* V sér., 5, 1855, p. 243-246.

2) *supra,* p. 246-250.

3) Bibliotheek der Rijksuniversiteit te Leiden, *Cod. Or.* 103.

4) I am indebted to Mr. A. J. W. Huisman, the head of the Oriental Department in the Library of the University of Leyden, for drawing my attention to these publications.

5) Cl. Cahen, *art. cit.,* p. 337, n. 22 and 23.

6) F. Woepcke, *art. cit.,* p. 249.

During my trip to Egypt in Spring 1961, I had an opportunity to consult another manuscript of *Kitāb al-manāzil*, consisting of an eleventh century copy of that treatise, in possession of the Dār al-Kutub al-Miṣrīyah. [1] I checked the chapter in question. It read simply: *Fī ikhtilāf al-akrār bi-al-Sawād wa al-bilād al-qarībah minha wa taṣrīfuhā* (fo. 168r). One can understand Woepcke's rendering of *Sawād* with Baṣrah and Kūfah, but one has to regret his failure to understand that the chapter in question dealt with different types of *kurr* (pl. *akrār*), i.e., with a measure of capacity, and not with the herds of camels. [2]

Table I

The *kurr* system in the Sawād

	kurr	*qafīz*	*makkūk*	*ʿashīr*	*kaylajah*	*rubʿ*	*thumn*
kurr	—	60	480	600	1440	5760	11520
qafīz [3]	1/60	—	8	10	24	96	192
makkūk [4]	1/480	1/8	—	1 1/4	3	12	24
ʿashīr [5]	1/600	1/10	4/5	—	2 2/5	9 3/5	19 1/5
kaylajah [6]	1/1400	1/24	1/3	5/12	—	4	8
rubʿ [7]	1/5760	1/96	1/12	5/48	1/4	—	2
thumn [8]	1/11520	1/192	1/24	5/96	1/8	1/2	—

1) Cf., Dār al-kutub al-miṣrīyah, *Fihrist al-kutub al-ʿarabīyah*, A. H. 1307, v/185. According to its colophon (fo. 226r) it was completed on the 3rd of the *dhū al-ḥijjah*, 487 (i.e. Dec. 14, 1094). Unfortunately, the Cairo copy of Abū al-Wafāʾ's treatise (thereafter *Cairo Ms*) is not complete either. A confrontation with the Leyden copy (thereafter *Leyden Ms*) reveals that the *Cairo Ms* lacks introduction, list of contents, all of the first 'station' (*al-manzilah al-ūlā*) and the first chapter (*al-bāb al-awwal*) of the second 'station'. Its fo. 1 r opens with the first section (*al-faṣl al-awwal*: *Fī marātib al-aʿdād*) which is the initial part of the second chapter (*Fi ḍarb al-aʿdād al-ṣiḥāḥ*) of the second 'station' (cf., *Leyden Ms*, fo. 29r, fo. 32 v; also F. Woepcke, *art. cit.*, p. 248). The text of the *Cairo Ms* continues through the sixth chapter (*al-bāb al-sādis*: *Fī ḥisāb al-maʾāṣīr wa al-jawāz*, fo. 207 r. Cf. Cl. Cahen's correct emendation, *art. cit.*, p. 337, n. 23, of Woepcke's misreading of the word *jawāz*, *art. cit.*, p. 250) which ends abruptly with the words *sittīn dirhaman* on fo. 207 v. Marginal words on that folio indicate that fo. 208 r should have started with *fa-idhā jamaʿnāhā*, but it begins instead with *nasabnā al-sittah wa al-ʿishrīn*. This is a part of the second chapter of the seventh 'station'. Beginning with the third chapter on fo. 208 v (*al-bāb al-thālith*: *fī ḥisāb al-ujarāʾ*—not *al-ajzāʾ*, as *Leyden Ms*, fo. 4 r, has it) the seventh and final 'station' is complete.

2) In fairness to Woepcke one has to admit that the word contained in the list of contents of the *Leyden Ms.*, (fo. 3 v) reads *al-akwār*.

3) Cf., W. Hinz, *Islamische Masse und Gewichte*, Handbuch der Orientalistik, Ergänzungsband 1, Heft 1, 1955, p. 48-50. (thereafter *Islamische Masse und Gewichte*). Also, Cl. Cahen, *art. cit.*, p. 331.

4) Cf., *Islamische Masse und Gewichte*, p. 45-46.

5) *Ibid.*, p. 37.

6) *Ibid.*, p. 40.

7) *Ibid.*, p. 50-51.

8) *Ibid.*, p. 52.

This chapter is an interesting one, indeed. In line with the whole character of a manual for administrative officials, it contains expert information concerning the different types of the *kurr*, and their mutual relationship. These instructions were absolutely indispensable to those in charge of perception and evaluation of different crops and commodities involved in tax operations. How informative Abū al-Wafā'’s contribution is one can appreciate by realizing that he lists 10 types of the *kurr*, 24 other capacity and weight measures, and that he refers to 33 geographical areas or inhabitants thereof, where or by whom these or other types of measures were used. It also seems to me that the manner in which Abū al-Wafā' arranged his materials—first: information about the types of the *kurr*; secondly: relationship between these various types; and lastly: a tabulation of different kinds of crops according to different types of the *kurr*, to expedite their evaluation—all this seems to convey a message of caution to those of the modern scholars who attempt to work out scales of prices and salaries prior to an adequate understanding of the nature of differences between so many types of weight, measure and coin units which were in use in Medieval Islam.

According to Abū al-Wafā', the measures of capacity in the Sawād and the adjacent areas were based on the *kurr* system. There were five basic types of the *kurr*: *mu-*

Table II

Size of the *kurr muʿaddal* and of its subdivisions expressed in terms of the *raṭl* of wheat.

Unit	*raṭl weight*
kurr	7200 [1])
qafīz	120 [2])
makkūk	15 [3])
ʿashīr	12 [4])
kaylajah	5 [5])
rubʿ	1 1/4 [6])
thumn	5/8 [7])

1) *Ibid.*, p. 43.
2) *Ibid.*, p. 48.
3) *Ibid.*, p. 44.
4) Such a specification is not listed in *Islamische Masse und Gewichte.*
5) Cf., *Islamische Masse und Gewichte*, p. 40.
6) No such specification is listed in *Islamische Masse und Gewichte.*
7) No such specification is listed in *Islamische Masse und Gewichte.*

'addal [1]), *kāmil*, [2]) *fālij*, [3]) *hāshimī*, [4]) and *sulaymānī*. [5]) The most widely used was the *kurr mu'addal* to which the remaining ones were related, and with which were measured crops in all the administrative districts (*A'māl*) of the Sawād in the lifetime of the author. All these basic types of the *kurr* had subdivisionary units based on the regular *kurr* system (see Table I), but they were not alike as far as their capacity was concerned. To explain and define their particular sizes, Abū al-Wafā' first indicated the size of the *kurr mu'addal* in terms of *raṭl* of wheat (see Table II), and then discussed other types of the *kurr*, supplementing information about additional measures of capacity. The basic information from this chapter of Abū al-Wafā''s treatise has been tabulated below (see Table III).

Table III

Different types of the *kurr* listed by Abū al-Wafā'
(*Cairo Ms.*, fos. 169r-171v) [6])

Type of *kurr*	Also known as:	Used in the regions or by the people of:	Function	Relation to the *kurr mu'addal*	Consists of	Weight in *raṭl* of Baghdād
kāmil		Wāsiṭ, Jāmidah, Baṭā'iḥ		1/2	30 *qafīz*	[3600]
	makhtūm [7])	Upper land of the Baṣrah Tigris,[8]) Kaskar, Nahr al-Ṣilah, Shaṭṭ al-Fāris				
	jarīb [9])	Coastal areas [10])				
qanqal [11])		Baṣrah	to estimate palm trees, to measure unripe and ripe dates, olives, date seeds, nabk, salt [12])	5/12] [13])	120 *qafīz* [at 25 *raṭl* each]	3000
fālij		Sawād	for assessment of winter and spring crops	2/5	24 *qafīz*	[2880]
	mursal			30 *ṭasq*		
	abrajī	Jundāy Sābūr, Abraj, Anbār		10 *jarīb* [14])		
hāshimī		Ahwāz [15])	to measure government crops	1/2	20 *qafīz* [or 240 *qafīz* at 10 *raṭl* each]	2400
sulaymānī		Mawṣil, Jazīrah, Diyār Muḍar		[4/15] [16])	16 *qafīz*[17])	1920
dīnawarī		Jibāl		[1/12] [18])	5 *qafīz*	[600]
yazīdī		Bedouin areas of the Yaman[19])	[?]	[?]	75 *qafīz*	[?]

1) ‚Ausgeglichene' or ‚genormte' according to W. Hinz, *Islamische Masse und Gewichte*, p. 42. Also, H. Sauvaire, ‚Matériaux pour servir à l'histoire de la numismatique et de la métrologie musulmanes', *JA*, VIII ser., 8, 1886, p. 117, (thereafter ‚Matériaux'). Also, Cl. Cahen, art. cit., p. 336.

2) Cf., Cl. Cahen, *loc. cit.* This type of the *kurr* is not referred to in *Islamische Masse und Gewichte.*

3) Cf., Cl. Cahen, *loc. cit.* Also, ‚Matériaux', *JA*, VIII ser., 7, 1886, p. 426. Also, al-Khuwarazmī, *Mafātīḥ al-ʿulūm*, ed. G. van Vloten, 1895, p. 67 (thereafter *Mafātīḥ al-ʿulūm*). No reference in *Islamische Masse und Gewichte.*

4) Cf., Cl. Cahen, *loc. cit.* Also, ‚Matériaux', *JA*, VIII ser., 8, 1886, p. 117. Also, *Mafātīḥ al-ʿulūm*, p. 67. No reference in *Islamische Masse und Gewichte.*

5) Cf., Cl. Cahen, *loc. cit.*, No reference in ‚Matériaux', *Mafātīḥ al-ʿulūm*, or *Islamische Masse und Gewichte.*

6) Positions in square brackets are computed on the basis of data from the same chapter.

7) *Cairo Ms.*, *fo* 170 *r*. Not to be confused with a standard measure of capacity known under this name. Cf. *Cairo Ms.*, fo. 170 v. Also, Cl. Cahen, *art. cit.*, p. 350. Also, *Islamische Masse und Gewichte*, p. 44.

8) *Ahl al-aʿālī min Dijlat al-Baṣrah*, *Cairo Ms.*, fo. 170 r.

9) Not to be confused with a land measure known under this name. Cf. *Islamische Masse und Gewichte*, p. 65-66.

10) *Baʿḍ ahl al-sawāḥil*, *Cairo Ms.*, fo. 170 r.

11) No reference to this type of the *kurr* is found in *Islamische Masse und Gewichte.*

12) *Wa hādhā al-kurr yukhraṣu bi-hi al-nakhl wa yukālu bi-hi al-busr wa al-tamr wa al-zaytūn wa al-nawan wa al-nabq wa al-milḥ*, *Cairo Ms.*, fo. 171 r.

13) According to Abū al-Wafā' (*Cairo Ms.*, fo. 171 r) *al-qanqal . . . huwa mi'ah wa ʿishrūn qafīzan bi-al-muʿaddal . . . wa hādhā al-kurr yukhraṣu bi-hi* . . . (etc., see *supra*) . . . *wa qafīz al-khirṣ khamsah wa ʿishrūn raṭlan bi-al-baghdādhī fa-yakūnu al-kurr thalāthat alf raṭl.* The first part of this statement is in agreement with information found in ‚*Matériaux*', *JA*, VIII ser., 8, 1886, p. 117. A difficulty arises from Abū al-Wafā''s statement concerning the size of the *kurr qanqal* in terms of the *raṭl* weight. According to the authorities of E. W. Lane, *An Arabic-English Lexicon*, 1, vii, p. 2601 (cf. ‚Matériaux', loc. cit.), and according to *Mafātīḥ al-ʿulūm*, p. 67, the *kurr qanqal* was twice the size of the *kurr muʿaddal.* See also A. Grohmann's remarks on the *qanqal* in his *Einführung und Chrestomathie zur arabischen Papyruskunde*, (Monografie Archivu Orientalního, vol. XIII/i), Praha, 1955, p. 159-160, 162. If one is to judge by the number of the *qafīz* alone, then this information appears to be borne out by the statement of Abū al-Wafa'. Considering that the *kurr muʿaddal* amounted to 7200 *raṭl* (see Table II) the size of the *kurr qanqal* would come to 14400 *raṭl.* However, Abū al-Wafa' explicitly recorded that that *kurr* amounted to 3000 *raṭl.* The solution to this apparent contradiction is to be found in the nature of the *qafīz* involved in the subdivisionary system of the *kurr qanqal.* This *qafīz*, 120 of which making up 1 *kurr qanqal*, was not the regular *qafīz* of 120 *raṭl* (see Table II), but a smaller one consisting of 25 *raṭl* only. In this way, although consisting of 120 *qafīz* and creating the impression of being twice the size of the *kurr muʿaddal*, the *kurr qanqal* really weighed only 3000 *raṭl*, being not twice but 5/12 of the size of the *kurr muʿaddal.* A similar pattern applied to the *kurr hāshimī*, see *infra*, n. 15.

14) *Wa ahl Jundāy Sābūr wa Abraj wa Anbār yakīlūna bi-hādhā al-kurr wa tusammūnahu* [*sic !*] *al-mursal wa yusammā ayḍan al-abrajī wa huwa ʿindahum thalāthūn ṭasqan wa al-ṭasq mikyāl la-hum wa yajʿalūnahu ʿasharat ajribah ayḍan*, *Cairo Ms.*, fo. 170 v.

15) . . . *bi-al-Ahwāz wa akthar kuwarihā wa yaqsimūnahā* [*sic !*]*ilā ithnāʿashar jarīban kull jarīb ʿasharat makhātīm kull makhtūm qafīzān fa-yakūnu al-kurr ʿindahum ithnā ʿashar jarīban wa mi'ah wa ʿishrīn makhtūman wa mi'atay wa arbaʿīn qafīzan wa alfay wa arbaʿ mi'at raṭl bi-al-baghdādhī*, *Cairo Ms.*, fo. 170 v. The nature of the subdivisionary system of the *kurr hāshimī* resembles that of the *kurr qanqal* (see *supra*, n. 13. The *kurr hāshimī* was also divided into 240 *qafīz* (12 *jarīb* = 120 *makhtūm* = 240 qafīz), creating the impression of being 4 times the

size of the *kurr muʿaddal*, if judged by the number of the *qafīz*. But the *qafīz* in the system of the *kurr hāshimī* amounted to 10 raṭl only. Thus the actual relation of the *kurr muʿaddal* to the *kurr hāshimī* was 1 : 3.

As for the *makhtūm* used in Ahwāz, its size amounted to 20 *raṭl*. This information of Abū al-Wafā' is corroborated by *Kitāb al-Ḥāwī* (cf., ‚Matériaux', *JA*, VIII sér., 8, 1886, p. 135; Cl. Cahen, *art. cit.*, p. 362) according to which 1 *makhtūm* = 1 *makkūk* [15 *raṭl*] + 1 *kaylajah* [5 *raṭl*] = 20 *raṭl*, and also by *Mafātīḥ al-ʿulūm*, p. 67, according to which 1 *makhtūm* = 1/6 of the *qafīz muʿaddal* [i.e. 1/6 of 120 *ratl* = 20 *raṭl*].

16) *al-kurr al-sulaymānī fa-innahu suds wa ʿushr al-muʿaddal, Cairo Ms.*, fo. 170 v. [i.e. 1/6 + 1/10 = 4/15].

17) *al-dīnawarī wa huwa niṣf suds al-kurr al-muʿaddal, Cairo Ms.*, fo. 171 r. [i.e. 1/2 1/6 of the *kurr muʿaddal*, i.e. 1/12].

18) If the *qafīz* in the *yazīdī* system is the regular 120 *raṭl* unit, then this *kurr* would be the most voluminous one, amounting to 9500 *raṭl*, thus being 1 1/4 the size of the *kurr muʿaddal.*

19) *Nawāḥī al-ʿarab min ahl al-Yaman, Cairo Ms.*, fo. 171 v.

XIII

THE *TASRĪF* AND *TAS'ĪR* CALCULATIONS IN MEDIAEVAL MESOPOTAMIAN FISCAL OPERATIONS

Professional activities of Mesopotamian fiscal agents in the Middle Ages were greatly complicated by the prevailing lack of a uniform system of the measures of capacity. The use of a uniform system of capacity measures would have facilitated assessment and perception of the *muqāsamāt*, i.e., taxes based on a percentage of the crops, as well as in the evaluation of taxes paid by means of deliveries in kind. In order to overcome the many difficulties arising from the lack of uniformity, fiscal authorities adopted a certain degree of standardization with regard to capacity measures and the value relationship between different species of agricultural produce. This standardization was helpful in the achievement of equation calculations between agricultural species differing from each other by their value, quantity, and the type of capacity measure with which they were handled. The equation or conversion processes were called *taṣrīf*. On the other hand, processes consisting of the apprizing of crops were known as *tas'īr*.

Some interesting information concerning the *taṣrīf* and *tas'īr* calculation methods is contained in the *Kitāb al-manāzil fī mā yaḥtāju ilayhi al-kuttāb wa al-'ummāl min ṣinā'at al-ḥisāb*, composed between A.D. 979 and 983, by al-Būzajānī [1]). An analogous text, found in

1) For further references concerning this treatise, as well as its preserved manuscript copies, *see* A. S. Ehrenkreutz, "The *kurr* system in Medieval Iraq", *JESHO*, 5, iii, 1962, pp. 309-310. This fairly close dating of the composition of the *Kitāb al-manāzil* may be inferred from personal references in the text, such as that occurring on fo. 171 r of the *Cairo Ms.*, or on fo. 1 v. of the Leyden Ms.: *Mawlānā al-Malik al-Sayyid Shāhānshāh al-Ajall al-Manṣūr 'Aḍud al-Dawlah wa Tāj al-Millah*. This means that al-Būzajānī wrote this treatise before the death of 'Aḍud al-Dawlah (i.e. A. H. 372) but after his assumption of the title Tāj al-Millah, which had taken place in A. H. 369.

Kitāb al-ḥāwī li-l-aʿmāl al-sulṭānīyah wa rusūm al-ḥisāb al-dīwānīyah and dating from the second quarter of the eleventh century of the Chr. era [1]), has been analyzed by Cl. Cahen [2]). However, the chronological precedence of al-Būzajānī's contribution, as well as its historical implications, seem to warrant a closer scrutiny of its contents.

As I have indicated in an earlier publication [3]), al-Būzajānī listed five types of the *kurr* which were established as the basic measures of capacity in the Sawād or Lower Mesopotamia. These were: *muʿaddal*, *kāmil*, *fālij*, *hāshimī* and *sulaymānī*. The first of them was regarded as the standard one since the remaining types of the *kurr* were related to it; furthermore, it was with the *kurr muʿaddal* that crops were measured in all administrative districts of that region in the lifetime of the author [4]). Al-Būzajānī also referred to a capacity measure called *jarīb* [5]), introduced in Fārs with the apparent intention of achieving uniformity in the local system. *This [measure] was established by our Lord al-Malik.... ʿAḍud al-Dawlah wa Tāj al-Millah. It is called al-ʿaḍūdī. It equals two and a half qafīz according to the muʿaddal [system]-(bi-al-muʿaddal), ten qafīz according to its own qafīz [system]-(bi-qufzānihi); each qafīz equals six kaff, each kaff ten ʿashīr. Each qafīz equals thirty raṭl according to the baghdādī [system] (bi-al-baghdādī), and twenty-four jarīb of this jarīb [system] equal one kurr according to the muʿaddal [system] (bi-al-muʿaddal)* [6]). The relation of the Mesopotamian types of *kurr* and of the *jarīb* to the *kurr muʿaddal* was as follows:

---

1) Cf., Cl. Cahen, "Documents relatifs à quelques techniques iraqiennes au début du onzième siècle", *Ars Islamica*, 15-16, 1951, p. 24.

2) *Idem*, "Quelques problèmes économiques et fiscaux de l'Iraq Buyide d'après un traité de mathématiques", *Annales de l'Institut d'Etudes Orientales*, 10, 1952, pp. 326-363.

3) A. S. Ehrenkreutz, *art. cit.*

4) *Idem*, p. 312.

5) Not to be confused with a land measure known under this name, cf., W. Hinz, *Islamische Masse und Gewichte*, Handbuch der Orientalistik, Ergänzungsband I, Heft I, 1955, pp. 65-66.

6) Cairo Ms., (thereafter: *Ms.*) fo. 171 r. For the nature of different capacity measures occurring in this text see W. Hinz, *op. cit.* ʿAḍud al-Dawlah ruled over Fārs from A. D. 944.

mu'addal	1
kāmil	1/2
fālij	2/5
hāshimī	1/3
sulaymānī	4/15
jarīb	1/24

In order to help fiscal agents and scribes to handle difficulties arising from differences between the various types of the *kurr*, al-Būzajānī composed a special section in his treatise, entitled *Fī taṣrīf hādhihi al-akrār ba'ḍihā ilā ba'ḍ* [1]). It consists of simple arithmetical formulas based on the relationship between the different types of the *knrr* measures, arranged in the following pattern:

To convert *al-mu'addal* into *al-kāmil*—take 1/2 of it
To convert *al-mu'addal* into *al-fālij* take 2/5 of it
To convert *al-mu'addal* into *al-hāshimī*—take 1/3 of it
To convert *al-mu'addal* into *al-sulaymānī*—take 1/6 plus 1/10 of it [i.e: 4/15]
To convert *al-kāmil* into *al-mu'addal*—multiply it by 2
To convert *al-kāmil* into *al-fālij*—subtract 1/5 of it
To convert *al-kāmil* into *al-hāshimī*—take 2/3 of it
To convert *al-kāmil* into *al-sulaymānī*—take 1/3 plus 1/5 of it [i.e. 8/15]
To convert *al-fālij* into *al-mu'addal*, etc., etc.

This section is followed by one entitled *Fī taṣrīf al-jirbān al-'aḍudīyah ilā al-akrār al-madhkūrah* [2]), and arranged in a similar pattern:

To convert *al-jirbān* (*sic!*) into *al-mu'addal*—multiply it by 24
To convert *al-jirbān* (*sic!*) into *al-kāmil*—multiply it by 12
To convert *al-jirbān* (*sic!*) into *al-fālij*, etc., etc.
To convert *al-mu'addal* into *al-jirbān* (*sic!*)—take 1/3 × 1/8 of it [i.e. 1/24]
To convert *al-kāmil* into *al-jirbān* (*sic!*)—take 1/2 × 1/6 of it [3]) [1/12]
To convert *al-fālij*, etc., etc.

---

1) *Ms.*, fo. 172r. 2) *Ibid.*, fo. 172 r-v.
3) *Ibid.*, fo. 172 v, reads *one half times one seventh.*

The following section was entitled by al-Būzajānī *Fī ajnās al-ḥubūb wa taṣrīfihā* [1]). According to its contents, different types of grain and of some other agricultural and horticultural produce were categorised by fiscal authorities into four basic value classes [2]). This was done in order to facilitate the assessment of these commodities. The four value classes were: sesame, wheat, barley and *jahjandum* [3]). The highest class as far as its value was concerned, was that of sesame (*simsim*). It included the following species: cumin (*kammūn*), mustard (*khardal*), coriander (*shūnīz*) [4]), caraway (*karawayā*), poppy (*khashkhāsh*), the seeds of lucerne (*bizr al-ratbah*). The species belonging to this class were the highest rank-wise and their value was always approximately twice the value of the wheat class. The species classed with wheat (*ḥinṭah*) consisted of the following: chick-pea (*ḥummaṣ*), haricot beans (*lubiyā*), lentil (*'adas*), linseed (*bizr al-kattān*), garden cress (*ḥabb al-rashād*) [5]), fenugreek (*ḥilbah*), safflower (*qurṭum*), *ḥabbat al-khaḍrā* [6]), raisin (*zabīb*), sumac (*summāq*), unshelled almonds (*lawz bi-qishrihi*), unshelled hazel-nuts (*bunduq bi-qishrihi*), hemp-seeds (*shahdānj*). This category constituted a middle class, the value of its species being always approximately twice that of the barley [7]), and half the value of the sesame class. As for the species classed with barley (*sha'īr*) they were: whole rice (*aruzz bi-qishrihi*), varieties of millet such as *jāwars* [8]), *dhurrah* [9]), *dukhn* [10]), variety of oat

---

1) *Ibid.*, fos. 172v-173v.

2) Cf., Cl. Cahen, art. cit., pp. 336-337. Also idem, 'Contribution à l'étude des impôts dans l'Égypte Médiévale', *JESHO*, 5, iii, 1952, p. 268.

3) With only one exception, when it is spelled *jahkandum*, this term consistently appears as *jahjandum* in the *Cairo Ms. Kitāb al-ḥāwī* (Cf., Cl. Cahen, loc. cit.) shows *jahgandum* which is much closer to its original Persian version. For explanation of its etymology see below, p. 50, n. 4.

4) Cf., F. Steingass, *Persian-English dictionary*, p. 767. Also, Cl. Cahen, 'Quelques problèmes économiques et fiscaux de l'Iraq Buyide. . . ,', p. 336.

5) Lepidium sativum, cf., A. Siggel, *Arabisch-deutsches Wörterbuch der Stoffe*, 1950, p. 27.

6) *Pistacia terebinthus*, cf., *supra*.

7) The same value relationship was maintained in Egypt, cf., D. Müller-Wodarg, 'Die Landwirtschaft Ägyptens in der frühen 'Abbāsidenzeit', *der Islam*, 32, 1955-57, p. 21.

8) Cf., F. Steingass, *op. cit.*, p. 354. Also, A. Siggel, op. cit., p. 25.

9) Cf., D. Müller-Wodarg, *loc. cit.*

10) Cf., *Ibid.*, p. 22. Also, Cl. Cahen, *loc. cit.*

called *hurtumān* [1]). Furthermore: the *kabīs* dates, a type of coriander called *kusbarah* [2]), and lentil seeds (*majj*), in Syrian regions: beans (*baqilā*), and *al-khullī* [3]) in the regions of the Jabal. This was the lowest of the three above-categories, estimated at half the value of the wheat and one fourth of the value of the sesame class. As for the *jahjandum* [4]), this category was made up by the two last classes thus corresponding to half a *kurr* of wheat and half a *kurr* of barley. This constituted a class by itself to which no other species were related. Its value amounted approximately ṭo one half plus one fourth [i.e. 3/4] of the value of the wheat class and to one fourth plus one eighth (i.e. 3/8) of that of the sesame.

There existed other species whose prices were not comprised in such a standardization. The most important of those in the districts of the Sawād were, according to al-Būzajānī [5]), shelled nuts and almonds *al-jawz wa-al-lawz al-muqashshar*), shelled pistachioes, chestnuts, jujubes and hazel-nuts (*al-fustaq, wa-al-shahbalūṭ wa-al-nabq* [6]), *wa-al-bunduq al-muqashshar*), dry pears (*al-kummathrā al-yābis*, and stoned peaches (*al-khawkh al-muqawwar*) and others of the kind.

As long as the *tasrīf* involving species belonging to different value classes was done by means of the same type of capacity measures, the following formulas could be used as suggested by al-Būzajānī: [7])

To equate sesame with wheat—reduce it by 1/2
To equate sesame with barley—reduce it by 1/4
To equate sesame with *jahjandum*—reduce it by 1/4 + 1/8 [i.e. 3/8]
To equate wheat with sesame—multiply it by 2

1) Cf., A. Siggel, *op. cit.*, p. 72.

2) Ms., fo. 173 r. reads al-kasīrah which I take to be a faulty rendering by the copyist of *kusbarah* or *kuzbarah*, cf., A. Siggel, *op. cit.*, p. 63.

3) '... a rel. n. from *khullah* as meaning the sweet kind of plants or herbage' (?), cf., E. W. Lane, *An Arabic-English Lexicon*, 1, ii, p. 781.

4) This term was obviously borrowed from Persian terminology in which *jawgandum* meant exactly barley-and-wheat (*hordeum et triticum*), cf., I. A. Vullers, *Lexicon Persico-Latinum etymologicum*, i. 534. Also, consult A. Siggel, *op. cit.*, p. 26, for the meaning of *jandum*.

5) *Ms.*, fo. 173 r-v.

6) *Zizyphus spina Christi*, i. e. jujube. Cf., A. Siggel, *op. cit.*, p. 70.

7) *Ms.*, fo. 173 v.

To equate wheat with barley—reduce it by 1/2
To equate wheat with *jahjandum*—reduce it by 1/2 + 1/4 [i.e. 3/4]
To equate barley etc., etc.

More complicated problems arose whenever fiscal agents or scribes in charge of the *taṣrīf* were confronted by various classes of species which were handled with different types of capacity measures. To cope with such situations, al-Būzajānī compiled extensive tabulations which were to simplify these rather complicated twofold conversion operations. They were presented in a long chapter entitled *Fī taṣrīf al-ghallāt baʿḍihā ilā baʿḍ, idhā kānat mukhtalifat al-kayl* [1]) and consisting of four sections.

First Section

Equation of sesame with all kinds of species and all types of measures [2]).

To equate *al-kurr al-muʿaddal* of sesame:
with wheat—
if *al-kurr al-kāmil* [3]):—take 1/4 of it [4])
if *al-kurr al-fālij*—take 1/5 of it
if *al-kurr al-hāshimī*—take 1/6 of it
if *al-kurr al-sulaymānī*—take 1/10 + 1/3 × 1/10 [i.e. 2/15] of it
with barley—
if *al-kurr al-kāmil*—take 1/8 of it
if *al-kurr al-fālij*—take 1/10 of it
if *al-kurr al-hāshimī*—take 1/2 × 1/6 [i.e. 1/12] of it
if *al-kurr al-sulaymānī*—take 2/3 × 1/10 [i.e. 1/15] of it
with *jahjandum*
if *al-kurr al-kāmil*—take 1/8 + 1/2 × 1/8 [i.e. 3/16] [5])
if *al-kurr al-fālij*—take 1/10 + 1/2 × 1/10 [i.e. 3/20] of it
if *al-kurr al-hāshimī*—take 1/8 of it

1) *Ibid.*, fo. 173 v-179 v.
2) *Ibid.*, fo. 174 r, reads literally: *Fī-mā yuṣarrafu ilā al-simsim min sā'ir al-aṣnāj wa sā'ir anwāʿ al-makāyīl.*
3) I. e. if the quantity of wheat consists of one *kurr kāmil.*
4) I. e. take $\frac{1}{4}$ of the *kurr muʿaddal* of sesame.
5) *Ms.*, fo. 174 r, reads $\frac{1}{8} + \frac{1}{2} \times \frac{1}{8}$.

if *al-kurr al-sulaymānī*—take 1/10 of it
To equate *al-kurr al-kāmil* of sesame:
with wheat
if *al-kurr al-mu'addal*—leave it intact
if *al-kurr al-fālij*—take 2/5 of it
if *al-kurr al-hāshimī*—take 2/3 of it
if *al-kurr al-sulaymānī*—take 1/6 + 1/10 [i.e. 4/15] of it
To equate *al-kurr al-kāmil* of sesame:
with barley
if *al-kurr al-mu'addal* etc., etc.

Second Section [1])

Equation of wheat with all kinds of species and all types of measures.
To equate *al-kurr al-mu'addal* of wheat:
with sesame
if *al-kurr al-kāmil*—leave it intact
if al-kurr al-fālij etc., etc.

Third Section [2])

Equation of barley with all kinds of species and all types of measures.
To equate *al-kurr al-mu'addal* of barley:
with sesame
if *al-kurr al-kāmil*—multiply it by 2
if *al-kurr al-fālij* etc., etc.

Fourth Section [3])

Equation of *jahjandum* with all kinds of species and all types of measures.
To equate *al-kurr al-mu'addal* of *jahjandum*:
with sesame
if *al-kurr al-kāmil* [4]) add to it 1/3 of it
if *al-kurr al-fālij* etc., etc.

---

1) *Ibid.*, fo. 175 v-177 r.
2) *Ibid.*, fo. 177 r-178 r.
3) *Ibid.*, fo. 178 r-179 v.
4) *Ibid.*, fo. 178 r, reads *al-kurr al-mu'addal.*

After compiling all of these detailed tabulations, al-Būzajānī presented a few chapters containing examples which demonstrated the applicability of the formulas. Examples listed in the first of them were to serve the trainees to practice the art of *taṣrīf* involving various species of grain and different types of capacity measures [1]). For instance:

> We have 10 *kurr muʿaddal* of sesame. We want to know what does it amount to in terms of one *kurr fālij* of barley? We multiply 10 *kurr* of sesame by 10 = 100, and this is the amount of barley in terms of the *kurr fālij*.
>
> Let us suppose that we have barley whose amount in terms of the *kāmil* system (*bi-al-kāmil*) has been established by converting (*taṣrīf*) a quantity of sesame measured in terms of the *kurr muʿaddal* (*bi-al-muʿaddal*). We wish to learn how much this basic quantity (*aṣl*) amounts to. This is like saying: What is the equivalent of barley *bi-al-kāmil* in terms of sesame *bi-al-muʿaddal*? Or it is like saying what does 424 *kurr*, 6 *qafīz*, 5 *ʿashīr* of barley *bi-al-kāmil* amount to in terms of sesame *bi-al-muʿaddal*? We take 1/8 of 424 *kurr*, or 6 *qafīz*, of 5 *ʿashīr*, which equals 53 *kurr*, 80 1/8 *ʿashīr*, and this is the quantity of sesame *bi-al-muʿaddal*.

Examples presented in another chapter [2]) consist of simple *tasʿīr* calculations requiring no *taṣrīf* processes. For instance: [3])

The prince of one *kurr muʿaddal* of sesame is 65 *dīnār*.

We wish to know the price of six *kurr fālij* of wheat.

One *kurr muʿaddal* of sesame equals 5 *kurr fālij* of wheat [4]). Thus 5 *kurr fālij* of wheat cost 65 *dīnār*. How much is 6 *kurr fālij* of wheat? Six times 65 *dīnārs* equals 390. Divide it by 5 and you get 78 *dīnārs*. This is the price of 6 *kurr fālij* [5]) of wheat.

Concluding remarks

The primary purpose of this paper has been to make known the

1) *Ibid.*, fo. 179 v-180 v.: *Fī amthilah yartāḍu bi-hā al-mutaʿallim fī taṣrīf aṣnāf al-ḥubūb bi-anwāʿ al-makāyil.*

2) *Ibid.*, fo. 188 r-191 v.: *Fī tasʿīr.*

3) *Ibid.* fo. 191 v-193 r *'Fī ḥisāb al-ghallāt al-muṣarrafah bi-al-makāyil al-mukhtalifah.*

4) Cf. above, p. 51.

5) *Ms.*, fo. 192 r. reads *muʿaddal.*

contents of the sections from the *Kitāb al-manāzil* which deal with the problem of the *taṣrīf* and *tas'īr*. It goes without saying that information derived from this and similar texts should contribute to a better understanding of technical procedures employed in the fiscal activities of Medieval Mesopotamian society. To obtain a good idea of the historical significance of such materials, one should consult the ingenious discussion of relevant chapters from the *Kitāb al-ḥāwī*, produced by Cl. Cahen who thoroughly analyzed most of the problems explicitly and implicity referred to by al-Būzajānī [1]). As a supplement to Cahen's analysis, I wish to illustrate below a practical method of utilising information obtained from al-Būzajānī's text for the purpose of historical criticism.

In the *Kitāb al-wuzarā'* one can find the following fiscal information referring to the *Sawād* in the beginning of the 4/10 century [2]):

A. The quantity of barley levied from the *Sawād* amounted to 340,000 *kurr muṣarrafan bi-al-fālij*.

B. The price of 2 *kurr bi-al-mu'addal* of wheat and barley amounted to 90 *dīnārs*.

C. The value of the levy [3]) was 4,080,000 *dīnārs*.

The meaning of item A is clear. Two *kurr mu'addal* of wheat and barley, in other words meaning : two *kurr mu'addal* of *jahjandum*—cost 90 *dīnārs*, the price of one *kurr mu'addal of jahjandum* amounting, thus, to 45 dīnārs. By applying the value scale of al-Būzajāni [4]), one may infer —as Cahen rightly suggested [5])—that the officially fixed price of one *kurr mu'addal* of wheat amounted to 60 *dīnārs*, while that of barley to 30 *dīnārs*. If one looks at item C, one can easily grasp that the figure indicating the total value of the levy cannot possibly imply the *mu'addal* type of the *kurr*, for in that case 340,000 *kurr* (as listed *sub* A) would produce 10,200,000 dīnārs and not 4,080,000. The explanation of this

1) See above, p. 47 and n. 2.
2) *The historical remains of Hilâl al-Sâbi*, ed., by H. F. Amedroz, Leyden, 1904, p. 188.
3) Literally: *fa-kāna thaman al-akrār*.
4) See above, p. 49.
5) Cl. Cahen, *art. cit.*, p. 342-343.

apparent discrepancy lies in the nature of the *kurr* system in which the amount listed *sub* A, has been recorded. Indeed, it is in terms of the *kurr fālij* (*bi-al-fālij*) that the 340,000 *kurr* of barley have been assessed. Since, according to al-Būzajānī [1]), the *kurr fālij* cost 2/5 of the *kurr mu'addal*, the price of one *kurr fālij* of barley in the light of the statement under consideration, amounted to 12 dīnārs. Hence the figure of 4,080,000 *dīnārs* obtained from 340,000 *kurr* of barley.

By applying the value scale of al-Būzajānī to these few price data, one could possibly reconstruct a list of official prices for agricultural produce. However, the prices listed in the above statement from *Kitāb al-wuzarā'* did not represent typical normal prices prevailing in Mesopotamia in the 4/10 century. The normal price of wheat fluctuated between 30 to 40 *dīnārs per kurr* (*mu'addal?*) as suggested by Cl. Cahen [2]). Al-Būzajānī's reference to the price of the *kurr mu'addal* of sesame [3]) implied the price of 32 1/2 *dīnārs* for one *kurr mu'addal* of wheat. Even if this reference was adduced by al-Būzajānī as a theoretical example, one would not be wrong in assuming that such a price was based on the author's personal experience with the prevailing level of prices. This plausible assumption with regard to the normal price of wheat as well as the availability of the value classification, as supplied by al-Būzajānī, make it possible to tabulate an index of normal prices of certain species of agricultural produce, prevailing in Lower Mesopotamia or the *Sawād* in the Tenth century of the Chr. era. To be sure, such an index does not positively reestablish the exact prices of the species under consideration, but it may nonetheless serve as a useful checking guide in our studies of Medieval economic source materials.

1) See above, p. 49.
2) Cl. Cahen, *loc. cit.* Also, E. Ashtor, 'Essai sur les prix et les salaires dans l'empire califien', *RSO*, 36, 1961, p. 31.
3) See above, p. 48.

Notes of page 56

1) Prices in this table are indicated only in terms of *dīnārs* in order to avoid—for the time being at least—the intricate problem of the exchange rate between the *dīnārs* and the *dirhams*.
2) See above, p. 49 and n. 6.
3) See above, p. 49 and n. 3.

Index of Prices of Agricultural Produce in 10th Cent. *Sawād*

Price of one kurr in dīnārs [1]

Species	*kurr muʿaddal*	*kurr kāmil*	*kurr fālij*	*kurr hāshimi*	*kurr sulaymāni*
almonds, unshelled (*lawz bi-qishrihi*)	30-40	15-20	12-16	10-13⅓	8-10⅔
barley (*shāʿir*)	15-20	7½-10	6-8	5-6⅔	4-5⅓
barley mixed with wheat *see jahjandum*					
caraway (*karawayā*)	60-80	30-40	24-32	20-26⅔	16-21⅓
chick-pea (*ḥummas*)	30-40	15-20	12-16	10-13⅓	8-10⅔
coriander (*shūnīz*)	60-80	30-40	24-32	20-26⅔	16-21⅓
cumin (*kammūn*)	60-80	30-40	24-32	20-26⅔	16-21⅓
dhurrah [a variety of millet]	15-20	7½-10	6-8	5-6⅔	4-5⅓
dukhn [a variety of millet]	15-20	7½-10	6-8	5-6⅔	4-5⅓
fenugreek (*ḥilbah*)	30-40	15-20	12-16	10-13⅓	8-10⅔
garden cress (*ḥabb al-rashād*)	30-40	15-20	12-16	10-13⅓	8-10⅔
ḥabbat al-khaḍra [2])	30-40	15-20	12-16	10-13⅓	8-10⅔
haricot beans (*Lubiyā*)	30-40	15-20	12-16	10-13⅓	8-10⅔
hazel-nuts, unshelled (*bunduq bi-qishrihi*)	30-40	15-20	12-16	10-13⅓	8-10⅔
hemp-seeds (*shahdānj*)	30-40	15-20	12-16	10-13⅓	8-10⅔
hurtumān [a variety of oat]	15-20	7½-10	6-8	5-6⅔	4-5⅓
jahjandum [3])	22½	11¼-15	9-12	7½-10	6-8
jāwars [a variety of millet]	15-20	7½-10	6-8	5-6⅔	4-5⅓
lentil (*ʿadas*)	30-40	15-20	12-16	10-13⅓	8-10⅔
linseed (*bizr al-kattan*)	30-40	15-20	12-16	10-13⅓	8-10⅔
lucerne, the seeds of (*bizr al-raṭbah*)	60-80	30-40	24-32	20-26⅔	16-21⅓
millet, see *jāwars, dhurrah, dukhn*					
mustard (*khardal*)	60-80	30-40	24-32	20-26⅔	16-21⅔
oat [a variety of], see *hurṭumān*					
poppy (*khashkhāsh*)	60-80	30-40	24-32	20-26⅔	16-21⅓
raisin [or dry raisin] (*zabīb*)	30-40	15-20	12-16	10-13⅓	8-10⅔
rice, whole (*aruzz bi-qishrihi*)	15-20	7½-10	6-8	5-6⅔	4-5⅓
safflower (*qurṭum*)	30-40	15-20	12-16	10-13⅓	8-10⅔
sesame (*simsim*)	60-80	30-40	24-32	20-26⅔	16-21⅓
sumac (*summāq*)	30-40	15-20	12-16	10-13⅓	8-10⅔
wheat (*ḥinṭah*)	30-40	15-20	12-16	10-13⅓	8-10⅔
wheat mixed with barley, see *jahjandum*					

XIV

AL-BŪZAJĀNĪ (A.D. 939-997) ON THE "*MĀʾṢĪR*"

Considering* how intensive and extensive was the scope of internal and external trade of Medieval Near East, the operations of customs houses must have constituted an important feature of the economic life of its society. Although M. ʿAwwād has published a useful compilation of Medieval texts pertaining to this problem,[1]) we must continue our search for additional source materials before an attempt is made at a systematic reconstruction of the organizational nature of that interesting fiscal institution.[2]) It thus goes without saying that relevant information furnished by al-Būzajānī (A. D. 939-997), an established authority in Mesopotamian fiscal

*) *Note de Cl. Cahen*: Réfléchissant aux douanes islamiques (voir JESHO 1964/3), j'ai demandé à notre ami A. S. Ehrenkreutz ce que contenait *à* cet égard le microfilm d'al-Būzajānī en sa possession; il m'a envoyé la présente note, dont je le remercie vivement.

1) Mikhāʾīl ʿAwwād, *al-Māʾṣir fī bilād al-Rūm wa al-Islām*, Baghdād, 1948.

2) Cf. methodological remarks and the contents of the most recent contribution by Cl. Cahen, "Douanes et Commerce dans les Ports Méditerranéens de l'Égypte Médiévale d'après le *Minhādj* d'Al-Makhzūmī," *JESHO*, 7, iii, 1964, pp. 217-314. A parallel study in the field of Byzantine history has been contributed by H. Antoniadis-Bibicou, *Recherches sur les douanes à Byzance*, (Cahiers des annales, 20) Paris, 1963.

procedures, should merit our special attention. I refer here to his *Kitāb al-manāzil* [1]) which includes a chapter (*al-bāb al-sādis of al-manzila al-sādisa*) dealing with the problem of customs establishments (*amr al-mā' ṣīr*, fo. 193 v). Its full title *Fī ḥisāb al-mā' ṣīr wa al-jawāz* is listed in the main table of contents (Leyden *ms.* fo. 5 v), as well as in the introductory index to the sixth *manzila* (Cairo *ms.* fo. 194 r). Unfortunately the Cairo manuscript containing this part of the *Kitāb al-manāzil*, shows a deplorable text *lacuna*, so that instead of announced three sections, only introductory comments have been preserved of the chapter in question. The text of the chapter, which begins on fo. 207 r, is dropped abruptly at the end of fo. 207 v. The text on the following page, i.e. fo. 208 r, belongs to another *manzila*.[2]) To make matters worse several words in the survived portion are so defaced that they are hardly if at all legible.

Truncated though it is, the text of al-Būzajānī contains a few interesting points which deserve being recorded here as a modest contribution to the study of Medieval Near Eastern customs organisation.

Al-Būzajānī's discussion begins with a few terminological remarks. It appears from them that in the Tenth century Lower Mesopotamia (Sawād) the term *al-mā' ṣīr* [3]) signified not only customs establishments themselves but also toll fees collected for the right of passing through (*jibāya ḥaqq al-ijtiyāz*, fo. 207 r). However, apart from *al-mā' ṣīr* the term *al-marākiz* (*ibid.*) was also in use.[4]) Customs examination (*al-taftīsh*, *ibid.*) administered by customs officials (*aṣḥāb al-marākiz*, *ibid.*; also, *al-mufattish*, fo. 207 v) was called *al-tafsīr* (fo. 207 r). So was the evaluation of customs dues (*mablagh al-tafsīr*, fo. 207 v).

As for the customs fees (*al-rusūm*, fo. 207 r) we learn from al-Būzajānī that the method of their assessment was not alike in all territories. Their nature was determined by the will of the sulṭān. There were customs assessed *ad valorem*. In such a case the sulṭān claimed a percentage of the value of all goods passing through the customs. Such was the tithe system (*a 'shār*) in Basra, 'Umān and the maritime districts (*sawāḥil al-baḥr*) down to the confines of India (*nawāḥī al-Hind*). Al-Būzajānī elaborated somewhat on the application of this system: "from every piece of cloth and from other goods a stipulated quantity of dirhams is collected, consisting of various amounts according to the value of the goods" (fo. 207 v).

The procedure of collecting customs dues was quite simple whenever arriving merchandise consisted of items covered by the same tariff. In that case there was no need for computations arising from difference in the value of the merchandise. How simple this procedure was is illustrated by another example furnished by al-

---

1) For further references concerning that treatise as well as its preserved manuscript copies, see A. S. Ehrenkreutz, "The *kurr* system in Medieval Iraq," *JESHO*, 5, iii, 1962, pp. 309-310; also, *idem*, "The *taṣrīf* and *tas'īr* calculations in Medieval Mesopotamian fiscal operations," *ibid.*, 7, i, 1964, p. 46, n. 1.

2) *Cf. JESHO*, 5, iii, 1962, p. 10, n. 1.

3) This spelling differs from the plural form *mā'ṣir* normally found with Medieval lexicographers. *Cf.* M. 'Awwād, *op. cit.*, p. 7-10.

4) *Cf.*, al-Ḥarīrī (d. 1122): *wa-yaqūlūna li-markaz al-ḍarā'ib al-mā'ṣir. Apud* 'Awwād, *op. cit.*, p. 7. It is also possible that the word *al-marākiz* has crept into the Cairo *ms.* because of a mistake of the copyist who failed to reproduce correctly a fitting word *marāṣid*, cf. M. J. de Goeje, *Index, Glossarium et addenda et emendanda*, (BGA, 4) 1879. p. 247.

Būzajānī: "If the customs charge per load (*ḥiml*) is 40 dirhams and 200 loads arrive at the *mā' ṣir*, one multiplies 200 by 40. This makes 8,000, which is the total of customs assessment" (fo. 207 v).

More sophisticated calculations were naturally required when the bulk of the merchandise arriving at the customs consisted of different commodities. Once again al-Būzajānī resorts to a practical example, to explain this more complicated procedure:" Of the total of 200 loads, 30 loads consist of perfumes, 40 loads of cloth and 130 [1]) loads are of cheapest kind (? *saqaṭ*) [2]). The charge collected from the perfumes amounts to 50 dirhams per load; that imposed on the cloth is 40 dirhams; and the last mentioned is charged 5 dirhams per load. To establish what is the charge on these 200 loads we multiply . . . and we add up. It turns out that the total charge imposed on the first category amounts to 1500 dirhams, that on the second category is 1600 dirhams; finally, that on the third category consists of 650 dirhams.[3]) If we added up . . . [4])

These observations of al-Būzajānī confirm rather than add to our knowledge about the operations of the 10th century customs in the Near East. Thus his statement about the prerogatives of the sulṭān in respect of the customs decisions, corresponds to the information found with Hilāl al-Ṣābī (A.D. 970-1056), another authority in the field of Buwayhid administration.[5]) Al-Būzajānī's implication that the assessment of customs charges was based on a system of tariffs is in agreement with his famous contemporary, al-Maqdisī. The latter recorded, for instance, that customs dues imposed at Jidda on the imports of *Shaṭawī* cloth amounted to 3 dīnārs per chest (*safaṭ*), but those collected from the *Dabīqī* cloth amounted to 2 dīnārs.[6]) Al-Maqdisī also indicated that customs fees varied from region to region. Thus customs fees per one load of wool were 2 dīnārs at Jidda but 1 dīnār at ʿAththar.[7]) Unfortunately, the available text of al-Būzajānī leaves us short of further information which one would expect to find in the continuation of his observations.

---

1) *Ms.* reads: 140.

2) This word may designate some kind of spices, as in the *Mahāsin al-tijāra of Abu'l-Faḍl al-Dimashqī*. Cf. Cl. Cahen, *art. cit.*, p. 231, n. 2.

3) *Ms.* reads: 560.

4) *Cf.*, a pertinent extract from the *Kitāb al-ḥāwī*, quoted by Cl. Cahen in „Quelques problèmes économiques et fiscaux de l'Iraq Buyide d'après un traité de mathématiques," Annales de l'Institut d'Etudes Orientales, 10, 1952, p. 337.

5) *Cf.*, *ʿAbd-al-ʿAzīz al-Dūrī, Ta'rīkh al-ʿIrāq al-iqtiṣādī fī al-qarn al-rābiʿ al-hijrī*, Baghdād, 1948, p. 202.

6) *Aḥsan al-taqāsīm fī maʿrifat al-aqālīm*, (BGA, 3) 1906, p. 104. Also R. B. Serjeant, "Material for a history of Islamic textiles up to the Mongol conquest," *Ars Islamica*, 13-14, 1948, p. 95.

7) *Supra.*

XV

THE CRISIS OF *DĪNĀR* IN THE EGYPT OF SALADIN *

IF ONE JUDGED SALADIN'S achievements solely by his monetary policy, that great Islamic hero would have been accused by history of dangerously jeopardizing the stability of the official Egyptian currency.[1] The existence of a monetary crisis manifested in the withdrawal of gold coinage from the circulation in Egypt was indicated by al-Maqrīzī (A. D. 1364-1422). This famous Egyptian chronicler recorded that following the abolition of the Fāṭimid caliphate in A. H. 567/A. D. 1171 Saladin had ordered the coins of Egypt to be struck in the name of the 'Abbāsid caliphs of Baghdād.[2] 'In that year,' continued al-Maqrīzī, 'a calamity overcame Egypt, because gold and silver left Egypt, not to return again . . .' The shortage was so acute that 'to say the name of a pure gold *dīnār* [3] was like mentioning the name of a wife to a jealous husband, while to get such a coin in one's hand was like crossing the doors of paradise.' [4]

This information has not been corroborated by other textual evidence. Nevertheless, the alleged crisis must have inevitably occurred considering the quality of the gold coinage issued by the administration of Saladin in Egypt. In the following discussion I propose to bring out these aspects of the reformed *dīnārs* of Saladin, which offer interesting evidence for the explanation of some of the contributory causes of the crisis in question.

The monetary reforms of Saladin certainly marked a new chapter in the numismatic history of the country of the Nile. One of the measures, alluded to by al-Maqrīzī, consisted of the substitution of the name of the orthodox (*sunnī*) caliphs of Baghdād for that of the heterodox (*s̲h̲ī'ite*) Fāṭimid caliphs in the inscriptions on Egyptian coins. This was a logical consequence of the policy of Saladin who put an end to the rule of the S̲h̲ī'ites in Egypt, and restored that country to its former *sunnī* allegiance. Such a measure implied also the invalidation and a mass exchange of the old Fāṭimid coins for the new coinage of Saladin.

Whatever its importance from the political point of view might be this big switch would not have produced any economic repercussions had the monetary issues of Saladin corresponded qualitatively with the coinage of the Fāṭimids. The issues of the latter were handled by number,[5] which was made possible by the maintenance of a fixed weight standard. The success of the Fāṭimids in this respect may be grasped with the help of the following weight-frequency table which also illustrates the relevant development under Saladin and his immediate Ayyūbid successors.[6]

---

* I wish to acknowledge the help of the authorities of the University of Michigan who, by providing me with a grant from the Charles L. Freer Research and Publication Fund, enabled me to carry out the examination of numismatic material at the Museum of the American Numismatic Society in New York.

[1] The official currency in the Egypt of Saladin consisted of gold coins (*dīnārs*) and pure silver coins (*nuqra dirhams*). For the exchange rate between the gold and silver coins see A. S. Ehrenkreutz "Contributions to the Knowledge of the Fiscal Administration of Egypt in the Middle Ages" *BSOAS*, XVI/3 (1954), p. 503-505.

[2] Al-Maqrīzī, *Kitāb as-sulūk li ma'rifat duwal al-mulūk* (Cairo, 1936), I, i, 46; also idem, *Shudhūr al-'uqūd* (Alexandria, 1933), p. 12; French transl. by A. I. S. de Sacy, *Traité des monnoies musulmanes* (Paris, 1797), p. 43.

[3] *Dīnār Aḥmar.* For such meaning of the term see H. Sauvaire, "Matériaux pour servir à l'histoire de la numismatique et la métrologie musulmane," *JA*, VII Série, 15 (1880), p. 272; also de Sacy, *loc. cit.*

[4] Supra, note 2.

[5] Cf. al-Muqaddasī, *Aḥsan at-taqāsīm fī ma'rifat al-aqālīm* (Leyden, 1906), p. 240.

[6] For a clear description of the weight frequency method applied to coinage, and pertinent references, see Ph. Grierson, "Visigothic Metrology," *Numismatic Chronicle*, Sixth Series, XIII (1953), p. 77-78. The frequency table under consideration is based on the material scrutinized in the following catalogues:

S. Lane-Poole; *Catalogue of Oriental Coins in the British Museum* (London, 1875-1888).

——; *Catalogue of the Collection of Arabic Coins preserved in the Khedivial Library at Cairo* (London, 1897).

H. Lavoix, *Catalogue des monnaies musulmanes de la Bibliothèque Nationale* (Paris, 1887-1894).

G. C. Miles, *Fāṭimid coins in the collection of the University Museum, Philadelphia, and the American Numismatic Society* (New York, 1951).

Some unpublished Ayyūbid *dīnārs* from the collection of

TABLE I

WEIGHT-FREQUENCY OF EGYPTIAN DĪNĀRS STRUCK BY THE FĀṬIMIDS AND THE AYYŪBIDS (DOWN TO THE REIGN OF AL-KĀMIL)

RULER: al-Mu'izz A. H. 341-365/A. D. 953-975	al-'Azīz A. H. 365-386/A. D. 976-996	al-Ḥākim A. H. 386-411/A. D. 996-1021	az-Ẓāhir A. H. 411-427/A. D. 1021-1036	al-Mustanṣir A. H. 427-487/A. D. 1036-1094	al-Musta'li A. H. 487-495/A. D. 1094-1101	al-Āmir A. H. 495-524/A. D. 1101-1130	INTERREGNUM	al-Ḥāfiẓ A. H. 526-544/A. D. 1131-1149	aẓ-Ẓāfir A. H. 544-549/A. D. 1149-1154	al-Fā'iz A. H. 549-555/A. D. 1154-1160	al-'Āḍid A. H. 555-567/A. D. 1160-1171	Salāḥ ad-Dīn (Saladin) A. H. 569-589/A. D. 1174-1193	al-'Azīz A. H. 589-595/A. D. 1193-1198	al-'Ādil A. H. 596-615/A. D. 1199-1218	al-Kāmil A. H. 615-635/A. D. 1218-1238	Weight group (in grams)
Number of specimens in each																
—	1	—	—	2	—	1	—	—	2	1	—	9	1	2	3	3.5 and below
—	—	—	—	—	—	—	—	—	1	—	—	2	—	—	—	3.51 — 3.55
—	—	—	—	—	—	2	—	—	—	—	—	—	1	—	—	3.56 — 3.6
—	—	—	—	1	—	2	—	—	1	—	1	—	—	—	—	3.61 — 3.65
—	—	2	—	—	—	1	—	1	—	—	—	1	—	1	1	3.66 — 3.7
—	1	—	—	2	—	—	—	—	—	—	—	3	1	—	—	3.71 — 3.75
—	—	—	—	—	—	1	—	1	—	—	—	1	1	1	—	3.76 — 3.8
—	2	2	1	2	—	5	—	—	—	—	—	—	—	3	—	3.81 — 3.85
2	—	—	—	7	—	3	—	3	—	—	—	2	1	—	—	3.86 — 3.9
—	—	—	2	4	1	2	—	1	—	—	1	2	—	—	2	3.91 — 3.95
4	2	2	1	8	3	5	—	4	—	1	2	3	—	—	—	3.96 — 4.
3	1	1	2	4	1	4	1	—	—	2	—	2	—	—	2	4.01 — 4.05
10	3	2	3	14	1	7	1	1	1	1	—	3	—	—	—	4.06 — 4.1
7	24	17	1	18	2	13	2	—	3	1	1	1	—	—	—	4.11 — 4.15
9	7	19	6	20	—	15	1	6	1	—	1	2	—	—	—	4.16 — 4.2
1	—	5	4	24	2	13	1	4	—	1	1	—	1	—	—	4.21 — 4.25
—	—	1	1	21	2	12	1	—	—	—	—	2	1	—	—	4.26 — 4.3
—	—	—	—	3	—	7	—	3	—	—	1	3	—	1	1	4.31 — 4.35
—	—	—	—	5	—	3	—	8	—	1	—	2	—	2	1	4.36 — 4.4
—	—	—	—	—	—	3	—	3	—	—	—	1	—	—	2	4.41 — 4.45
—	—	—	—	—	—	—	1	1	1	—	—	2	—	2	1	4.46 — 4.5
—	—	—	—	—	—	—	—	1	—	—	—	2	—	2	1	4.51 — 4.55
—	—	—	—	—	—	1	—	—	—	—	—	2	—	1	—	4.56 — 4.6
—	—	—	—	—	—	—	—	1	—	—	2	2	—	2	2	4.61 — 4.65
—	—	—	—	—	—	1	—	—	1	—	—	1	2	1	1	4.66 — 4.7
—	—	—	—	—	—	—	—	1	—	—	—	1	1	1	1	4.71 — 4.75
—	—	—	—	—	—	—	—	1	—	—	—	1	—	2	—	4.76 — 4.8
—	—	—	—	1	—	—	—	—	—	1	—	—	—	—	1	4.81 — 4.85
—	—	—	—	—	—	—	—	—	—	—	—	1	—	—	—	4.86 — 4.9
—	—	—	—	—	—	—	—	—	—	—	—	—	—	—	1	4.96 — 5.
—	—	—	—	—	—	—	—	—	—	—	—	1	—	—	2	5.01 — 5.05
—	—	—	—	—	—	—	—	—	—	—	—	—	—	—	2	5.06 — 5.1
—	—	—	—	—	—	—	—	—	—	—	—	—	—	1	1	5.11 — 5.15
—	—	—	—	—	—	—	—	—	—	—	—	—	—	2	2	5.16 — 5.2
—	—	—	—	—	—	—	—	—	—	—	—	1	—	—	—	5.21 — 5.25
—	—	—	—	—	—	—	—	—	—	—	—	—	—	1	1	5.31 — 5.35
—	—	—	—	—	—	—	—	—	—	—	—	—	—	—	2	5.36 — 5.4
—	—	—	—	—	—	—	—	—	—	—	—	—	1	—	1	5.46 — 5.5
—	—	—	—	—	—	—	—	—	—	—	—	2	—	—	3	5.56 — 5.6
—	—	—	—	—	—	—	—	—	—	—	—	—	1	—	3	5.76 — 5.8
—	—	—	—	—	—	—	—	—	—	—	—	—	—	—	1	5.81 — 5.85
—	—	—	—	—	—	—	—	—	—	—	—	—	—	—	1	5.86 — 5.9
—	—	—	—	—	—	—	—	—	—	—	—	—	—	2	—	5.91 — 5.95
—	—	—	—	—	—	—	—	—	—	—	—	—	1	—	2	5.96 — 6.

(In that last group falls also the single specimen of al-Manṣūr, A. H. 595-596/A. D. 1198-1199).

A study of this table permits one to realize that an overwhelming majority of the available Fāṭimid *dīnārs* (311 out of 466; or 69.7%) weighs between 4.06 g and 4 g. In the case of three rulers: 'Azīz, al-Ḥākim and al-Mustanṣir, the number of coins in particular weight groups is sufficient enough to permit the drawing of hypothetical conclusions concerning the actual weight standard adopted by the mints of these respective caliphs.[7] These standards seem to have been fixed at c. 4.128 g under al-'Azīz, 4.188 g under al-Ḥākim, and 4.229 g under al-Mustanṣir. It should be added however that the average weight of the largest group of the coins of al-Āmir suggests a standard of 4.186 g which is similar to that of his three above-mentioned predecessors.

As far as the *dīnārs* of Saladin and of his successors are concerned it is obvious that they totally lack any fixed standard of weight. Moreover it is significant that only 10 out of 133 specimens (i. e. 7.5% only) fall within the weight limits 4.06-4.3 g most commonly met with the Fāṭimid issues. It seems that the new development constituted another attempt by Saladin to eradicate the *shī'ite* reminiscences in Egypt. Apart from introducing the *sunnī* legends and abandoning a fixed standard of coinage (probably in imitation of the practice of the 'Abbāsids) Saladin and his successors appear to have ordered their dīnārs to be struck outside the weight limits current under the Fāṭimids.

When an administration abandons the tale-system, switching thus to weight method, the safeguarding of a fixed standard of fineness, of purity of coinage, becomes the most imperative, unflexible necessity, vital for the economic stability of such an administration. Consequently the question of the maintenance of a fixed standard of fineness of coinage should have become of paramount importance to the administration of Saladin. But in this respect also the *dīnārs* of Saladin contrast sharply with those of the Fāṭimids and of his Ayyūbid successors. This is evidenced by the results of an analysis of the specific gravities of 214 Fāṭimid and Ayyūbid coins of Egypt, disclosing drastic fluctuations in the standard of Saladin's *dīnārs*.[8]

Only the period of al-Āmir bears certain resemblance to that of Saladin.[9] There are, however two essential differences between the quality of the examined coinage of the two periods. First, the debased *dīnārs* of al-Āmir constitute only 13.3% of the whole lot. Those of Saladin as much as 29.8%. And secondly, whereas 53.3% of the examined *dīnārs* of al-Āmir show an excellent standard of c. 100% purity, there is not a single specimen of Saladin of such a high quality. The temporary debasement in the period of al-Āmir and the sharp fluctuations during the reign of Saladin, are the only established symptoms of deterioration in the standard of the Egyptian *dīnārs* during a period of almost one and a half centuries. A more detailed idea about the occurrence of *dīnārs* of different degrees of purity, struck by the rulers of Egypt during the period in question, may be obtained from the following fineness-frequency table:

Again this table illustrates the superiority of the Fāṭimid specimens over those issued under Saladin. The largest group of the Fāṭimid specimens, consisting of forty *dīnārs* of al-Āmir, falls within the 100% limit. The second largest group, the twenty-one *dīnārs* of al-Ḥāfiẓ, also shows a similarly excellent standard. It is true that a

the American Numismatic Society (App.) have also been included in the surveyed material.

[7] In difference from the legal *dīnār* whose prescribed weight appears to have amounted to 4.233 g. Cf. W. Hinz, *Islamische Masse und Gewichte*, in *Handbuch der Orientalistik, Ergänzungsband* 1, Heft 1 (Leyden, 1955), p. 2.

[8] A full list of the examined coins can be found in the Appendix. I wish to acknowledge the kindness of Dr. John Walker of the British Museum, Dr. G. C. Miles of the American Numismatic Society Museum in New York, Professor Ph. Grierson of Cambridge University, and of Mr. A. D. H. Bivar of Oxford University, who either allowed me to carry out necessary examinations of the coins under their curatorship, or have provided me with pertinent information. Those who have seen my article on "The Standard of Fineness of Gold Coins Circulating in Egypt at the Time of the Crusades," *JAOS*, LXXIV, iii (1954), may be struck by the fact that the fineness of the *dīnārs* of al-Kāmil differs from that in the present article. The difference results from the fact that I had previously considered the specific gravity of 19.4 as being 100% pure gold. It was only after perusing the enlightening articles by Prof. Grierson, "The debasement of the bezant in the eleventh century," *Byzantinische Zeitschrift*, XLVII (1954), and that by E. R. Caley, "Estimation of Composition of Ancient Metal Objects," *Analytical Chemistry*, XXIV (1952), p. 678-81, that I have decided to follow these authorities in adopting S. G. 19.3 as 100% purity of gold.

[9] The monetary difficulties of al-Āmir were undoubtedly caused by the havoc produced by the invasion of the Crusaders, cf. A. S. Ehrenkreutz, "Contributions to the Knowledge of the Fiscal Administration of Egypt in the Middle Ages," *BSOAS*, XVI/3 (1954), p. 507-508.

FINENESS-FREQUENCY TABLE

Name of the ruler (dates in H years)	Number of specimens of different degrees of purity											
	Under 90%	90%	91%	92%	93%	94%	95%	96%	97%	98%	99%	100%
al-Musta'li (487-495)	—	1	—	—	—	—	1	—	—	1	—	4
al-Āmir (495-524)	10	1	2	—	1	3	—	8	3	9	8	40
Interregnum (495)	—	—	—	—	—	—	—	—	—	—	—	1
al-Ḥāfiẓ (526-544)						—	—	—	—	1	2	21
aẓ-Ẓāfir (544-549)						—	—	—	—	—	—	8
al-Fā'iz (549-555)	—	—	—	—	—	—	—	—	—	—	—	2
al-'Āḍid (555-567)	1	—	1	—	—	—	1	—	—	—	—	1
Saladin (569-589)	13	1	3	1	—	2	6	6	5	2	5	—
al-'Azīz (589-595)	—	—	—	—	1	—	—	—	—	1	1	6
al-'Ādil (596-615)	—	—	—	—	—	—	—	—	—	1	1	6
al-Kāmil (615-635)	—	—	—	—	1	1	4	4	2	4	6	5

group of ten *dīnārs* of al-Āmir features a standard inferior to 90% of purity, but there are also three other groups of specimens of that same ruler, consisting of eight, nine and eight specimens, which show 99%, 98%, and 96% degrees respectively. As for Saladin, the largest group of his specimen, consisting of thirteen *dīnārs,* falls under the 90% limit. The standard of the remaining thirty-one *dīnārs* fluctuates between 99% and 90%, whereby two groups of six coins show 95% and 96% respectively, and two groups of five specimens display 97% and 99% respectively.

The number of specimens dating from the reign of Saladin's immediate successors is scanty. But even so one is struck by the lack of any specimen with a standard inferior to 93%. A group of six coins of al-'Azīz, a similar group of al-'Ādil, and a group of five coins of al-Kāmil, all of them fall within the 100% limit. A group of six coins of al-Kāmil shows an equally high standard of 99%.

The contrast between the standard of the coinage of Saladin and that of both his Fāṭimid predecessors and the Ayyūbid successors is well illustrated by the following and final table:

DISTRIBUTION OF THE EXAMINED SPECIMENS ACCORDING TO THEIR STANDARD OF FINENESS

Degree of purity in %	The Fāṭimids (al-Musta'li — al'Āḍid)	Saladin	The Ayyūbīds al-'Azīz — al-Kāmil)
100	79	—	11
99	10	5	7
98	11	2	5
97	3	5	2
96	8	6	4
95	2	6	4
94	3	2	1
93	2	—	2
92	—	1	—
91	3	3	—
90	1	1	—
under 90	12	13	—

It is clear from the above evidence that the *dīnārs* of Saladin were not only lacking a fixed weight standard, but also suffered from an acute deterioration of the standard of fineness. One might perhaps argue that the fluctuation in the standard, the appearance of debased *dīnārs,* could be attributed to the inefficiency of the minters, or their dishonesty. Such an idea has to be rejected, however, in the light of our knowledge of the organization of the minting production under Saladin.[10] Thus, regardless of the efficiency of the actual minting technique, the alloys themselves were submitted to strict control exercised by the chief judge or by his representatives.[11] This supervision was applied by the Fāṭimids and the Ayyūbids, including Saladin as well.[12] There were too many supervisory elements involved in the control of the standard of *dīnārs*, to overlook the striking of so many debased specimens within such a relatively short stretch of time. In my opinion, therefore, most of the bad issues were the result of a monetary debasement deliberately undertaken by the administration of Saladin. And as the decision concerning the standard of fineness in most of Islamic lands, particularly in Egypt, belonged to the sultan,[13] the responsibility for that debasement rested with Saladin. That his administration was up to such disruptable methods, is quite obvious. A good proof here is the fact that in spite of the debasement, the Egyptian administration continued to maintain the exchange rate between the Egyptian and foreign coinage at the old rate of the Fāṭimids, that is to say of the pre-Saladin period, when both the weight standard and the standard of fineness had been rigidly observed.[14]

The foregone facts ascertained from numismatic sources, constitute very important evidence in support of the information of al-Maqrīzī. According to the well-known economic law of Gresham 'bad coins drive away good coins.' The appearance of debased coinage under Saladin must have produced similar effect. Gold influx from abroad must have slowed down because the enforced course of Egyptian *dīnārs* did harm to foreign merchants. In Egypt itself, people tended to keep the good coinage in their possession in expectation of more stable times. Thus the stoppage of gold influx and the hoarding of gold must have resulted in the withdrawal of gold pieces from circulation, which fact was referred to by al-Maqrīzī.

On the other hand, this very shortage of gold had to affect detrimentally the minting production of Saladin's administration. For with decreased deliveries of gold bullion, the mints had to debase the qualitative value of their issues if they wanted to meet quantitatively the monetary demands of the day. Thus, the debased coinage caused the shortage of gold, and the shortage of gold in turn produced the minting of debased coinage. It would, therefore, be interesting to investigate the initial causes of this vicious circle and to establish what might have been the roots of the crisis in question, remembering that the Fāṭimids had been so successful in maintaining the high standard of gold coinage.

It can hardly be disputed that Egypt reached the climax of economic development in the Middle Ages during the rule of the Fāṭimid dynasty. But the economic situation of the valley of the Nile at the time of Saladin's rise to power differed greatly from that which Egypt enjoyed after the Fāṭimid conquest.

While the invasion of the Fāṭimids, because of its bloodless character, did not disturb the agricultural and industrial production of Egypt, the accession of Saladin was preceded by long years of destructive internal struggles between various factions. Moreover, the industrial centers were recurrently raided by the Crusaders.

The territory acquired by Saladin was limited to Egypt only while the Fāṭimids, by conquering Egypt, became masters of the whole southern coast of the Mediterranean Sea. Syrian ports under the Fāṭimids were submitted for about one century to the commercial monopoly of Fāṭimid Egypt. At the time of Saladin's rise they belonged to the Crusaders.

Under the Fāṭimids, the traffic along Egyptian trade routes was extremely intensive because of general security both on land and at sea. This was not the case when Saladin seized power. Egyptian trade routes were then cut off from the East by the Crusaders. The North-south trade axis was also exposed to the attacks of the Crusaders and of the partisans of the overthrown Fāṭimid regime.

---

[10] For the description of the organization of the minting production in Egypt, see A. S. Ehrenkreutz, *art. cit.*, p. 506-514.

[11] Ibid. p. 510-511; for a description of minting processes in the Egypt of the Ayyūbids, see A. S. Ehrenkreutz, "Extracts from the Technical Manual on the Ayyūbid Mint in Cairo," *BSOAS*, XV, 3 (1953), p. 433-443.

[12] Idem, "Contributions to the Knowledge of the Fiscal Administration of Egypt in the Middle Ages," *BSOAS*, XVI/3 (1954), p. 511.

[13] Ibid., p. 510.

[14] Thus for instance the exchange rate of the North African *dīnārs* of the Almohades (called *al-mū'minī*) against the *dīnārs* of Saladin was 2: 1. Cf. Ibn Jubayr, *The travels of Ibn Jubayr*, ed. W. Wright (Leyden), 1907, p. 43. This rate resulted from the fact that the *mū'minī dīnārs* weighed half as much as the *dīnārs* of the Fāṭimids.

The routes leading westward were disrupted by customs barriers erected by new states which were established on the ruins of the Fāṭimid empire. The sea trade and naval hegemony in general was lost to the Europeans.

Finally, while the period of the Fāṭimids was notable for abundant influx of gold bullion, this was not the case with the Egypt of Saladin. The gold mines of Western Sudan, 'the Alaska of the Middle Ages,' passed under the influence of the Almohades. On the other hand, the output of gold mines situated on the Egyptian-Nubian frontiers must have suffered because of the general unrest created by the pro-Fāṭimid agents supported by the Nubians. The latter had a good reason to be hostile to the new regime because Saladin, in the course of the consolidation of his position, 'liquidated' the Fāṭimid regiments composed of Nubian slaves. This ruthless measure was followed by the looting of Nubian territory by Saladin's troops.[15]

Considering all these factors, it is obvious that the finances of Egypt, at the time of the accession of Saladin, were seriously undermined. Had his rule been accompanied by a period of peace, it might have proved possible, by adopting drastic economy measures, to maintain the financial balance and, consequently, a stabilized coinage, despite the decrease in the influx of gold. What happened was that Saladin mobilized the resources of Egypt in pursuance of his warlike activities. The whole economy of the country was directed to support Saladin's policy to restore internal security, to unify Syria with Egypt, and to proceed with a showdown with the Crusaders.

Despite the magnitude of his operations, there is sufficient evidence indicating that from the very beginning of his activities in Egypt, Saladin suffered from a lack of gold which continued throughout the duration of his rule. With the build up of his armed forces and navy, with profuse fortification constructions, and especially with big purchases of war material with European merchants, it was obvious that Saladin was in great need of 'hot' cash. And it is this factor, in my opinion, that forced his administration to proceed with qualitative debasement of coinage.

Although the appearance of the debased coinage resulted in the crisis of the *dīnār*, the ultimate achievements of Saladin seem to have justified such a measure. The restored military power and internal security in Egypt, which were produced through Saladin's successes, lay at the foundation of the high standard of Egyptian *dīnārs* issued by his immediate successors.[16]

[15] It is worth mentioning that gold production among the pagan gold diggers suffered whenever some Islamic rulers directly interfered with their activities; cf. al-'Omarī, *Masālik el-abṣār fī mamālik el-amṣār*, transl. Gaudefroy Demombynes (Paris, 1927), I, 58. It was probably for that reason that the exploitation of gold in Nubia was left to private enterprise; cf. C. H. Becker, *Islamstudien* (Leipzig, 1924), i, 189.

[16] Cf. A. S. Ehrenkreutz, "The Standard of Fineness of Gold Coins Circulating in Egypt at the Time of the Crusades," *JAOS*, LXXIV, iii (1954).

APPENDIX I

LIST OF DINARS EXAMINED FOR THE ANALYSIS OF THE STANDARD OF FINENESS

Reference and rulers *	Fineness of gold in %	Reference and rulers *	Fineness of gold in %	Reference and rulers *	Fineness of gold in %
al-Musta'li		M-405	97	BM-202-iv-51	98
M-393	100	BM-Mrs. Loeve	76	M-410	100
M-394	100	BM-199p-Add-325	98	M-454	100
M-400	100	M-406	94	BM-204-iv-51	90
M-401	95	M-447	100	M-455	100
M-395	98	M-448	100	M-456	100
M-402	100	BM-200-iv-51	81	M-411	100
al-Āmir		BM-201-iv-51	96	M-412	100
		M-449	100	M-413	100
BM-197-iv-50	96	M-407	94	M-457	100
M-403	98	M-408	96	M-458	100
M-444	99	Ashmolean	99	Ashmolean	99
BM-198-iv-51	100	M-450	100	BM-206-iv-52	96
BM-199-iv-51	98	M-451	100	BM-206c-Add.-325	91
M-404	100	Ashmolean	99	M-459	100
M-445	100	M-452	100	M-414	100
M-446	100	M-409	100	M-460	100

Reference and rulers *	Fineness of gold in %	Reference and rulers *	Fineness of gold in %	Reference and rulers *	Fineness of gold in %
BM-207-iv-52	96	ANS	100	ANS	66
M-461	100	M-502	100	ANS	98
M-416	100	M-503	99	ANS	94
M-418	100	M-504	99	BM-252-iv-65	97
M-462	100	M-488	100	BM-253-iv-65	97
BM-208-iv-52	85	M-489	100	BM-254-iv-65	91
M-417	96	M-505	100	ANS	95
BM-208d-Add.-325	91	M-506	100	ANS	91
BM-209-iv-52	97	M-508	100	ANS	90
BM-210-iv-52	98	M-509	100	ANS	91
M-463	100	M-490	100	BM-255-iv-66	Less than 50%
M-464	100	M-491	100	BM-256-iv-66	Less than 50%
BM-211-iv-52	99	M-492	100	BM-257-iv-66	64
M-465	100	M-512	100	ANS	83
M-422	100	M-493	100	BM-258-iv-66	89
M-466	99	az-Zāfir		Ashmolean	96
BM-213-iv-52	98	M-513	100	BM-259-iv-66	96
M-467	100	M-519	100	ANS	96
M-423	100	M-520	100	al-'Azīz	
BM-215-iv-53	89	M-514	100	BM-287-iv-76	93
BM-217-iv-53	80	M-515	100	al-'Ādil	
M-469	85	M-517	100	ANS	100
BM-222-iv-54	81	M-518	100	ANS	100
BM-221-iv-53	76	M-521	100	ANS	100
BM-219-iv-53	75	al-Fā'iz		ANS	100
M-470	98	M-522	100	ANS	100
M-475	100	M-524	100	ANS	99
M-476	96	al-'Āḍid		ANS	100
M-424	100	M-526	Less than 50%	BM-354-iv-96	98
BM-223-iv-54	(false coin?)	M-525	95	al-Kāmil	
M-425	93	M-527	91	BM-373-iv-103	99
M-477	99	M-528	100	ANS	100
M-471	99	Saladin		ANS	100
M-478	96	ANS	95	BM-375-iv-104	99
M-472	98	ANS	86	ANS	100
M-426	100	BM-243-iv-63	96	ANS	99
M-427	94	BM-244-iv-63	94	ANS	99
M-473	100	ANS	96	BM-376-iv-104	99
M-479	97	ANS	Less than 50%	BM-380-iv-105	98
M-474	100	BM-246-iv-64	62	ANS	95
M-428	100	BM-245-iv-64	95	BM-383-iv-106	99
M-429	98	ANS	56	BM-388-iv-107	93
M-430	100	BM-247-iv-64	96	ANS	96
Interregnum		Ashmolean	97	BM-384-iv-106	97
M-481	100	ANS	74	ANS	100
M-482	100	Ashmolean	99	BM-389-iv-107	95
M-484	100	ANS	95	ANS	100
al-Ḥāfiẓ		ANS	97	BM-392-iv-107	98
M-485	100	ANS	99	Ashmolean	96
M-494	Less than 50%	ANS	97	BM-393-iv-108	97
M-495	98	ANS	99	BM-394-iv-108	96
M-496	100	BM-248-iv-64	99	BM-396-iv-108	96
M-486	100	ANS	99	Ashmolean	95
M-497	100	BM-249-iv-65	95	BM-398-iv-108	99
M-498	100	ANS	83	BM-400-iv-109	98
M-499	100	BM-91.4-Prideaux	98	BM-402-iv-109	95
M-500	93	ANS	92	BM-403-iv-110	94
M-501	100	ANS	97		
M-487	100	BM-251-iv-65	95		

* Key to abbreviations:

M = G. C. Miles, *Fatimid Coins in the Collections of the University Museum, Philadelphia, and the American Numismatic Society* (New York, 1951).

BM = British Museum Collection. Vol. / page ref. to Lane-Poole, *Catalogue of Oriental Coins in the British Museum* (London, 1875-1888).

Ashmolean = Collection of the Ashmolean Museum, Oxford.

ANS = Collection of the American Numismatic Society.

XVI

THE STANDARD OF FINENESS OF GOLD COINS CIRCULATING IN EGYPT AT THE TIME OF THE CRUSADES

IT HAS BEEN generally known that the official monetary system in Medieval Islam was based on gold (dinars) and silver (dirhams) currency. Little attention, however, has been devoted to the problem of the great variety of types struck of these respective metals. The limited knowledge concerning the nature of the specific differences and the relationship characterising the types of coins, results chiefly from scarcity of textual sources relating to this problem. This serious shortcoming could be made up by the availability of vast quantities of Islamic coins preserved in various numismatic collections, provided that those in charge of numismatic collections will be willing to submit at least some of the duplicate specimens to the appropriate tests aiming at ascertaining the composition of alloys.

It is in this light that the information contained in the treatise composed by Manṣūr ibn Ba'ra, entitled "*An Inquiry in the Technical Secrets of the Egyptian Mint*,"[1] acquires particular significance. It was written during the reign of the Ayyūbid Sultan, al-Kāmil (A. H. 615-635/A. D. 1218-1238),[2] but only one early eighteenth century copy has been preserved, in the collection of the Egyptian Library in Cairo.[3] The contents of the work of Ibn Ba'ra deal chiefly with technological problems of the Cairo mint during the reign of the Ayyū-

* This paper was presented at the annual meeting of the American Oriental Society, 1954. I am indebted to the Department of Near Eastern Languages of Yale University for awarding me the Kohut Fellowship which enabled me to investigate the economic aspects of Egyptian history during the period of the Crusades.

[1] *Kashf al-Asrār al-'Ilmiya bi Dār aḍ-Ḍarb al-Miṣriya.*

[2] For the dating of this work see A. S. Ehrenkreutz, "Extracts from the Technical Manual on the Ayyūbid Mint in Cairo," *BSOAS* 15 (1953), 423-4.

[3] Cf. *Fihris Dār al-Kutub al-'Arabiya*, A. H. 1308, V, 390.

bids.[4] The second chapter, however, called "*Description of gold coins of different standards and shapes,*" [5] not only lists the various types and the exchange rates of gold coins in circulation in Ayyūbid Egypt (A. H. 569-648/A. D. 1174-1250), but it also offers enough ground to understand the basis of differentiation.

The contents of this chapter are arranged according to the following pattern:

1. Type of gold coins;
2. loss suffered by 100 *mithqāls* [6] of this gold in the refining process aiming at the adjustment of its alloy to the official standard of Egyptian gold coinage; [7]
3. tax imposed by the state, the costs of production and the salaries of the minters, the total of which amounted to 5 *mithqāls* or 5%; [8]
4. the exchange value of the type of gold coinage against the *waraq* dirhams,[9] based on the exchange rate between the Egyptian gold coinage and the *waraq* dirhams, which stood at 1 : 40.[10]

For an easier understanding of this chapter it was thought advisable to reproduce its substance in a tabulated form.

Type of Gold	*Loss*	*Tax, etc.*	*Remains*	*Exchange Rate*
Ya'qūbī (gold)[11]	very	pure[12]		
Ṣūriya (dinars)[13]	2½%	5%	92½%	1 : 37
Dimishqī (gold)[14]	5%	5%	90%	1 : 36
Muẓaffariya (dinars)[15]	11%	5%	84%	1 : 33⅗[16]
Murābiṭiya (dinars)[17]	15%	5%	80%	1 : 32
Atābakiya (dinars)[18]	"	5%	"	"
Dūqiya (dinars)[19]	30%	5%	65%	1 : 26
Tūriya (dinars)[20]	35%	5%	60%	1 : 24[21]

[4] For the analysis of the content of Ibn Ba'ra's treatise see Ehrenkreutz, *art. cit.* p. 424-5.

[5] *Fī ma'rifa nuqūd adh-dhahab al-mukhtalif al-'iyārāt wa-ash-shakl*, fol 4 r-4 v.

[6] The fiscal administration of Saladin (A. H. 569-589 / A. D. 1174-93), the founder of the Ayyūbid dynasty, abandoned the weight standard for its monetary issues. Cf. P. Balog, "Quelques dinars du début de l'ère Mamelouke Bahrite," *Bull. de l'Inst. d'Égypte* 32 (1951), 251. From then on the coins were no longer taken by tale, but had to be weighed. One of the weight units employed for gold coins was *mithqāl*. As Muslim weights and measures varied from town to town, and from one period to another, it is impossible to establish what a *mithqāl* represented precisely in Cairo during the lifetime of Ibn Ba'ra.

[7] (!) *naqṣuha fi-t-ta'līq ḥattā tulḥaqa bi-l-'iyār al-miṣrī*. For the meaning of *ta'līq*, see Ehrenkreutz, art. cit. p. 428 n. 6.

[8] For the problem of the administrative aspect of the Cairo mint see A. S. Ehrenkreutz, "Contributions to the Monetary History of Medieval Egypt," *BSOAS* 16 (1954), forthcoming.

[9] The *waraq* dirhams which circulated in Cairo and Alexandria under the Ayyūbids were destined for the internal Egyptian market, to meet the needs of the local retail trade. Cf. A. S. Ehrenkreutz, "Extracts from the Technical Manual on the Ayyūbid Mint in Cairo," *BSOAS* 15 (1953), 425 n. 1.

[10] This exchange rate was based on the quality of alloy of the *waraq* dirhams. As the exchange rate of pure silver dirhams was fixed at 1 : 13⅓ (Cf. H. Sauvaire, "Matériaux pour servir à l'histoire de la numismatique et de la métrologie musulmanes," *Journal Asiatique* 19 [1882], 111), the *waraq* dirhams, whose alloy consisted of 30% silver only (cf. A. S. Ehrenkreutz, art. cit. p. 441-2), had to be rated at 1 : 40.

[11] This term was applied to the issues struck by the Muwaḥḥid ruler of North Africa, Ya'qūb ibn Yūsuf ibn 'Abd al-Mū'min (A. H. 558-580/A. D. 1163-84). Cf. H. Sauvaire, art. cit. *JA* 1882, 68.

[12] Ibn Ba'ra does not provide any figures for this type of gold, but makes it understood that it was of a very high quality. Cf. A. S. Ehrenkreutz, *art. cit.* p. 426. This is corroborated by the statement of M. Amari who, referring to this type of dinars, stated that: "le métal en est très pure." *Voyage en Sicile de Mohammed-ebn-Djobaïr* . . . (Paris, 1846) (extrait de *JA* 1845), p. 95, n. 78.

[13] Ms. reads الصورية, which I render as *aṣ-ṣūriya*, i. e., the dinars struck in Tyre (*Ṣūr*). This type of coin occurs frequently in the sources relating to the period of the Crusades (cf. H. Sauvaire, art. cit. *JA* 1880, 471-4). It is also reported that their standard was only slightly inferior to that of the Egyptian dinars. Cf. C. Cahen, *La Syrie du Nord à l'époque des Croisades* . . . (Paris, 1940), 470, n. 16. It does not seem that this term was applied to dinars with Arabic legends which were struck in Tyre after the conquest of that town by the crusaders. Cf. Ibn Khallikān (M. de Slane, transl.), *Biographical Dictionary* (Paris, 1843-71) iii, 455. The examination of some Christian dinars with Arabic legends showed their standard as fluctuating between 65.5% and 75% fineness only. I am indebted for this information to Professor P. Grierson of Cambridge University, who was kind enough to carry out the examination in question.

The interpretation of the above data should begin with ascertaining the nature of the official standard of the Egyptian coinage. Here, again, Ibn Ba'ra provides an interesting piece of information. From fol 2 v of the copy of his treatise, we learn that in A. H. 514/1120 A. D., the Fāṭimid Caliph, al-Āmir (A. H. 495-524/A. D. 1101-1130) proceeded with an inquiry "*investigating the secrets of gold production in the mint. This investigation resulted in fixing the standard of gold to a level which could not be surpassed. Later on, Sultan al-Kāmil was interested in the standard of al-Āmir, and eagerly desired to excel it. Consequently, there existed neither in the West nor in the East dinars of a standard excelling the standard al-Āmirī al-Kāmilī.*"

The report of Ibn Ba'ra is corroborated by the Egyptian chronicler al-Maqrīzī (A. D. 1364-1442), in so far as he stated that in A. H. 518/A. D. 1124, al-Āmir had ordered the opening of a mint in Cairo, whose issues surpassed in standard the dinars struck by other Egyptian mints.[22] The numismatic evidence also speaks in favour of Ibn Ba'ra's allegation. The specific gravity of some dinars struck by the Cairo mint indicates that the issues of that mint reached 99.71% purity of alloy, already in the fifth year after the opening of that minting centre.[23] Of the eighteen dinars of al-Kāmil which I was able to examine, only four show the standard inferior to 95% purity of alloy. The standard of the remaining fourteen dinars fluctuates between 96.29% and 98.83% purity, that is to say, well within the limits of 23-24 carats. The high quality and the stability of their standard may be best grasped with the help of the following graph.[24]

---

[14] Ms. reads: يبرس Ibn al-Qalānisī reports that the standard of dinars struck in Damascus was fixed in A. H. 530/A. D. 1136 at 87.5% fineness. *Dhayl ta'rīkh Dimishq* (Beyrut, 1908), 257.

[15] Ms. reads: . . . *al-muẓaffariya ḍuriba Irbil*. . . . The reference is most probably made to dinars struck by Muẓaffar ad-Dīn Kukburī, who ruled over Irbil from A. H. 586-630/A. D. 1186-1233. Cf. Ibn Khallikān, op. et ed. cit. ii, 535.

[16] Ms. reads: 33½, which is an obvious mathematical error.

[17] Ms. reads: *al-murābiṭa*. These coins were struck by the Almoravids who ruled over Morocco, part of Algeria, and Spain, A. H. 448-541/A. D. 1056-1147. Cf. H. Sauvaire, art. cit. *JA* 19 (1882), 41-2.

[18] Ms. reads: *al-tābakiya*. This term probably refers to dinars struck by the rulers who descended from the Atābeg 'Imād ad-Dīn Zangī. Cf. E. de Zambaur, *Manuel de généalogie et de chronologie pour l'histoire de l'Islam* (Hanover, 1927), i, 226-7.

[19] This name, according to Sauvaire (*art. cit. JA* 1880, 449), was given to coins struck by Norman rulers of Sicily.

[20] This term presents a real problem. I was inclined to read it as *nūriya* but an-Nābulusī spells it *ṭūriya* (cf. *Lumā' al-qawānīn al-muḍiya fī dawāwīn ad-diyār al-miṣriya*, Ms. Landberg 39, Yale Univ. Coll., fol 34 r), which corroborates the spelling found in Ibn Ba'ra's treatise. An-Nābulusī (loc. cit.) also reports that the *dhawqi* (sic!) type of gold was superior to the *ṭūrī* gold. I am inclined to consider the term *tūrī* to be the Arabic rendering of *tari*, which was the name given to gold coins struck in Sicily and southern Italy in the Middle Ages, their standard of fineness being 75% (cf. A. Nagl, "Die Goldwährung im Mittelalter," *Numismatische Zeitschrift* 30 [1898], 269). If this interpretation is correct, would the distinction between the *dūqiya* and *tūriya* coins consist of the difference between their respective standards of purity?

[21] The manuscript gives the loss of *tūriya* dinars as 10%. This is incompatible with the exchange rate of 1 : 24, and the information of an-Nābulusī; see the preceding note.

[22] *Kitāb al-mawā'iẓ wa-l-i'tibār* (Cairo, A. D. 1853) i, 445.

[23] Dinar struck in A. H. 523, now in the Collection of the University of Pennsylvania, deposited in the American Numismatic Society. I am indebted to Dr. G. C. Miles for permission to carry out the examination of the coins in the American Numismatic Society.

[24] The composition of this graph is based on the examination of specific gravities of the following dinars:

Nr. of coin on the graph	Reference	Mint	Year	Degree of fineness in %
1	BM 373	Cairo	1219	98.48
2	BM 375	Miṣr	1226	98.55
3	BM 376	Cairo	1227	98.73
4	BM 380	Cairo	1228	97.43
5	BM 383	Cairo	1229	98.85
6	BM 388	Alexandria	1230	94.02
7	BM 384	Cairo	1230	97.36
8	BM 389	Cairo	1231	95.6
9	BM 392	Alexandria	1231	98.17
10	Ashmolean Museum	Illegible	1232	96.81
11	BM 393	Alexandria	1232	97.03
12	BM 394	Cairo	1233	96.71
13	BM 396	Cairo	1234	96.53
14	Ashmolean Museum	Cairo	1234	96.29
15	BM 398	Cairo	1235	98.83
16	BM 400	Cairo	1236	97.93
17	BM 402	Alexandria	1236	95.47
18	BM 403	Cairo	1237	94.9

The abbreviations: BM = S. Lane-Poole, *Catalogue of Oriental Coins in the British Museum* (London, 1875-1888) vol. iv. I am indebted to Dr. John Walker, the Keeper of the Department of Coins and Medals in the

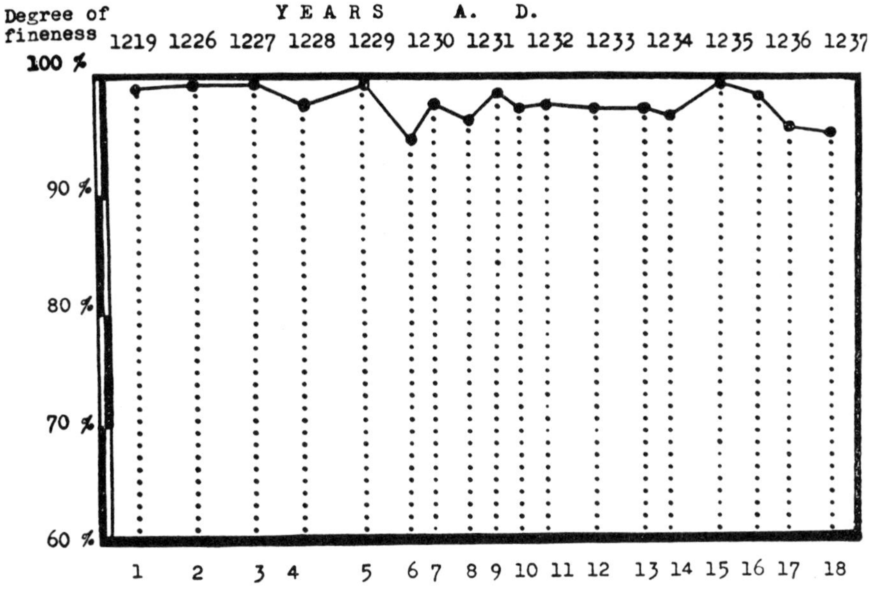

TABLE I. The quality of Egyptian dinars during the rule of al-Kāmil (A.D. 1218-38).

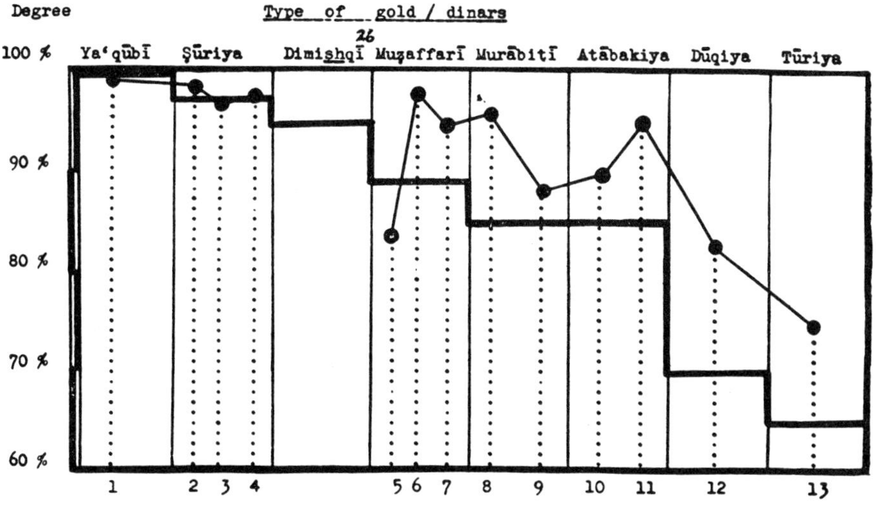

TABLE II. The heavy line indicates the standard of fineness as given by Ibn Ba'ra. The heavy circles indicate the degree of fineness yielded by the analysis of specific gravities.

It seems, therefore, reasonable to assume that the alleged high standard *al-Āmirī al-Kāmilī* amounted to almost 100% degree of purity. Thus the adjustment of the alloy of the gold coins to the official Egyptian standard seems to have been tantamount to a complete refining of the gold contained in the alloys in question. Hence the percentage of the losses as listed by Ibn Ba'ra indicates also the purity of the alloy of these various types of gold coins, prior to the adjusting process.

Consequently, it is extremely interesting to compare the data provided by Ibn Ba'ra with the purity of coins of the corresponding types, in so far as the analysis of the specific gravities allows us to ascertain such information. The following table serves the purpose of confronting the details contained in the manuscript, with those yielded by the analysis of the numismatic material available for the examination.[25]

What can be deduced from the above chart? Firstly a negative remark, namely, that there is a definite discrepancy between the figures listed by Ibn Ba'ra and those yielded by the examined coins. This discrepancy may result not so much from the inaccuracy of the information of Ibn Ba'ra, or from the lack of precision of medieval chemists,[27] as from the inadequate methods of analysis which had to be applied. On the other hand the various classes of the examined specimens really differ from one another in their respective standards of fineness and what is more interesting, the qualitative gradation sequence displayed by the coins corresponds more or less to that given by Ibn Ba'ra.

Although no definite conclusions can be reached without ascertaining the standard of fineness of a great many more coins, two important facts concerning the monetary history of Medieval Egypt may be established on the basis of the information of Ibn Ba'ra. Firstly, that the distinction between various types of gold coinage consisted of the difference in their '*bonitas intrinseca,*' that is to say their standard of fineness. And secondly, that the distinction was being made even between types of very high quality, whose respective standards excelled the limit of 22 carats, or 91.66% purity.

Finally, it is my belief that a proper exploitation and coordination of numismatic and textual evidence may decisively improve our knowledge of the Islamic monetary system, which constitutes an important element in the study of the economic history of the Mediterranean World.

British Museum, for allowing me to analyse the coins in B. M. Collection.

Ashmolean Museum = Collection of the Ashmolean Museum, Oxford. My thanks are due to Mr. A. D. H. Bivar for the information concerning the coins in the Ashmolean Museum Collection.

[25] The composition of this table is based on the examination of specific gravities of the following dinars.

Nr. of coin on the table	Reference	Year H.	Ruler	Mint	Degree of fineness in %
1	UM	—	Ya'qūb ibn Yūsuf	—	100
2	Miles 435	514	al-Āmir	Ṣūr	99.22
3	" 436	515	"	"	97.52
4	" 437	516	"	"	98.6
5	ANS	609	Muẓaffar ad-Dīn	Irbil	84.26
6	ANS	618	"	"	98.87
7	BM/Add/ 651 xxyy	619	"	"	95.
8	UM	519	'Alī b. Yūsuf	Almeria	96.55
9	BM/v/24	559	Tashfīn b. 'Alī	Ishbīlīya	88.5
10	BM/iii/196		Nāṣir ad-Dīn Maḥmūd	Mawṣil	90.27
11	UM		"	"	95.39
12	BM-unpublished-S. 1860		Roger I	Palermo	83.4
13	See above note 20.				

Abbreviations:

BM = S. Lane-Poole, *op. cit.*

BM-unpublished = an unpublished specimen in the British Museum Collection.

UM = University of Philadelphia Collection, now deposited in the American Numismatic Society.

Miles = G. C. Miles, *Fāṭimid Coins in the Collections of the University Museum, Philadelphia, and the American Numismatic Society* (New York, 1951).

ANS = Collection of the American Numismatic Society.

[26] The only specimens from Damascus for which I have been able to secure the necessary data were issued in A. H. 583, during the rule of Saladin (A. H. 569-89/A. D. 1174-93). These coins show an extremely low percentage of gold. As the reign of Saladin was notorious for the shortage of gold in circulation (cf. al-Maqrīzī, *Shudhūr al-'uqūd*, ed. L. A. Mayer [Alexandria, 1933] p. 12), the specimens in question are not included in the composition of the above table.

[27] For refining processes practised in the Egyptian mint see Ehrenkreutz, *art. cit.* p. 428-33.

XVII

ARABIC *DĪNĀRS* STRUCK BY THE CRUSADERS

A CASE OF IGNORANCE OR OF ECONOMIC SUBVERSION*

The phenomenon of gold coins struck by the Crusaders in imitation of contemporary Arabic *dīnārs* has attracted the attention of several generations of numismatists. There exist many publications containing interesting discussions about the historical background of the appearance and circulation of these *sarracenati*, as well as meticulous descriptions of surviving specimens preserved in various numismatic collections [1]). Although the authors of these contributions have succeeded in correlating textual and numismatic evidence, they have traditionally neglected certain basic historical questions concerning the function of the gold coinage of the Crusaders and the impact of its circulation on the monetary situation in the Mediaeval Mediterranean area. More recently, however, there have appeared two publications in which treatment of the coinage in question is different from the traditional approach of the numismatists. In one of them, entitle "Monnaies à legendes arabes de l'Orient Latin", Paul Balog and Jacques Yvon [2]) propose the following interpretation of the role of the gold coins in the monetary system of the Crusaders. "A côté d'une monnaie locale, émise par chaque principauté ou chaque fief, il existe une monnaie de valeur, internationale, dirons-nous, capable d'être le moyen d'échange

---

*) This paper was read at the XXVI International Congress of Orientalists, New Delhi, India; January 1964.

1) For bibliographical details concerning these publications, *see* Paul Balog et Jacques Yvon, "Monnaies à legendes arabes de l'Orient Latin", *Revue Numismatique*, 6e serie, 1, 1958, p. 133, n. 1.

2) *Ibid.*, p. 133-168.

par excellence dans les transactions de cette partie de l'Orient méditerranéen" [1]). In the other contribution, entitle "Back to Gold, 1252", Robert S. Lopez [2]) considers the gold coinage of the Crusaders as an abortive, typological forerunner of the Genoese gold coins [3] In the present paper I wish to communicate additional evidence concerning the gold coins of the Crusaders. It is my belief that a proper interpretation of this evidence permits one to attribute to this coinage a more significant historical function than has so far been suggested.

Before presenting this new evidence, I wish to provide a background to my discussion by stating certain well established facts about the monetary pattern which confronted the Crusaders upon the establishment of their regime in the Near East. To begin with, one must remember that Christian leaders responsible for the administrative and fiscal organization of the Frankish kingdom in the Near East originated from the countries of Western Europe, the coinage system of which had been for many centuries based on silver. On the other hand, it is obvious that in establishing their regime in Syria, the Crusaders had to align their monetary concepts and practices with the conditions existing in that part of the Mediterranean world. As it has been discussed by Carlo M. Cipolla, since the end of the seventh century of the Christian era the Mediterranean area had been dominated by two strong coins that enjoyed a predominant international prestige: the Muslim *dīnār* and the Byzantine *nomisma* [4]). The international success of these "dollars of the Middle Ages" [5]) was achieved through their high unitary value, their intrinsic stability, and because of the powerful economic assets,

---

1) *Ibid.*, p. 138.

2) *Economic History Review*, 9, ii, 1957, p. 219-240.

3) *Ibid.*, p. 228; Cl. Cahen in his "Notes sur l'Histoire des Croisades et de l'Orient Latin. III. Orient Latin et Commerce du Levant", *Bulletin de la Faculté des Lettres de Strasbourg*, 29e année, 8, 1951, p. 337, conceded that the gold coinage of the Crusaders should be regarded "comme quelque chose de plus important qu'une curiosité locale, explicable par des besoins locaux".

4) Cf. Carlo M. Cipolla, *Money, Prices, and Civilization in the Mediterranean World. Fifth to Seventeenth Century*, 1956, p. 20.

5) Cf. *Ibid.*, p. 22; also, R. S. Lopez, "The Dollar of the Middle Ages", *Journal of Economic History*, 11, 1951, p. 209-234.

productive activities, and commercial vitality of the Byzantine and Muslim societies [1]). Although many of the factors which had originally contributed to the success of Byzantine and Muslim gold coinage were no longer operative in the late eleventh century, the basic monetary pattern at the time of the invasion of the Crusaders remained the same: the coinage system of Western Europe continued to be based on silver, while that of the Mediterranean East rested on gold. Consequently, if the Crusaders were to conform with the monetary pattern prevailing in the area falling under their domination, they had to make a decision in favor of introducing gold coinage into their monetary system. Although silver and copper coins were struck locally by Frankish principalities and other feudal territorial units, gold coinage was to acquire the status of an official, full-fledged, international currency, serving the Crusaders in their internal and external monetary transactions [2]).

How were the Crusaders to procure that gold coinage, however? They could possibly rely on the influx of Byzantine and Muslim coins, but this solution entailed a number of disadvantages. For instance, the demand for gold coinage in the Frankish kingdom would be dependent upon the supply of coins from foreign mints. Furthermore, by not undertaking to strike gold coins in their own mints, the royal authorities in Jerusalem would deprive themselves of income produced by such minting operations [3]). Another solution was to produce gold coins in the royal mints of the Frankish kingdom. This alternative was not without certain problems either. Frankish authorities had no gold minting traditions of their own to draw upon in producing gold coinage which could be identified as their own. Even if they did try to issue a new type of coin, they could hardly expect to see this coinage accepted in Mediterranean markets along with the traditional gold coins of the Byzantines or of the Muslims. The economic and political foun-

1) Cf. C. M. Cipolla, *op. cit.*, p. 24.
2) Cf. above, p. 168 and n. 1.
3) Cf. Ph. Grierson, "Mint output in the tenth century", *Economic History Review*, 9, iii, 1957, p. 464.

dations of the Frankish kingdom were certainly too shaky to lend enough prestige and support to such a monetary venture. Under these circumstances, if the gold coinage of the Crusaders was to serve its economic purpose it had to resemble typologically the traditional and commonly recognized gold coinage of the Mediterranean, i.e., the *nomisma* and/or the *dīnār*. In other words, the Crusaders had no other viable solution but to imitate the local gold coinage.

Which of the Near Eastern gold types were they to imitate, however? Although presently one can indulge in classifying Mediaeval gold coins into two generic categories: the Byzantine *solidi* and the Muslim *dīnārs*, Mediterranean markets in the eleventh century saw the circulation of various types of Byzantine and Muslim gold coins. In regard to Byzantine coins, one could refer to two basic types, such as the regular *nomismata* and the light-weight *tetartera* [1]). Apart from the early history the Muslim minting production was also characterized by a proliferation of particular types of *dīnārs* [2]). Thus in the course of the eleventh century there existed a definite distinction between the ʿAbbāsid and Fāṭimid *dīnārs* [3]). Furthermore, the former category consisted of different types of *dīnārs* struck by various local dynasties or political regimes of the Eastern caliphate, such as the Sāmānids, the Ghaznawids, the Buwayhids and the Saljūqids. As for the Fāṭimid *dīnārs*, there were those issued by Egyptian mints and others which originated in Syria. Which of these types were the Crusaders to imitate? If one assumes that they proceeded with a calculated decision at all, it stands to reason that in order to accomplish their purpose, the Crusaders had to select a type of gold coin which currently constituted the best coinage in that area.

Such a criterion disqualified Byzantine gold coinage, which in that period suffered from a serious debasement. That its intrinsic quality

1) Cf. *idem*, "Nomisma, tetarteron et dinar: un plaidoyer pour Nicephore Phocas", *Revue de la Numismatique Belge*, 100, 1954, p. 75-84.

2) Cf. A. S. Ehrenkreutz, "Studies in the Monetary History of the Near East in the Middle Ages", (Hereafter, "Studies . . .") *Journal of Economic and Social History of the Orient*, 2, ii, 1959, p. 129-131.

3) Cf. *idem*, "Studies in the Monetary History of the Near East in the Middle Ages: II. The Standard of Fineness of Western and Eastern *Dīnārs* before the Crusades", (Hereafter, "Studies . . . II"), *JESHO*, 6, iii, 1963, p. 264.

greatly deteriotared may be seen from evidence compiled by Phillip Grierson, who has applied the method of examining the specific gravity in analyzing Byzantine gold coinage [1]. Thus, out of twenty-six *nomismata* struck between A.D. 1025 (the initial year of the reign of Constantine VIII) and A.D. 1081 (the final year of the reign of Nicephorus III), which were examined by Grierson, only two specimens were better than 95 per cent fine. Eight specimens fell within the 91 to 95 per cent degree of fineness; another group of eight *nomismata* belonged to the class of 86 to 90 per cent; the remaining eight specimens displayed a standard of fineness lower than 84 per cent. As for the *tetartera*, twenty-six specimens dating from the same period were examined by Grierson. Four of them fell within the 91 to 95 per cent category of fineness; one specimen displayed a standard of 86 per cent; four belonged to the class of 71 to 75 per cent; one to the class of 66 to 70 per cent; one to 61 to 65 per cent; three to 55 to 60 per cent; and

TABLE I

Distribution of Byzantine Gold Specimens Dating From 1025-1081 A.D., According to Their Standard of Fineness

Standard of Fineness in Percents:

Type of coin	Below 50	57	58	59	61	66	72	73	77	81	82	83	86	90	91	92	93	94	95	96	98
Nomisma	—	—	—	—	—	—	1	2	1	2	1	1	4	4	1	1	2	2	2	1	1
Tetarteron	11	1	1	1	1	1	2	2	—	—	—	—	1	—	—	1	3	1	—	—	—
Total	11	1	1	1	1	1	3	4	1	2	1	1	5	4	1	2	5	3	2	1	1

finally, eleven specimens showed a standard of fineness inferior to 50 per cent degree of purity [2]. One should also stress the fact that the ten

1) Cf. Ph. Grierson, "The Debasement of the Bezant in the Eleventh Century", *Byzantinische Zeitschrift*, 47, 1954, p. 379-394; also, *idem*, "Notes on the Fineness of the Byzantine Solidus", *Byzantinische Zeitschrift*, 54, 1961, p. 91-97.

2) In evaluating the data produced by Grierson I relied on the conversion tables of Earle R. Caley, "Estimation of Composition of Ancient Metal Objects. Utility of Specific Gravity Measurements", *Analytical Chemistry*, 24, iv, 1952, p. 678.

nomismata displaying a standard of fineness better than 90 per cent were struck before A.D. 1056. This serious debasement, which began during the reign of Michael IV (A.D. 1034-1041), was the most significant feature of the Byzantine coinage on the eve of the invasion of the Crusaders.

A similar negative development may be observed in the *dīnārs* struck in the eleventh century by the mints of the ʿAbbāsid caliphate. Beginning with the late tenth century uniformity in the weight standard of the coins was abandoned [1]). More serious was a deterioration in their standard of fineness. This was particularly true of the *dīnārs* struck during the domination of the Buwayhids (A.D. 946-1055). An examination of the specific gravity of eleven Buwayhid *dīnārs* has disclosed that only four of them, struck in the early period of their regime, possess a standard of fineness of 90 per cent or more.

TABLE II

Buwayhid Dīnārs

Name of Ruler	Mint	A.H.	Standard of Fineness in Percents
Rukn al-Dawla	al-Muḥammadīyah	341	97
Rukn al-Dawlah	Sawāh	346	94
Muʿizz al-Dawlah	Madīnat al-Salām	349	90
Rukn al-Dawlah	Madīnat al-Salām	356	89
ʿAḍud al-Dawlah	Madīnat al-Salām	366	93
Bahāʾ al-Dawlah	Sūq al-Ahwāz	397(9)	less than 50
Bahāʾ al-Dawlah	Sūq al-Ahwāz	397	less than 50
Bahāʾ al-Dawlah	Sūq al-Ahwāz	397	less than 50
Bahāʾ al-Dawlah	Sūq al-Ahwāz	398	less than 50
Sulṭān al-Dawlah	Madīnat al-Salām	409	62

Buwayhid *dīnārs* struck during the eleventh century are characterized by an extremely poor metallic quality [2]), a fact confirmed by textual sources [3]). A debased standard of fineness charac-

1) Cf. A. S. Ehrenkreutz, "Studies ....", *JESHO*, 2, ii, 1959, p. 147.
2) Cf. *idem*, "Studies ... II", *JESHO*, 6, iii, 1963, p. 256.
3) Cf. A. Grohmann, *Einführung und Chrestomathie zur arabischen Papyruskunde*, Praha, 1954, p. 193; also ,G. C. Miles, *The Numismatic History of Rayy*, (*Numismatic Studies*, No. 2), New York, 1938, p. 176-177.

terized the *dīnārs* issued by the mints of the Sāmānids (A. D. 892-1004) and of the Ghaznawids (A.D. 962-1186), with the exception of those produced by the mint of Naysābūr [1]). Table III illustrates the quality of Sāmānid and Ghaznawid *dīnārs* (excluding those struck in Naysābūr) [2]).

A certain improvement in the quality of the ʿAbbāsid *dīnārs* took place with the establishment of the Saljūqid regime in the middle of the eleventh century. Although forty-eight such specimens, which I have had occasion to examine, come from different mints of the ʿAbbāsid caliphate, they display a rather uniform and good standard of fineness, with the exception of four *dīnārs* with a standard inferior to 90 per cent.

TABLE III
Distribution of ʿAbbāsid *Dīnārs*
According to Their Standard of Fineness

		Standard of Fineness in Percents										
Dynasty	Below 90	90	91	92	93	94	95	96	97	98	99	100
Sāmānids	4	—	—	—	1	2	2	2	1	2	—	—
Ghaznawids	8	—	2	2	4	8	3	6	1	—	1	—
Saljūqids	4	1	2	4	3	5	9	8	7	5	—	—

In spite of this improvement, it seems unlikely that the ʿAbbāsid *dīnārs*, the reputation of which had been undermined by the pre-Saljūqid debasement, could compete with gold coins struck by Egyptian and Syrian mints following the establishment of the Fāṭimid regime in the second half of the tenth century [3]). Fāṭimid *dīnārs* struck in Egypt and Syria prior to the invasion of the Crusaders were characterized not only

1) Cf. A. S. Ehrenkreutz, *art. cit.*, p. 253-255.
2) Tables II-VI are based on coin data listed by A. S. Ehrenkreutz in the following journals: *BSOAS*, 16, iii, 1954, p. 507; *JAOS*, 76, iii, 1956, p. 183-184; *JESHO*, 6, iii, 1963, p. 266f. Five additionally examined *dīnārs* of Al-Āmir (cf. Table VI) are listed in the appendix to the present article.
3) Cf. A. S. Ehrenkreutz, "Studies . . . II", p. 258 f.

by a fixed standard of weight [1]) but by excellent intrinsic quality as well. Thus, out of 142 examined Fāṭimid specimens struck in Egypt before the end of the eleventh century, 121 (or 85.2 per cent) show a standard of fineness of 98 per cent and above. An equally impressive degree of purity is evident in Syrian *dīnārs* of the corresponding period. Of forty-three specimens, thirty-five (or 81.3 per cent) fall within a standard of 96 to 98 per cent.

TABLE IV

Distribution of Egyptian and Syrian *Dīnārs*, Struck Between 969 and 1094 A.D., According to Their Standard of Fineness

Standard of Fineness in Percents

	Below 90	90	91	92	93	94	95	96	97	98	99	100
Egyptian *dīnārs*	3	—	—	—	—	—	1	6	11	53	52	—
Syrian *dīnārs*	—	1	—	—	—	3	4	7	8	15	5	—

TABLE V

Comparison of the Metallic Quality of Byzantine and Muslim Gold Coinage

Percentage of Specimens with a Standard of Fineness in Percents

Type of Coin	Total Number of Examined Specimens	Below 90	90	91	92	93	94	95	96	97	98	99	100
Byzantine:													
Nomisma	26	46.1	15.3	3.8	3.8	7.6	7.6	7.6	3.8	—	3.8	—	—
Tetarteron	26	80.7	—	—	3.8	11.5	3.8	—	—	—	—	—	—
Muslim:													
ʿAbbāsid *Dīnārs*	108	21.2	1.8	3.7	5.5	8.3	14.8	12.9	14.8	9.2	6.4	0.9	—
Fāṭimid *Dīnārs*:													
Egyptian	142	2.1	—	—	—	—	—	0.7	4.2	7.7	37.3	36.6	11.2
Syrian	43	—	2.3	—	—	—	6.9	9.3	16.2	—	—	—	—

1) Cf. *idem*, "The Crisis of *Dīnār* in the Egypt of Saladin", *JAOS*, 76, iii, 1956, p. 178.

To obtain a better appreciation of the intrinsic difference between the Byzantine, ʿAbbāsid, and Fāṭimid gold, a special table has been prepared, indicating the distribution of the specimens considered in the preceding discussion, according to the standard of fineness. (See above Table V).

In the light of the above evidence it becomes clear that if the Crusaders based their decision on the evaluation of the merits of different types of gold coins circulating in the Near East, their choice must have fallen on the Fāṭimid *dīnārs*. Lack of pertinent textual evidence does not allow us to establish whether the precedent of striking gold coins in imitation of Fāṭimid *dīnārs* was really a deliberate act in the monetary policy of the Crusaders, or the result of some accidental, spontaneous, local decision. Neither is it possible to establish positively on the basis of available data the chronological background of that undertaking. All that one learns from textual evidence is that the Crusaders struck gold coins in imitation of Fāṭimid *dīnārs*, a fact fully supported by abundant numismatic evidence [1]).

The introduction by a basically West European feudal regime of gold coinage into its monetary system constituted a new development in the monetary history of the Middle Ages. In interpreting this phenomenon one should be careful not to overlook its real historical significance. The fundamental question to be raised is: To what extent did the appearance of the gold coins struck by the Crusaders bring about a change in Mediaeval monetary history? After all, Muslim *dīnārs* had been imitated by Christian rulers on earlier occasions [2]). Newcomers though they were, the Crusaders accepted many other social and economic habits of the local Near Eastern society. The striking of *dīnārs* by the Crusaders may thus be regarded as a continuation of the practice of their political predecessors in Syria. It is true that by imitating Fāṭimid *dīnārs* the Crusaders usurped minting prerogatives reserved for the sovereigns of Egypt. Aside from this diplomatic misdemeanor, however, and besides their cutting in on proceeds derived from minting

---

1) Cf. above, p. 167 and n. 1.

2) Cf. P. Balog and J. Yvon, *art. cit.*, p. 137, n. 2.

operations [1]), no significant change would develop in the overall monetary situation as long as the Crusaders exactly imitated Fāṭimid *dīnārs* [2]). This condition of the identity between the original Fāṭimid *dīnārs* and their Frankish counterparts was of great significance. Especially crucial was the problem of their intrinsic identity, or at least similarity. Relatively minor deviations or inaccuracies in the external appearance would not disqualify Frankish Fāṭimid *dīnārs* from circulation, particularly among the Crusaders or their Italian mercantile allies. On the other hand, any intrinsic discrepancy between the regular Fāṭimid coins and their Frankish imitations could be of significant economic consequence.

To obtain information about the relationship between the Fāṭimid and Frankish *dīnārs* from the point of view of their respective intrinsic quality, I examined the specific gravity of pertinent numismatic specimens. In imitating Fāṭimid gold coinage the Crusaders used chiefly the *dīnārs* of al-Mustanṣir (A.D. 1036-1094) and those of al-Āmir (A.D. 1101-1130) as prototypes. The coins of al-Mustanṣir must have been extremely popular in Egypt and Syria since their production had been going on for almost sixty years. The *dīnārs* of al-Āmir began to circulate almost concurrently wiht the spread of the Crusaders in Syria. For this reason I decided to investigate the metallic fineness of *dīnārs* of those two Fāṭimid caliphs and to compare it with the intrinsic quality of Frankish *dīnārs*.

The results yielded by my investigation are quite revealing. As one can see from Table VI, the *dīnārs* of al-Mustanṣir are of excellent intrinsic quality. Of 105 specimens only three (or 2.8 per cent) are less than 90 per cent pure. On the other hand, ninety-three specimens (or 88.5 per cent) show a standard of fineness of 96 per cent or above. Examining the *dīnārs* of al-Āmir, one can detect a deterioration in their

---

1) Cf. A. S. Ehrenkreutz, "Contributions to the Knowledge of the Fiscal Administration of Egypt in the Middle Ages", (Hereafter, "Contributions . . ."), *BSOAS*, 16, iii, 1954, p. 509, 513.

2) For the best discussion of the accomplishments of the Crusaders in this respect, *see* P. Balog and J. Yvon, *art. cit.*

intrinsic level. Thus, out of ninety-four specimens, fifteen (or 15.9 per cent) are inferior to 90 per cent standard, and twenty-two (or 23.4 per cent) are less than 96 per cent fine. One is impressed, however, by the fact that seventy-two specimens (or 76.5 per cent) fall within the excellent category of 96 per cent and above. It is also interesting to note that no *dīnār* with a standard of fineness of less than 90 per cent was struck after 1124 A.D. [1]).

TABLE VI

Distribution of Fāṭimid *Dīnārs*
According to Their Standard of Fineness

Standard of Fineness in Percents

Ruler and Origin of Coins	Below 90	90	91	92	93	94	95	96	97	98	99	100
al-Mustanṣir												
Egyptian *Dīnārs*	3	—	—	—	—	—	—	4	10	33	19	3
Syrian *Dīnārs*	—	1	—	—	—	3	5	7	8	8	1	—
al-Āmir												
Egyptian *Dīnārs*	15	1	2	—	1	3	—	8	3	10	8	40
Syrian *Dīnārs*	—	—	—	—	—	—	—	—	1	1	1	—

In spite of the occurrence of debased Egyptian *dīnārs*, the standard of Fāṭimid gold coinage was far superior to the *dīnārs* of the Crusaders. Table VII fully demonstrates the extremely poor intrinsic quality of *dīnārs* struck in imitation of Fāṭimid coins [2]). Only two of fifty-five specimens (or 3.6 per cent) have a standard of fineness better than 90 per cent; eighteen (or 32.7 per cent) are not even 75 per cent fine. The sharp contrast in intrinsic quality between the Fāṭimid and Frankish *dīnārs* is illustrated in Table VIII.

In the light of this evidence the striking of "Arabic" *dīnārs* by the Crusaders acquires meaningful significance. It is apparent that although the Crusaders imitated Fāṭimid *dīnārs* in external characteristics, they did not emulate their intrinsic quality. Whether the poor standard of the

1) Cf. below, p. 179.
2) For references to examined specimens, *see* Appendix.

TABLE VII

Distribution of the *Dīnārs* Struck by the Crusaders According to Their Standard of Fineness

Standard of Fineness in Percents

Below 60	60-64	65-69	70-74	75-79	80-84	85-89	91	99
6	4	7	1	18	16	1	1	1

gold coins struck by the Crusaders should be attributed to their technological ignorance or to a policy of monetary subversion, the consequences remained the same: Mediterranean markets were penetrated by pseudo-Fāṭimid *dīnārs* of cheap intrinsic quality. Consequently, the in-

TABLE VIII

Comparison of the Metallic Quality of the Original and Imitated *Dīnārs*

Percentage of Examined Coins Falling Within the Following Classes of Fineness in Percents

Dīnārs of the	Total Number	Below 60	60-64	65-69	70-74	75-79	80-84	85-89
Fāṭimids	199	1.0	—	—	—	2.5	4.0	1.5
Crusaders	55	10.9	7.2	12.7	1.8	32.7	29.0	1.8

Dīnārs of the	90	91	92	93	94	95	96	97	98	99	100
Fāṭimids	1.0	1.0	—	0.5	3.0	2.5	9.5	11.0	26.1	14.5	21.6
Crusaders	—	1.8	—	—	—	—	—	—	—	1.8	—

ternational reputation of Fāṭimid gold currency was compromised. The unavoidable loss of confidence in the integrity of Egyptian *dīnārs* must have caused a widespread tendency toward gold hoarding. Alarmed by the new situation, Fāṭimid authorities instituted measures to preserve the quality of Egyptian gold coinage. In A.D. 1120 a special investigation was undertaken into problems of the minting production. "This investigation resulted in fixing the standard of gold to a level which could not be surpassed" [1]). In A.D. 1122 an additional mint was set up

1) Ibn Baʿrah, *Kashf al-Asrār al-ʿilmīyah bi-Dār al-Ḍarb al-Miṣrīyah*, Ms., Dār al-

in Cairo; yet another began to function in Qūṣ [1]). These new mints were undoubtedly established to compensate for the loss of Syrian mints, the most important of them—that of Tyre (Ṣūr)—succumbing to the Crusaders in A.D. 1124. It is possible that Egyptian mint authorities succeeded in safeguarding the high standard of their *dīnārs*. As has been mentioned above, examined Fāṭimid *dīnārs* struck after A.D. 1124 do not include any debased specimens [2]). These measures, however, could not reverse the operation of the Gresham Law. Furthermore, the Fāṭimid caliphate was by then too weak politically and economically to offer sufficient backing for its *dīnār* which was shaken in prestige by the circulation of the Crusaders' coins. The fact that the mint of Qūṣ closed its operations after a brief period [3]) may be explained as an indication of a decrease in the circulation of gold [4]). At the time of the rise of the Ayyūbids in Egypt the shortage of gold was so acute that, to repeat the statement of al-Maqrīzī, "to say the name of a pure *dīnār* was like mentioning the name of a wife to a jealous husband, while to get such a coin in one's hand was like crossing the doors of paradise" [5]). The change in the political regime in Egypt was of no practical consequence to the status of the Muslim *dīnār*. The fate of the Mulim "dollar of the Middle Ages" had been sealed before the overthrow of the Fāṭimid caliphate. The Ayyūbids were politically and militarily successful in dealing with the Crusaders but they could not salvage the international credit of Egyptian gold coinage [6]). Ayyūbid *dīnārs* might have been temporarily of high intrinsic value,

---

Kutub al-Miṣrīyah, fo. 2 v. Cf. A. S. Ehrenkreutz, "The Standard of Fineness of Gold Coins Circulating in Egypt at the Time of the Crusades, (Hereafter, "The Standard of Fineness . . ."), *JAOS*, 74, iii, 1954, p. 164.

1) Cf. A. S. Ehrenkreutz, "Contributions . . .", *BSOAS*, 16, iii, 1954, p. 508.

2) Cf. above, p. 177.

3) Cf. A. S. Ehrenkreutz, *art. et loc. cit.*

4) Cf. Cl. Cahen, *art. cit.*, p. 332.

5) Cf. *Kitāb al-Sulūk li-Maʿrifat Duwal al-Mulūk*, Cairo, 1936, I, i, p. 46.

6) Ayyūbid *dīnārs* had no fixed standard of weight. They suffered from a serious debasement during the rule of Saladin (A.D. 1174-1193). Cf. A. S. Ehrenkreutz, "The Crisis of *Dīnār* in the Egypt of Saladin", *JAOS*, 76, iii, 1956, p. 178-184.

but they stood no chance of rising to the status of their Fāṭimid predecessors [1]).

It thus appears that the Arabic *dīnārs* struck by the Crusaders were an important instrument in precipitating a significant change in Mediaeval monetary history which for many centuries had witnessed the domination of the Byzantine and Muslim gold coins. While the decline of the former had begun before the Crusaders, the collapse of the Muslim *dīnār* may be attributed to subversive minting activities of the Crusaders. With the fading away of the early Mediaeval "dollars" a demand was created for a new strong gold coinage to serve the needs of international markets. The Crusaders paved the way for the new coinage. It was for the Italian mercantile republics [2]) to produce the "dollars" of the late Middle Ages and to inaugurate a new period in international monetary history.

APPENDIX

All of the specimens listed below belong to the American Numismatic Society in New York. Reference details used by me correspond to identification labels with which these coins are provided, or to classification numbers established by P. Balog and J. Yvon in their "Monnaies à legendes arabes de l'Orient Latin", *RN*, 1958, p. 133-168, here abbreviated as: Bal.

Dīnārs of al Āmir (original, not imitated)

Reference	*A.H.*	*Mint*	*Degree of Fineness in %*
57-114/16	508	Miṣr	81
57-114/14	510	Miṣr	80
57-114/17	510	Miṣr	82

1) A temporary improvement of Ayyūbid *dīnārs* took place during the rule of al-Kāmil (A.D. 1218-1238). Towards the end of the Ayyūbid Dynasty serious irregularities were reported in the operations of the mint of the sultan. Cf. A. S. Ehrenkreutz, "The Standard of Fineness ...", *JAOS*, 74, iii, p. 162-166; also, ʿUthmān ibn Ibrāhīm al-Nābulusī, *Kitāb lumaʿ al-Qawānīn al-Miṣrīyah fī Dawāwīn al-Diyār al-Miṣrīyah*, ed. by Cl. Cahen, (Extrait du *Bulletin d'Études Orientales*, 16, 1958-1960), p. 52-54.

2) For a more recent treatment of Italian gold coinage, *see* R. S. Lopez, "Back to Gold, 1252", *Economic History Review*, 9, ii, 1957, p. 219-140; *idem*, "Settecento Anni Fa: il Ritorno all'Oro nell'Occidente Duecentesco", *Rivista Storica Italiana*, 1955, p. 20-55; 161-198; C. M. Cipolla, *Money, Prices, and Civilization in the Mediterranean World. Fifth to Seventeenth Centry*, Princeton University Press, 1956, p. 20-26; Ph. Grierson, "La Moneta Veneziana nell'Economia Mediterranea del Trecento e Quattrocento", *La Civiltà Veneziana de Quattrocente*, Florence, 1957, p. 77-97.

57-114/15	514	al-Iskandarīyah	less than 50
57-114/3	518	al-Muʿizzīyah al-Qāhirah	77

Dīnārs Imitated by the Crusaders

	Reference	*Degree of Fineness in %*
al-Mustanṣir	52.115	56
	57.2143 (Bal. 1)	less than 50
	(Bal. 1)	99
	61.89	88
	Newell Coll. 1917 (Bal. 15)	58
	53.177 (Bal. 14)	54
	52.115 (Bal. 16)	56
	57.2143	57
al-Āmir	57-114/7	75
	57-114/8	77
	57-114/9	80
	57-114/10	77
	57-114/11	75
	57-114/12	74
	57-114/13	66
	57-114/18	75
	57-114/19	75
	57-114/20	81
	57-114/21 (top)	75
	57-114/21 (bottom)	75
	57-114/22	75
	57-114/23 (top)	66
	57-114/23 (middle)	76
	57-114/23 (bottom)	66
	57-114/24	80
	57-114/25	78
	57-114/26	81
	57-114/27	75
	57-114/32	78
	57-114/33	66
	57-114/34	80
	57-114/35	61
	59.203/39	81
	59.203/40	76
	59.203/41	81
	59.203/42	80
	59.203/43	81
	59.203/44	81
	59.203/45	76
	59.203/46	80
	59.203/47	81

XVII

182

59.203/48	81
59.203/49	84
59.203/50	76
Bal. 21	81
50.70	64
Another of this type	66
Newell Coll. 1917	64
Wright Coll. 49.163	66
Bal. 27c	76
57.161	81
Acquisition 1924 (Bal. 27a)	76
55.68 (Bal. 26, fig. 26b)	91
62.78	63
62.125	66

XVIII

CONTRIBUTIONS TO THE KNOWLEDGE OF THE STANDARD OF FINENESS OF SILVER COINAGE STRUCK IN EGYPT AND SYRIA DURING THE PERIOD OF THE CRUSADES

Two research projects recently undertaken at the University of Michigan have yielded new information concerning the intrinsic quality of silver coins struck in Egypt and Syria during the era of the Crusades. They involved the application of the neutron activation analysis (NAA) to two different samples of silver coinage: one consisting of Crusaders deniers and oboles, and the second of Mamlūk dirhams[1]). Technical data gathered from these inquiries not only furnished evidence concerning the purity of the specimens in the respective samples, but invited speculative conclusions regarding a linkage between the standards of fineness of the contemporaneaous Crusader and Muslim silver coinage.

I. *Royal issues of the Latin Kingdom of Jerusalem*

The first study involved the examination of the Gillman collection of coins of the Crusaders, made up of specimens gathered in the nineteenth century in Palestine. Belonging to the Kelsey Museum of Art and Archaeology at the University of Michigan[2]), the Gillman collection includes coins from the two extant series minted under the auspices of the Latin Kingdom of Jerusalem. These series were minted in the names of King Baldwin and King Amalric. A chronological check up has revealed that the monarchs involved were Baldwin III (A.D. 1143-1163) and his successor Amalric (A.D. 1163-1174).

The results of the NAA performed upon the coins from these series serve to expand the data published in the recent work of D. M. Metcalf, *Coinage of the Latin East in the Ashmolean Museum*, (London, Royal Numismatic Society, 1982). Metcalf provided the results of NAA for 22 royal coins of the Latin Kingdom[3]). The following frequency table shows the fineness of these coins.

This table reveals that 17 of the 22 coins (77.2%) have a standard of fineness of between 31 and 33 percent silver; nine of those (40.7%) being at 32 percent. Although the royal issues from the Gillman collection at the Kelsey Museum have a wider range of fineness stretching from 18 to 46 percent fine, they serve to reinforce Metcalf's data as the following tables demonstrate.

When the seventeen Kelsey specimens are added to the coins of Metcalf, one can see that twenty six of the coins (66.6%) are between 30 and 34 percent fine, with the highest concentration remaining at 32 percent fine. This high frequency of coins between 30 and 34 percent seems to point out a standard adopted by the Crusaders.

In searching for the basis of the establishment of this standard one should perhaps look to the Fāṭimids. In his article "History of the Dirhem in Egypt from the Fāṭimid Conquest until the Collapse of the Mamlūk Empire, 358 H./968 A.D.-922 H./1517 A.D."[5]), the late modern numismatist Paul Balog includes a table showing that Fāṭimid silver, which had been minted at a relatively high standard, began to take a rapid decline in the middle of the eleventh century i.e. during the rule of Caliph al-Mustanṣir (A.D. 1036-1094). Balog obtained his data by melting down a number of Fāṭimid specimens and using chemical analysis to determine their metallic composition. The following chart illustrates Balog's results.

When al-Mustanṣir's reign came to a close, the fineness of Fāṭimid coinage had already fallen to approximately one-third silver. It is possible that this phenomenon was connected with a catastrophic socio-economic crisis experienced by Lower Egypt during the middle part of al-Mustanṣir's regime. This drop in fineness of Fāṭimid silver is substantiated by evidence from the Geniza materials published by S. D. Goitein in his article, "The Exchange Rate of Gold and Silver Money in Fāṭimid and Ayyūbid Times." An entry dating from A.D. ca. 1060-1080 (A.H. 452-473) reads, "Please write me how the dirhams are in Fusṭāṭ. The rate of exchange here [Alexandria] is fifty per one dīnār''[6]). If we assume that the classic rate of exchange of 'pure' silver dirhams to 'pure' gold dinars was 13 1/3 to 1, and that Fāṭimid dīnārs were characterized by an excellent standard of fineness, the reference from the Geniza document implies a low standard of ca. 30 percent silver.

The production of such low quality silver in Egypt continued beyond the Fāṭimid dynasty until the coinage reforms initiated by the Ayyūbid Sultan al-Kāmil (A.D. 1218-1238)[7]). The question arises whether there was not a deliberate linkage between this low standard of fineness of Muslim silver and that of Crusader deniers. It is possible that by adopting a standard similar to that prevailing in Egypt, the monarchs of the Latin Kingdom of Jerusalem desired to supply silver coins which would facilitate trade because such a measure would allow for one to one exchange by weight of Crusader silver with Egyptian late Fāṭimid and early Ayyūbid dirhams.

II. *The Standard of Fineness of Early Mamlūk Dirhams*

Although Ayyūbid Sultan al-Kāmil began to reform the production of coinage, the dirham wavered at approximately 30 percent silver[8]) until a major improvement in its quality was made by the regime of Mamlūk Sultan Baybars (A.D. 1260-1277). This suggestion is based upon the statement of al-Maqrīzī[9]) and on the recent NAA examination of silver coins originally from the Karak hoard of the Department of Antiquities of the Jordanian Archaeological Museum in Amman. This hoard accidentally unearthed in 1963 A.D. near the tower of Sultan Baybars in Karak in southern Jordan, consists of 2244 early Mamlūk coins of which 1452 were identified by Salih Sari and submitted to NAA at the University of Michigan[10]).

Statistical results of the NAA testing reveal that the majority of the coins appears to have been struck of an alloy composed of between 65 and 75 percent silver with the balance being largely copper. This is true of both the Egyptian and the Syrian specimens irrespective of denominational units.

III. *Concluding Remarks*

King Baldwin and King Amalric set a standard of ca. 33% silver for their coinage in a probable attempt to facilitate trade with their neighbors in Egypt. Because this 33% standard inherited from the late Fāṭimid era was considered low, attempts were made by the Ayyūbid Sultan al-Kāmil to reform the Egyptian coinage, but the Karak hoard reveals that the real success in the efforts to improve and standardize Egyptian and Syrian silver coinage was achieved only by sultan Baybars and his immediate successors whose dirhams enjoyed a higher standard of 70 percent purity. Because of the concurrent catastrophic disintegration of first, the central authority of the Latin Kingdom, and then of the kingdom as a whole, the Crusaders had hardly any chance to institute coinage reforms to match the improved silver coinage of the Mamlūks.

Andrew S. Ehrenkreutz, Theresa K. Toman Emington,
and Ṣāliḥ Kh. Sārī

1) Prof. Adon Gordus and his staff graciously performed this analysis at the University of Michigan.

2) We wish to acknowledge our indebtedness to the Museum for its permission to use this collection for our research project.

3) *Op. cit.*, Tables 6 & 7.

4) The coin at 18 percent fine although omitted from the second chart is included in the compilations.

5) *Revue Numismatique*, 1961, p. 122.

6) *Journal of the Economic and Social History of the Orient.* 8, 1965, p. 21.

7) A. S. Ehrenkreutz, "Contributions to the Knowledge of the Fiscal Administration of Egypt in the Middle Ages," *Bulletin of the School of Oriental and Aftican Studies*, 16, 1954, p. 504.

8) *Ibid.*

9) Al-Maqrīzī, *Shudhūr al-ᶜUqūd Fī-Dhikr al-Nuqūd,* ed. Muḥammad al-Sayyid ᶜAlī Baḥr al-ᶜUlūm, 1967, pp. 30-31.

10) For a detailed description and analysis of the hoard see "A Note on al-Maqrīzī's Remarks Regarding the Silver Coinage of Baybars," and the unpublished Ph. D. Dissertation of Salih Kh. Sari, *A Critical Analysis of a Mamlūk Hoard from Karak,* The University of Michigan, 1986. Copies may be obtained through *University Microfilms,* 300 N. Zeeb Rd., Ann Arbor, MI 48103, U.S.A.

XIX

CONTRIBUTIONS TO THE KNOWLEDGE OF THE FISCAL ADMINISTRATION OF EGYPT IN THE MIDDLE AGES [1]

I. The Nature of the Exchange Rate between the Silver and Gold Issues in Egypt of the Baḥrī Mamlūks

ALTHOUGH the ratio between Egyptian gold coins (dinars) and those of silver (dirhams) is known to have fluctuated throughout the history of Islamic Egypt,[2] no attempt has been made to explain the principles underlying the rate of exchange.[3] Any such research is handicapped from the start by a deplorable failure on the part of numismatists to provide their fellow-historians with details concerning the alloys of various Egyptian coins.[4] This drawback deprives us of any means of counterchecking the textual evidence. Nevertheless, it is the belief of the present writer that the material contained in written sources relating to the period of the Ayyūbids (A.H. 569–648/A.D. 1174–1250), allows us to ascertain certain facts concerning the contemporary exchange pattern. The analysis of the nature of that pattern shows clearly that the exchange rate of the gold and silver issues of the Baḥrī Mamlūks (A.H. 648–784/A.D. 1250–1390), which remained fixed at 1 : 20, 1 : 25, and 1 : 28½,[5] had its roots in the system of the Ayyūbids.

The administration of the Ayyūbids, so important for the crystallization of the social and economic structure of the Mamlūk state,[6] marks a distinct phase in the monetary history of Islamic Egypt. For some unknown reasons, the fiscal administration of Saladin (A.H. 569–589/A.D. 1174–1193), the founder of the Ayyūbid dynasty, abandoned the weight standard for its issues.[7] From

[1] Acknowledgement is made to the members of the Department of Near Eastern Languages of Yale University, who by the award of the Kohut Fellowship enabled the author to undertake a study of the economic background of the Near East in the period of the Crusades. The present paper is a by-product of this research.

[2] cf. K. W. Hofmeier, ' Beiträge zur arabischen Papyrusforschung, I : Das System arabischer Steuerverrechnung im 9. Jahrhundert n.Chr. ', *Der Islam*, 4, 1913, pp. 100 and 101 ; A. Grohmann, ' Texte zur Wirtschaftsgeschichte Ägyptens in arabischer Zeit ', *Archiv. Or.*, 7, 1935, p. 443.

[3] The contribution of J. A. Decourdemanche, ' Du rapport légal de valeur entre l'or, l'argent et le cuivre chez les peuples anciens et les arabes ', *Revue d'Ethnographie et de Sociologie*, Paris, 1911, deals merely with the metrological aspect of the reform of ʿAbd al-Malik.

[4] Some seventy years ago the famous French scholar H. Sauvaire emphasized this problem in the following words : ' . . . il serait à souhaiter, pour le progrès de la numismatique orientale, que les grands cabinets de médailles de Londres, Paris, Saint-Pétersbourg, etc., sacrifiassent quelques-uns de leurs doubles pour les faire analyser et en déterminer le titre. Ce serait un grand service rendu à la science '. (' Matériaux pour servir à l'histoire de la numismatique et de la métrologie musulmanes ', *JA*, 19, 1882, p. 111.) Alas, the appeal of H. Sauvaire has remained unanswered up to the present.

[5] cf. E. Strauss, ' Prix et salaires à l'époque Mamlouke ', *Rev. des Ét. Islamiques*, 1949, p. 52 ; D. Ayalon, *L'esclavage du mamelouk*, Jerusalem, 1951, p. 42 ; Sauvaire, loc. cit., p. 129.

[6] cf. C. H. Becker, *Islamstudien*, Leipzig, 1924, i, 157 ; W. Björkman, *Beiträge zur Geschichte der Staatskanzlei im islamischen Ägypten*, Hamburg, 1928, p. 31.

[7] cf. P. Balog, ' Quelques dinars du début de l'ère Mamelouke Bahrite ', *Bull. de l'Inst. d'Égypte*, 32, 1951, p. 251.

then on the coins were no longer taken by number, but had to be weighed.[1] Under the new arrangements the problem of the alloys of the coins, their *bonitas intrinseca*, acquired a particular significance, since it was this factor which decisively influenced the ratio between the various monetary types.

While there was only one type of gold coins (dinars) in Egypt,[2] several types of silver coinage (dirhams) were in circulation in the period under discussion. Five of them: *nuqra*, *waraq* or *miṣrī*, *nāṣirī*, *kāmilī* or *mustadīra*, and finally *ẓāhirī*, have a direct bearing upon the present discussion.

The *nuqra* dirhams were the silver coins *par excellence*.[3] They were the official currency which served as the base of all big scale calculations and financial operations where both gold and silver were involved. They were struck of pure silver,[4] and their exchange value was 13⅓ per 1 unit of gold coinage.[5]

The *waraq* or *miṣrī* dirhams were struck for the use of the internal Egyptian market, to meet the needs of the local retail trade. Their alloy consisted of 30 per cent silver and 70 per cent copper.[6] Their exchange value was 40 to 1.[7]

In the winter A.D. 1187/88 (Shawwāl A.H. 583) Saladin introduced a new type of dirhams called *nāṣirī*.[8] Their alloy consisted of 50 per cent silver and

[1] Down to the reign of sultan al-Ashraf Sha'bān (A.H. 764–778/A.D. 1363–76), when new attempts were made to restore the weight standard. cf. al-Qalqashandī, *Ṣubḥ al-a'shā*, Cairo, 1914, iii. p. 440.

[2] The examination of about 100 dinars struck in Islamic Egypt shows that the standard of the gold issues was maintained well above 22 carats. Temporary debasements should be regarded as an exception to the rule. My thanks are due to Dr. J. Walker, Keeper of the Department of Coins and Medals in the British Museum, and to Dr. G. C. Miles, Curator in the Museum of the American Numismatic Society, for granting me permission to carry out the examination in question.

[3] For the etymology of this term see R. Dozy, *Supplément aux dictionnaires arabes*, Leyden, 1881, ii, p. 710. For further references see H. Sauvaire, loc. cit., pp. 61–4.

[4] cf. A. S. Ehrenkreutz, 'The Technical Manual on the Ayyūbid Mint in Cairo', *BSOAS*, xv, 1953, pp. 438–9. Notice the misleading information given by al-Qalqashandī (op. cit.). In one place he says that the alloy of the *nuqra* dirhams consisted of 70 per cent silver and 30 per cent copper (iii, 443). In another place, he says that the *nuqra* silver (*al-fiḍḍat an-nuqra*) was struck of 70 per cent copper and only 30 per cent silver (iii, 466). In the latter case al-Qalqashandī refers to the authority of Ibn Mammātī, who did not discuss at all the standard of fineness of the *nuqra* dirhams but that of the *miṣrī* (or *waraq*) dirhams. (cf. Ibn Mammātī, *Kitāb qawānīn ad-dawāwīn*, Cairo, 1943, p. 333.)

[5] Similar exchange rate (13⅛) is met in the papyri dating from the 3rd century A.H./9th century A.D., cf. Grohmann, loc. cit., p. 443. In A.H. 469/A.D. 1077 the ratio also stood at 13 : 1, cf. C. Cahen, *La Syrie du Nord à l'époque des Croisades* . . ., Paris, 1940, p. 470. For the exchange under the Ayyūbids, see Sauvaire, loc. cit., p. 122. It is, however, uncertain what kind of weight units was involved in the exchange figures.

[6] For the etymology of that term see A. I. S. de Sacy, *Traité des monnoies musulmanes, traduit de l'arabe de Makrizi*, Paris, 1797, p. 44, note. For its spelling, see Ziyada's edition of Maqrīzī's *Kitāb as-sulūk li ma'rifat duwal al-mulūk*, Cairo, 1936, i, 506, note 6. The *waraq* dirhams were already in circulation in Fāṭimid Egypt, cf. Ibn Muyassar, *Annales d'Égypte* (*Les Khalifs Fātimides*), ed. H. Massé, Cairo, 1919, p. 107. For the alloy of the *waraq* dirhams, see Ehrenkreutz, loc. cit., pp. 440–2.

[7] cf. Ibn Ba'ra, *Kashf al-asrār al-'ilmiya bi dār aḍ-ḍarb al-miṣriya*, MS., (*Fihris Dār al-Kutub al-'Arabiyah*, A.H. 1308, V., 390), fo. 4 v.

[8] From an-Nāṣir, the honorific name of Saladin.

50 per cent copper.[1] Considering that the 100 per cent silver *nuqra* dirhams stood at 13⅓ to 1, and the 30 per cent silver *waraq* dirhams stood at 40 to 1, it is reasonable to assume that the exchange value of the *nāṣirī* dirhams was 26⅔ to 1.

In the autumn of A.D. 1225 (*Dhū al-qa'da* A.H. 622) sultan al-Kāmil (A.H. 615–635/A.D. 618–638) substituted a new type of dirhams, called *kāmilī* or *mustadīra* (rounded), for the *waraq* and *nāṣirī* dirhams. The alloy of the new dirhams consisted of 70 per cent silver and 30 per cent copper. This is what was reported by al-Maqrīzī,[2] the chief authority on Egyptian coinage. Yet, when confronted with the information contained in the *Chronicle of the Patriarchs of Alexandria*,[3] the report of al-Maqrīzī proves to be misleading.

Firstly, contrary to the allegation of al-Maqrīzī, the *waraq* and the *nāṣirī* dirhams remained in the official circulation long after the reform of al-Kāmil.[4] Secondly, the alloy of the *kāmilī* or *mustadīra* dirhams could not by any means consist of 70 per cent silver. This can be established on the basis of the exchange rates which are reported in the *Chronicles of the Patriarchs of Alexandria*,[5] in connexion with the account of the reform of al-Kāmil. We find that the exchange rate of the new dirhams was fixed by the authorities at 37 : 1, and later at 35 : 1, which would amount to only 32·4 per cent and 34·2 per cent silver respectively. Thus, although the alloy of the new dirhams was slightly improved, its percentage of silver still wavered at 30 per cent, and not at 70 per cent silver.

In the light of these data I am inclined to dismiss the information of al-Maqrīzī as far as the alloy of the *kāmilī* or *mustadīra* dirhams is concerned. As for the nature of the reform in question, I think, that it consisted not so much in the improvement of the intrinsic value of the coins, but in the change in the shape of the inscriptions on the coins in question. The old square type of inscription on Egyptian coins was temporarily replaced in A.H. 622/A.D. 1225 by a round legend carried out in *naskhī* script.[6] And it was probably because of that conspicuous innovation that the new dirhams of al-Kāmil acquired the name of *al-mustadīra*. Thus as far as the exchange value is concerned the new reformed coins appear to have been identical with the pre-reform *waraq* dirhams. This inference is corroborated by the fact that the exchange rate of the *waraq* dirhams is listed in A.H. 637/A.D. 1240 as 35¼,[7] which ratio corresponds exactly with that of the reformed *kāmilī* dirhams.[8]

[1] cf. al-Maqrīzī, *Shudhūr al-'uqūd*, ed. L. A. Mayer, Alexandria, 1933, p. 12. In another work, however, the same author reports that the new dirhams of Saladin were to be struck of pure silver (cf. *Kitāb as-sulūk.*, ed. cit., I, i, 99).

[2] cf. al-Maqrīzī, *Shudhūr*, loc. cit.

[3] Published in E. Blochet (transl.), *Histoire d'Égypte de Makrizi*, Paris, 1908.

[4] ibid., p. 427, note. This is also reported by al-Maqrīzī himself in *Sulūk*, I, i, 508.

[5] cf. Blochet, op. cit., p. 362, note.

[6] cf. P. Balog, ' Études numismatiques ', *Bull. de l'Inst. d'Égypte*, 32, 1951, p. 30.

[7] cf. *Chronicle of the Patriarchs of Alexandria*, p. 427, note.

[8] This is also corroborated by a remark of H. Lavoix, who classified the metal of a few specimens of the reformed dirhams of al-Kāmil, as being of ' argent du bas titre ', (cf. *Catalogue des monnaies musulmanes de la Bibliothèque Nationale*, Paris, 1887–1894, iii, 245.)

No further changes are reported down to the rule of the Mamlūk sultan Baybars (A.H. 658–676/A.D. 1260–1277). Concerning his rule there is firstly the evidence of the *nāṣirī* dirhams being still in circulation.[1] On the other hand the rate of exchange of dirhams during his rule is recorded at 28½ : 1.[2] It seems beyond doubt that both, this exchange ratio as well as that of 25 : 1,[3] refer to the *nāṣirī* dirhams which were rated at 26⅔ : 1 on the basis of their 50 per cent silver alloy.[4]

The main contribution of Baybars in the field of monetary activities was the issue of *ẓāhirī* dirhams,[5] whose alloy consisted of 70 per cent silver and 30 per cent copper. The source of information in question is again al-Maqrīzī.[6] This time, however, his report is corroborated by additional textual[7] and numismatic evidence. The latter consists of a detail concerning the alloy of a dirham struck by Baybars. The chemical analysis of this specimen showed the percentage of purity of that dirham at 0·672[8] which almost perfectly corresponds with the reported alloy of the *ẓāhirī* dirhams.

Considering that 100 per cent silver dirhams stood at 13⅓ : 1, that 50 per cent silver dirhams were rated at about 26⅔, and that 30 per cent silver dirhams at 40 : 1, the exchange value of the *ẓāhirī* dirhams had to be consequently 20 : 1. And it is this very ratio which appears most frequently in the sources dealing with the exchange rates between the monetary types of the Baḥrī Mamlūks.

It appears, therefore, that the fixed exchange system of the Baḥrī Mamlūks depended on the purity of the alloy of their silver issues. The whole pattern of various rates of exchange was evolved from the basic ratio of 13⅓ silver units to 1 gold unit, which had become crystallized under the preceding dynasty of the Ayyūbids.

Finally, here is a table of the exchange value of Ayyūbid and Baḥrī Mamlūk dirhams, reconstructed on the basis of the above conclusions (the *kāmilī* dirhams are not included because of the contradictory evidence concerning their nature).[9]

Type of dirhams	*Alloy*	*Exchange rate per 1 gold unit*	
Nuqra	100 per cent	13⅓	
		correct	*reported*
Ẓāhirī	70 per cent	20	20[10]
Nāṣirī	50 per cent	26⅔	25 and 28½[11]
Waraq or *miṣrī*	30 per cent	40	40 and 35¼[12]

[1] See p. 504, note 4.
[2] cf. Sauvaire, loc. cit., p. 129.
[3] See p. 502, note 5.
[4] See above, p. 503.
[5] From adh-Dhahir, the honorific name of Baybars.
[6] cf. Al-Maqrīzī, *Shudhūr*, pp. 12/13.
[7] cf. al-Qalqashandī, op. cit., iii, 467.
[8] cf. Sauvaire, loc. cit., p. 106.
[9] See p. 504.
[10] The dirhams of that exchange value are not called by any specific name in the sources.
[11] The dirhams of such exchange value are not specified by name in the sources.
[12] See p. 504, note 8.

II. The Organizational Structure of the Cairo Mint at the Time of the Crusades

The following discussion will survey the administrative features of the famous Islamic mint at Cairo during the period of the Crusades, which constituted the most flourishing phase in the life of that institution. Scarcity of textual sources relating to the subject of Islamic mints [1] will perhaps never make it possible to achieve anything comparable with works dealing with medieval European mints.[2] It is, nevertheless, hoped that the material presented in this paper will contribute to our knowledge of Islamic minting organization,[3] and also enable those concerned with the subject of the institutional history of medieval Europe to follow parallel developments south of the Mediterranean.

The establishment of the mint in Cairo

The establishment of the mint in Cairo took place at the time, and as a result, of the impact of the Crusaders. Hitherto Cairo, the capital of Egypt since A.D. 970, had no mint of its own. Occasional issues of coins with the name of

[1] Oriental texts bearing on the subject of Islamic mints come not only from various areas, ranging from North Africa to India, but also from different periods. Thus the treatise of Haj Lassen (?) gives an account of the 14th-century Moroccan mint. A French translation of this treatise, by M. Viala, has been published in the work by J. D. Brethes, *Contribution à l'histoire du Maroc par les recherches numismatiques*, Casablanca, 1939. As this translation is not accompanied by any critical notes, or by the Arabic text itself, it must be treated with reserve. The treatise of ibn Baʿra (*Kashf al-asrār al-ʿilmiya bi dār aḍ-ḍarb al-miṣriya*, MS., *Fihris dār al-kutūb al-ʿarabiya*, A.H. 1308, v, p. 390), which deals exhaustively with the Ayyūbid mint of Cairo, was written in the first quarter of the 13th century A.D. For a detailed analysis of its contents, together with extracts describing minting operations, see A. S. Ehrenkreutz, ' Extracts from the Technical Manual on the Ayyūbid Mint in Cairo ', *BSOAS*, xv, 1953, pp. 423–447. There are also two published Oriental books on administration, containing chapters entirely devoted to the problems of mints. Those in *Ain i Akbari by Abul Fazl Allami* (tr. H. Blochmann, Calcutta, 1873, vol. 1) deal with the 16th-century mint of Moghul India. Those in *Tadhkirāt al-mulūk, a manual of Safavid administration* (c. 1137/1725), tr. V. Minorsky, London, 1943, examine the 18th-century mint of Ṣafāvid Persia. In addition to these major sources, scattered fragmentary information can be found in the works of various Oriental chroniclers, moralists, or authors dealing with administrative problems, such as Ibn Saʿīd, al-Ghazzālī, Ibn Mammāṭī, al-Qalqashandī, an-Nābulusī, or al-Maqrīzī, to which frequent reference is made in the present paper. Al-Maqrīzī's *Treatise on Coins* (*Shudhūr al-ʿuqūd*, ed. L. A. Mayer, Alexandria, 1933 ; French transl. by A. I. S. de Sacy, *Traité des monnoies musulmanes, traduit de l'arabe de Makrizi*, Paris, 1797), although essentially dedicated to Islamic coins, provides a good deal of useful information on the subject of mints. The task of collecting and systematizing these various scattered texts was attempted by H. Sauvaire (' Matériaux pour servir à l'histoire de la numismatique et la métrologie musulmane ', *JA*, 1897–1887), and by Père Anastase-Marie (*An-nuqūd al-ʿarabiyah wa ʿilm an-nummiyat ou Monnaies Arabes et Numismatique d'après les meilleurs auteurs de langue arabe*, Cairo, 1939).

[2] cf. for instance F. Mazerolle, *L'hôtel des monnaies, les batiments — le musée — les ateliers*, Paris, 1907 ; U. Cabrol, *Histoire de l'atelier monétaire royal de Villefranche-de-Rouergue*, Villefranche-de-Rouergue, 1913 ; or more recently, J. Craig, *The Mint, a History of the London Mint from* A.D. 287 *to* 1948, Cambridge, 1953 ; R. S. Lopez, ' An Aristocracy of Money in the Early Middle Ages ', *Speculum*, 28, 1953, pp. 1–43.

[3] For the importance of the studies on this subject, cf. J. Sauvaget, *Introduction à l'histoire de l'orient musulman*, Paris, 1946, p. 51.

Cairo as the mint of their origin,[1] were probably struck in the old capital of Moslem Egypt, Fusṭāṭ. The output of that Egyptian mint was supplemented by a great number of mints in Syria, where even minor localities like Tiberias or Ramla possessed mints of their own.[2] As long as the Fāṭimid caliphs exercised an effective control over their provinces, there was no need for increasing the minting production in Egypt. The 11th century A.D., however, witnessed a rapid shrinking of the Fāṭimid state. With the withdrawal of the Fāṭimids, Syria was plunged into a state of political chaos from which the Saljūqs and the Crusaders were to emerge as the chief rivals for the Fāṭimid heritage. In consequence, the flow of trade was diverted from Syria to Egypt. This circumstance and the successive loss of various Syrian mints must have created the problem of raising the minting production in Egypt itself. Already in the first half of the 11th century A.D. another mint began to operate in Alexandria.[3] Of the Syrian mints, Aleppo, Damascus, Ramla, and Tiberias fell into the hands of the Saljūqs. And in consequence of the invasion of the Crusaders, the mint of Tripolis (the latest available Fāṭimid coin dates from A.D. 1101), of 'Akkā (A.D. 1101), Ayla (A.D. 1120), and Tyre (A.D. 1122),[4] interrupted their operations for the Fāṭimids. The loss of these several important minting centres appears to have shaken the stability of the gold coinage of the Fāṭimids. The Egyptian dinars struck in A.D. 1122 and 1123 reveal a considerable deterioration in the standard of fineness, as illustrated by the following graph.[5]

[1] cf. G. C. Miles, *Fāṭimid coins in the Collections of the University Museum Philadelphia, and the American Numismatic Society*, New York, 1951, p. 50.

[2] ibid. [3] ibid.

[4] For all these dates see Miles, loc. cit. Although Ascalon was captured by the Crusaders in A.D. 1153 only, the last available coin from that mint dates from A.D. 1116.

[5] The composition of this graph is based on the examination of the specific gravity of the following dinars :—

A.H.	A.D.	Mint	S.G.	Percentage of purity	Reference	
510	1116	Alexandria	19·4	100	PhC	418
510	1116	Alexandria	18·627	96·01	PhC	417
510	1116	Alexandria	18·031	92·94	BM	208 d
510	1116	Miṣr	17·104	88·16	BM	208
511	1117	Miṣr	18·885	97·34	BM	209
511	1117	Alexandria	19·018	98·03	BM	210
512	1118	Alexandria	19·22	99·07	BM	211
514	1120	Alexandria	19·336	99·67	PhC	422
514	1120	Miṣr	18·973	97·79	BM	213
514	1120	Miṣr	19·275	99·35	PhC	466
515	1121	Miṣr	19·31	99·53	PhC	467
515	1121	Alexandria	19·4	100	PhC	423
515	1121	Alexandria	17·708	91·27	BM	215
516	1122	Miṣr	16·505	85·07	BM	217
517	1123	Miṣr	17·271	89·02	PhC	469
517	1123	Miṣr	16·78	86·49	BM	222
517	1123	Miṣr	16·152	83·25	BM	221
517	1123	Alexandria	16·048	82·72	BM	219

(Reference Abbreviations : PhC—University of Philadelphia Collection, now deposited in the American Numismatic Society. BM—British Museum Collection.) I am indebted to Dr. J. Walker of the British Museum and to Dr. G. C. Miles of the American Numismatic Society Museum for their kind permission to examine some specimens.

To cope with the situation the caliph al-Āmir ordered an investigation of the problems of the minting production.[1] Following this inquiry the vizir of the caliph, al-Mā'mūn ibn al-Baṭā'iḥī, ordered the construction of a new mint in Cairo, in December, A.D. 1122.[2] The new mint was to become the most important coining centre of medieval Egypt. Yet another mint was opened for a short period of time, in Qūṣ (the available coins date from A.D. 1123, 1124, 1125).[3]

Altogether the number of the Egyptian mints issuing gold currency amounted under the Fāṭimid caliph al-Āmir to four, though within the very reign of that ruler the production of the mint of Qūṣ was brought to a standstill. With the subsequent destruction of Fusṭāṭ in A.D. 1168, its mint ceased to operate,[4] so that the number of mints taken over by Saladin, the founder of the Ayyūbid dynasty (A.D. 1171–1250), was reduced to only two, Cairo and Alexan-

DIAGRAM

showing the degree of fineness of Egyptian dinars in A.H./A.D.

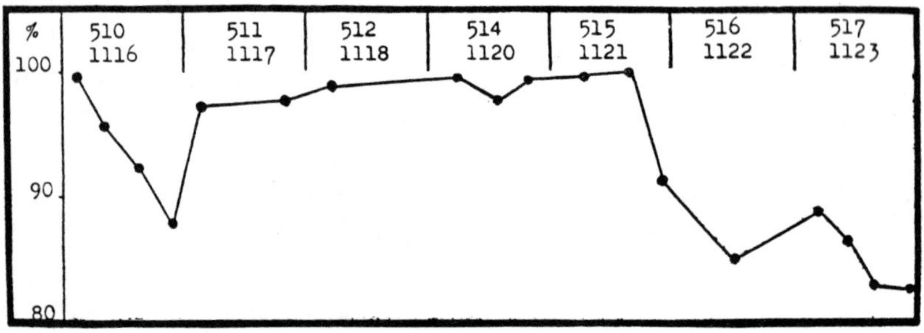

dria.[5] These were destined to be the sole minting centres of the Ayyūbids in Egypt, although in A.D. 1126 sultan al-Kāmil (A.D. 1218–1238) was compelled to open temporarily two additional mints in the capital, in order to supplement the needs of coinage demand, connected with his monetary reform.[6]

The Location of the Mint at Cairo

According to al-Maqrīzī, the famous chronicler of 14th-century Egypt, the first mint of Cairo, erected during the reign of the caliph al-Āmir, was situated

[1] cf. Ibn Ba'ra, op. cit., fo. 2 v.

[2] cf. al-Maqrīzī, *Kitāb al-mawā'iz wa-l-i'tibār*, Cairo, A.D. 1853, i, 445; de Sacy (transl.), *Extrait de la description historique et topographique de l'Egypte par Makrizi*, in *Traité des monnoies musulmanes*, pp. 76–77. For further references see G. Wiet, 'Matériaux pour un Corpus Inscriptionum Arabicarum', *MIFAO*, 52, pp. 183–184.

[3] cf. Miles, op. cit., p. 50; also al-Qalqashandī, *Ṣubḥ al-a'shā*, Cairo, 1913, iii, 369. For the importance of Qūṣ see W. J. Fischel, *Über die Gruppe der Karimi-Kaufleute*, Rome, 1937, p. 74.

[4] Last available coin dates from A.D. 1125, cf. Miles, op. cit., p. 51.

[5] cf. Ibn Mammātī, *Kitāb qawānīn ad-dawāwīn*, Cairo, 1943, p. 331.

[6] cf. *Histoire des patriarches d'Alexandrie* in E. Blochet (transl.), *Histoire d'Egypte de Makrizi*, Paris, 1908, p. 362, note 1. While one temporary minting centre was established in the citadel of Cairo, another one was set up in the old suburb of Miṣr, a fact confirmed by the existence of coins from that mint and corresponding date, cf. S. Lane-Poole, op. cit., iv, 104.

in the vicinity of the '*Sūq al-qashshāshīn*'.[1] This new establishment was known by the name of *ad-dār al-āmiriya* (the house of al-Āmir). The place indicated by al-Maqrīzī corresponds with modern Sanadiqiya Street, not far from the Azhar mosque. When Saladin seized power in Egypt (A.D. 1168), he transferred the mint to a building in the neighbourhood of the *Īwān Kabīr* (the Great Hall), where it still remained in al-Maqrīzī's time (A.D. 1364–1422). This new site is identical with the external hall of ablutions of the Ḥasanayn mosque.[2]

The Function of the Cairo Mint

The mint of Cairo performed a double function in the fiscal administration of Egypt at the time of the Crusades. Primarily concerned with the production of coinage, it served also as an ancillary treasury. There is an allusion to this aspect of the activities of the Cairo mint in the treatise of Ibn Ba'ra, for instance. He calls that mint '*the most abundant of the treasuries*'.[3] Large quantities of precious metal, stored in the mint, contributed to the importance of this institution as a treasury depot. Moreover, it seems that the mint in question was also a place of exchange of money at the time of monetary reforms. I base my assumption on an analogy drawn from an incident from the reign of the Fāṭimid caliph al-Ḥākim (A.D. 996–1021). When this ruler undertook his monetary reform, the population was ordered to hand over the abrogated currency to the mint.[4] When the inhabitants of Cairo were, on the occasion of a similar reform,[5] ordered by the Ayyūbid sultan al-Kāmil to exchange the money in their possession, they probably did it in the same way.

The Status of the Mint

Whereas under Mamlūk rulers (A.D. 1250–1517) the Cairo mint was farmed out as a fief, this was not the case during most of the period of the Crusades. This assertion is borne out by the existing evidence concerning the nature of financial obligations imposed on the mint. According to the information given by Ibn Mammāṭī, describing the mint of Saladin, the levy of the state from the mint was based on a fixed percentage.[6] Ibn Ba'ra, describing the mint of al-Kāmil, repeats that the tax imposed on the mint consisted of a percentage derived from the coined material.[7] He warns that any dishonesty in the course of production would cause inevitable loss to the state revenue.[8] An-Nābulusī, who wrote in the last years of the Ayyūbid dynasty (A.D. 1174–1250), also warns against similar danger resulting from inadequate supervision of the mint.[9] Thus the income yielded by the mint of Cairo varied in accordance with the quantities

[1] The 'Market of the produce-gatherers'?
[2] cf. G. Wiet, loc. cit.
[3] cf. Ibn Ba'ra, op. cit., fo. 1 v.
[4] cf. al-Maqrīzī, *Shudhūr*, pp. 11 and 12.
[5] cf. *Histoire des patriarches* in Blochet, op. cit., p. 362, note 1.
[6] cf. Ibn Mammātī, op. cit., pp. 332 and 333.
[7] cf. Ibn Ba'ra, op. cit., fo. 4 v.
[8] ibid., fo. 8 v.
[9] cf. An-Nābulusī, *Luma' al-qawānīn al-muḍiya fī dawāwīn ad-diyār al-miṣriya*, MS., Landsberg 39 (Yale University Coll.), fo. 33 v; also, C. Cahen, 'Quelques aspects de l'administration égyptienne médiévale vus par un de ses fonctionnaires', *Bull. Fac. des Lettres de Strasbourg*, 26, 1948, p. 113.

of bullion passing through the mint. This fact seems to indicate clearly that the mint of Cairo, prior to the period of the Mamlūks, could not have been farmed out, since farming involved payment of a fixed sum at agreed periods, apart from the real proceeds or the efficiency (read honesty) of the minters.

Thirteen years after the fall of the dynasty of the Ayyūbids, in the second year of the reign of the Mamlūk sultan Baybars (A.D. 1263) the mint was already farmed out. Muḥyī ad-Dīn, the chronicler of Baybars, not only mentions the term *ḍamān dār ad-ḍarb* (guarantee of the mint), but even specifies the sum which the farming involved.[1] This change in the status of the mint might have been brought about by the rapid decline in its production and the consequent dwindling of profits obtained by the state.[2] Farming out the institution in question would secure a steady income to the treasury.

The System of Control

Control of the mint in Egypt, as elsewhere in Islamic lands, was the prerogative of the ruler himself.[3] For the exercising of his prerogatives the ruler relied on a two-channelled system of control. On the one hand, legal authorities, charged with the task of protecting the integrity of the coinage, as well as the interests of general public. On the other hand, officials of the fiscal machinery of the state, who saw to it that the levy from the mint was duly delivered.

The responsibility for the first type of supervision rested with the chief judge (*qāḍī'l-quḍāt*),[4] who used to be charged with this task directly by the

[1] Sultan Baybars cut the rent from 250,000 dirhams (silver coins) to 200,000 dirhams, cf. Ibn 'Abd-aẓ-Ẓāhir, *Sīrat al-Malik aẓ-Ẓāhir Baybars*, MS., BM, Add. 23,331, fo. 20; also, al-Maqrīzī, *Kitāb as-sulūk*, ed. Ziyāda, Cairo, 1934–42, i. 508.

[2] cf. An-Nābulusī, loc. cit.; C. Cahen, loc. cit.

[3] Some Egyptian rulers took a personal interest in the working of their mints. Aḥmad ibn Ṭūlūn (A.D. 868–883), the founder of the first semi-independent Muslim dynasty of Egypt, is said to have improved the standard of fineness of his gold coinage (cf. Ibn ad-Dāya, *Sīrat Aḥmad ibn Ṭūlūn* in *Fragmente aus dem Mugrib des Ibn Sa'īd*, ed. K. Vollers, Berlin, 1894, pp. 33 and 34; al-Balawī, *Sirat Aḥmad ibn Ṭūlūn*, ed. Muḥammad Kurd 'Alī, Damascus, A.H. 1358, p. 196; al-Maqrīzī, *Shudhūr*, p. 10; de Sacy, *Traité*, pp. 38–40). The founder of the Ikhshīdid dynasty, Muḥammad ibn Tughj (A.D. 935–946), personally fixed the standard of fineness of his coinage (cf. Ibn Sa'īd, *Kitāb al-mughrib*, p. 31; Ismā'īl Kāshif, *Miṣr fi 'aṣr al-Ikhshīdiyīn*, Cairo, 1950, p. 191). The Fāṭimid caliph al-Ḥākim (A.D. 996–1021) undertook a large scale reform of the monetary issues (cf. al-Maqrīzī, *Shudhūr*, pp. 11–12). Another Fāṭimid caliph al-Āmir (A.D. 1101–1130) ordered an investigation of the operations of his mint and set up a new standard of fineness for his dinars (cf. Ibn Ba'ra, op. cit., fo. 2 v). Among the Ayyūbids, Saladin was responsible for the transfer of the Cairo mint to a new place (see, above, p. 509); he also undertook some measures aiming at the improvement of the standard of his coinage (cf. al-Maqrīzī, *Shudhūr*, p. 12; idem, *Kitāb as-sulūk*, i, 99). The interest of al-Kāmil (A.D. 1218–1238) in the operations of the Cairo mint, had the effect of producing dinars of a standard which was superior to the standard of the issues of other contemporary states (cf. Ibn Ba'ra, op. cit., fo. 2 v). The standard of 12 Cairo dinars of al-Kāmil, which I had the opportunity to examine in the British Museum, ranged from 22·77 carats (No. 403, vol. iv, p. 110 of S. Lane-Poole's *Catalogue*) to 23·72 carats (No. 383, ibid., iv, 106). In the Mamlūk period, mints were farmed out, but decisions concerning monetary issues continued to be made by the sultan (cf. al-Maqrīzī, *Shudhūr*, p. 12).

[4] cf. idem, *Kitāb al-mawā'iẓ*, i, 404. Similar duties were fulfilled in the first half of the 11th century A.D. by a *qāḍī* in Baghdād, cf. A. Mez, *Renaissance des Islams*, Heidelberg, 1922, p. 213; G. Bergsträsser (review), 'The governors and judges of Egypt . . .', *ZDMG*, 68, 1914, p. 407; R. Levy, *An Introduction to the Sociology of Islam*, London, 1931–33, ii, 236.

supreme ruler.[1] The chief judge performed this function by means of his representatives,[2] whose duties originally consisted of the following functions: [3]

(*a*) being present at the opening of the mint,
(*b*) being present at the process of the refining of precious metals,
(*c*) checking the degree of fineness of the adjusted alloys,
(*d*) being present at the closure of the mint, to be attested by the sealing of its premises.

During the early phase of the Fāṭimid domination, the control over the mint rested chiefly with the juristical, religious bodies. Later on the emphasis was shifted on to the civil administration.[4] Already under the Fāṭimid caliph al-Āmir, a new official, called *mus̱ẖārif dār aḍ-ḍarb* (controller of the mint), came into prominence.[5] He served as a link between the mint and the vizir, the head of the civil administration.[6] The *mus̱ẖārif* received instructions concerning monetary types directly from the vizir who remitted to him the bullion required for coining.[7] Under the Ayyūbids the administrative subordination of the mint was fully crystallized. As its revenues belonged to the category of special taxes (*ḍarā'ib*),[8] the mint of Cairo came under the authority of the Porta (*Bāb*) which constituted a subsection of the department of finances (*dīwān al-māl*).[9] Most of the supervisory functions, previously discharged by legal authorities, were taken over by the *mus̱ẖārif*, a member of the staff of the mint. He was responsible for the stocks of precious metal, for the coin-dies, for instruments of precision, and other implements. He also kept under his guard the samples of standard gold and silver, and finally he had to examine the accounts which had to be signed by him.[10] But the presence of judicial authorities was still required during the refining processes,[11] as well as for the approval of the adjusted alloys.[12]

This limitation of the prerogatives of the outside supervision exposed the proceedings of the mint to abuse by the staff of the mint. One of the important tasks of the inspectors of the *dīwān* was to prevent losses resulting from the inefficiency and dishonesty of the minters. By the administrative reform of

[1] cf. Al-Kindī, *Kitāb al-wulāh wa kitāb al-quḍāh*, ed. R. Guest, London, 1912, pp. 562, 575, 589, 597; al-Qalqas̱ẖandī, op. cit., x, 384, 385, 388, 466.

[2] cf. Ibn Mammātī, op. cit., p. 332; M. Gaudefroy Demombynes, *La Syrie*, Paris, 1923, p. lxxvii; al-Maqrīzī, *Kitāb al-mawā'iẓ*, i, 110.

[3] cf. ibid., i, 450; de Sacy (transl.), *Extrait de la description de l'Egypte*, p. 80.

[4] cf. Al-Maqrīzī, *Kitāb al-mawā'iẓ*, i, 450. Ibn K̲h̲aldūn also mentions the curtailment of the initially exclusive authority of the judicial authorities, cf. M. de Slane (transl.), *Les prolégomènes d'Ibn Khaldoun*, Paris, 1863–1868, i, 460.

[5] For a description of the office of *mus̱ẖārif* under the Fāṭimids, see R. Levy, op. cit., ii, 244.

[6] ibid., ii, 235.

[7] cf. Al-Maqrīzī, *Kitāb al-mawā'iẓ*, i, 450.

[8] cf. Ibn Mammātī, op. cit., p. 333.

[9] cf. An-Nābulusī, op. cit., fo. 19 r; Cahen, op. cit., pp. 102 and 103.

[10] cf. Ibn Ba'ra, op. cit., fo. 8 v.

[11] ibid., fo. 9 r. The officers in question were *al-'udūl*, for their status and functions, see R. Dozy, *Supplément aux dictionnaires arabes*, Leyden, 1881, ii, 103.

[12] cf. Ibn Mammātī, op. cit., p. 332.

A.D. 1233 the mint of Cairo was placed under the authority of a special inspector (*nāẓir dīwān al-wajh al-baḥrī*) entrusted with the supervision of all branches of state revenue in Cairo.[1] But even that measure did not prevent a serious drop in the revenue from the mint towards the end of the Ayyūbid dynasty.[2]

The Staff of the Mint

The operations of the mint were directed by the master, referred to as *mutawallī dār aḍ-ḍarb* (lit. man in charge of the mint),[3] but also as *ṣāḥib dār aḍ-ḍarb* (lit. master of the mint).[4] Other employees of the mint can be divided into two categories, the clerks and the manual workers. Among the former are the *mushārif* and the *shāhid* (assessor). Among the latter the *naqqāsh* (die sinker), the *sabbākūn* (melters), and *ḍarrābūn* (minters), with the *muqaddam* as their foreman.

The duties of the *mushārif* have been described above.[5] As for the *shāhid*, he supervised the carrying out of the transactions of the mint. He had to assess the value of the material delivered for coining, to take care of the registers, and to write out receipts which had to be signed by him.[6]

A special position among the manual workers was occupied by the *naqqāsh*. To ensure his loyalty his arm had to be stamped (branded ?).[7] To improve his skill, his professional activities were restricted to engraving only. The engraving of the dies was done in seclusion.[8]

The *muqaddam* was in charge of the actual technical operations. He tested the alloys of the raw material and adjusted them to the official standard. In order to prevent forgeries he had to test personally every quantity of raw material delivered to the mint, and to seal the furnaces used for the tests.[9] If a mistake occurred in the proportions of the components of the alloy, the *muqaddam* was held responsible for the loss.[10]

The remaining members of the staff (the *sabbākūn* and the *ḍarrābūn*) carried out various minting processes under the direction of the *muqaddam*.[11] Whenever a mistake was made in the course of these operations it was they who were charged with loss incurred by the mint.[12]

[1] cf. An-Nābulusī, op. cit., fo. 24 v ; Cahen, op. cit., p. 105.

[2] cf. An-Nābulusī, op. cit., fo. 33 v ; Cahen, op. cit., p. 113.

[3] cf. Ibn Ba'ra, op. cit., fo. 1 v.

[4] cf. An-Nābulusī, op. cit., fo. 33 v ; Cahen, op. cit., p. 113. For the use of terms *mutawallī* and *ṣāḥib* in medieval Egyptian administration, see Gaudefroy Demombynes, op. cit., p. lxxii, note 1.

[5] See p. 511.

[6] cf. Ibn Ba'ra, op. cit., fo. 8 v.

[7] This custom was practised in early Islam, cf. Balādhurī, *Futūḥ al-buldān*, Cairo, 1932, p. 454.

[8] cf. Ibn Ba'ra, op. cit., fo. 8 v.

[9] cf. ibid., fo. 8 v/9 v.

[10] cf. ibid., fo. 9 v.

[11] cf. ibid., fo. 4 v ; 7 v ; 8 r ; 9 r ; 9 v ; also, an-Nābulusī, op. cit., fo. 24 r ; Cahen, op. cit., p. 114.

[12] cf. Ibn Ba'ra, op. cit., fo. 9 v.

The Proceeds of the Mint at Cairo

Scattered details concerning the financial arrangement of the mint can be tabulated as follows :—

A.D.	INCOME IN DINARS			EXPENDITURE disposed according to to the following key :		
	TOTAL		derived from charges imposed on gold delivered to mint and fixed at	levy of *dīwān*	salaries of the minters	costs of production
	PER MONTH	PER YEAR				
1190 [1]	non datum	non datum	3·425 per cent	0·166 per cent	non datum	non datum
1191 [2]	,, ,,	,, ,,	3 per cent	less than 1 per cent	0·3 per cent	c. 2·6 per cent
1218 1235 [3] 1236	,, ,,	,, ,,	5 per cent	non datum	non datum	non datum
1237 [4] 1240	3,000	c. 80,000	non datum	,, ,,	,, ,,	,, ,,
1249 [5]	less than 100	non datum	,, ,,	,, ,,	,, ,,	,, ,,
1263 [6]	non datum	between 18,750 and 15,000	,, ,,	,, ,,	,, ,,	,, ,,

It appears from this table that the charges for coinage of gold demanded from the customers, which in A.D. 1190 amounted to 3·425 per cent, were in A.D. 1191 reduced to 3 per cent. This measure, accompanied by a simultaneous reduction of the levy, might have been enacted to stimulate deliveries of gold to the mint, since the circulation of gold in that period was hampered by Saladin's military preoccupations.[7] Some thirty years later the charges were raised again, since they then amounted to 5 per cent. The levies cashed from the customers were spent on the tax of the *dīwān*,[8] on the wages of the minters, and on costs connected with minting operations.[9] Unfortunately, except for A.D. 1191, no information is available about the exact percentage allotted to the minters.

As for the coining of silver, the charges borne by the customers, according

[1] cf. Ibn Mammātī, op. cit., p. 332. The revenue from the mint of the very active commercial centre of Aleppo, amounted to 100,000 dirhams during the domination of Saladin over that city (A.D. 1183–1193) ; cf. E. Blochet, ' L'histoire d'Alep de Kamal-ad-Din ', *Revue de l'Orient Latin*, 6, 1898, p. 38. Applying the exchange rate of 1 Egyptian dinar against 9 Syrian dirhams, as reported by Abū Shāma (cf. C. Cahen, *La Syrie du nord à l'époque des Croisades*, Paris, 1940, p. 470, note 16), the revenue of the Aleppo mint would equal 11·111 Egyptian dinars.

[2] cf. Ibn Mammātī, loc. cit.

[3] cf. Ibn Ba'ra, op. cit., fo. 4 v.

[4] cf. An-Nābulusī, op. cit., fo. 33 v.

[5] cf. ibid., loc. cit.

[6] This is implied in the financial settlement between sultan Baybars and the farmers of the mint (see above, p. 510). The conversion of the sum of dirhams into dinars is based on the exchange rate 1 dinar against 13⅓ dirhams, which was valid during the period of the Ayyūbids (cf. H. Sauvaire, loc. cit.).

[7] cf. E. Minost, ' Au sujet du traité des monnaies musulmanes de Makrizi ', *Bull. de l'Inst. d'Egypte*, 19, 1936/37, p. 58.

[8] Ibn Mammātī, op. cit., p. 332, refutes the criticism concerning the raising of this levy by the state, which was expressed by public opinion.

[9] cf. Ibn Ba'ra, op. cit., fo. 4 v ; Ibn Mammātī, op. cit., p. 333.

to the information dating from A.D. 1191,[1] amounted to 1·45 per cent, the tax levied by the *dīwān* being 0·255 per cent.

The costs of production, entirely covered by the customers,[2] included the purchase of raw material, instruments and tools, chemicals, and other ingredients required for the coining processes.[3]

The last decade of the Ayyūbid dynasty was notable for a considerable drop in the revenue of the mint. This process continued throughout the period of the Mamlūk rule (A.D. 1250–1517). Some Arab writers ascribed this decline in the output of the mint to the administrative mismanagement of its staff.[4] It is obvious, however, that the gradual decadence of the mint was a consequence of great economic difficulties [5] which were brought about by the outcome of the Crusades. The ever-increasing privileges granted to the Italian mercantile republics, and the establishment of their agencies in Egyptian towns,[6] resulted in the intensification of the circulation of European coins in the country of the Nile, and ended finally in the capture of the Egyptian market by the issues of Italian provenance.[7]

Thus the mint of Cairo completely lost its importance because of the ultimate results of the activities of the Crusaders, the very Crusaders whose initial impact had led to the establishment of that most flourishing of medieval Islamic mints.

[1] ibid., loc. cit.

[2] cf. *supra*.

[3] cf. Ehrenkreutz, loc. cit., p. 443 ff.

[4] cf. Al-Maqrīzī, *Kitāb al-mawā'iẓ*, i, 110 ; an-Nābulusī, op. cit., fo. 33 v.

[5] Even al-Maqrīzī admits it, when he says that the reduced revenue from the mint resulted from the scarcity of wealth (cf. *Kitāb al-mawā'iẓ*, loc. cit.).

[6] cf. W. Heyd, *Histoire du Commerce du Levant*, Leipzig, 1923, i, 393 ff.

[7] cf. A. R. van Gennep, ' Le ducat vénitien en Egypte ; son influence sur le monnayage de l'or dans ce pays au commencement du xv-e siècle ', *RN*, 1897.

XX

Extracts from the Technical Manual on the Ayyūbid Mint in Cairo

The Manuscript of ibn Ba'ra

IN the Manuscript Collection of the Cairo Library (Dār al-Kutub al-Miṣriya), there is an unpublished and practically unknown manuscript (*Kashf al-Asrār al-'Ilmiya bi Dār aḍ-Ḍarb al-Miṣriya*),[1] which contains a treatise dealing with problems of the Egyptian mint. It was composed by Manṣūr ibn Ba'ra aḏẖ-Ḏẖahabī al-Kāmilī. Although the manuscript is only a late copy of the original work, it constitutes an important source for the study of the monetary system and minting problems of medieval Egypt.

The manuscript, of which I was able to obtain a photostat copy, consists of nine folios measuring 25 × 18 cm. (the written text, of 25 regular lines, measures 20·5 × 12 cm.). It is written in fair *naskẖī* script with diacritical points, but few vowel signs. The text is on the whole well preserved and consists of an introduction and seventeen short chapters.

Nothing is known about the author himself, apart from the conclusions derived from the name and the contents of the treatise. The *nisba aḏẖ-Ḏẖahabī* suggests that he was professionally concerned with the smelting and refining of gold.[2] That he possessed such technical qualifications is confirmed by the contents of his treatise, whose value from the point of view of medieval chemistry has been summarized by Prof. E. J. Holmyard as follows : ' The contents of the book show that Arab chemists of the 13th century were well acquainted with cupellation, the parting of gold and silver by means of nitric acid, the extraction of silver by amalgamation with mercury, and with the quantitative chemical analysis of gold-silver alloys. The *Probierbuechlein* and Agricola's *De Re Metallica*, of the middle of the 16th century, contain scarcely any improvements upon the methods described by Manṣūr al-Kāmily '.[3]

C. Brockelmann, who has registered the manuscript in the paragraph called ' Die Politik ', reports that ' Manṣūr b. Ba'ra . . . wrote in 1135/1722 '.[4] A critical examination of the contents of this treatise makes this remark untenable. The very words ' *mawlānā as-sulṭān al-Malik al-Kāmil* ', which appear on fo. 2v, constitute sufficient evidence that ibn Ba'ra wrote his book during the reign of the Ayyūbid sultan al-Kāmil, that is to say between A.H. 615–635/A.D. 1218–1238.[5] This is corroborated by the *nisba al-Kāmilī*,

[1] *Fihris Dār al-Kutub al-'Arabiya*, A.H. 1308, v., p. 390.

[2] «هذه النسبة الى الذهب وتحليصه واخراج الغش منه», as-Sam'ānī, *Kitāb al-Ansāb*, London, 1912, p. 241 ; cf. as-Suyūtī, *Lubb al-Lubāb*, 1840, p. 112. For the problem of the acquiring of professional names by the Arabs, see Kremer, *Culturgeschichte des Orients unter den Chalifen*, Vienna, 1875–7, ii, p. 185.

[3] *The Makers of Chemistry*, Oxford, 1931, p. 77.

[4] *Geschichte der Arabischen Litteratur*, Leyden, 1937–1942, ii, p. 356.

[5] al-Malik al-Kāmil Nāṣir ad-Dīn Abu 'l-Ma'ālī Muḥammad ruled Egypt from 7 Jumādā II, 615, till 22 Rajab, 635. Cf. Zambaur, *Manuel de généalogie et de chronologie pour l'histoire de l'Islam*, Hanover, 1927, i, p. 97.

which shows the relation of its bearer to that sultan, and also by his references to certain monetary reforms carried out by this Ayyūbid ruler. The year 1135/1722, mentioned by Brockelmann as the date of the Cairo MS., is correct, as far as the origin of the preserved copy is concerned.

While ibn Baʻra's expert knowledge of minting operations, and of chemical processes especially, cannot be questioned, this is not true of his knowledge of Arabic. In addition to many grammatical mistakes, probably committed by ibn Baʻra himself, the preserved manuscript contains many corrupt terms which should be ascribed to the fact that the copyist lacked the necessary scientific knowledge. Thus the existing copy of ibn Baʻra's treatise presents a very difficult text. While attempting an edition of such a corrupt Arabic text on the basis of a single manuscript would certainly be a risky undertaking, the exploitation of its substance for the purpose of research proves extremely rewarding.

The material contained in the treatise of ibn Baʻra can be divided into two categories. The first, to which I shall refer as historical material, consists of all fragments bearing upon the economic history of Egypt, such as details concerning—

(*a*) the origin of gold reaching Egyptian mints (ch. i, fo. 2v),
(*b*) the monetary reforms carried out by the Fāṭimid Caliph al-Āmir and the Ayyūbid sultan al-Kāmil (ch. i, fo. 2v),
(*c*) the standard of fineness of dinars issued by these rulers (ch. i, fo. 2v ; ch. ii, fo. 4v),
(*d*) the alloy of dirhams issued by al-Kāmil (ch. x, fo. 6v–7r ; ch. xiii, fo. 7v),
(*e*) the exchange-rate of several types of dinars which were in circulation in Ayyūbid Egypt (ch. ii, fo. 4v),
(*f*) the function of the mint in the Ayyūbid administration of Egypt (introd., fo. 1v),
(*g*) the staff of the mint and their duties (cf. xvii, fo. 8v–9v).

The bulk of ibn Baʻra's information belongs to the second, essentially scientific, category. This should be divided into four subsections. The first of them consists of—

(i) details about gold and silver ore (ch. i, fo. 2v, 3v),
(ii) descriptions of chemical processes, such as—
 (*a*) The smelting and refining of gold (ch. i, fo. 3r, 3v ; ch. iv, fo. 5r–5v) and of silver ore (ch. ix, fo. 6v ; ch. xii, fo. 7r–7v),
 (*b*) the extraction of gold and silver, absorbed by the earthy residue, by means of amalgamation with mercury (ch. i, fo. 4r ; ch. viii, fo. 6r, 6v ; ch. xvi, fo. 8r, 8v).

To the second subsection belong descriptions of actual minting operations, such as—

(*a*) the qualitative testing of gold (ch. iii, fo. 5r),
(*b*) the quantitative testing of gold (ch. v, fo. 5v),
(*c*) the adjusting of the alloy of dinars (ch. vii, fo. 6r),

(*d*) the polishing of gold flans (ch. v, fo. 6r),
(*e*) the qualitative testing of silver (ch. ix, fo. 6v),
(*f*) the method of producing *nuqra* dirhams (ch. x, fo. 6v, 7r),[1]
(*g*) the polishing of *nuqra* flans (ch. xi, fo. 7r),
(*h*) the method of producing *waraq* dirhams (ch. xiii, fo. 7v),
(*i*) the quantitative testing of the alloy of *waraq* dirhams (ch. xiv, fo. 8r),
(*j*) the polishing of *waraq* flans (ch. xv, fo. 8r).

As the third subsection I would classify all scattered descriptions and mentions of various instruments, tools, weights and measures, fuel, chemicals, and other ingredients (see Appendix).

The fourth subsection consists merely of a digression contained in chapter i, fo. 3v, 4r, in which ibn Ba'ra refers to medicinal properties of gold.

Although I am primarily concerned with the historical source material, I have had to postpone an analysis of its substance pending an exhaustive examination of numismatic evidence.[2] It is, therefore, the two principal subsections of the 'scientific' material of ibn Ba'ra's treatise that are dealt with in the following part of this paper. I must stress, however, that lacking necessary scientific preparation, I have limited my task to giving what is, I hope, an accurate—though not literal—translation of the minting operations, and a summary of chemical processes, without analysing them from the technical point of view. The purpose of this exposition is to convey the 'scientific' contents of this 13th-century Arabic manuscript to those who are directly interested in technological problems.

Gold and Silver Ores

The high standard of alloy of 'Āmirī' dinars [3] was obtained by blending three kinds of gold [4] :—

«وهم معدنى وتربة ونبات. فامّا المعدنى فهو الذى خلقه الله تعالى فى الحجر يشبه العروق المغرعة فيه، وهو بالمغرب. وامّا التربة فهى التبر المشبه بالجص والرمل. والنبات فهو الذى ينبت فى بحر النيل خلف جبل القمر. ولطيف هذا النبات يحمله النيل الى

[1] Ibn Ba'ra distinguishes two kinds of dirhams : *nuqra* and *waraq* (for the spelling of *waraq*, cf. note 6 in Ziyāda's edition of Maqrīzī's *Kitāb as-sulūk li-ma'rifat duwal al-mulūk*, Cairo, 1936, i, p. 506). While the former were produced of pure silver, the latter were made of an alloy of base quality. The *waraq* dirhams, obviously destined for the internal Egyptian market, to meet the needs of the local retail trade, were in circulation in Cairo and Alexandria. Cf. Maqrīzī, *Shudhūr al-'Uqūd*, ed. L. A. Mayer, Alexandria, 1933, p. 12.

[2] One of the essential requirements in this respect is the ascertaining of the specific gravities (indicating the standard of fineness) of Egyptian dinars issued in the period extending from the accession of al-Āmir (A.D. 1101) down to the death of al-Kāmil (A.D. 1238).

[3] Dinars struck by al-Āmir. cf. Sauvaire, 'Matériaux pour servir à l'histoire de la numismatique et de la métrologie musulmane', *JA.*, xv, 1880, p. 425.

[4] fo. 3r :—«فجمع الآمر من هذه الاصناف الثلاثة . . . . واى صنف حضر من هذه الثلاثة».

426

ارض اسوان [1] بجمع ترابها منه. وهو ظاهر فى الفخار الاسوانى اذا تاملته كالدر
اللطيف. ولطيف هذا اللطيف يحمله النيل من اسوان الى بحر مصر تراه ظاهرا فى
الرمل لمن يتامله بشاطى بحر مصر، إلاّ انه لا يفى بما يغرم عليه من العمالات بضعفه
وترازينه [*sic*]. وامّا الذى لايقدر النيل على حمله ويبقى مستقر فى مكانه، وهو كالجص
المستطيل. وهذه الاصناف. اول ما تطلع فى معادنها وتظهر فضة ملونة بذهب. ثم
يقوى الذهب فيها على الفضة اولا فاولا على قدر قوة نجاز معدنها. فيصل منها الى دار
الضرب ما يكون خالصا [2] ،قد انضجته الطبيعة وكملت مزاجه. ومنها ما يكون ذهبا
دونا [3] لم ينته فى الطبخ الى غايته.» (fo. 2v)

'The three types of gold are: *mineral, sand, and vegetal*. As for the *mineral gold*, God has created it in rocks in the shape of ramified branches. It is found in the Maghrib. *Sand gold* consists of nuggets mixed with gypsum and sand, and *vegetal gold* is that which grows in the Nile beyond the Mountain of the Moon. The fine parts of this plant are carried down the Nile to the territory of Aswān, where they are deposited in the earth and are seen in Aswān pottery in the shape of small pearls. The finest particles of this fine *vegetal gold* are carried from Aswān down the lower reaches of the Nile, appearing to those who look for them in the sand on the banks of the river. But the efforts spent on extracting them do not pay as this gold is very weak. As for the gold which the Nile cannot carry away it remains stuck in its place and looks like oblong layers of gypsum. These, then, are the three kinds.

It is the silver tinged with gold, which appears first in the ore; but gradually gold prevails in it over the silver, owing to the strength of its nature. Gold reaching the mint consists of the pure gold, whose process of ripening was completed by nature, and of the inferior, under-developed one.'

Although ibn Baʿra does not say what was exactly the origin of gold imported from the Maghrib,[4] it is quite probable that it was that high quality gold which merchants of Sijilmasa used to obtain in Ghana, famous for its resources in precious ore.[5] In another place ibn Baʿra mentions the *yaʿqūbī* gold (الذهب اليعقوبي—fo. 4v) as an example of high quality gold. This kind of ore, which was certainly of Maghribī origin,[6] is said to possess such a degree of purity that it suffered no losses in the refining process (fo. 4v). As for the *sand gold*, it is safe to assume that it originated from the renowned veins in the Nubian

[1] MS. سرار   [2] MS. حايف   [3] MS. دون

[4] For gold imports from Maghrib, see Kremer, *Culturgeschichte*, i, p. 355.

[5] cf. Abu 'l-Fidā' (transl. M. Reinaud), *Géographie*, Paris, 1848, ii, p. 220. Also, *Description de l'Afrique septentrionale par el-Bekri*, ed. De Slane, Paris, 1911, p. 177; French transl. by de Slane, Paris, 1913, p. 331.

[6] Named after the Muwaḥḥid ruler Yaʿqūb ibn Yūsuf ibn ʿAbd al-Mūʾmin (A.H. 558–580/A.D. 1163–1184). Cf. dinars *yaʿqūbiya*, Sauvaire, op. cit., *JA.*, xix, 1882, p. 68.

desert,[1] considering that the description given by ibn Ba'ra corresponds with the accounts of many geographers.[2]

The most interesting, however, is his statement about the third kind of gold. It shows, namely, that ibn Ba'ra, though himself an expert in practical chemical processes, nevertheless believed in the existence of floral gold, a conception which two centuries earlier had been declared as legendary by al-Birūnī.[3] The gold in question could be nothing else but the float or wash gold found in the Nile, a fact well known to medieval geographers.[4]

Ibn Ba'ra's description of the gradual ' ripening ' of ore which transforms from silver into gold, is an example of the popularity of the theory of transmutation of metals.[5] It also implies the nature of silver, at least of one type of silver, that was used in the mint of ibn Ba'ra. Elsewhere, describing the smelting of gold ore, he mentions the ' golden silver ' (فضة ذهبية) and explains that he means by it ' *that silver which oozes out of gold, and which would have become gold, if it had remained in the ore* '.[6] Another characteristic of the ' golden silver ' is given on fo. 6r, in connexion with the adjusting of the standard of gold mixed with copper (الذهب المنحس).[7] ' *Its standard cannot be adjusted and its loss*

[1] cf. E. A. Floyer, ' The mines of the Northern Etbai or of the Northern Æthiopia ', *JRAS.*, 1892, pp. 811 ff. For gold in Wādī 'Allaqī, see Ya'qūbī (transl. G. Wiet), *Les Pays*, Cairo, 1937, p. 190, and note 1 on that page. Also Monneret de Villard, *Storia della Nubia cristiana*, Rome, 1938, p. 109. Its mines were well known to ancient writers, cf. Sabatier, *Production de l'or, de l'argent et du cuivre chez les anciens . . .*, St. Petersburg, 1850, p. 22.

[2] cf. *Ḥudūd al-Ālam*, tr. V. Minorsky, London, 1937, p. 81 : ' Other sands are those east of which are the Gulfs of Barbar and Ayla ; south of them, the desert of Buja ; west of them, the countries of Nubia and Egypt ; north of them, the Qulzum Gulf. These sands are called *Sands of the Mines* (*Ma'dan*) *because there is much gold, and much gold is* (*actually*) *found there* '. For methods employed for recovering that gold see Idrīsī, *Description de l'Afrique et de l'Espagne*, ed. R. Dozy et de Goeje, Leyden, 1866, p. 31/32. A similar account can be found with a medieval Chinese traveller Ch'ang Te, who writes : ' . . . the kingdom of Mi-Si-Ra, a very rich country. There is gold in the ground. In the night at some places a brightness can be seen. The people mark it with a feather and a charcoal. When digging in the daytime pieces as large as a jujube are brought to light '. *Apud* Bretschneider, *Mediaeval Researches from Eastern Asiatic Sources*, London, 1910, i, pp. 141–2.

[3] *Kitāb al-jamāhir fī ma'rifat al-jawāhir*, ed. A.H. 1355, p. 240 :—«وقد يضاف الى ماقلنا أساطير اخرى نبت الذهب فى تلك البرارى كالخرز».

[4] cf. *Ḥudūd al-'Ālam*, p. 69 : ' Jabal al-Qamar possesses mines of silver and gold, and the river comes out of it '. Birūnī, op. cit., pp. 240–1, states that the current of the Nile carried pellets of gold :—.«فيحمل الماء اليها بقوته القطع الكبار من الذهب سبائك تشبه الخرز» Also ad-Dimishqī :—«ونهر شقرّ يمرّ على لاردة ويوجد به تبر كثير مختلط بطينه وأجزاء لطيفة منه بمائه كما ترى أجزاء التبر اللطيفة فى طين النيل». (*Nukhbat ad-dahr fī 'ajā'ib al-barr wal-baḥr*, ed. Mehren, St. Petersburg, 1866, 2nd ed., Leipzig, 1923, p. 112).

[5] A similar description of the formation of gold from silver can be found in Dimishqī, op. cit., p. 51. An exponent of this theory was another 13th-century chemist al-'Irāqī, cf. G. Sarton, *Introduction to the History of Science*, vol. ii, part 2, p. 1045.

[6] Fo. 3v :—.«الفضة الخارجة منه التى لو بقيت فى معدنها صارت ذهبا»

[7] Terms such as *dhahabī*, *fiḍḍī*, or *nuḥāsī* were used not only with reference to colours, but as an indication of alloys. Cf. J. Ruska, *Ar-Rāzī's Buch Geheimniss der Geheimnisse* Berlin, 1937, p. 43.

is enormous, unless a quantity of "golden silver", amounting to $\frac{1}{10}$ *the weight of the gold, is melted with it. The silver extracts the whole copper and permits the gold to reach the standard.'* [1] But ibn Ba'ra speaks also of another kind of silver, the *gharība* silver (الفضة الغريبة) or the non-golden silver (الفضة الغير الذهبية), '*which attracts all the "golden silver", separating it from gold and turning into silver*'.[2] On fo. 3r he says again: '*The fire ... dissolved (the admixtures) contained in the body of gold and silver, which God has created and nature failed to turn into pure gold*' [3] and a little further: '*silver eliminated ... because of ... the imperfection of its nature*'.[4]

The Refining of Gold Ore

The description of the purification of gold from silver resembles closely that contained in the 10th-century scientific book *Rutbat al-Ḥakīm.*[5] The ore is melted down, cast into ingots, flattened, and cut into leaves thin as finger nails. These are placed, in alternate layers with earthy compound (تراب التعليق), in special cups. The cups are closed, sealed with clay, and deposited in the furnace, where their contents are submitted to the refining fire.[6] The gold is exposed to fire for one night whereupon the cups are taken out and the earthy compound containing the residue is removed, while the gold is submitted to further refining in the same way. This operation is repeated until *sirsīm* (سرسيم) appears instead of silver in the earthy compound. What ibn Ba'ra means by *sirsīm* is not clear. I am inclined to read this undoubtedly corrupt alchemical term as sirr as-sīm [7] (سر السيم) with the meaning 'the essence' or 'the core' of gold, which would fit the context.

As the result of the refining process all admixtures are melted down and absorbed by the earthy compound. The longer the gold is refined the higher its standard becomes. When the amount of gold has been reduced to three-quarters of its original weight, it never suffers any loss again (?).

[1] «الذهب المنحس اذا علّق وتردد فى التعليق ولايخلف العيار ويكون نقصه عظيما ان لم يسبك معه مثل عُشر وزنه فضة ذهبية. فان تلك الفضة تستخرج جميع ما فى جسمه من النحاس بسهولة ويلحق العيار».

[2] Fo. 3v :—«تستجذب جميع ما فى بطن جسم الذهب من الفضة الذهبية لتجانسها فى الفضة».

[3] «فاذابت النار ما فى جسمهم من الذهب والفضة التى خلقها الله تعالى فى جسمها وقصرت الطبيعة عن نضجها حتى تعود ذهبا».

[4] «الفضة فارقته . . . . لنقص كمال طبيعتها».

[5] cf. E. J. Holmyard, 'Maslama al-Majriti and the Rutbatu'l Hakim', *Isis*, vi, 1924, pp. 304–5.

[6] تعليق. cf. Ja'far ibn 'Alī ad-Dimashqī, *Al-ishārah īlā maḥāsin at-tijāra*, ed. A.H. 1318, p. 8. Also H. Ritter, 'Ein arabisches Handbuch der Handelswissenschaft', *Der Islam*, vii, 1917, p. 37. Also ibn Mammātī, *Kitāb Qawānīn ad-dawāwīn*, Cairo, 1943, p. 332. Also F. Wuestenfeld, *Die Geographie und Verwaltung von Ägypten*, Göttingen, 1879, p. 165, note.

[7] For the meaning of *sīm* as gold, see *al-Mukhaṣṣaṣ*, xii, p. 22.

The Refining of Silver

Silver is separated from copper [1] and chrysocolla by fusing it with lead. This is carried out by dissolving the two substances in deep crucibles which are kept under strong fire sustained by the blowing of bellows. The lead attracts all impurities and is in turn absorbed by the compound of which the crucibles are made, leaving the silver pure. Again this method does not differ from the description of a corresponding process which can be found in *Rutbat al-Ḥakīm*.[2] There are, however, two points which require comment. Firstly the term *ṭalgham* which in the language of Muslim medieval chemists meant *amalgam*,[3] but is used by ibn Ba'ra with reference to pure silver.[4] Secondly, the term *ḥabaq*, which appears in connexion with the refining of silver. This must be treated more fully.

What is ḥabaq ?

This question was raised for the first time in 1910 by E. Wiedemann,[5] who was puzzled by the appearance of this technical term in a passage of Bernhauer's *Mémoire sur les institutions de police chez les arabes, les persans et les turcs*,[6] which was a translation of a treatise written in the 12th century A.D. by an-Nabrawī. Wiedemann did not suggest any solution to the query. Neither did al-'Arīnī, the editor of the Arabic version of the same treatise, whose author has been identified as 'Abd ar-Raḥmān b. Naṣr ash-Shayzarī. 'Arīnī provided the term in question with a footnote stating that he was unable to offer any explanation at all.[7] The relevant passage in ash-Shayzarī's text reads as follows :—

«فى الحسبة على النحّاسين والحدّادين»

«لا يجوز لهم أن يمزجوا النحاس بالحبق الذى يخرج للصاغة وسبّاكى الفضة عند السبك، فإنه يصلّب النحاس ويزيده يبساً، فإذا أفرغ منه طاسة أو هاون انكسر سريعاً مثل الزجاج».

[1] The text reads نفس السواد (fo. 6v) which I take as code-name for copper. cf. Siggel, *Decknamen in der arabischen alchemistischen Literatur*, Berlin, 1949, p. 35.

[2] cf. E. J. Holmyard, ' Maslama al-Majriti and the Rutbatu'l Hakim ', *Isis*, vi, 1924, p. 304 ; also idem, *The Makers of Chemistry*, p. 79.

[3] cf. E. Wiedemann, ' Zur Chemie bei den Arabern ', *Beiträge*, xxiv, 43, 1911, p. 102. Also J. Ruska (transl.), *Al-Razi's Buch Geheimniss der Geheimnisse*, Berlin, 1937, p. 65.

[4] Ibn Ba'ra says on fo. 6v : الفضة اذا كانت سالمت من نفس السواد واللحام وكانت كأنّها الطلغم. cf. the statement by ad-Dimishqī : «الفضة الخالصة من شوائب الرصاص والزيبق والنحاس هى الفضة الطلعم». ([*sic*] *ṭal'am*) (*Nukhbat ad-dahr fī 'ajā'ib al-barr wal-baḥr*, ed. cit., p. 51. Such rendering of the meaning of the word *ṭalghām* may be the answer to the difficulty faced by Cl. Cahen in connexion with the appearance of that term in his ' Documents relatifs à quelques techniques iraquiennes au début du onzième siècle ', *Ars Islamica*, xv–xvi, 1951, pp. 23 ff.

[5] cf. *Beiträge*, xxiii, 42, 1910, p. 322.

[6] cf. *JA.*, xvii, 1861, pp. 34–5.

[7] 'Abd ar-Raḥmān b. Naṣr ash-Shayzarī, *Kitāb nihāyat ar-rutba fī ṭalab al-ḥisba*, ed. al-Bāz al-'Arīnī, Cairo, 1946, p. 79, note 1.

‘[Regulations of] *ḥisba* for the coppersmiths and blacksmiths

‘They are not allowed to mix copper with *ḥabaq* which is produced by jewellers and founders of silver in the course of casting operations. *Ḥabaq* stiffens the copper and increases its dryness. If a bowl or mortar is cast of it, it breaks quickly like glass.’ [1]

Ibn Ba‘ra not only mentions *ḥabaq* in his description of the refining of silver, where he says: ‘the substance that oozes out of silver is called *ḥabaq*’ (والذى يخرج من النقص يسمى حَبَق—fo. 6v), but he devotes a whole chapter to the process of extracting silver from the lead substance called *ḥabaq*, given here *in extenso*.

نى استخلاص الفضة من جسم الرصاص الذى يسمى حبق.

يؤخذ الحبق يدق كالفتيت ويُجعل فى بوطة مقعرة من رماد وحده مندى بالمآء. ويبنى عليها بناية[2]، صفة: برج عال[3] طوله ذراعين ووسع قطره شبر ونصف، واسفله اوسع من اعلاه. وفيه الروباش مبنى عليه. ليس له باب مفتوح. ثم يُملأ فحم بعد حريقه بالحطب. ويُجعل عليه من الرصاص لكل قنطار من الحبق حسابا عشرون رطلا رصاصا. فاذا استوعبه دعت [*sic*] جميع الحبق وهو علقة فحم وعلقة[4] حبق. ثم تحققت دوران الجميع. تكون الى جانب هذا التنور خارج عنه بوطة مقعرة من جير ورماد نصفين بالسوية منخفضة عن ارض البوطة. فيجرى جميع ما دار فيها من الحبق وغيره الى البوطة [5] البرانية، والنفخ مستمرا. وعلى وجه ذلك اقليميا الفضة[6] كالزجاج البوليس، وهو وسخ يجتمع من الحصى والرماد. فيرمى بها ويكشف وجه الحبق منها بماسك حديد. ثم يصير ذلك الحبق قرصا واحدا. فعند ذلك يهدم التنور. ويجعل مكانه بوطة اخرى مقعرة من رماد وجير مطفى نصفين بالسوية مندى [7] بقليل مآء كما جرت به العادة ويبنى فوقها قبة قصيرة العلو ولها باب واسع. وقبالة الباب طاقة لطيفة، وفم الروباش مبنى فى جنبها. وتملأ تلك البوطة فحم، وينفخ عليها ويجعل القرص على الفحم، والنفخ مستمر الى ان يدور ذلك القرص. فسد باب القبة جميعا بطين ورمل[8] ولايزال النفخ مستمرا[9] الى ان يخرج من تلك الطاقة المتقدم ذكرها دخان متغير اصفر. ثم يعود ازرق وهو علامة بخارها. فيتفتح[10] باب القبة فتجد الحبق قدنشف وصار جنبارا [*sic*]

[1] Similar regulation can be found in 14th-century text of Ibn al-Ukhuwwa, which is an abbreviation of the preceding book, except that the term *ḥabaq* is intentionally left out: «ويلزم الصنّاع الاّ يكثروا الرصاص فى النحاس المفرغ فانه اذا فعل منه هاون او طاسة او غير ذلك ثم وقع انكسر سريعاً مثل الزجاج». (*Ma‘alim al-qurba*, ed. R. Levy, London, 1938, p. 148).

[2] MS. بغابة [3] MS. عالى [4] MS. علفة [5] MS. البوط [6] MS. اقلبها فضة

[7] MS. مندا [8] MS. بطين رمل [9] MS. مستمر [10] MS. فينفتج

كالجفنة. وفى وسطه قرص وهو كالفضة النقرى، فيؤخذ، ثم تصفى فى بوطة ثالثة
مكشوفة بغير بناء كالتصفية [1] الاولى. فيعود مابقى فضة طلغم. ويؤخذ ذلك الجلنبار [*sic*]
ويستعمله[2] العطارون[3] فى دهان الزبادى وغيرها. (fo. 7r–7-).

'Crumble the *ḥabaq* and put it into a deep crucible made of moistened ash only. Erect over this crucible a construction of the following shape. A chimney two ells high,[4] its diameter being a span and a half. The bottom of this construction is larger than its top. A *rūbāsh* [5] is built on top of it. This construction has no door. Light the fire with wood, fill the furnace with charcoal, and blow continuously with the *rūbāsh* until the *ḥabaq* melts. Add to every qinṭār of *ḥabaq* 20 raṭl of lead. When this is absorbed introduce all the *ḥabaq*, one load of *ḥabaq* and one load of coal.[6] Make sure that it is melted. Close to the furnace is another deep crucible made of equal amounts of ash and lime. It is placed lower than the bottom of the first crucible, so that the *ḥabaq* and the contents of the crucible flow down into that external crucible. On its top appears silver *iqlīmīya* [7] like *zujāj al-būlīs*,[8] which is dirt coming from gravel and ash. Throw it away by skimming the surface of the *ḥabaq* with an iron ladle, whereupon the *ḥabaq* takes the shape of a cake. Thereupon the furnace is destroyed and in its place you put another deep crucible made of equal parts of ash and slaked lime, moistened with a little water in the usual way. Construct over this crucible a low cupola with a wide door. At the opposite side of the cupola is a small opening. The mouth of the *rūbāsh* is introduced into the side of the cupola. Fill this crucible with charcoal and blow on it. Thereupon place the cake on the

[1] MS. كالمصية   [2] MS. تستعمله   [3] MS. العطاريون

[4] As Muslim weights and measures varied from town to town, and from one period to another, it is impossible to establish what شبر, ذراع, رطل, and قنطار represented in Cairo during ibn Ba'ra's lifetime. H. Sauvaire mentions a great number of different types of *raṭl* (op. cit., *JA.*, Sér. viii, 4, 1884, pp. 210–240). He calculates the legal *raṭl* at 397·26 gr. and the legal *qinṭār* (100 *raṭls*) at 39 kg. and 726 gr., according to one source, and 401·674 gr. and 40 kg. 167·4 gr., according to another source ; ibid., 5, 1885, p. 502.

[5] A special kind of bellows, for its description see Appendix.

[6] For such rendering of the word '*allaqa*, cf. Spiro, *Arabic–English Vocabulary*, Cairo, 1923, p. 302 : علّق على اللحمة—put the meat on the fire.

[7] *Iqlīmīya*, one of the volatile products formed in the manufacture of silver and copper. cf. H. E. Stapleton and R. F. Azo, ' Alchemical equipment in the eleventh century A.D.', *Mem. As. Soc. Beng.*, 1, iv, 1905, p. 56, note 7. J. Ruska : ' wenn das Gold mit einem anderen Mineral vermengt ist . . . so reinigt seine Substanz und treibt sie hoch ein Stein, mit Schwarz gemischt, zum Teil auch von der Farbe des Glases. . . . Auch dem Silber wird bei Qazwini ein ähnlicher Stein zugeschrieben. Nach Vullers soll iqlimiya die Schlacke sein '. (*Al-Razi's Buch Geheimniss der Geheimnisse*, p. 50). Also *Memorandum Book of a Tenth Century Oculist. . . . A translation of the Tadhkirat of Ali ibn Isa of Baghdad* (c. A.D. 940–1010), by Casey A. Wood, Chicago, 1936, p. 51.

[8] While this word does not figure in any dictionary, various authorities translate it as follows : Kremer, *Culturgeschichte.*, i, p. 278 -(*bolus*) *armenische Siegelerde.*

De Slane, *Les Prolégomènes d'ibn Khaldoun*, Paris, 1863–8, i, p. 364, -(*bol d'Armenie*)-*terre sigillé.*

M. Sobernheim, *CIA.*, *Syrie du Nord*, p. 60, note -(*al-bals*)-*potasse.*

Règlements fiscaux ottomans : les provinces Syriennes, tr. Mantran et Sauvaget, Beirut, 1951, p. 69, note -*belis-cendres alcalines.*

cf. *az-zujāj al-būlīṣ* in ibn Mammātī's *Kitāb qawānīn ad-dawāwīn*, Cairo, 1943, p. 361. Also ad-Dimishqi, *Cosmographie*, tr. Mehren, Copenhagen, 1874, p. 94.

coal, continuing the blowing until the cake is dissolved. Then the door of the cupola must be closed with the clay and sand, and blowing continues. Yellow smoke, which later turns blue, escaping through the above-mentioned opening, is a sign that the contents of the cupola are boiling. Subsequently you open the door of the cupola and find dried *ḥabaq* which has turned جنبارا. In the middle is a cake of molten silver, which must be removed. This silver is placed in a third crucible, open and without any construction over it, where it is submitted to primary refining,[1] until it is rendered pure. This الجلنبار [2] is used by druggists for the greasing of bowls, etc.' [3]

For the explanation of the term *ḥabaq* I applied to Dr. D. MacKie (Department of History of Science, University College, London) and to H. H. Coghlan (Honorary Curator of the Borough Museum, Newbury). The former, having consulted Dr. E. J. Holmyard and Prof. J. R. Parlington, suggests that *ḥabaq* might mean ' litharge ' (by-product in separation of silver from lead), although in Arabic this is usually called *martak*. It is well known that the liquid litharge, when allowed to cool, solidifies into a hard, stone-like mass, a property which appears in ibn Ba'ra's description. Moreover, litharge is used for the manufacture of oil varnishes. Mr. Coghlan is much more inclined to suggest that the word denotes *bismuth*, a common and very harmful impurity in ancient copper tools. It causes extreme brittleness, which defect recalls the statement of Shayzarī, quoted above, that *ḥabaq* produces brittleness in copper.

The description of the process discussed above, although detailed, is unfortunately far from clear from the chemical point of view. It is obvious, however, from the information given by ibn Ba'ra, that the term *ḥabaq* referred to an unwanted by-product obtained during the refinement of silver.

The Extraction of Gold and Silver from the Earthy Residue

This operation is based on principles of amalgamation. The earthy compound containing residue is pounded, mixed with mercury, and dipped into a vessel full of water. When the water is removed from the vessel, the earthy compound is

[1] That is to say to the refining with lead, see above, p. 429.

[2] I am unable to give any satisfactory reading for this undoubtedly deformed word. In the first instance it may well be a corrupt rendering of *jinzār* (جنزار), which means verdigris. In that case the translation of the sentence would read : ' *ḥabaq*, which has become the colour of verdigris like (that on) a vessel '. The last sentence of the chapter discussed above would not apply, therefore, to the *ḥabaq* itself but to the verdigris. But in the second instance this word looks more like *jullanār* (جلنار) which was used as a code name for sulphur by Muslim chemists in the Middle Ages (cf. Siggel, *Decknamen in der arabischen alchemistischen Literatur*, p. 37). But it may be as well a compound word, the second part of which being *abār* (lead—ابار—cf. Siggel, *Arabisch-Deutsches Wörterbuch der Stoffe aus den drei Naturreichen*, Berlin, 1950, p. 76).

[3] It is interesting to notice that 16th-century writer Abū 'al-Faḍl 'Allāmī, describing the process of refining of silver with lead, says : ' . . . As soon as it (silver) is hardened in the middle, they sprinkle it with water . . . it then forms itself into a dish, and is perfectly refined. If this dish be melted again, half a surkh in every tólah will burn away. . . . The ashes of the dish, which are mixed with silver and lead, form a kind of litharge. . . .' cf. '*Ain i Akbarī*, tr. H. Blochmann, Calcutta, 1873, i, pp. 22–3.

washed away, while the precious residue, mixed with mercury, remains at the bottom. It is then squeezed out with a parchment so that the mercury is filtered through the pores of the parchment. The precious residue, with remnants of mercury sticking to it, is put into a special container filled with potsherds. The container is placed in a jug of water. When exposed to fire, the remaining mercury condenses into the jug, leaving the precious metal pure.[1]

The Minting Operations

The Qualitative Test

The first step in the minting operations consisted of assaying the raw material. The assaying of raw gold was carried out by means of a qualitative test, that is to say by using a touchstone and a set of touchneedles.[2] Ibn Ba'ra describes this testing set and the assaying as follows.

وعدة هذه العيارات ثمانية عشر عيارا. وزنها ثمانية عشر مثقالا، فيها من الذهب عشرة[3] مثاقيل ونصف وربع وثمن. ومن الفضة الذهبية سبع مثاقيل وثمن. هذا العيار[4] غير الجائز. والجميع متقوية مسكوكة فى قلب فضة مع المحك على التوالى[5]، اولهم الجائز واخرهم عيار رباعى.

فاذا وقع لك ذهب مجهول[6] تحكه على جانب العيارات المقدم ذكرها، فيظهر لك من كونه ولونه شبهه من العيارات مبلغ قيمته على الوضع الصحيح المحرر بعد الحمى. فانه ربما كان فى جسمه نحاس، فيكون لونه على المحك احمر عال، وهو ناقص فى العيار. وهو اذا حمى تغير لونه وركبه سواد وغيره، على قدر مافيه نحاس من الكثرة والقلة (fo. 5r).

'The number of touchneedles should be 18, weighing together 18 *mithqāls*,[7] of which $10\frac{7}{8}$ is gold and $7\frac{1}{8}$ is *golden silver* (الفضة الذهبية). All these touchneedles are affixed to a silver form together with the touchstone, one after another, beginning with the (one that is of the highest) official standard, and ending with the *rubā'iy* standard.[8]

[1] Again this process does not differ from the corresponding one discussed by Holmyard in his article on the *Rutbat al-Ḥakīm*. cf. op. cit., p. 305. Also *idem*, *The Makers of Chemistry*, p. 80.

[2] This is how I translate *'iyārāt*. Although they differ in shape from ordinary touchneedles, their function is exactly the same.

[3] MS. عشر [4] MS. عيار [5] MS. التولى [6] MS. ذهبا مجهولا

[7] Decourdemanche calculates the Egyptian *mithqāl* at 5·95 gr. cf. 'Etude métrologique et numismatique sur les misqals et les dirhems arabes', *Revue Numismatique*, Paris, 4e sér., xii, 1908, pp. 232–3.

[8] We must distinguish between the standard of gold in general and the standard of gold coinage. The standard of gold that is declared as officially accepted (جائز) by ibn Ba'ra extends from pure gold to an alloy consisting of 7 parts of pure gold and 17 parts of *golden silver*. An alloy containing a proportion of gold to silver of 1 : 3 is declared as 'out-of-course'

'If you happen to meet some unknown gold, you should assay it close to those touchneedles. And the colour of this gold after heating, when compared with that of the touchneedles, reveals to you the real value of the assayed metal. For it may happen that this gold contains copper and though it shows fine red colour on the touchstone, its standard is deficient.[1] But if you heat it its colour will change and darken and turn to other colours, in proportion to the copper contents of this metal.' [2]

The Quantitative Test

Refined Islamic gold, which ibn Ba'ra calls *haraja*,[3] had to be submitted to a quantitative analysis.

فى اعتبار الهرجة

يسبك الذهب الذى علق بسبائك ويقطع طرفى كل سبيكة وتسبك[4] الاطراف جملة. ثم يؤخذ منها وزن مثقالين. ثم يضرب منه ورقين مساويين فى القدر والوزن. ويضرب من الآمرى، الذى هو الاصل، مثلهما[5] والوزن على قالب فولاذ[6] هذه صورته، ثم يصور فى النسخة[7]. ثم يجعل الاربعة اوراق فى القدح على المخلوط متقابلات، والمخلوط فوقهم. ثم تجعل اوراق الاصل وهما فوقهم فى بعينه. فتغطيهم بالمخلوط متقابلات وتكتب عليه قدح العيار. وتشد الوصل كما جرت به العادة، وتختم عليه

(غير الجائز). The lowest standard accepted at the court of the Moghul emperor al-Akbar was set at 6 bán, which was the degree of the alloy consisting of 5¼ gold, $\frac{11}{8}$ silver, and $\frac{11}{8}$ copper. All baser compositions were rejected (cf. *'Ain i Akbarī*, i, p. 19). The standard of gold coinage, on the other hand, was fixed at a certain limit. In modern England the standard of gold used for plate and jewellery consists of 9, 12, 15, 18, and 22 carats, the alloying metals being silver and copper in varying proportions. But the British standard of gold coinage is based on 22 carat gold, that is to say, consisting of 91·67 per cent gold and 8·33 per cent copper.

[1] For forgeries and methods for discovering them, see H. Ritter, 'Ein arabisches Handbuch der Handelswissenschaft', *Der Islam*, vii, 1917, pp. 51 ff.

[2] The method of assaying by means of touchstone was well known all over medieval Islamic territories. cf. 14th-century Arabic manuscript of Hadj Lahsen (describing the operations of the mint of the Marinids) transl. by M. Viala, and published in J. D. Brethes' *Contributions à l'histoire du Maroc par les recherches numismatiques*, Casablanca, p. 258. Also *'Ain i Akbarī*, i, p. 19.

[3] Ibn Ba'ra consistently uses the term *al-haraja* with reference to gold, and distinguishes it from *Rūmī* gold (الذهب الرومى—fo. 8v). Maqrīzī gives a full explanation of the term *haraja* as follows: الذهب الهرجة . . . . هو الذهب الاسلامى الخالص من الغش (*Kitāb as-sulūk*, Brit. Mus. MS. Or. 2902, fo. 22b). The explanation of M. M. Ziyāda—given in his edition of *Kitāb as-sulūk*, Cairo, 1942, ii, p. 393, note—is not only erroneous but absolutely out of place, since the quoted remark of de Sacy (*Traité des monnoies musulmanes, traduit de l'arabe de Makrizi*, Paris, 1799, p. 46, note 88) does not refer to هرج but to حراج. cf. Maqrīzī, *Shudhūr al-'uqūd*, ed. L. A. Mayer, Alexandria, 1933, p. 13.

[4] MS. يسبك [5] MS. مثلها [6] MS. فولاد

[7] This is obviously an addition made by the copyist indicating that he intended to provide his copy with the drawing of the mould, contained in the original. There is no trace of an illustration in the existing MS. and no space was left for one.

بالطين ويودع الاتون اللطيف اعتد برسم العيار. وتوقد عليه يوما وليلة. ثم تخرج[1] اوراق الاصل والفرع وتمسح كل ورقة منهم على لوح خشب بخرقة صوف مسحا يزيل الشك والوهم. ثم تعدل[2] عيارات التعليق عليهم. ويكون قد حرر وزن الاوراق بالمثقال والحبوب من قبل لتعلم ما قطعت النار منهم ، ومقدار مس زدت به الهرجة من حبة. ثم يقابل باوراق الوزن فى كفتى الميزان، فان رجح عن الاصل، ولو بعُشر حبة، فقد جازت. تعمل دنانير وتختم بعد جلاها. واعلم انه متى عمل اوراق اصل برسم العيار من دينار آمرى[3]، واعتبار العيار على ذلك (fo. 5v).

' The testing of the standard of the *haraja*

' Refined gold is cast into ingots. The two ends of each ingot are sliced off and all of these bits are melted down together. Two *mithqāls* of this gold are taken and hammered into two leaves, equal in shape and weight. Two other similar leaves are made of the *Āmirī* gold. They are the check plates. The hammering is done on a steel form. The four plates are put in a cup. Firstly the two test plates are placed on a layer of the earthy compound, facing each other, and are covered with another layer of that mixture. Then the two check plates are placed in a similar fashion. The cup is filled with that mixture and labelled " test cup ". Its lid is fastened in the usual way and sealed with clay. Then it is deposited in a small furnace, built for that purpose, where it is kept under fire for one night and one day. Afterwards both the check and test cups are taken out, and each of them is cleaned with a woollen rag on a wooden board, until all doubt disappears.[4] The calculations concerning the refining of the *haraja* are based upon the results of this experiment.[5] The weight of the plates was previously taken down in *mithqāls* and grains [6] so that the loss caused by the fire can be calculated. The plates are now weighed on scales and the loss of the test plates is compared with that of the check plates. If the difference does not exceed 0·1 grain, the *haraja* is passed, and can be turned into dinars after polishing and stamping.' [7]

The Adjusting of the Standard of the haraja

Should the degree of fineness of the *haraja* prove to be either too low or too high in relation to the official standard, its alloy had to be adjusted, and this was done by the following method.

تعديل كل هرجة من الذهب وما يحتاج من الذهب من النقص فى التعليق ليبلغ الجائز من غير حيف ولا نقص. مثاله ان الهرجة اذا اردت تنقص حبة فى كل مثقال.

[1] MS. يحرج [2] MS. تعلق [3] MS. آميرى

[4] Probably ' about the identity of the plates ', which might have been fraudulently exchanged. Ibn Ba'ra describes on fo. 9r the precautions taken by the staff of the mint in order to prevent substitution of deficient plates in the course of this operation.

[5] See below.

[6] Decourdemanche puts the Egyptian and the legal ḥabba (grain) at $0 \cdot 08\frac{10}{72}$ gr. (loc. cit.).

[7] Similar, though incomplete, description of the quantitative analysis is given by ibn Mammātī, op. cit., p. 332. Also *'Ain i Akbari*, i, p. 21.

ووزنها مائة. فاردنا تعليقها ليلة، فلا تنقص تلك الحبة. وكما علمنا اذا علقت ليلة نقصت حبتين فى المثقال[1]، وهذا حيف. فيتحيل حتى لا ينقص الحبة المذكورة. والطريق فى ذلك ان تعلق من المائة خمسين، فانها تنقص حبتين فى المثقال. ثم تجعلها بالسبك مع الخمسين الاخرى فتجئ حبة تنقص من كل مثقال. فتعدله، وعلى مثل ذلك فقس جميع الهرج (fo. 6r).

'The adjusting of the standard of *haraja* by calculating the loss incurred by it in the refining process. Example: the *haraja* weighs 100 *mithqāls*. To reach the official standard the *haraja* must lose 1 grain per *mithqāl* in one night. The test shows that this *haraja* loses 2 grains per *mithqāl*, excelling thus the official standard.[2] The following is the method by which the *haraja* will lose only 1 grain per *mithqāl*. Only 50 *mithqāls* are submitted to the refining process. The loss amounts to 2 grains per *mithqāl*. Afterwards these 50 *mithqāls* are melted together with the remaining lot (50 *mithqāls*), so that the loss of the whole *haraja* (100 *mithqāls*) amounts to 1 grain per *mithqāl*. This method of splitting permits the adjusting of the standard of *haraja*.'

The Polishing of Gold Flans

The last stage in the production of dinars, which is described by ibn Ba'ra, consisted of polishing the flans.

فى جلاء الذهب ليختم

يجعل الذهب بعد تدويره فى قدح فخار احمر. وتجعل ملحا مدقوقا مندى بقليل ماء حلو. وتوقد بنار الحطب القوية الى ان يدور الملح كما يدور الرصاص ويجرى ويقلب سبائك فتخرج الدنانير منه. وتغسل بالماء البارد والرمل الناعم وتجفف فى قدح على نار لطيفة وتختم (fo. 6r).

'On the polishing of gold before stamping

'Gold—*ba'da tadwīrihi*—is placed in an earthenware cup, together with crushed salt, moistened with a little fresh water. It is submitted to strong wood-fire until the salt dissolves like lead. It is poured out, whereupon strips are cast of which dinars are made These are cleaned with cold water and fine sand, dried in a cup over a gentle fire, and finally stamped.'

The meaning of this important passage of the manuscript is far from being clear. Thus, for instance, it is difficult to establish what ibn Ba'ra means by *tadwīr* in this context. Is it 'dissolving'? This would imply that melted gold was placed in the cups with salt (?). Should it mean 'giving round shape', the first sentence would read: 'Gold, after being given round shape . . .' This

[1] MS. حبتين المثقال

[2] *ḥaif* is consistently used by ibn Ba'ra in contraposition to *naqṣ*.

could be taken as gold flans, which translation would be incompatible with the detail about the casting of strips. Whatever the interpretation of this passage might be, it is obvious that the flans were produced by cutting the strips into pieces and subsequently trimming them, in the same way in which the *nuqra* dirhams were produced (see below, p. 438). This method was widespread in the middle ages.[1] As for the stamping, the shape of the existing examples of medieval Islamic coin-dies leaves no doubt about the imprint being produced by means of a hammer-blow,[2] which expedient was still in use in Persia towards the close of the last century.[3]

Another interesting problem arises in connexion with the problem of producing the inscription on the dies. There is no doubt concerning the *sikka* of the Almoravids, where the engraving was carried out directly on the steel. The idea of considering this method as having been applied for the manufacture of the Ayyūbid coin-dies has been recently rejected by Prof. P. Balog.[4] Having thoroughly examined the preserved obverse die apparently made in Cairo in A.H. 635/A.D. 1238, he states that it was manufactured indirectly, by means of a mould. A discovery of two small lead plates, bearing the two negative faces of a dinar struck in Mah al-Kūfa (?) in A.H. 251/A.D. 865, is in Prof. Balog's view a conclusive argument in favour of his theory. These were made of so soft a metal that they cannot have been employed for stamping blanks, but only for imprinting the moulds in which the stamp-dies were cast. This was the way in which the *sikka* of A.H. 635 is also said to have been manufactured. According to Prof. Balog this method possessed many advantages. ' Le travail du graveur était infiniment plus facile sur le plomb que sur le métal dur du coin en bronze même, de plus, en cas d'erreur, l'artisan n'avait qu'à effacer le tout et recommencer sur la même feuille de plomb. La présence ou l'absence de traces de moulage dépendait donc uniquement du plus ou moins de soin et d'habileté du mouleur.' [5]

[1] This is how M. Viala translates the passage from Haj Lahsen's manuscript, describing the hammering of flans : ' La première opération que fait subir l'ouvrier monnayeur aux lingots d'or, est l'applatissage au marteau. Il les chauffe ensuite au rouge, les brosse et les réchauffe ; les tourne et les retourne jusqu'à ce qu'ils soient prêts à être débités. Il les coupe pièce par pièce à la taille des dinars, les rogne au gaz (?), les calibre et les vérifie. Il obtient ainsi ce qu'on appelle des " flans ". Si ce sont des dinars, il leur donne la forme ronde à la dimension voulue, il les martelle un par un, jamais deux par deux, ni trois par trois, en vérifie le pourtour et les met en rouleaux à raison de quarante ou cinquante par rouleau. Il frappe ce rouleau sur l'enclume en le tenant entre le pouce et l'index, à trois reprises. Au cours de cette opération, il change les pièces de position, mettant celles du centre aux extrémités et celles des extrémités au centre, jusqu'à ce que leur pourtour soit bien régulier '. Cf. J. D. Brethes, op. cit., p. 260. See also '*Ain i Akbari*, i, p. 21. Also *Tadhkirat al-mulūk, A Manual of Safavid Administration (circa 1137–1725)*, transl. and explained by V. Minorsky, London, 1943, p. 58, and fo. 36 a.

[2] Cf. G. Marçais, ' Un coin monétaire almoravide du Musée Stéphane Gsell ', *Annales de l'Inst. d'Etud. Orientales*, ii, 1936, pp. 180–8. Also L. A. Mayer, ' A Fatimid Coin-Die ', *QDAP.*, i, 1932, pp. 34–5.

[3] Cf. A. Smith, ' Mode of Coining Hammered Money in Persia ', *Num. Chronicle*, 3 ser., ii, 1882, pp. 299–300.

[4] ' Nouvelles observations sur la technique du monnayage ', *BIE.*, xxxiii, 1950–1, pp. 34 ff.

[5] ibid., p. 40.

I fully agree with Prof. Balog that this method makes the task of a ' graveur ' easier. The responsibility for the successful manufacture of dies would, in fact, have rested chiefly with the moulder. On the other hand the engraving, in soft material, of a pattern-die which was to suffice for a whole series, possibly for a whole year, would have reduced the occupation of the die-sinker to a rather easy, occasional, or to use a modern term, part-time job. This conception of the die-sinkers' profession, implied in the theory of Prof. Balog, is incompatible with the information found in ibn Ba'ra. The latter emphatically stresses the peculiar significance of that artisan's task. ' A *naqqāsh* (engraver, sculptor, in this case die-sinker) must be engaged exclusively in engraving (*naqasha*) dies. This increases his skill and dexterity and makes the dies difficult to imitate. The workers must have no access to a new die. The dies are stored by the *mushārif* ' (fo. 8v).

Ibn Ba'ra's information is, in my opinion, a convincing argument for challenging Prof. Balog's view with reference to dies manufactured in al-Kāmil's mints. It is not necessary to assume that the process outlined by Prof. Balog represented the usual one employed in the mints, as we can by no means be sure that the isolated examples on which he bases his conclusion are genuine. Should they be proved to be forgers' tools, his argument would be automatically void. Against this theory we have an unequivocal statement of ibn Ba'ra, whose expert knowledge could not be questioned, that dies were engraved, not cast.

The Testing of Purity of Silver

Silver delivered to the mint was tested in the following way.

فامتحان [الفضة] ان تبرد منها موضع. ثم تحمى ويرى الموضع المبرد[1] .فان اسود
او تغير فهى مغشوشة. وان لم يتغير فهى طلغم. (fo. 6v).

' The testing of silver consists of filing it at a certain point and exposing the silver to fire. If its colour changes or turns black, this silver is adulterated. If the colour does not change the silver is pure.' [2]

The Method of Producing the nuqra *dirhams*

The *nuqra* dirhams were produced of pure silver.

صفة عمل الدراهم النقرة

تسبك الفضة ومهما دار منها اولا فاولا يقلب فى الدرسل بعد تغطية ما فى البوتقة من الفضة. ان يدور جميعا فانها تنضج وتتصعد. وانما التوفير فى اقلابها اولا فاولا. ثم تؤخذ

[1] MS. موضع المبرد

[2] Abu'l-Faḍl mentions the same process : ' Practical men can discover from the colour of the compound which of the alloys is prevailing, whilst by filing and boring it the quality of the inside is ascertained. They also try it by beating it when hot, and then throwing it into water, when blackness denotes lead, redness copper, a white greyish colour tin, and whiteness a large proportion of silver '. '*Ain i Akbari*, i, p. 22.

السبائك، فتقطع قطعا بالقسمة، اكثر من درهم كل قطعة. مثاله ان السبيكة وزنها عشرون درهما، فتقطع خمس عشره[1] قطعة، وتعمل دراهم. فاذا احتجت مائة قيراط تحرر ايضا بصنجة المائة، تحريراً ثانياً لتصح[2] اوزانها مجتمعة متفرقة. فادا نقصت القطعة عن درهم فيعمل منها نصف. وتجلى وتختم. (fo. 6v–7r).

' Silver should be melted in a crucible. As it gradually liquefies, the dissolved substance is poured out into a *darsal*, while the crucible with the remaining silver is covered. This gradual pouring out is an economic method. The pouring out of the whole lot would result in losses caused by evaporation. The cast ingot (strip) is cut into pieces, each of them weighing more than 1 dirham.[3] Thus, for instance, an ingot weighing 20 dirhams should be divided into 15 pieces, of which dirhams are made. The whole lot should equal 100 *qirāṭs*,[4] the weighing constituting another check, apart from weighing each piece separately. If a piece proves smaller than 1 dirham, then it should be made into a half-dirham. Then the flans are polished and stamped.'

It does not appear clearly whether these dirhams weighed $1\frac{1}{3}$ or 1 dirham only. In the next paragraph, however, the existence of filings is mentioned, which is an indication that the pieces cut from the strips were trimmed to give these flans a round shape. In that case one could assume that the flans were cut at $1\frac{1}{3}$ dirham each, so that some allowance was made for the losses incurred during the process of reducing the flans to a round shape of 1 dirham each.

The Polishing of nuqra *dirhams*

Before being stamped the adjusted flans had to be ' whitened '[5] and polished.

صفة جلاء الدراهم النقرة

اذا احكم تدويرها وتحريرها، احميت واطفيت فى مآء الليمون والملح وعركت به. فاذا ظهر بياضها جليت بالرمل الناعم المغربل. ويختم عليها بعد ان تنشف فى النخالة

[1] MS. خمسة عشر

[2] MS. ليصح

[3] Decourdemanche calculates 1 dirham at $3 \cdot 96\frac{2}{3}$ gr. and 1 Egyptian qīrāṭ at $0 \cdot 24\frac{19}{24}$ gr. (loc. cit.).

[4] This passage of the manuscript is a good example of how complicated was the medieval Islamic weight system. Whereas normally 1 dirham constituted $\frac{2}{3}$ the Egyptian mithqāl (ibid.), the dirham with ibn Ba'ra equals $\frac{5}{24}$ mithqāl. As ibn Ba'ra states on fo. 4v that the mithqāl consists of 24 qīrāṭs, the following relationship between some of the troy weights, used in the Cairo mint, can be reconstructed :—

qīrāṭ . .			1
dirham . .		1	5
mithqāl . .	1	$4\frac{4}{5}$	24

[5] For the method of whitening flans, see Luschin von Ebengreuth, *Allgemeine Münzkunde und Geldgeschichte des Mittelalters und der neueren Zeit*, Berlin, 1926, p. 60. Also, *Tadhkirat al-mulūk*, p. 59, and fo. 36a.

وتغربل منها. والحمى يكون فى كف حديد. والقراضة تسبك وتعمل دراهم كالعمل الاول حتى لا يبقى الا درهم واحد يسبك ويدور، ويجلى[1]. ويختم عليه. (fo. 7r).

'When the flans have been turned round and adjusted, you heat them and rub them with lime-water. When the flans turn white you polish them with soft sifted sand. Dried out with bran and subsequently cleaned, the flans are ready for stamping. The flans are heated in an iron ladle.[2] As for the filings, they are cast together and made into dirhams in the usual way, until finally there remains but one dirham which, too, is molten, made round, polished, and stamped.'

The Casting of the waraq *dirhams*

The process of producing the *waraq* dirhams consisted of two operations: the adjusting of the alloy and the casting itself.

تعديل الدراهم المصرية ورق

يؤخذ لكل صنف منها لكل جزء منها جزئين وثلث نحاس احمر، غير حبوب النار مثاله ان الالف وثمانمائة درهم من الفضة النقرة عليها من النحاس اربعة الاف ومائتين درهم. فتصير[3] الجملة ستة الاف درهم ومائتى درهم. وعلة حبوب النار لحفظ العيار ثلثين درهما ولكن سقط المائتين الزايدة عن الستة الاف فيصير سوآء عليه حبوب النار لحفط العيار ثلثين درهما نقرة.

اول ما تسبك النحاس فاذا دار وصار كالمآء الجارى ارم عليه الفضة بعد حماها. فانها تدور لساعتها فتغطى بفحم مسحوق خشية ان لا يفتح ويتصور علدا.[4] خذ من هذه الفوتقة وزن درهم واحد او عشرة او مائة، وصفى بالروباص، يخرج منها جزء واحد فضة وجزان وثلث نحاس، محرر كالتعديل الاول. مثاله ان العشرة يخرج منها ثلاثة دراهم فضة ولولا زيادة حبوب النار لم يصح هذا المقدار فى العيار.

ثم يتناول السباك من الفوتقة التى فى الكور ببوتقة صغيرة بالكلبتين الحديد من الفضة الذايبة والنحاس الجارى ويقلب على راس خشبة كالحوذة، قائمة فى وسط دن

[1] MS. يجلا

[2] Iron ladles could be used for silver and baser metals, but not for gold, for which special clay tools had to be prepared. cf. F. Mazerolle, *L'Hôtel des Monnaies, Les Bâtiments—Le Musée—Les Ateliers*, Paris, 1907, p. 140.

[3] MS. فيصير

[4] MS. يتصور علوا

مملوا جالمآء الحلو. وعلى تلك القبة قليل من تراب الفحم المسحوق. فيكون ذلك سبب تدوير الفضة[1] مدحرجة. وهى كالمآء على القبة وتنزل فى المآء الذى فى الدن، فيصير نقط مستديرة كبار وصغار. ويكون الى جانب السباك صانع اخر، يكون بيده فحم مدقوق متواصل رشه على القبة كلما قلب[2] عليها السباك الفضة، يمنع ذلك من الالتصاق بعضها ببعض، وتعين على صحة تدويرها. ثم تؤخذ تلك النقط من قعر الدن فتغسل من وسخ الفحم وتنشف على الباب. ثم يوخذ عيارها. (fo. 7v).

'The adjusting of the Egyptian *waraq* dirhams

'Add to one part of pure silver $2\frac{1}{3}$ of red copper, besides the *ḥubūb an-nār*.[3] Thus, for example, to 1,800 dirhams of pure silver you should add 4,200 dirhams of copper, making the total 6,000 dirhams and 200 dirhams (of *ḥubūb an-nār*). The *ḥubūb an-nār* are used in order to maintain the standard of 30 dirhams. The loss of 200 dirhams which occurs in 6,000 is thus replaced with the additional 200 dirhams of the *ḥubūb an-nār*.[4]

'Copper is melted first, and as it dissolves, becoming fluid like water, throw hot silver into it. It will dissolve immediately. It should be covered with crushed charcoal so that it does not become stiff. If you take from the crucible any quantity, be it 1, 10, or 100 dirhams, and refine it in the rūbāṣ,[5] you will always obtain 1 part of silver and $2\frac{1}{3}$ parts of copper, according to the first adjustment. Ten dirhams, for instance, should produce 3 dirhams of silver. But this proportion cannot be achieved without the addition of the *ḥubūb an-nār*.

'Subsequently the moulder removes the small crucible containing the dissolved silver and copper with iron tongs from the *fūtaqa* in the furnace, and pours the substance on top of a wooden cupola which has the shape of a helmet. This cupola, which stands in the middle of a container with fresh water, is covered with a layer of crushed charcoal. This causes the liquid silver, which is poured on the cupola, to assume a round shape and to fall into the water. In the water-container it takes the shape of irregular small and large pellets. Close to the moulder there should be another craftsman holding crushed charcoal which he should scatter on the cupola whenever the moulder pours out the silver. This method prevents the drops from sticking to each other and gives the pellets correct shapes. Afterwards the pellets are collected from the bottom of the water-container, washed from the coal dirt, and dried in the open air. The next step consists of testing the standard of the *waraq* flans.'

[1] MS. التدوير الفضة

[2] MS. اقلب

[3] The same proportions are given by ibn Mammātī, op. cit., p. 333. Also *Guide de Kātib*, MS. Bibl. Nat. 4441 (Sup. 1912), *apud* Sauvaire, op. cit., *JA*., xix, 1882, p. 103.

[4] If every 30 dirhams lose 1 dirham in the fire, requiring thus 1 additional dirham to maintain the standard, then 6,000 dirhams, losing 200 dirhams, require 200 additional dirhams.

[5] As distinct from *rūbās* with *sīn* or *rūbāsh*, *rūbāṣ* written with *ṣād*, seems to mean refining. cf. Dozy, i, p. 564.

The Quantitative Checking of the Alloy of the waraq *dirhams*

The standard of the *waraq* dirhams was ascertained by means of a quantitative analysis.

اعتبار عيار الدراهم

يؤخذ من مجموع هذه الدراهم بعد تخليطها وزن خمسة عشر درهما، وتجعل تحت الروباش مع رطلين رصاص[1]...... فيخرج الرصاص ما فى جسم الفضة من النحاس[2]....... وقد خلصت الفضة من جميع ما فيها الرصاص والنحاس. فحينئذ تحقق وزنها وتحرره. فان كان اربعة دراهم ونصف او ارجح فتعلم ان العيار صحيح. فعند ذلك تسلمها الضرابون ويضربونها، ويجمعونها، ويجلونها ويختمونها. (fo. 8r).

'On testing the standard of the *waraq* dirhams

'Take 15 dirhams weight from the whole lot of alloyed *waraq* dirhams and melt it down under the *rūbāsh* with 2 raṭls of lead. . . . The lead attracts copper contained in the silver. . . . When the silver has become free from both lead and copper, you should ascertain its weight. If it amounts to 4½ dirhams' weight or more, then the standard of the *waraq* alloy is correct.[3] Then they are taken by the minters who hammer them, put together, polish, and stamp.'

The Polishing of the waraq *flans*

Also the *waraq* dirhams were submitted to the process of 'whitening' and polishing, which preceded the stamping.

فى جلاها ليختم عليها

يؤخذ الخل الحاذق ويغلى فى دست نحاس. وتحمى الدراهم وترمى فى تلك الخل. وتعرك فيه بالملح الى ان يخرج سوادها ويظهر بياضها. فتغسل[4] بالمآء الحلو دفوعا الى ان ينقى بياضها فى دست من خشب. ثم تعرك[5] فيها[6] بالسماق الى ان يزداد بياضها وترجع كالفضة الطلغم. فتنشف بالنخالة حتى تجف وتغربل من النحالة وتختم عليها بالسكة. (fo. 8r).

[1] Here follows a description of the crucible and of the *rūbāsh*.

[2] Follows a description of purification of silver by fusing it with lead, and by subsequent removal of lead.

[3] cf. similar description in ibn Mammātī, loc. cit.

[4] MS. فيغسل

[5] MS. يعرك

[6] MS. فيه

Polishing *waraq* dirhams

'Boil sharp vinegar in a copper vessel and having heated the dirhams dip them in that vinegar. Rub them with salt until they cease to be black and become white. Rinse them with fresh water in a wooden tub, and rub them with wood of sumaq tree, until the whiteness intensifies so that their colour resembles that of pure silver. Dry them with bran and when you have finished it, clean them from bran. Thereupon you can proceed to stamp them with a die.'

Conclusions

Although many obscurities in ibn Baʿra's treatise on the *Secrets of the Mint* still remain to be clarified, the following information about the working of the Egyptian mint under al-Malik al-Kāmil can be extracted from it :—

(*a*) The advanced standard of knowledge of chemical processes made it possible to prepare gold and silver of a high degree of purity.

(*b*) Effective check-measures secured great accuracy in the adjusting of alloys.

(*c*) The flans of dinars and of *nuqra* dirhams were made by cutting ingots into small pieces which were given round shape by means of trimming and hammering. The flans of *waraq* dirhams were produced by casting small pellets and subsequent hammering.

(*d*) The whitening and polishing processes indicate that great care was taken about the external appearance of the coins.

(*e*) To carry out all these complicated and extensive operations, the Egyptian mint of Cairo must have been a well organized, permanent establishment, and not an improvised workshop, as it has been suggested by Marçais in his reference to Islamic 'hôtels des monnaies'.[1]

To what extent the picture of the mint drawn by Manṣūr ibn Baʿra corresponded with the real state of affairs requires further investigation and the analysis of numismatic material.[2]

Appendix

Tools, Instruments, Weights, and Measures

In his description of various technical processes of the mint ibn Baʿra mentions the following implements.

Furnaces

There are three types of furnaces, *atūn* (اتون), *tannūr* (تنّور), and *kūr* (كور), used for refining, for extracting silver from the *ḥabaq*, and for fusing alloys necessary for casting the *waraq* dirhams. The *atūn* is quadrangular on

[1] G. Marçais, op. cit., p. 188.

[2] My thanks are due to Dr. D. S. Rice for his help in revising this paper.

the outside and round inside. The surface is plastered with fine clay mixed with salt. On its top is a small earthenware chimney. The door of this construction, resembling that of an oven, is shut with a bolt. The bottom of the *atūn*, which has an earthenware fire-grate, is raised from the ground to the height of two courses of bricks (fos. 3r, 5r, 5v, 8v, 9r).

The *tannūr* is larger at the bottom than at the top, its diameter being 1½ span. Its tall chimney is two cubits long. A *rūbāsh* (bellows) is built on top of this furnace. The tannūr has no door (fos. 7r, 8v).

The *qubba* (cupola—قبة) is a slightly different furnace of the *tannūr* type. It is not very high. It has a large door which is sealed with clay and sand in the course of the operation. In front of this door is an opening through which the smoke escapes (fo. 7r). An interesting feature of the furnaces of this type is their temporary character. They are erected over crucibles and taken down as soon as the required chemical results have been obtained. As for the *kūr* (fos. 7v, 8r, 8v, 9r) ibn Ba'ra says only that it was used for heating crucibles.

A special kind of bellows, called *ar-rūbāsh* (الروباش), was used for intensifying the heat (fos. 6v, 7r, 8r, 8v, 9v). Ibn Ba'ra gives a description of the rūbāsh, which provides a fair indication of the precise meaning of this word.[1] He says: ' It is a kind of bellows turned upside down. The wind comes out of their mouth to the middle of the crucible '. («الروباش منفخ مكبوب الراس يخرج ريحه من فمه الى اسفال فى وسط البوط»—fo. 8r).

Crucibles

There are three types of crucible, *būtaqa* (بوتقة), *fūtaqa* (فوتقة), and *būṭa* (بوطة), sometimes called *būṭ* (بوط). While the first two were used for melting down silver alloys (fos. 6v, 7r, 7v, 8r, 9r, 9v), the last one was also used for adjusting the standard of gold (fo. 9r). The material of which it was made varied according to its particular use. Thus the *būṭa* used for refining silver was made of slaked lime, sifted ash, and a little water (fo. 6v). Another, used for the extraction of silver from the *ḥabaq*, was of ash mixed with water only (fo. 7r). Still another, for the same process, was made of equal amounts of slaked lime and ash (fo. 7r). A third *būṭa*, in the course of the same operation, was made of equal amounts of slaked lime, ash, and water (fo. 7r). The *būṭa* made of a compound consisting of $\frac{1}{3}$ lime and $\frac{2}{3}$ ash was required for testing the standard of the *waraq* dirhams (fo. 8r).

The crucibles were removed from the furnaces with iron tongs (كلبتان حديد—fo. 7v). They were skimmed off with iron ladles (ماسك حديد or ماسكة حديدة—fos. 7r, 9v).

[1] cf. discussion in *Ma'ālim al-qurba*, p. 103. Also Wiedemann, *Beiträge*, xxxii, p. 37.

Vessels

Gold was refined and heated before polishing in earthenware cups (فخار احمر—fos. 3v, 5r, 6r, 6v, 8v, 9r). When put into the *atūn* the cup was placed on a brick (لبنة—fo. 5r). An earthenware vessel (قصرية فخار) was placed under the riddle (غربال) in the course of refining gold (fo. 5v). An earthenware pot (قدر فخار—fos. 6v, 8r) and earthenware vessel (مطر فخار fo. 6v) were used for distilling mercury. Still another vessel (ماجور), was used in the process of extracting silver from the earthy residue (fo. 6r). The *nuqra* blanks were heated before polishing in an iron ladle (كفّ حديد—fo. 7r). Vinegar, in which the *waraq* flans were dipped, was boiled in a copper vessel (دست نحاس—fo. 8r). These blanks were then rinsed in a wooden tub (دست من خشب—fo. 8r). A wooden cupola (خوذة) in the shape of a helmet (fo. 7v), used for casting the *waraq* flans, was placed in a container called *dann* (دن—fo. 7v).

Other Tools

A grindstone (?) (حجر السبك—fos. 6r, 6v, 8v), an oblong stone (صلاية—fo. 4r), and a roller (فهر—fo. 4r) of the size of a hand, the two last of hard stone, were used for crushing the earthy residue. Gold test and check plates were shaped on a steel mould (قالب فولاذ—fo. 5v). A hammer (مطراق) and anvil (سندان) were used for annealing silver (fo. 6v). Silver, of which *nuqra* dirhams were produced, was cast in a mould (?) (درسل) fo. 6v). Gold plates were wiped on a wooden board (لوح خشب—fo. 5v) with a woollen rag (خرقة صوف—fo. 5v). Weighing was done with a balance (ميزان) with two scales (كفتان—fo. 5v) and troyweights (صنجة—fos. 7v, 8v).

A touchstone (محك—fos. 4v, 5r, 5v) was used for assaying. A special set of 18 touchneedles (عيارات) was required for that purpose. Each touchneedle weighed 1 *mithqāl*. The highest quality of needle consisted of 23 *qīrāṭs* of pure gold and 1 q. of 'golden silver' (الفضة الذهبية). In the remaining needles the 'golden silver' was gradually substituted for the fine gold, so that the 18th needle contained 18 q. 'golden silver' and only 6 q. pure gold. This standard called *rubā'iyy* (رباعى) was below the official rate (غير الجائز). All these touchneedles were affixed to a silver form, together with the touchstone (fos. 4v–5r). Finally, polished flans were stamped with a coin-die (سكة fos. 5v, 6r, 8r, 8v, 9v).

Weights and Measures

The following weight and measure units are found in the treatise of ibn Baʿra :—

حبة *ḥabba* (fos. 5v, 6r, 7v),

درهم *dirham* (fos. 6v, 7r, 7v, 8r),

مثقال *mithqāl* (fos. 3v, 4r, 4v, 5r, 5v, 6r),

كيل *Kayl* (fo. 5r),

ويبة *wayba* (fo. 8r),

رطل *raṭl* (fos. 6r, 6v, 7r, 8r),

قنطار *qinṭār* (fo. 7r),

شبر *shibr* (fos. 5v, 7r),

ذراع *dhiraʿ* (fo. 7r).

Apart from a few hints discussed in note 4, p. 439, no details are given which would permit a full reconstruction of the relationship between the respective units.

Fuel, Chemicals, and Other Ingredients

The following articles were required for various processes of converting raw material into coins.

Fuel

Both wood (fos. 6r, 6v, 7r) and charcoal (fos. 3r, 6v, 7r, 7v, 9v) were used as fuel. Wood was not only needed for lighting (fo. 7r) but also to obtain a strong fire (fo. 3r). Thus the strong fire for refining gold was made of the wood of the acacia tree (سنط—fo. 3r), or of the charcoal of the same wood (fo. 3r). The glow was sustained by blowing the bellows.

Chemicals

A special compound (تراب التعليق) was placed in the cups in which the refining and testing of gold was carried out. This compound consisted of 1 *kayl* of salt, 2 *kayls* of fine powder, obtained by crushing and sifting a new, soft, red brick, and a little water (fo. 5r). The refining of silver (fo. 6v) and extracting it from *ḥabaq* (fo. 7r) required lead, while the extracting of silver and gold from the earthy residue was done by amalgamating it with mercury (fos. 6r, 8v). Salt was required in the process of polishing gold (fo. 6r) and silver blanks (fo. 8r). For that purpose both *nuqra* and *waraq* blanks had to be dipped in lime-water (ماء الليمون—fo. 7r) and sharp vinegar (خل حاذق—fo. 8r).

Other Ingredients

Crushed coal was used during the process of pouring the molten *waraq* alloy on the *khūdha* (fo. 7v). Cups and furnaces were sealed with clay (fos. 3v, 5r, 5v, 7v, 9r). The polishing of blanks was done with soft sifted sand (رمل ناعم مغربل—fos. 6v, 8r, 9v), the wood of the sumaq tree and bran (fos. 7v, 8r). Finally potsherds (fos. 4r, 6r, 8v) and parchment (fos. 6v, 8r) were used for distillation and filtering.

INDEX